ALSO BY CHARLES RAPPLEYE
with Ed Becker

All American Mafioso: The Johnny Rosselli Story

Sons of

The Brown Brothers,
and the

CHARLES RAPPLEYE

Simon & Schuster

New York   London   Toronto   Sydney

Providence

the Slave Trade,
American Revolution

SIMON & SCHUSTER
Rockefeller Center
1230 Avenue of the Americas
New York, NY 10020

SIMON & SCHUSTER and colophon are registered trademarks
of Simon & Schuster, Inc.

For information about special discounts for bulk purchases,
please contact Simon & Schuster Special Sales at
1-800-456-6798 or business@simonandschuster.com.

Designed by Karolina Harris

Original maps by Tulsa Kinney

Title page art © CORBIS

Manufactured in the United States of America

10   9   8   7   6   5   4   3   2   1

Library of Congress Cataloging-in-Publication Data

Rappleye, Charles.
    Sons of Providence : the Brown brothers, the slave trade, and the American Revolution/Charles Rappleye.
        p.   cm.
    Includes bibliographical references and index.
    ISBN-13: 978-0-7432-6687-1
    ISBN-10:   0-7432-6687-0
    1. Brown, Moses, 1738–1836.   2. Brown, John, 1736–1803.   3. Abolitionists—Rhode Island—
Providence—Biography.   4. Merchants—Rhode Island—Providence—Biography.   5. Providence
(R.I.)—Biography.   6. Slave trade—Rhode Island—Providence—History.   7. Antislavery movements—
Rhode Island—Providence (R.I.)—History.   8. Rhode Island—History—Revolution, 1775–1783.
9. Providence (R.I.)—History—18th century.   10. Brown family.   I. Title.

F89.P953A2 2006
326'.809227451—dc22
[B]   2006042320

To my mother Ann Crompton

Contents

Sons

of Providence

Introduction

THIS IS THE STORY of two brothers whose lives spanned the course of the American Revolution and whose sibling rivalry encompassed all the painful dilemmas that attended the dawn of the new era. John and Moses Brown were partners in business and in raising their community, and their legacy is commemorated in the university that bears their name. But the brothers fell out over the great moral dilemmas posed by the new prospect of human liberty. They divided over questions of war and peace, of faith and conscience, but especially, and for more than twenty years, they wrestled over the question of slavery.

For most readers, these two men will be new faces in the pantheon of the founding generation. But the Brown brothers were men of action who lived lives of commitment and zeal, deeply engaged in the challenges and the achievements of their time. In their exploits and in their passionate disputes they breathe new life into our mythic understanding of the early years of the republic.

The tale unfolds against the backdrop of colonial Rhode Island, a tiny outpost on the fringe of England's vast empire, but situated at the epicenter of an unprecedented upheaval in politics and ideas. Rhode Island was from its inception a distillate of what America would become—democratic, ambitious, and fiercely independent. By the time John and Moses appear on the scene, they represent their family's fifth generation in the New World and they exercise political and religious liberty as their birthright. As they grow into the prominence of their later years, we are able to share their thinking, their setbacks, and their triumphs through an extraordinary archive of documents and personal letters. This is a living history of war, politics, and revolution, but one rooted in the faith and aspiration, the blood bonds and internecine betrayals of a single founding family.

The period of the brothers' coming of age covers familiar terrain—the rising resentment against England, the mortal struggle of the Revolution, the writing of the Constitution—but it takes on new vitality when seen through the lives of these two men. They lose their father at an early age but follow in his path, sending crews and cargoes to sea aboard a growing fleet of sailing ships. We see them go underground to join the secret Sons of Liberty in plotting their defiance to the edicts of the British crown. And we see them challenge each other over the best way to run a business, to win an election, to run the government.

What raises their saga to the level of tragedy, what provides it spine and dramatic energy, is the brothers' mutual struggle over slavery. The book opens with the family's first venture in the trade, staged by patriarch James Brown the year John was born. Thirty years later, the brothers establish a personal stake in the trade when they stage their own voyage to Africa. It results in a human and financial disaster: after a journey attended by disease and shipboard rebellion, more than half the slaves perish, an ordeal illuminated by detailed notes from the captain's log. Here the brothers divide. Moses recoils and becomes an early abolitionist, but John remains active in the slave trade and grows to be one of its most vocal defenders. Neither is willing to concede moral ground to the other, and they take their battle public, trading broadsides in print, in the legislature, and finally in the new United States Congress. This is a personal struggle for identity, but it illuminates the first great stage of the abolition movement in America, a period often overlooked in the general fascination with the founding era. Watching the story unfold affords the sobering realization that long before the nation paid the horrific price of the Civil War, Americans had the opportunity to square the rhetoric of human rights with their institutional practice. For the Browns, as for the nation, the system of human bondage presented an impasse that admitted no middle ground. And for the Browns, as for the founding fathers at Philadelphia, efforts at compromise only delayed a final, painful reckoning.

As much as their mutual rivalry stands at the center of this yarn, John and Moses each emerge as distinct and complete characters. Moses is the better known, famous in his day and in the annals of Rhode Island as a principled reformer, a man of faith and conviction who wrote laws and founded institutions that embodied the highest ideals of the new nation. His name is recalled in two of the schools he helped to establish, Brown University and Moses Brown School, both situated in his hometown of Providence, Rhode Island. He was a civic leader in the pioneer tradition, called upon by fellow citizens to lay out the streets of his town and serving as clerk and political captain to the colonial governor.

Moses was sober and abstentious; he read deeply in the Bible and sat out the Revolution as a conscientious objector. But he was also worldly and sophisticated, with strong opinions on the proper course of social and economic development for his state and for the nation. These were not just theoretical concerns; with his brother, Moses founded and helped lead one of America's first banks, and on his own initiative, he established on the shores of the Blackstone River the first mechanized cotton mill on this side of the Atlantic, allowing American weavers to compete on equal footing with England and inaugurating the Industrial Revolution. His story defies category: readers will find startling insights into American political, business, and social history, all in the skein of this long and remarkable life.

As much as Moses contributed in the fields of business and education, his most passionate engagement was his opposition to slavery and the slave trade. Here Moses waged a quarter-century campaign of public persuasion and legislative action, winning a succession of major battles he fought through a combination of will and unshakable conviction, and personally writing the first law ever to decree slave trading illegal. His achievements in the first phase of the American abolition movement serve as a case study of idealism in action, when the new apparatus of democracy matched the aspirations of its founders. But the story also reads as tragedy, demonstrating the limits of institutions when confronted with the insinuating power of individual interest.

John was born in the same house with Moses and raised with the same values, but the two could not have been more different. Where Moses was slight and reserved, John had an outsized physique with a character to match. He loved to drink and to wager, to boast and to denigrate. Toward the end of his life, his children called him Old Thunder. But while Moses' exploits were extolled in two biographies during the last century, John's story has never been told—in part, perhaps, because so much of it smacked of the unsavory.

John was as cynical as Moses was idealistic, and his adventures take the reader on an eye-opening tour of the underside of the new republic. He leads a brazen attack on a British revenue ship, earning the wrath of the king and pushing New England to the brink of war. He wheels and deals with the Continental Congress and Washington's army, finding avenues to profit while the nation wallows in privation. And in an episode remarkable for sheer audacity, John's obstinate refusal to shoulder his share of the first tax authorized by the American Congress pushes the new federal government to the brink of collapse.

But when John's interests coincide with those of the nation, he could be just as constructive as he was sometimes divisive. Even more than Moses, John was instrumental in raising the college that later bore his family name. And when a reactionary rural party won a large enough following to keep the former colony out of the new union, John became Rhode Island's most vocal and most effective advocate for the new federal Constitution.

Neither brother is an easy read. Each has his foibles, his contradictions, his strengths and weaknesses. And they are men of their times, deeply committed to the conventions of family and community. While they get angry at each other, they never break with each other. But each is fully engaged in the life of their times, John as the thunderer, lashing out against every adversary, and Moses, equally willful, determined to honor his inner light. By following both brothers in their collaborations, their collisions, and their separate pursuits, we get a panoramic view of a seminal period. Seen through the prism of the lives of these two brothers, the founding era comes across as rich, rollicking, and more chaotic than most readers could possibly expect.

With the Browns' wide range of interests and influence, their story inevitably intersects with those of other key players, some familiar and some less so, and all of them fascinating. Samuel Adams and Nathanael Greene take turns here, as do Stephen Hopkins, Rhode Island's great revolutionary leader and theorist, and his brother Esek, first commodore of the United States Navy. We meet the Philadelphia abolitionists Anthony Benezet and James Pemberton, and Providence printer John Carter, one of the pioneers of the American press. George Washington is revealed here as well—for among all the chronicles of America's primary patriarch, none documents, as this book does, his sole public performance in opposition to the slave trade.

Sons of Providence provides a fresh excursion into American history, certainly, but it is also a study in American character. Raised in a culture of freedom and self-expression, Moses and John devoted their lives to the pursuit of their own vision of individual liberty. In so doing, each emerges as an American archetype—Moses as the social reformer, driven by conscience and dedicated to an enlightened sense of justice; John as the unfettered capitalist, possessed of the prerogatives of profit and defiant of any effort to constrain his will. The story of their collaboration and their conflict has a startlingly contemporary feel. It's hard to see their achievements and their failures without recognizing something enduring, at once hopeful and daunting, in our national character. Like any good yarn, the story of the Browns tells us something about ourselves.

1

James Brown Puts Out to Sea

DURING THE MONTHS of April and May in 1736, as the winter snows melted off the rocky hillsides of New England, the sloop *Mary* lay careened on the marshy west bank of the Great Salt River in the tiny British colony of Rhode Island. Her masts were taken down and laid alongside, and the graceful lines of her oaken hull exposed to be scraped of barnacles and rot and then sheathed in copper. Daytimes found the little ship swarmed by workers clad in leather breeches and homespun cotton shirts, the teams supervised by shipwright John Barnes and, occasionally, by James Brown, owner of the *Mary*, registered freeman of the town of Providence, and an entrepreneur of restless, seemingly limitless energy.

From his vantage above Barnes's shipyard on Weybosset Neck, James was able at once to watch the progress on the *Mary* and to survey the domain of his youth and enterprise. On the point where he stood there were just a handful of farm buildings, and a dirt track that ran south and west across lowlands and tidal flats to the banks of the Pawtuxet River. To the north, past a broad, shallow cove, meadows and rolling hills stretched another fifteen miles to the border of the Massachusetts Bay Colony. To the east, across the brackish tidal flow, Prospect Hill rose sharply to an elevation of just under two hundred feet, crowned by great stands of old oak and cedar. Arrayed at its foot, running along a single lane, lay Providence itself, its taverns and proud new homes facing the street; below them, leading down to the water, stood a row of warehouses, and back of those, a dozen tarry wharves jutting into the river, one of them belonging to James. Directly south, in a vast expanse that opened until it occupied half the horizon, lay Narragansett Bay, a small inland sea of two hundred square miles fed by the streams of the Woonasquatucket and the Pawtuxet, and the surging Seekonk River. Fifty miles farther, past the busy and prosperous harbor at Newport, Narragansett Bay opened onto the chill waters of the Atlantic.

The town of Providence had been founded a century before by Roger Williams, a religious visionary banished for heresy by the rigid Puritans of Salem. For generations, the residents of Williams's bayside settlement lived simply, raising livestock and orchards and devoting themselves to a range of religious doctrines, including Baptist, Congregationalist, and Quaker. It was a new model for a community based on the Enlightenment ideals of religious freedom and political democracy, and protected by grace of a royal charter that endorsed a "lively experiment" in "religious concernments."

Now that close and simple world was changing. The more ambitious men of the colony were turning their backs to the gloomy hinterland and looking to the Atlantic for opportunity. Lacking the craftsmen of Massachusetts and the fertile soil of the southern colonies, Rhode Island produced little that could find a market back in England. But her wood and livestock were mainstays for the plantation colonies of the Caribbean. In addition, the head of the Narragansett Bay provided a convenient depot for the farmers of Connecticut and western Massachusetts. More and more, the sons of Providence farmers grew up in the maritime trade.

The first shipyard in Providence commenced business in 1711, building small, shallow-draft sloops to move cargoes down the bay to Newport, where they were loaded onto heavier craft for shipment to the other ports along the eastern seaboard, from Nova Scotia to the Carolinas, or farther, to the British, French, and Dutch colonies of the West Indies. Before long, the ship captains of Providence were making those voyages themselves, taking great barrels of pork and beef and cheese, along with loads of board and shingles and barrel staves, and returning with the fruits of the British empire — coffee, salt, rice, flour, milled fabrics, pewter and stoneware, silk, guns and gunpowder, and, especially from the Caribbean, sugar, molasses, and rum.

James Brown was among the earliest of these seafaring entrepreneurs. His first recorded voyage past the bluffs of Point Judith, at the mouth of Narragansett Bay, took him to Martinique, in 1727. Thereafter he'd made a score of such journeys, supplying himself enough merchandise to open a store on the main street in Providence, and enough molasses to supply two stills, where he converted the sticky brown syrup into rum. Nine years later, at the age of thirty-eight, James was all but retired from the sea, but he owned outright or in partnerships with the town's other leading merchants a dozen ships, and he managed their affairs, commissioning captains, issuing sailing orders, and distributing the cargoes.

With the *Mary*, recently returned from the West Indies, James was taking the next great step, for himself and for his hometown. Once she was overhauled and sheathed to endure the long duration and heavy beating of a

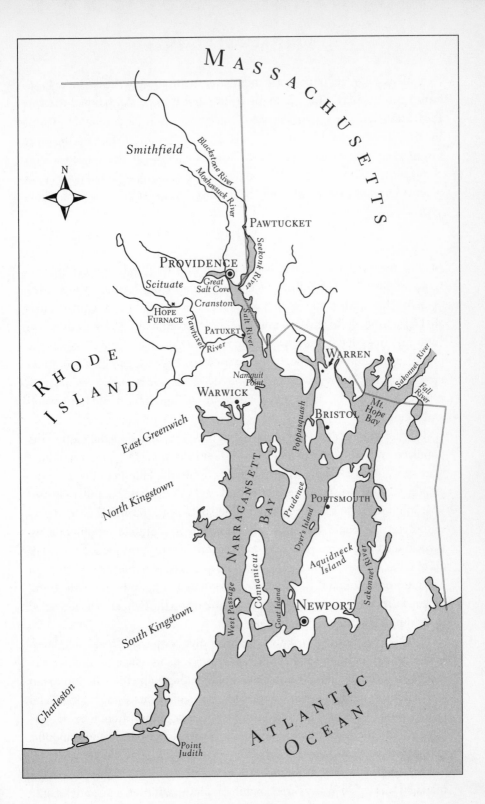

Narragansett Bay

transatlantic voyage, James was sending her to the coast of Africa, there to secure a cargo of slaves for sale to the British and French plantation owners in the Caribbean. The slave trade was at once the most hazardous and the most lucrative business of the time, and had served as the foundation for the great fortunes of Newport, a city twice the size of Providence, which rivaled Boston as the commercial center of New England. The *Mary* represented James's bid to join their ranks; the vessel would be the first slaver ever to put out from Providence.

Making his way back to town, James passed over the Weybosset Bridge—or, more prosaically, Muddy Bridge—a sturdy expanse eighteen feet wide with a creaking draw in the middle that was the town's first public enterprise, operated for a time by Roger Williams himself. It served mainly to carry droves of cattle and hogs that farmers brought to town for slaughter. Directly across the bridge at the foot of Prospect Hill stood Market Square, an open common crowded during the day with carts, loose livestock, and shoppers seeking produce. Stalls lined the "cheapside," where artisans and tinkers sold housewares and handicrafts.

There were four churches in town, but no spires, a mark of the piety of the populace and a measure of their still-meager resources. The largest buildings were inns, of which there were half a dozen, but the tallest entities were the great spreading elms that shaded the yards in front of several popular taverns. The population of Providence had doubled between 1708 and 1730, to nearly four thousand people, but the sale of home lots was restricted to other townsmen, and if there were occasional strangers on the street, the place retained its air of sober industry and religious zeal. People carried names like Mercy and Toleration, Pardon and Resolved. Local ordinances barred any sports, hunting, or common labor on Sundays, and drinking on the Sabbath was restricted to "no more than necessity requireth."

As well as James Brown knew the town, the people of Providence knew James. Stocky and powerfully built, his various pursuits engaged him in every facet of community life. Beyond his shipping interests and his stills, James ran a slaughterhouse and a retail store. He also loaned money at interest, and rented out draft animals and space on his wharf or in his warehouse. His customers often included friends and family, whose debts he carried for months and sometimes years before calling them in.

Crossing the market, running north to south, ran Towne Street; below the market it was called Water Street, but it was all the same avenue, and the only one in Providence until the middle of the century. The street was bordered for more than a mile on both sides by third-generation houses, shops, and inns. Gone were the rude, single-story houses of the early settlement, now replaced by capacious two- and three-story homes, built around massive stone fireplaces that served as kitchen, hearth, and center of family life. Some were painted in bright colors; others were clad in raw, weathered wood. Steps of stone or wood led up from the mire of the unpaved road, and served as a perch in the late afternoons for old men who puffed tobacco from long-stemmed clay pipes.

Close by the market, "amid heaps of stones and rubbish," according to one description, stood the town whipping post, employed for the punishment of thieves and misdemeanants through the middle of the next century. This stern sentinel carried special meaning for James, recalling a seminal chapter from the family annals. That was the story of Obadiah Holmes, the father of James's great-grandmother and among the most fervent of the religious dissidents to reject Puritan orthodoxy and establish a haven in Rhode Island. Holmes returned to Massachusetts in 1651, traveling with two acolytes to defy official edict and preach an optimistic doctrine of baptismal redemption.

Once Holmes commenced services, two local constables arrived, produced a warrant, and arrested the three schismatics. At trial a week later, presided over by the colonial governor, a verdict of heresy was found and fines assessed. Holmes's tiny Baptist congregation quickly raised the funds to secure their leaders' release, but Holmes stood on principle and forbade that his fine be paid. In forfeit, he was sentenced to a public flogging. The punishment was meted out at the whipping post on Boston Common, where Holmes endured thirty heavy strokes from a three-tailed whip across his bare back. According to legend, Holmes stayed silent through the beating until he was cut down from the whipping post, whereupon he turned to the magistrate-witnesses and declared, "You have struck me as with roses." Thereafter he remained in Newport, where he presided over his church for another thirty years.

Holmes's counterpart in Providence was Chad Brown, one of the town's original settlers and the first pastor of the first Baptist church in America. Like Roger Williams, Chad had been exiled from Massachusetts "for conscience' sake," as his gravestone recorded. Chad's only son, John, followed his father as a Baptist pastor; John's union with the daughter of Obadiah Holmes, then, was a match of ecclesiastic moment. The Browns were a family steeped in the sort of conviction that led the Pilgrims to leave Europe and risk their lives in a strange new wilderness. In Rhode Island that ideal was taken to its extreme; the colony was distinguished in all the world as the first place to guarantee religious freedom, welcoming a freewheeling mix of antinomians, Congregationalists, Sabbatarians, and Quakers—dissidents all. Its neighbors dubbed the little colony Rogue's Island, the "island of errors," but those who lived there made freedom of conscience a point of pride.

Heading south from the market, James would pass two doors down to arrive at his own home. It was a busy and comfortable household, maintained by his wife, Hope, and occupied by a growing brood. The oldest, James, was then twelve years of age, followed by Nicholas, six; Mary, five; Joseph, three; and John, born January 27, 1736, and still in his crib. The family enjoyed the best furnishings the times might offer: they slept in feather beds and ate from pewter and stoneware at a table spread with linen. Leaded glass windows admitted light, and in the cold winter months, even a little warmth. In addition, like most of the established men of Providence, James owned four black slaves. At least one lived at home and worked in the kitchen; the others labored in the warehouse and other enterprises.

Little is known about Hope save for her ancestry, but that fragment of lore speaks volumes about the young family and its progeny. She was the eldest daughter of Col. Nicholas Power, who earned his rank in the colonial militia, sported a silver-hilted sword and an ivory-topped cane, and boasted the first home in Providence to feature its own dining room. The colonel was the leading Providence merchant of his time and proprietor of the town's first still. It was Colonel Power who underwrote James's first voyage to the West Indies, at the helm of a forty-five-foot sloop, in 1723.

Toward the end of his life, James's father, the last of the family to take the pulpit at the First Baptist Church, grew concerned that the strict principles that guided his forebears were beginning to lose sway. In one of his final sermons, Elder James exhorted his congregation to "refuse Eror and Chuse Truth"—"Truth" residing in "the man of God" who "laboreth under a promise of salvation," and "Eror" embodied in "the marchant man." The admonishment might well have been addressed to his own son, by then a captain sailing for Nicholas Power. James gave a clear response in his decision to marry Hope. He would follow in the path blazed by Hope's father, and not the one laid down by his own.

Nor was he alone. Among James's several partners in the African venture was his brother Obadiah, namesake of their courageous ancestor. Fourteen years younger than James, the eighth of Elder James's ten children, Obadiah had shipped out to sea under his brother's charge, and served as captain on the *Mary*'s late trip to the Caribbean. Obadiah would not take the helm on the voyage across the Atlantic, but he was commissioned as supercargo, in charge of the ship's commercial transactions. Obadiah would buy the slaves in Africa and sell them at auction in the West Indies.

In outfitting a ship to make the voyage to Africa, James was joining a vast mercantile system that united four continents in a single great economic endeavor. The logic of slavery was simple: of all the peoples of the world, Africans had proven the best suited to withstand the heat, disease, and backbreaking toil required to raise and process cane sugar in the American tropics. White men and indigenous Indians had been put to the test, but they died in such numbers that their impressment was abandoned. Africans succumbed as well—as many as a third died during the first two years on a plantation, a phenomenon known as "seasoning"—but most survived, and the African trade thrived as a result. Slaves were used to raise coffee, tobacco, indigo, and other plantation staples, but most—as many as 90 percent in the period before 1820—were employed exclusively in growing and processing sugar.

By the end of the seventeenth century, slavery and the products of slave labor comprised the single largest economic enterprise on earth. Over the course of more than two hundred years, European carriers—British, Spanish, French, and Portuguese—had shipped more than 2 million Africans across the Atlantic in chains. But that was just the beginning. Spurred by an exploding European demand for sugar, traffic in slaves surged, and in the eighteenth century alone more than 6 million Africans were taken from their homeland to plantations in Brazil, the Caribbean, and, to a much smaller extent, British North America.

The increase in demand wrought fundamental changes in the trade. Up to the end of the seventeenth century, most of the slaves were carried on ships owned by monopolies operating under royal charters. Beginning in 1698, however, in a bid for still greater volume, the British opened the trade to private carriers. The French followed suit in 1725, and by 1730, most of the trade was being conducted by private enterprise. And while most of the slave ships continued to sail from European ports, mariners from Britain's North American colonies answered the call as well.

At the outset, the nascent North American slave trade sprung up at all the major colonial ports. Ships put out for the Guinea Coast, as the slave-trading region of West Africa was known, from Boston, New York, Charleston, and Philadelphia, as well as from Newport. But Rhode Island soon emerged as the dominant player on this side of the Atlantic, due in large part to its isolation. For the merchants and sea captains of Rhode Island, ever hampered by the limited range of exports they could offer, the opening of the slave trade represented a crucial new opportunity. If they could raise the capital to finance the twelve-thousand-mile voyage, they might realize dramatic profits, gains far surpassing the single-digit margins produced by even the most successful coasting run. Moreover, the African trade prized the single export that Rhode Islanders had so far learned to manufacture: rum.

In the first centuries of the slave trade, African and European middlemen on the western coast of Africa had narrowed the list of commodities that they would barter for slaves to guns, gold, and spirits—primarily French brandy. Around 1700, interlopers from the West Indies introduced rum, and the stronger stuff quickly supplanted brandy as the preferred libation. By 1725, British traders at Sierra Leone reported to their home office that there was "no trade to be made without rum."

This development accrued to the benefit of Rhode Island, as craftsmen there had learned to distill their spirits at a higher proof and consistently better quality. African chiefs and their European trading partners quickly learned to tell the difference, which led the governor of one British trading fort to acknowledge, in 1775, that "West India rum never will sell here while there is any Americans here." Consequently, almost from the time they entered the trade, New England slavers specialized in rum—the Rhode Island captains came to be known as Rum Men—and their merchandise took precedence in the slave markets of Africa. Rum became the practical currency on the coast and at the European forts, with prices for slaves denominated in gallons of rum as well as ounces of gold.

Rhode Island rum first appeared in quantity on the African coast in 1725, when three slaving voyages sailed from Newport. Over the course of the next ten years, Newport merchants sent twenty-five ships to Africa, where they traded barrels of rum for an estimated four thousand slaves. Once their cargo was loaded, they sailed a southerly route to reach the Caribbean, where they disposed of their captives and invested the proceeds in molasses, which they brought home to Rhode Island to make more rum. This was the triangle trade, and a successful run brought profits from each leg. How much depended on the particulars of the voyage, and ledgers giving specific figures are rare. But one 1747 letter sent from a slave captain to a Liverpool shipmaster gives a sense of the high end: "Negroes at Jamaica £50 to £55 a head bought on the Coast of Affrica at from £4 to £6 a head."

In trying to keep tabs on his competitors at Newport, James Brown was sure to hear talk about the ten-to-one margins that could be realized in the slave trade. He was just as sure to hear of the pitfalls of trade on the African coast.

Trading for slaves was a dangerous business, where a soured deal could suddenly turn violent, and where, once secured on board, the human cargoes often rebelled, sometimes overwhelming their captors. Even the normal hazards of maritime commerce increased exponentially in the slave trade. The West African coast was a notorious haunt for pirates, and tropical disease carried off white seamen at an alarming rate.

But as a sea captain and a maritime merchant, James was accustomed to long odds and high risk. Besides, his two stills were producing more rum than he could move in the local market. In March of 1736, one consignment of molasses had been sitting on his wharf untouched for six months. James had spent years supplying Newport slavers with rum; now he was determined to join their ranks.

James kept no journal in the months preceding the dispatch of the *Mary*, but a cache of his letters survives, and they make it clear this was a critical project, demanding all of his resources and capital. In January of 1736, he notified one correspondent that "I should be very glad if you would come over & Settel accounts with me, I am at present in great want of Money." The same month, addressing a Mr. Turtolow, he was even more direct: "I want my money verry much." And as late as June, he requested of a Captain Remington that "if you have any money to lett I will take it at two shillings per pound to the quantity of five hundred pounds," a small fortune at the time.

James had to call in his accounts in order to finance the thorough overhaul required to convert his coastal freighter into a slave ship. Aside from copper sheathing, that meant raising the deck to allow more room beneath, where the slaves would be confined during much of the passage from Africa. A wooden barrier, known as a barracoon, had to be constructed amidships to separate the crew from their cargo.

No physical description of the *Mary* survives, but in all probability she was about the same size as James's other single-masted sloops — about fifty feet in length, no more than twenty feet across, and less than ten feet deep. A raised quarterdeck in the rear made room below for an officer's cabin that looked over the sea through a row of cut-glass windows. The *Mary* was a good deal smaller than the average European slaver, but fit the norm for those putting out from the colonies. The smaller craft required less up-front capital, and allowed captains to assemble their cargoes more quickly, which meant a shorter stay on the pestilential African coast. With a second deck, really little more than a shelf, rigged below to provide cramped sleeping quarters of between eighteen inches and two feet high, the little ship could carry a cargo of about a hundred disconsolate Africans.

Other modifications were required. All of the hatches, gangways, and other portals through which a slave might attempt escape had to be reinforced. A ledger of James's accounts shows a bill from the blacksmith for an assortment of iron spikes, a "scuttle bar" and a "hach bar" weighing about eight pounds apiece, along with "35 pare of handcoofs." That last entry gives some indication of the size of the cargo James anticipated; male slaves were commonly shackled together, so the handcuffs would suffice for seventy men; females were kept separate and often unfettered.

James's letters also indicate the cargo he was sending to Africa. In March, he wrote to Boston to obtain precise current prices for rum, sugar, and molasses and, separately, contacted a fellow merchant who was due to receive a vessel "loden with staves." James asked him to set aside a thousand, to make barrels suitable for shipping rum.

By June, all the preparations were complete. The *Mary* was fitted and stocked, and a captain and crew had been enlisted. Certainly there was a final gathering of the Brown clan, with James, Hope, and their five children, along with Obadiah and perhaps Jeremiah, another seafaring brother, and Elisha, the youngest son of Elder James and always a favorite in the family. Widow Mary Brown would have presided, the ailing matriarch having arrived at her sixty-fifth year; her household slave, a black woman named Quassie, would have tended the table, serving roasted meat, stewed squash, and coarse corn-meal bread. There would be toasts of rum or cider drunk to the success of James's most daring venture, and prayers for Obadiah's safe return from his first trip across the sea.

Soon after, James looked on as Obadiah climbed the gangway from the wharf on the banks of Salt River to join the captain and crew on the *Mary*, her rails gleaming with a new coat of varnish. Comparable slave ships of the time carried a remarkably small complement of sailors, with a mate or two, half a dozen seamen, and perhaps a cabin boy. With the wind at their backs and the tide flowing out, the crew raised the canvas, a billowing, triangular mainsail behind the mast, two or three headsails toward the bow, and a square-rigged topsail above. Silently gaining way, she slipped down to Fox Point, at the southern end of town, and out onto the choppy waters of the bay. Even if all went well, she would not return for the better part of a year.

The passage to Africa was the quiet leg of the journey. With the cargo secure in the hold, the crew had little to do but get to know one another and the ship. The seas beneath their bow shifted from green to blue as they entered the Gulf Stream, and then back to green as they crossed through, en route to Sierra Leone, at the western edge of Africa. The water was streaked with pale yellow gulf weed and broken by the splash of flying fish and dolphins. Reaching the Tropic of Cancer, the mariners marked their passage by celebrating the baptism of the tropics, a ribald and time-honored ceremony that called for dousing any novice to the southern climes, regardless of rank, with bracing pails of seawater. From there the *Mary* would steer farther south, into the steady flow of the Guinea current, which would carry them up into the Bight of Benin, and along the shores of the storied slave coast.

In the weeks before his departure, Obadiah would have learned what he could of the state of trade on the coast. He would know about the two primary modes of trade—either at the forts maintained by the major European powers, or in direct transactions with African chiefs or white freelancers, usually at the mouth of the scores of rivers that cleaved the thousand-mile stretch of coastline where most of the English-speaking slavers conducted business. The forts presented the easier option, mud-walled garrisons where Dutch, British, or French factors held as many as a thousand slaves in stockades or underground dungeons awaiting the arrival of ships seeking cargo. But the large stocks were reserved for European captains; for Yankee interlopers, the middlemen exacted a premium, and the supply of slaves was sporadic. During lean years, or if a slaver was seeking bargains, he made his deals with the Africans in person.

That was a decidedly tricky option. Grounded as it was in kidnapping, the slave trade bred fear and mistrust on both sides. Some slavers liked to shorten the bargaining process by grabbing the African traders as well as those captives offered for sale; retribution might be exacted upon the next slave crew to arrive. And even the most routine transactions involved an elaborate series of payments of tribute to the local king or his lieutenants, to various interpreters and intermediaries, and to the African trader on the beach. Wrangling over what was paid and what was delivered might quickly escalate into a "palaver," a dispute that required a formal sit-down between the parties, usually resolved through still another payment of rum, gold, or possibly tobacco. Both slavers and their African counterparts frequently resorted to "panyaring," or seizing hostages, to ensure the terms of trade.

The greatest drawback in direct deals with Africans was time. Slaves were rarely available in quantity, and usually purchased one or two at a time. Even trading at the European forts, American slavers rarely made their cargo through a single transaction, or even several. Far more often, a slave ship would languish for three to five months on the south-facing coast, her crew members exposed to malaria, dysentery, and other mortal threats; some slave ships tarried as long as eight months to assemble a full complement of Africans.

Obadiah had proven himself in the markets of the West Indies, which were notoriously dicey; as one ship captain put it, there was "more honor and honesty in so many highwaymen in England than in the merchants" of the Caribbean. Still, the ports of Surinam and Martinique must have seemed tame by comparison. The strange surroundings, the bewildering conventions, and the high stakes of trade on the coast—literally life-and-death—had to pose a challenge to a young trader making his first trip to the continent.

Obadiah and the *Mary* reached Africa sometime in early August, not long after the close of the rainy season, when sudden squalls and offshore tornadoes made the seas especially dangerous. Under quiet skies, the long, low profile of the Guinea Coast hovered over a border of soft white breakers, rolling steadily in the tropical haze. The captain had completed his primary mission. It was now up to Obadiah to make his way to shore, contact the nearest slave merchant, and begin trading for captive Africans, who would be sent off in chains aboard the *Mary's* longboat. The trips ashore became a routine that lasted for months, broken only to weigh anchor and move farther east, carried by the Guinea current, first along the Gold Coast, then the Slave Coast, the stifling quarters between decks slowly filling with people.

The *Mary* soon had company. A Newport captain reported in October that "we have had nineteen sail of us at one time . . . so that these ships that are said to cary prime slaves off is now forced to take any that comes." Many of the rival slavers were French—"the whole coast is full of them"—but several others were from Rhode Island. "Heair is 7 sail of us Rume men that we are Ready to Devur one another; for our Case is Despart."

The writer went on to describe what amounted to the grim existence of the slave trader: "I beg that you will exist my family in what they shall want for I no not when I shall git home to them myself. I have had the misfortune to bury my Chefe Mate on the 21st of September, and one man more; and lost the Negro man primus, and Adam Overboard on my pasedge one three weeks after another. That makes me now Very weak handed: for out of what is left theair is two that is good for nothing. Cap Hamond hath bin heair six months and has but 60 slaves on bord."

Aside from competition for scarce slaves, the prevalence of so many Rhode Island traders meant that the market for rum was glutted, making trades that much more difficult. Yet for all the adversity other slavers encountered that season, Obadiah appears to have had a successful voyage. It may have been that the *Mary* beat the rush, moving her rum before the rest of the Rhode Islanders arrived. And it may be a measure of Obadiah's mercantile skills. But the *Mary* must have departed Africa sometime in October, for she had arrived in the Caribbean by November 25, when Obadiah got a letter off to his brother. Unfortunately, Obadiah reported, he had encountered a "poor market" for selling his captive cargo. James addressed an answer to his "Loveing brother" in March, reflecting the long delays in seaborne communications.

"But you are well, which is good news, for health in this world is better than welth," James wrote. "By all means make dispatch in your business if you cannot Sell all your Slaves to your mind bring some home I believe they will Sell well, get molasses if you can, and if you Cannot come without it, leave no debts behind upon no account, get some Sugar & Cotten if you Can handily, but be Sure make dispatch for that is the life of trade."

Obadiah completed the final leg of his passage in May, returning to Providence eleven months after his departure with a full cargo of guns, gunpowder, salt, cordage, coffee, fabrics, and still more rum. Obadiah also delivered three slaves, whom James promptly put up for sale. On May 11, 1737, he notified a correspondent: "Sir, if I remember Rite you dezaired me to Right you a few lines at the Arivol of my Ginemon. Theas may in forme you that she is Arived and you may have A slave if you Cum or send Befoar they air Gon." James added that salt and other goods were available, but advised his customer to hurry: "You Cannot be two soon."

Obadiah's African voyage came at a time of transition in the life of the Brown family. While he was at sea, his mother died, closing the books on the third generation of the Browns in Providence. Mary Brown's will completed the distribution of her late husband's estate, including several parcels of land and her personal servants. To one son she left an "apprentice boy, Othniel Herndon"; to another, a young slave named Cuffey, the son of Quassie. In June, after a month ashore, Obadiah married Mary Harris, his first cousin, daughter of his mother's brother. The following year, both Obadiah and James each celebrated the birth of children; Obadiah's first, a daughter, Phebe, and James's sixth, a son, whom he named Moses.

Also in 1738, James suffered the injury that would lead to his demise, sustained during a weight lifting contest at a spring fair. In May, he penned a public letter "to all my neighbours, that if it be the pleasure of the heavens to take the breath out of my mortal body . . . I am quite free and willing that my body may be opened, in order that my fellow creatures and neighbours may see whether my grievance hath been nothing but a spleen or not." James survived another year, during which he continued to dispatch ships and issue detailed sailing orders to his captains, but he succumbed in April of 1739. Obadiah was again at sea when his brother died. Writing home to his grieving sister-in-law, he commiserated in "ye heavy nuse of ye death of my brother which is no small Con sarn to me for he was ye only frind to me." Obadiah promptly followed James's example, retiring from the sea to operate a store, underwrite shipping ventures, and invest in a range of local industry. And as they came of age, he introduced his nephews into the ways of commerce.

John and Moses Brown grew up with no memories of their father, but their lives were closely bounded by conventions of culture, community, and family. In their free time, they were turned loose to wander; the town was crowded with friends and relations, and the Brown boys were known by a singsong jingle that survives to this day, "Nick and Josie, John and Mosie." Providence provided ample opportunity for play. The woods were safe; Indian raiders had torched the town in 1675, but it had been a death spasm for the tribes of Rhode Island, and those not slain had been sold into slavery. Yet the forest still held its mystery, as well as wolves, martens, foxes, and wildcats. In the tidal shallows of Mile-End Cove, off the Great Salt River to the south of town, lay rich beds of clams, quahogs, and oysters, some as much as a foot long. And on the wharves, children could treat themselves to a taste of the molasses oozing from the seams of barrels awaiting shipment. An old story tells of a merchant trying to select his purchase. When he inquired, "What casks are your best?" he was answered with a shrug. "Ask that little molasses-faced Moses, he will tell you."

Hope Brown made sure the boys attended school, probably at the one operated by George Taylor, a disciple of the Church of England who also served as the town scrivener. Classes were held about a half mile from the Brown home; their trek up Towne Street took the boys past landmarks as familiar as the furniture in their living room. There were the fanciful signs of the shopkeepers— the Bunch of Grapes, or the leering Turk's Head—totems carved from heavy chunks of wood and swinging from ornate iron brackets. Entering Market Square, they passed on their right the apothecary run by Jabez Bowen. His brother Ephraim, also a physician, lived next door, their homes resting at the foot of Prospect Hill. Ephraim had fourteen children; the oldest, Jabez, a year younger than Moses, was a classmate who became a lifelong friend. Fronting the north side of the square lived Arthur Fenner, a judge and a distant cousin of the Browns who traced his lineage back to Chad. Of Obadiah Brown's four daughters, one would marry a Fenner; another, young Jabez Bowen. And to the left, on the south shoulder of the market, stood the home of Joseph Jenckes, recently retired as governor of the colony and a giant of a man, standing more than seven feet tall. Jenckes's wife, Martha, was a Brown; their daughter Catherine was married to William Turpin, proprietor of the town's largest inn, which doubled on occasion as the seat of the colonial legislature.

Continuing up past the square, the boys passed the home of their uncle Obadiah and his daughters, which faced across the avenue the squat, austere lines of the Baptist meetinghouse, forty feet square, where the Browns' forebears had presided for generations. Should they venture farther, beyond the schoolhouse to the northern reach of town, they would arrive at the shop kept by their uncle Elisha. For John and Moses, the lines between family and community were often blurred.

The boys learned to read and write in the fashion of the day—syntax and spelling, even among the leading intellectuals of the time, was haphazard, sometimes comically so. More exacting was the training in arithmetic, a critical skill at a time when merchants dealt with half a dozen currencies—French livres, Dutch stivers and guilders, Spanish pieces of eight, and British pounds, shillings, and pence, as well as several different issues of colonial scrip from Rhode Island and Massachusetts.

The boys learned those lessons well, if John's testimony can be taken at face value. A "cypher book" from his school days is inscribed with the date 1749— when he was twelve years old—and the legend "John Brown the Cleverest boy in Providence Town." What follows is exercises and instructions that today seem utterly confounding. An example is "The Golden Rule, or rule of 3. This is the Golden Rule for the excellency thereof." The rule is illustrated in rhyme:

If the 4th of the Second must Exceed then See
By the great Extream It Multiplyed be
But if it must be Less than Second Aim
To multiply it by the Less Extream.

Examples were taken from the life of commerce. Under the heading "Variety," pupils solved problems like these: "A Tobaconist would mix 20 lb. of Tobaco at 9*d.* a lb. with 40 lb. at 12*d.* a lb. and with 30 lb. at 18 Pence and with 12 lb. at 2 Shillings a Pound, What will a Pound of this mixture be worth?" John gave the answer of "2*s*.2.2 6-17 farthing."

Practical as they were, the lessons also included nautical problems. The boys learned to calculate a ship's latitude using sextant readings taken from the sun at zenith, a skill that opened all the seas of the globe to an intrepid mariner. And they learned the method for determining a ship's tonnage, which was more a factor of volume than weight—"Rule first say as 1 : Breadth :: Half the Breadth : a fourth Number. Again as 94 : the fourth Number :: her length : Tunnage."

Studies occupied only part of the day. Even in their teens, the boys were frequenting the taverns in town, playing cards and drinking "punch," commonly braced with rum. Weekends brought "frolicks," open-house parties that featured reels or jigs, danced to the tune of a fiddle, and games like Who's Got the Button, intricate contests that ended with the "loser" exchanging kisses with a laughing, longhaired girl. And there were pranks. Moses was away from Providence on a visit when he received a letter from his friend Jabez Bowen. It notified that "Brothers J. Brown and J. Updike have Broke the Meeting Hous windows. You must make haste home." Glass being precious at the time, this was a fairly serious case of vandalism. But John was rambunctious through all his years, and Moses would grow familiar with the task of bailing his brother out of trouble.

John and Moses ended their formal education early—Moses recalled later that he left school after his thirteenth year—and graduated to Obadiah's countinghouse. There they joined Nicholas, who was already keeping accounts and running the distilling operation, and Joseph, who did as he was asked but never developed the flair for business that distinguished his brothers. Obadiah needed his nephews' help as soon as they became useful. The business grew steadily, and in several new directions. Around 1752, Obadiah opened a chocolate mill—cocoa rivaled coffee as a favorite brew and was routinely listed on the cargo manifests from the West Indies, yet the beans had to be shipped on to Boston or New York for grinding. Obadiah's water-driven mill was the colony's first, and he was soon offering his services to merchants in Providence and at Newport.

About the same time, Obadiah invested in a chandlery to manufacture high-grade candles from refined whale oil. This served another pressing need in colonial households, which relied on pine knots or tallow candles fabricated over the kitchen stove for interior lighting. Whale-oil candles, called spermaceti for the thrice-pressed head matter from which they were made, gave off three times the light of tallow candles, from a tall, clear flame.

The method for producing spermaceti candles was an arcane process of pressing and cooling that lasted all through the cold winter months. Developed on the continent, it was brought to Rhode Island by Jacob Rodriguez Rivera, a Portuguese merchant and leader of the Jewish community at Newport. Soon after, in 1753, Obadiah had erected a candle works at Tockwotton, a district at the southern end of Providence sometimes known as Fox Point. There was a primary workshop and a collection of outbuildings that grew steadily over time until they sprawled over eleven acres. By then the Browns were processing more than a hundred tons of whale oil each year. The gloomy manufactory was operated by Joseph, whose abilities ran more in a mechanical than a commercial vein. Family lore holds further that John Vanderlight, a physician who trained in his native Holland and maintained a drugstore on Towne Street, revealed to Obadiah the secrets of spermaceti. Vanderlight was the husband of Mary Brown, the sole daughter of Captain James.

Some historians dispute Vanderlight's role, but the story reflects the insular nature of the Brown family enterprises. Nicholas ran the distillery and kept books in Obadiah's countinghouse. John and Moses joined in as they came of age; John appears to have specialized in assembling cargoes for the coastal trade, while Moses became expert in prices and markets in the West Indies and at the whaling center of Nantucket. Both of the younger brothers served as supercargo on coasting voyages, but it was James, the eldest, who followed in the path of his father and uncle as a captain at the helm of Obadiah's growing fleet.

For all their innovation, the family's primary interest remained on the sea. Records show that between 1748 and 1760, Obadiah and his nephews owned outright or jointly more than sixty vessels. Most were away at any given time, carrying freight from Surinam to Nova Scotia, and occasionally as far as Honduras, London, and, as we have seen, Africa. While the slave trade was never its primary concern, the family firm maintained an active interest in that line of business. In 1758, Obadiah listed ten black slaves in the cargo manifest of a ship dispatched to New Orleans on a trading venture. The next year, he sent the schooner *Wheel of Fortune* to the Guinea Coast. She never returned, apparently captured by French pirates. The event was recorded in the simple entry in Obadiah's insurance ledger: "Taken."

Raiders were a fact of life on the high seas during the period of Europe's near-incessant imperial conflicts, and the Browns gave as well as they got. As early as the 1740s, Obadiah was fitting vessels with cannon and shot, arming his crews with pistol and saber, and sending them out to prowl for ships flying foreign flags. These were privateers, marauders deputized by royal decree to harass enemy shipping. Through the hostilities that climaxed with the French and Indian War of the 1750s, Dutch, Spanish, and French captains all struck their colors under the threat of Obadiah's guns, and their ships and cargo were sold at auction at Newport, the proceeds divvied up as spoils of war.

Young James's correspondence from distant ports reflected the nature of the firm's business and the tenor of Brown family relations. A letter posted from New Bern, North Carolina, in February 1749, and addressed to "Mr. Nicholas Brown Distiller" described a voyage "With Such Gales of Wind that It Is Impossibel to Expres Beat and tore my Sails and Riging more than I should have Dun In Six months moderate wether. the Vessel Sprung A Leak the second Night after I came and Continewed the Whole Passage So that Wee had a smart Spel at a pump Every half hour . . . markets Are Very Bad so that our Goods Will Not fetch the firs Cos . . . Remember my harty and obedient Respect to my dear mother Brothers and Sister Likewise to Unkel Elisha."

The following September James put out as captain of the sloop *Freelove*, bound for Maryland. It was his last journey. He died at York, Virginia, February 21, 1751. There is no record of the cause of death, nor of the reactions in Providence, but it may have prompted the family's decision that Moses move from the home of his birth to his uncle's house, also on Towne Street but a few doors north of Market Square. Obadiah and his wife produced eight children, but each of their four sons died in infancy, and Moses was embraced as the surrogate. He reciprocated with unswerving devotion, and later came to refer to Obadiah as "Father Brown."

By persevering through bereavement, by building on the legacy of their forefathers, by exploiting the opportunities their particular situation offered to them while responding to its limitations, the Browns by the middle of the eighteenth century secured their position as the leading family of their growing town. That they succeeded as a clan seems to have been dictated by circumstance; more than in other, better established colonial centers, the fortunes of Providence rested on the achievements of families, rather than individuals.

This was due in part to the limited resources of the town: individual initiative alone did not guarantee success so well as concerted enterprise. It also shows how isolated Providence was. It was a juncture for commerce but not a crossroads, its overland approaches consisting of rutted trails, bridle paths, and old Indian tracks through the forest. Strangers were accepted only gradually, and the founding families held on to their prerogatives. Within that tight-knit community, however, there was easy familiarity and frequent collaboration.

The Browns pursued their business interests in concert with a handful of other leading families in Providence who also made up their circle of friends; together they constituted the town's elite. The Angells, partners in several Brown shipping ventures, were another clan that maintained vessels, a store, and a still for making rum. The sons and nephews of Joseph Jenckes, James's august neighbor on Towne Street, also traded with the West Indies and ran a shop in Providence; Joseph's brother Ebenezer preceded Elder James Brown as pastor of the Baptist Church. As Joseph Jenckes wed Martha Brown, so did Nicholas Brown, two generations later, marry Rhoda Jenckes, in 1762. Nicholas was an occasional business partner — and sometime rival — of Rhoda's father.

But the Browns' most important association, in the life of the family and the life of the colony, was with Stephen and Esek Hopkins, two of ten brothers and sisters raised on a homestead in Scituate, a rural district west of Providence. Stephen and Esek both moved to "the compact part of town" along Towne Street in the 1740s, where both became actively engaged in the life of the community. Esek was a mariner and a trader who routinely sailed on commission for James and then Obadiah Brown; in 1758, sailing at the helm of the Brown ship *Providence,* Esek and two other privateers from New York captured a five-hundred-ton, sixteen-gun Dutch freighter loaded with flour and brandy after a seven-hour firefight near Cape Francois.

Stephen Hopkins was a merchant and entrepreneur, but more than that, he was a born statesman, an autodidact renowned for his wide reading in the classics, law, and philosophy. He was elected to the colonial assembly from Scituate, and was named speaker the year he moved into Providence. The diarist Ezra Stiles, an early president of Yale, described Stephen as "a man of penetrating astutious Genius, full of Subtlety, deep Cunning, intriguing and enterprising." Moses Brown was thirty years younger than Stephen Hopkins, but even as a teenager Moses adopted him as a mentor and father figure, and Stephen accepted him as a peer.

These several families were distinguished by their expansive homes on Towne Street, most of them built on the original lots parceled out by Roger Williams and Chad Brown a century before; by their settled position in the several congregations in town; and by their rank as freeholders of the colony, a status conferred on landholders that included suffrage in local elections. They kept slaves to labor in their kitchens and their workshops, and spent the muggy summers in country homes outside the town. They were recognized on the street by the finery of their clothes: instead of coarse cloth and leather breeches, they wore cut velvet coats over brocaded silk vests, and below the knee, fine cotton hose. Powdered wigs were rare — these were not the grandees of Newport or New York—but the upper class favored silver buckles on their shoes instead of the more plebian pewter.

Like the Browns, most of the leading clans in Providence could trace their ancestry back to one of the founders of the town, and they owed their prominence as much to the generous land holdings passed down through the generations as to their own ingenuity. But they understood that with their prosperity came an obligation to lend a hand in raising up a new society on the edge of the wilderness. Obadiah served as a member of the Providence town council and later the colonial assembly, whose members were selected twice annually by the councils of the various towns. On the assembly he joined the Hopkins brothers, the Jenckeses, and others at biannual meetings that rotated between Providence, Newport, and three other county seats. When at Providence, the assembly would convene at Turpin's tavern, whose high, projecting eaves shaded the largest building in town. Meetings were held in a converted dance hall before a stone fireplace large enough to stand in. There the delegates wrangled over disputes with Great Britain and the neighboring colonies as well as local questions like financing the town jail. Administration was in the hands of the delegates; in 1754, Obadiah Brown and James Angell were commissioned to purchase "a large water engine" to augment the leather buckets of the town fire brigade.

Not all the advances were fostered through government associations. About 1750, Stephen Hopkins donated his collection of books to help launch a lending library in Providence; the titles included full sets of Pope, Swift, Milton, and Shakespeare, along with Greek and Latin classics and standards in politics, law, and medicine. Housed in the council chamber at the courthouse, it was one of the first public libraries in all the colonies, after Boston and Newport. The original subscribers included Obadiah, Nicholas, John, and Moses Brown, not yet fifteen years old. Nicholas was the first librarian, attending the desk from 2 to 5 P.M. on Saturday afternoons. Separately, Joseph, John, and Moses became Freemasons, joining the order when Saint John's Lodge was chartered in Providence in 1757.

Yet as much as their lives were circumscribed by family and town, the young men of the Brown clan each followed his own course to maturity. Nicholas emerged as the most conscientious of the four surviving brothers, keeper of accounts for the family firm and, as the eldest, the clan's first voice within family and local government councils. His instincts tended toward cautious and conservative; he rarely broke new ground, but made sure to consolidate whatever gains a given venture might yield. Joseph, by contrast, was indifferent to the affairs of business. He focused instead on esoteric questions of mathematics, architecture, and engineering. He joined with his brothers in service in the colonial assembly, and presided for years over the meetings of the Freemasons, but never attained the worldly stature of his siblings.

The two younger boys were more venturesome. John and Moses each practiced the arts of navigation as apprentices on the family ships, and both learned to dicker and drive bargains on Newport's bustling waterfront, at the great wholesale houses of Boston, and on the tarry wharves of Nantucket. The two were frequent collaborators, traveling together on business and, in the summer months, on pleasure cruises across the sparkling waters of Narragansett Bay. Just two years apart in age, they shared similar duties at the family firm and the same circle of friends. Growing up, they forged a bond of friendship that was often tested but never renounced.

Yet for all they shared, John and Moses were distinctly different in character, temperament, and even physical bearing. Both were short men, just over five feet tall, but where Moses was slim, John was stout, his girth broadening as the years went by. Even in his early years, John was a great talker and loved large entertainments; Moses was more reticent, more apt to listen, more thoughtful in his responses. Where John was an egotist, Moses was painfully humble. Where John sought out conflict, Moses looked for conciliation.

And while Moses was always comfortable with the disciplined pieties of the Baptists and other moral leaders of the town, John openly rebelled. He made a show of his independence in the spring of 1762, when a theater troupe from New York, after a successful season at Newport, moved on to Providence and commenced to raise a building to house a "histrionic academy." Their efforts spurred an emergency meeting of the town council, which voted to ban "all Kinds of Stage plays or Theatrical Shows." When the visitors persisted, the council petitioned the colonial assembly on grounds that "So Expensive Amusements and idle Diversions cannot be of any good Tendancy among us." The petition carried 405 signatures.

John Brown's was not among them. Toward the end of the troupe's stay in Providence, a mob gathered in front of their theater to demand their expulsion. John was outraged, and decided to stage a performance of his own to break up the demonstration. With the help of some other young men, John went to the local militia depot and secured the loan of a cannon, which he dragged back to the theater and trained on the assembled protesters. The show went on that day, but in August the assembly endorsed the Providence petition; the town would not host another theatrical performance until 1795.

But John's primary concern was always business. While still serving out his apprenticeship to Obadiah, John took in side work, keeping books for Esek Hopkins and others to earn a few extra shillings. Soon after, when the expanding state of the candle business began to drive up the cost of whale oil, John organized a consortium of four candle manufacturers in a bid to set a ceiling on the price. The agreement also specified a minimum price for the sale of finished candles, and required that all parties use any "fair and honorable" means to prevent any new chandlers from entering the trade. John put his stamp on the agreement by proposing that members of the consortium meet twice yearly "at the best tavern in Taunton," in Massachusetts.

John distinguished himself early as a shrewd and reliable arbiter of accounts. By 1757, at just twenty years of age, he was deputized at the admiralty court at Newport to help supervise the auction of prize ships sailed home by Rhode Island privateers. These captured vessels brought windfall profits for the owners of the privateers and handsome bonuses for their daring crews. Their arrival created a sensation along the waterfront, and John's official position placed him at the center of the action. He cut a striking figure on the docks and in the great stone market buildings of Newport, an upstart from Providence, short and stout but brash and cocksure, shouldering his way among swarthy seamen and the merchants and port officials with their ruffled cuffs and powdered wigs, some more than twice his age.

Moses also proved useful and reliable in the affairs of the family firm, but his creativity found different avenues of expression. Like Joseph, Moses became engrossed with the technical questions that arose at the chocolate and candle manufactories. And he was constantly looking for ways to diversify. While still in his teens, Moses began investigating ways to produce silk by raising silkworms on homegrown mulberry bushes. The scheme never reached fruition, though silk production caught on for a time in nearby Connecticut.

Nor was his intellect confined to affairs of commerce. He wrote to friends in New Haven and New York to request books on advanced mathematics and various topics in medicine and horticulture. He was fascinated by the new procedure of inoculation, then being introduced to combat the deadly threat posed by smallpox. Inoculation was illegal in Rhode Island, so Moses traveled to New Jersey to inspect a hospital that specialized in the practice. He made a second trip to get inoculated himself, marking a lifelong interest in public health.

The pronounced difference between the younger Browns was illustrated in their marriages. When John was wed, in 1760, at the age of twenty-four, he reached outside the family congregation and chose a Quaker, Sarah Smith, the daughter of a successful merchant and distiller. Their wedding was a gala celebration attended by most of the town's elite; the Browns borrowed coaches and carriages to ferry their guests from the nuptials to the reception. The next day, John moved his new bride into a new home, one of the first brick buildings to be erected on Towne Street. He furnished it with new chairs and looking glasses imported from Philadelphia, along with burnished walnut desks and bookcases made by John Goddard at Newport, regarded ever since as exemplars of colonial craftsmanship.

Moses was married four years later, at age twenty-six, in a quiet family ceremony, to his cousin Anna, the third of Obadiah's four daughters. The newlyweds continued to reside at Obadiah's drafty old house along with Moses' mother and his sister Mary Vanderlight, by then a widow, as well as Anna's younger sister. Like John, Moses also undertook a construction project in the year of his marriage, but his task, assigned by the town council, was to supervise the paving of Towne Street.

It seems likely that Obadiah would have rejoiced at the union of his daughter and his favorite nephew—after all, Obadiah had also chosen a first cousin as his wife, a practice that persisted in the colonies through the rest of the century. But the venerated uncle was not there to grant his blessing. Obadiah died a year before the ceremony, felled by a stroke while riding from Providence to his country house. John and Moses were in Newport when they heard the news. Moses headed immediately for Providence, riding hard up the east side of the bay and arriving in time to share a few last words with his uncle; John stayed behind "to compleat sum business of importance."

Obadiah's passing brought the tutelage of his brother's sons to an abrupt close. No longer could the Brown brothers turn to a seasoned elder for direction and advice. Yet their uncle had lived long enough to complete James's work of raising up the next generation. Each of the four young men had completed his apprenticeship in business, and each had assumed his home on Towne Street. John already stood out as the most aggressive and enterprising businessman in the family, and possibly Rhode Island, but he was not the best endowed. That distinction belonged to Moses, a consequence of his close bond with his uncle. In his will, Obadiah left Moses the same share of his fortune as he left his own children—this in addition to Moses' bequeathal from his own father, which included 145 acres of light farmland fronting the Seekonk River, east of town. That estate was increased further by his marriage to Anna, described in a contemporary account as "an agreeable young lady, with a handsome fortune."

In November 1762, the four Brown brothers reorganized the family firm as Nicholas Brown & Company. Nicholas was then thirty-three years old, and

Moses just twenty-four, but together the young men presided over the largest shipping concern in Providence, the largest chocolate mill in the colony, and the largest candle manufactory in North America.

The Brown brothers would grow and prosper, their fortunes entwined with those of their colony and the new society taking shape along the shores of North America. They were defined by concentric circles of powerful influence—family and town, colony and empire, God and king—and yet within that framework they were essentially, intrinsically autonomous, guided by instinct and character. In the coming years, those bulwarks of influence would be tested in the forge of war and revolution. The older Browns, Nicholas and Joseph, would hunker down, clinging to institutions and their own comforts as they rode out the tumult. But as much as their brothers turned inward, John and Moses looked outward, each grappling for his own answer to the questions of freedom and independence, both personal and political. And as much as the times were marked by the struggles of empire, by generals and armies and fleets, the greatest challenge the brothers faced would come from each other.

2

Brown Brothers Inc.

IN THE DECADES before the idea of America even took shape, the interior of North America loomed as a forbidding wilderness, and Rhode Island stood as an outpost on the western fringe of Britain's sprawling oceanic empire. Opportunity lay to the south, where the patrician planters of the Caribbean vied for the favor and the markets of their continental sponsors, and relied on Yankee sea captains for livestock, boards, and barrel staves, and for the fish and meat that sustained the slave gangs that labored under the tropical sun.

John and Moses Brown learned to work the creaking interstices of that unwieldy system from the family wharves on the Great Salt River and from their stores and countinghouse on Towne Street. By the middle of the 1760s, their firm had more than eighty-five vessels afloat, some making three or more trips a year, some, hauling whale oil from Nantucket, making that many trips in a month. That meant almost daily departures, the shouts and curses of the supercargoes and the rumble of the great, hundred-gallon barrels of oil and molasses easily heard from their homes and offices, all of which lay less than a hundred yards from the waterfront.

In counsel among themselves, and in offhand conversations with the other traders in town, the Brown brothers were constantly discussing what destinations and which markets would yield the highest returns for their cargoes. The elaborate trade laws of the British empire presented obstacles, but also opportunities.

One reliable course to profit was smuggling. The configuration of Narragansett Bay served to abet the subterfuge, as it afforded three distinct openings to the Atlantic, entrances divided by the islands of Aquidneck, home to the towns of Portsmouth and Newport, and Connanicut, where the Beavertail lighthouse stood atop windswept headlands overlooking the Atlantic. All three channels were navigable to oceangoing craft. British patrols traditionally focused on the center passage, which led between low, rocky bluffs to the harbor at Newport; smugglers tended to veer west, under the lee of Point Judith, or east, into the mouth of the Sakonnet River. James Brown used that geography to advantage when he advised his captains in 1736 that "it is ticklish times here, my neighbors threaten to informe against us, so I hope you will not be too bold when you come home, enter in the West Indias if you can"—a reference to the westerly passage.

Smuggling was a mainstay for Rhode Island merchants from early times, prompting the Earl of Bellomont, governor of all New England, to complain of his southernmost district in 1699: "I know that government and people to be the most piraticall in the King's dominions." When British plantation owners from the Caribbean persuaded Parliament to pass the Molasses Act in 1733, imposing a sixpence-per-gallon duty on imports from any non-British colony, it only alienated the northern colonies, and swelled the ranks of the smugglers.

Tobacco was another staple regulated by the Board of Trade, which required that all colonial leaf be sent directly to Britain. The Browns routinely ignored that edict, shipping tobacco grown in Rhode Island and Connecticut to the Dutch colonies at Saint Eustatius and Surinam. In 1738, Obadiah spent five days in the brig of a British man-o'-war and had his ship confiscated for carrying an illegal cargo of tobacco. Nonetheless, thirty years later, John Brown led the family firm and two other Providence merchants in a bid to corner the market in New England tobacco. The cartel was legal but the destination, a Dutch port, made the entire project unlawful.

England's intermittent wars with France and Spain presented new avenues for gain, and raised the stakes of illicit trade in the Caribbean and North America. Under Obadiah's direction, the Browns invested heavily in privateering, and some of their captains achieved a string of captures. But the risks were high; as one historian put it, "Conditions favored trade against raid." After Obadiah's decease, his nephews followed that dictum, dispatching their ships to the Caribbean and routinely trading with the enemies of the British crown.

Imperial conflicts, as old as Europe, flared on the American continent in 1754 when the French and the English clashed at Fort Duquesne, near present-day Pittsburgh, in a struggle for control of the frontier. For most of the next decade, the French and Indian War occupied British and colonial troops—and the ships of His Majesty's Navy—in a global conflict that ranged from Canada to the Caribbean, and from India to Europe. That brought bloody fighting in North America—and the first military action seen by Col.

George Washington of the Virginia militia—but the merchants of the northern colonies looked askance on the quarrels of Europe. They believed that the mercantile policy of Parliament was designed to benefit London, not her dominions, and had few qualms about trading with neutral parties or directly with the French; embargoes served only to drive prices up. The French sugar planters were happy to do business, as British naval power virtually severed the connections to their home countries. Without supplies from English colonials, the French plantations would simply collapse.

The traders of the North American colonies pursued their ends through several ingenious schemes. The simplest was to submit false papers to customs authorities warranting that cargoes were destined for British ports, and then rely on the wits of their captains to evade royal patrols and make for French harbors. It was the most direct route, but also the most hazardous, and seizures were commonplace.

Another strategy, much favored by the Browns, was to dispatch ships to ostensibly neutral harbors where cargoes would be traded for contraband French molasses. One favorite destination was Monte Christi, a "desolate little hole," as one writer termed it, on the northern—Spanish—coast of Hispaniola. A sailor on one of the Brown's trading sloops described the place in a letter to Moses: "Their houses are built of cabbage trees—they have a church, a gaol, six pieces of cannon for to guard the town, wherein there is about fifty houses, about one dozen chairs in the place to sit in, they ride on jackasses, for the most part, with a saddle made of straw." Desolate, perhaps, but in the war years, the seat of a thriving trade between British colonists, Spanish middlemen, and French planters. By 1760, the British navy reported finding as many as 130 ships anchored in Monte Christi's shallow harbor on a single day.

The most elaborate ruse perpetrated by the North American merchants involved "Flags of Truce," issued by colonial authorities. The idea was to facilitate the removal of French sailors or soldiers taken at sea by privateers or in fighting on the continent. Ship captains sailing under flags of truce would transport these prisoners to French ports, where they might be exchanged for British sailors or troops. This plausible design soon gave rise to widespread abuse, with merchants and their captains using the flags, and carrying a handful of prisoners or less, to authorize trading voyages to the enemy. The flags did not guarantee immunity, as many English naval commanders seized the ships anyway, but they were usually honored in the colonial courts, and the profits from such voyages could be stunning.

Obadiah Brown and his nephews were among the leaders in the ongoing imperial subterfuge; Obadiah was empowered to cover his own tracks through his appointment, in 1757, to a government committee investigating allegations of trade with the enemy. A year later, at the urging of the Board of Trade, the colony appointed a committee to inspect the holds of flag-of-truce ships to ensure they carried no trading goods, but only such provisions as required for the crews and their ostensible prisoners. That committee was likewise compromised, however, by the appointment of Uncle Elisha Brown and family friend Daniel Jenckes. For the Browns, at least, passage through customs was a breeze.

Several colonies refused to countenance trading under flags of truce, but for some, traffic in bogus documents became itself a thriving trade. In Pennsylvania, the governor began selling flags of truce for roughly $1,500—a very substantial sum. His successor detailed the business in a letter to English authorities in 1760: "Having once relished the sweets of this traffic, he became more undisguised, and as it were opened a shop at lower prices to all customers. . . . But toward the end of his administration, the matter was carried to such a pitch, that he scruple not to set his name to, & dispose of great numbers of blank Flags of Truce, at the low price of twenty pounds sterling or under."

Where Pennsylvania was the seat of illicit traffic in the middle colonies, Rhode Island was notorious in New England. Beset by complaints from the more restrained traders of Boston, Massachusetts governor Francis Bernard expressed his outrage to the Board of Trade in London: "These practices will never be put an end to, til Rhode Island is reduced to the subjection of the British Empire; of which at present it is no more a part than the Bahama Islands were when they were inhabited by the buccaneers."

How many voyages the Browns sponsored under flags of truce is hard to say, but certainly they were numerous; the ones cropping up in the family correspondence usually involved those vessels taken by the British. In 1758, their brig *Prudent Hannah* was seized by a British warship off the coast of Virginia. Two years later, the Browns lost a pair of ships, *Polley's Revenge* and the *Speedwell*, both condemned in admiralty courts at the Bahamas for engaging in "wicked, illegal unwarrantable, clandestine and prohibited trade." For the *Speedwell*, it was the last of seven trips to enemy ports; for her final voyage, Governor Hopkins had certified that she was to carry a single French prisoner.

For the illegal traders operating out of Rhode Island, and for the Browns especially, Stephen Hopkins played a key role. As early as 1755, the General

Assembly ordered that "every master of a vessel bound to sea" take whatever Frenchmen might be on hand, and by his own admission, Hopkins issued at least thirty flags of truce over the next five years. Other observers put the figure much higher; one British traveler recorded this account from a sojourn in Rhode Island:

> To my certain knowledge, in the course of the late war, many scores of vessels went loaded with beef, pork, flour, etc. under the pretext of flags, which, for a certain consideration, could at any time be procured from the Governor, when at the same time perhaps they carried not more than one or two French prisoners, dividing the crew of one of the French merchantmen they had taken, among a whole fleet of Flags of Truce, laden with articles more welcome to the enemy than all the prisoners, with the ship and cargo, they took from them.

These illegal trading ventures, from Providence and elsewhere, did more than raise the fortunes of the merchants who financed them: they confounded the British authorities and extended the war with France. Already by 1757 the governor of New York was reporting to London that, unless trade with the French were "soon prevented, I fear the enemy may avail themselves in great measure of the distresses I should hope will fall upon them." By August of 1760, William Pitt, the great architect of England's imperial expansion, could no longer contain his umbrage, denouncing "an illegal and most pernicious trade, by which the enemy is, to the greatest reproach and detriment of government, supplyed with provisions, whereby they are principally, if not alone, enabled to sustain, and protract, this long and expensive war." Writing to all the British governors in North America and the West Indies, Pitt ordered strict measures to end "such flagitious practices, so utterly subversive of all law, and so highly repugnant to the honor and well-being of this kingdom." In closing, he demanded an accounting from each governor of the state of illegal trade in his jurisdiction.

Most recipients of this blistering directive responded with contrition and fealty, but not Stephen Hopkins. Since his first term as governor, in 1755, Hopkins had been assiduous in answering the requests of his king, especially in raising troops to fight the French on the colonial frontier. But trade was a different matter. In a carefully crafted response to Pitt, Hopkins drew a clear, and insouciant, distinction between Pitt's view of the question and his own. While no military provisions had been shipped to the French, Hopkins averred, Rhode Island vessels "have indeed carried lumber and dry goods of

British manufacture to sell to the French, and in return have brought back some sugars, but mostly molasses." Moreover, he conceded, "'tis highly probable" that other ships, having sworn before customs they were headed for friendly ports, then "deviated from the voyage pretended," reaching French ports instead. Since such practices were secret, Hopkins said, the identity of the smugglers "may never come to the knowledge of any officers of the colony, by whom they are sure to be prosecuted should they be discovered."

Here Hopkins proposed his novel view of the illicit trade. Leaving aside the question of starving out the French, Hopkins observed that the northern colonies produced surpluses of flour, boards, meat, and fish, which, when sold at foreign ports, raised the funds whereby colonists earned the hard currency necessary to pay for British manufactures. Thus, Hopkins proposed, free trade had established a central role in the welfare not just of the colonies, but of England as well.

Hopkins closed with a promise to "put a total stop" to all future trade with the French, but he had broached a debate that would simmer through all the tumultuous years that ensued. His exposition on the benefits of trade contradicted not only Pitt's military strategy, but the reigning mercantile theory of the British Empire, which held that the produce of the colonies should accrue to the sole benefit of the home country. Hopkins's argument sparked immediate outrage; Joseph Sherwood, Rhode Island's colonial agent in London, reported to Hopkins that "some of our leading men have taken great disgust at the trade with the French mentioned in thy letter."

Stephen Hopkins was an iconoclast, a complex and often contradictory figure who loomed large in the life of the colony, of Providence, and of the Browns. He was a merchant from a family of sea captains, but he was drawn early on to the life of politics. A Quaker by birth, he was always distinguished at public meetings by his shoulder-length white hair and the broad-brimmed black hat of his sect. Yet he set aside his vows of peace to preside over a war administration as Rhode Island contributed troops and arms to British expeditions against the French. His political prose exhorted modesty and self-sacrifice, yet he assumed the title of "Governor, Captain General, and Commander in Chief," and profited handsomely by his office, collecting outsized fees for issuing flags of truce and commissions for privateers. And like the Browns, Hopkins sent his own ships out as privateers—one, the *Game Cock*, under command of the storied sea captain Abraham Whipple, captured twenty-three French vessels during a single Caribbean cruise in 1759. On other occasions Whipple helmed ships belonging to the Browns, but never with such spectacular results.

Hopkins rose to power through a succession of public offices, culminating in his appointment, in 1754, as Rhode Island's delegate to the Albany Conference, where Benjamin Franklin first proposed his plans for a colonial union. Hopkins endorsed the design, but when he presented it to the General Assembly it was roundly rejected as a threat to the colony's charter and independence.

Undaunted, Hopkins made his defense of the plan the centerpiece of a campaign for governor, and in 1755, at age forty-eight, he won the office for the first time. Upon his elevation, Hopkins eschewed the convention of residing at Newport, and the scions of his hometown's leading families gravitated around their eloquent and charismatic leader. "So social and hospitable was his nature," one early chronicler recalled, "that the young men of Providence used to come and spend the evening at his house, to hear him talk." Those young men, huddled around the fireplace in the study at Hopkins's modest wood-frame house on Towne Street, included Moses and John Brown, as well as their brother Nicholas, their brother-in-law Jabez Bowen, Captain Abe Whipple, still not thirty years old, and Silas Downer, a diminutive young attorney recently emigrated from Massachusetts.

Though most of this tight circle were just half the governor's age, they already comprised some of the most influential men in the colony. The Brown brothers were the leading merchants outside Newport, and Bowen and Downer boasted college education, a rarity in colonial Providence. Bowen had graduated from Yale, and Downer from Harvard; Downer's legal clients included Stephen and Esek Hopkins as well as the Brown family, but he made his living primarily as a scrivener, penning documents in a flowing hand for private clients and as a clerk for the General Assembly.

Their allegiances were cemented by family bonds. Moses Brown's wife, Anna, was the sister of Jabez Bowen's wife, Sarah; both were daughters of Obadiah Brown, and their husbands addressed each other in correspondence as "loving brother." Abraham Whipple's wife, Sarah Hopkins, was a niece to the governor, and a cousin to the Browns through her grandmother Martha Brown Jenckes.

Moses Brown and Silas Downer came to fill a special role for Hopkins. The governor, for whom letters and tracts were stock in trade, was afflicted with a palsy so severe that "when he wrote at all, which was seldom, he was compelled to guide the right hand with the left." Thus Hopkins relied upon Moses and Silas to serve as amanuenses, to whom he dictated his copious communications. The young men may have filled another role as well: in 1753, Hopkins was devastated by the loss of two of his five sons, the wages of a family that pursued its fortunes at sea. One was cast away on the coast of Nova Scotia and slain by Indians; the other contracted smallpox during a trading voyage to Spain. That same year, his wife perished "from the mental distress induced by the aggravating circumstances of these bereavements." Certainly, Hopkins found some solace in the company of his sons' contemporaries. Just as likely, Moses found in Hopkins a reflection of his departed father and uncle.

Their close relations with Governor Hopkins ushered the Brown brothers—primarily Nicholas, John, and Moses, but later Joseph as well—into the world of politics. Obadiah and James had each held positions in colonial government, but the boys of the next generation became far more deeply involved. Moses served for seven years as a Providence deputy to the General Assembly, chosen for the post by the town council twice each year beginning in 1764; later, John would sit for twelve terms. More important, the Browns learned how politics worked, taking on the roles of manager, bursar, and strategist for Hopkins's gubernatorial campaigns, some of them hard-fought.

The first order of business was to raise their hometown from its rustic origins. Trade was growing steadily, and new buildings were going up on Weybosset Neck across the Great Salt River, but Providence remained a one-street country market, the thoroughfare crowded with wagons and livestock, and for much of the year mired in mud. Using lotteries as a painless means to finance public works, Hopkins and his young cohort effected a series of dramatic improvements. A second road, cut into the hill parallel to Towne Street, was established in 1760. The new road represented a tangible break with the past, as many of the graves of the town founders, including Chad Brown's, stood in the lane and had to be removed to a common graveyard. But it also brought a sudden upgrade in the daily life of the town, and was soon dubbed Benefit Street.

A couple of years later, Towne Street was paved at last, in the Roman style, with cut stones crowned at the peak with larger, heavier stones; John Brown sat on the lottery committee for the north end; Moses, with Esek Hopkins, chaired the committee for the south. When a flood tide washed out the Great Bridge in the fall of 1761, it was promptly rebuilt; likewise, when the wood-frame county meetinghouse burned down, it was replaced with a stately brick-and-brownstone Colony House, capped by a two-stage wooden cupola.

This last project required the fiscal support of all the freemen in Providence, and provoked an identity crisis of some moment. The residents and business interests at the north end of town, including Uncle Elisha as well as tavern owners Turpin and Olney, called for locating the new statehouse near them, where Towne Street met the road leading to Connecticut. The residents at the waterfront held out for the status quo. And while such disputes were usually sorted out at town meetings, this question was settled through more primitive means. As John recalled years later, the disputants "did absolutely git a long large rope to pull each way, those for the north to pull up and those for the south or down town as then call'd pulled to the south and they being then the strongest it was built [there]." To John, this test of strength set the tone for decades to come: "Have you not seen ever since," he asked his correspondent, "is not the businesses constantly crowding that way?"

Not all the improvements were physical. Postal service was introduced, a sailing packet began regular trips to Newport, and in 1762, the *Providence Gazette* launched weekly publication, offering a partisan answer to the *Newport Mercury*. Stephen Hopkins is sometimes credited with recruiting the paper's founding editor, William Goddard, then twenty-two years old, and while no record confirms that role, the governor was a regular contributor. Observed one historian, "the *Gazette* was his personal organ for many years." John and Moses became close associates with Goddard; they placed advertisements in the paper and on occasion wrote letters and articles of their own.

The advances made by Providence, and the rise of Stephen Hopkins as its champion, were regarded with dismay by the old elite of Newport. By tradition in Rhode Island, "downright democracy" that it was, the governor was elected as the head of a slate that exercised virtually unlimited powers to make executive and judicial appointments, and set fees and tax rates. British officials could advise, but they couldn't interfere, as the colony's autonomy was guaranteed under its royal charter.

For generations, Rhode Island government had been headed by a clutch of leading families—the Greenes, from the small port of Warwick, on the western shore of Narragansett Bay; the Wantons of Newport; the Cranstons, from a rural district south of Providence; and Joseph Jenckes, who hailed from Providence but moved to Newport during his tenure as governor. But with the advent of Hopkins, the politics of the colony turned distinctly sectional. Hopkins spoke for Providence and its rising merchant class, while Samuel Ward, a Baptist who presided over an estate in rural Westerly, represented Newport, the town where he was raised and where his father sat as governor in 1740. The geographic division was breached by two distinct exceptions: the Wantons, a leading family of Newport that had produced three previous governors, enlisted for Hopkins; while in Providence Elisha Brown, irascible brother to

Obadiah and James, defected to the Ward camp. So influential was Elisha that he was twice elected deputy governor from the Ward slate.

The contest between north and south turned intensely personal during Hopkins's first term when Ward, sitting as a delegate to the assembly, issued a derisive pamphlet charging the governor with acting in a "tyrannical and arbitrary manner . . . not even pretended to by any King of England since James ye Second." More pointedly, Ward accused Hopkins of profiting from inflated fees for authorizing privateers and flags of truce.

The charges were largely true, but Hopkins was indignant and sued for defamation in Providence court, seeking the astronomical figure of twenty thousand pounds in damages. Ward petitioned the General Assembly to obtain a change of venue, citing Hopkins's "very extensive influence" and death threats he had received at the hands of Hopkins's allies. The case was tried in Massachusetts, where Hopkins was represented by famed Boston attorney James Otis, but Ward prevailed on the facts, and Hopkins was forced to pay the costs of the suit.

For most of the following decade, policy and issues were set aside, and Rhode Island politics were dominated by the simple question of whether Hopkins or Ward would take the governor's chair. Hopkins prevailed seven times and Ward three, but the contests were close, and increasingly hot. "During all this time, party virulence had been increasing, until one general hostility pervaded the whole colony," the *Newport Mercury* reported. Another chronicler later described the years of controversy as "a chapter in a madman's life."

As the dispute escalated, the Browns, John and Moses especially, took a leading role in the Hopkins camp. This was politics at its most elemental: votes were openly bought and sold, for coin, for rum, for promises of advancement. "Generally he that distributes the most cash, and gives the best entertainment . . . is the man who obtains a majority," according to one contemporary account. The brother's firm became a clearinghouse for campaign funds, and their parchment ledgers provide a detailed breakdown of payments made and votes secured. In the campaign of 1765, Moses distributed kegs of rum, bushels of corn, caked sugar, and sacks of flour, as well as various amounts of cash, to district organizers and prospective voters. Other documents record funds raised; the roster of contributions collected in 1763 reads like a guest list for a Brown family dinner party. Stephen Hopkins topped the list, with eight hundred pounds, but Nicholas, John, and Moses weighed in with four hundred apiece; other donors included Nicholas's father-in-law Judge Daniel Jenckes, and the ever-helpful Jabez Bowen. The funds were dedicated to "procuring the free votes of the poorer sort of Freemen in this county."

When duty called, John and Moses hit the road to stump for Hopkins. The brothers couldn't help but notice when, in the spring of 1765, upwards of forty men tramped into town from Glocester, a country seat in the northwest corner of the colony. The rustic crew located a distiller and purchased "rum enough for a small Guinea cargo," apparently to provision a rally for Samuel Ward. Anticipating "a hard battle," Moses and Jabez Bowen rode out the next day over rutted lanes through the low hills and tangled woods of the Rhode Island hinterland to make sure Hopkins was represented. On another occasion, John Brown made it his business to alert the citizens of Johnston that their deputies in the assembly had deserted the Hopkins party. In case they'd forgotten why their interest lay with the mercantile faction in the government, John spelled it out: "It is well known the farmers get their estates by selling the produce of their farms to the traders."

A letter to the Browns from Joseph Wanton Jr., an occasional business partner who twice served as deputy governor from the Hopkins slate, captured the tenor of the times. "The flame is broke out to a violent degree," he wrote. "The battle would be a pleasure if the troops were more equal, however the more difficult the greater the glory, for victory we will have if you to the northern stand your ground." He added, optimistically, "I make no doubt from the violence of our enemies that it is their last effort." The Browns shared Wanton's partisan sense that the evils in the dispute arose solely from the opposition. John Brown saw the question starkly, writing to another Newport correspondent, "Mr. Ward and Uncle Brown have kept the government in a rage for seven or eight years past by opposing Mr. Hopkins while they at the same time they have known the majority of freeholders in this colony have been in favor of his administration."

⁓

While John and Nicholas Brown were active members of the Hopkins machine, Moses played a more central role. The game of politics suited his nature, as he discovered a gift for finding avenues to compromise while holding on to the principles guiding his faction. And along with Joseph, Moses was more intellectually inclined than John or Nicholas, and thus more taken with the abstractions propounded by Stephen Hopkins. At the same time, Moses' emergence in the political arena was an important step for him personally. As the youngest of the four brothers, he was engaged to some degree in a struggle to establish his own identity.

When the brothers restructured the family firm in the late summer of 1762 after Obadiah's death, the ownership was divided into five shares; each brother held one, and Nicholas and John divided the last, as they generally initiated the firm's sailing ventures. That Moses chafed under this distinction is apparent in a letter he addressed to his brothers two years later: "That it be not again said that I never propose any business and as no voyage is determined for the ship I now propose that she be immediately sailed to sea . . . and that she proceed directly to Curacao. This is humbly offered for your consideration."

In these early days of his career, Moses could be punctilious and sometimes peevish. Charged with administering Obadiah's estate, he dogged his uncle's creditors until they howled. One, who filed a lawsuit to block the estate's efforts to collect a small disputed debt, said he took the step as an act of "revenge," and denounced "that damned little Moses."

Moses displayed his insecurities in another exchange not long after his uncle's death. While planning his wedding to Anna in the summer of 1763, Moses ordered a set of furniture from John Goddard, the renowned cabinetmaker. When Moses learned later that Goddard had in the interim delivered finished pieces to Stephen Hopkins, Moses fired off a surly dispatch. "This you was to do," he wrote in October. "Finish the work ye work I wrote for ye first you did after my brother's wife's furniture were done, but instead of this you have made work for Governor Hopkins' family spoke for in May and delivered it before ours. . . ." Worse, Moses accused Goddard of selling off a table promised to Moses for which he obtained a higher price. "I should be very sorry to think you have not acted agreeable to your engagement to me. . . ."

Goddard answered the accusation promptly, and with dismay. "I cannot conceive how it could enter thy heart to suppose such a thing," he wrote. The table was ready but he was delaying shipment until a set of chairs was complete. As to Hopkins, Goddard conceded, "Is true, and thou must have expected that I should [have] engaged work to keep my boys employed if it should a little retard thy work, for we must do so or we should be out of employment."

At this point in his life, Moses seems distinctly concerned with material things. Soon after his engagement to Anna, he ordered the creation of a family coat of arms, copied from that used by the Browns of Essex, England, of no known relation to the Browns of Providence. Moses had the insignia, which featured an eagle posed over a field with three lion's paws, engraved on his wedding silver; writing to a Boston silversmith, he requested the set be "made in the neatest manner and in ye same fashion of those you lately made for Mr. Jabez Bowen of this place." John Brown later adopted the same coat of arms in his own household.

The Brown family arms

If Moses was acquisitive, John was outright aggressive. As the primary shipping agent for the family firm, he traveled far afield in his pursuits. His correspondence places him in Boston, New York, and Philadelphia, hammering out deals and pushing sales of Brown & Co. candles and other goods in the great ports of the colonial seaboard. And while Moses handled much of the direct contact with the whaling magnates of Nantucket, it was John who assembled the chandlers of New England into a cartel in an effort to keep a lid on the price of head matter, the part of the whale prized for candle making. He opened the first talks under the auspices of Obadiah Brown, and when his uncle died, John continued to press to expand the family firm's share of the market.

John's problem was not knowing when to stop. In a letter of July 1, 1764, John rails to a contact at Boston that the Rotch family of Nantucket was selling head matter at less than cost. John took this as a sign of skulduggery: "You will excuse me for yet believing that he bought it with a desire to ship it home, as I have often heard him say that it will answer to ship head to England. . . ." What stood in the way was the high duties charged in England on imported head matter—though not on oil. Members of the cartel believed that Rotch and others were shipping their head matter in barrels marked as plain oil, thereby dodging both the import tax and the cartel.

What happened next was recounted by patriarch Joseph Rotch in a July 31 letter to the Newport members of the cartel. Someone had alerted Boston port authorities that a Rotch ship had a hidden cache of head matter onboard, and the vessel was seized and searched. "But to the informant's shame and disappointment, we had cleared it out properly, as we always did. . . ." Rotch then offered some insinuations about the suspected culprits. "We are surprised that such men should turn informers about an honest trade, when we may reasonably suppose (considering where they belong) that if ever they traded at sea at all, they cheated both King and country as much as was in their power. . . . We shall seek revenge if ever we hear of their carrying on any illicit trade." If there were any question who topped Rotch's list of suspects, he made it clear with a postscript. "Please to let all the manufacturers of head matter read this letter," he wrote, "and especially the Browns."

On the last week of October in 1763, Elisha Brown asked his nephew Nicholas for help in rallying the merchants of Providence in the face of a grave new threat. The Seven Years War had ended that spring in near-total victory for the British, and a new ministry in London was forced to confront the bloated national debt. Britons were already being taxed to the limit; in a new initiative, the government had decided to raise funds by taxing colonial trade.

The opportunistic Elisha might carry the opposition banner in the local political wars, but there was no division of allegiance in a confrontation with customs officials. As Elisha put it in a note to Nicholas, "These comes to acquaint you that I have a great minde, that all the merchants or as many as sees fit in this town, should meet some afternoon in order to consult what method will be best to take when any of our vessels arrives which is liable to pay duties — so as wee may stand by each other."

While no record of the meeting called by Elisha survives, events would show that the traders of Providence paid close attention, with Nicholas, John, and Moses in the forefront, and Stephen Hopkins in the lead. The duties Elisha mentioned were taxes on molasses, the key commodity in New England trade with the West Indies. The Molasses Act had been on the books for thirty years, but was roundly ignored both by merchants and by customs officials. Now, with the fighting over and the armies recalled, Parliament could turn to the long-neglected fiscal crisis. The easiest source of revenue was to enforce the dormant trade laws; enforcement would be assigned to the ships of the Royal Navy. The decision carried the added satisfaction of punishing those merchants who engaged in illegal shipping during the war.

The news first reached Providence in September, in a letter to the Brown brothers from Tench Francis, their commercial agent in Philadelphia. "What are the people of England now going to do with us?" Francis asked, and answering his own question, he attached a list of twenty-seven men-of-war assigned to cruise off the American coast. By October, the Lords of Trade in

London issued an explicit order for "suppression of the clandestine trade with foreign nations and the improvement of the revenue," and appointed a new chief of customs for all of New England, to be quartered at Boston.

The aggressive new posture of the home country sent a charge through the mercantile cities of the eastern seaboard. That November, the merchants of Boston had organized into a "grand committee," whose first order of business was to "open a correspondence with the principal merchants in all our sister colonies, endeavoring to promote a union, and a coalition of all their councils."

In Rhode Island, the growing sense of dread was given tangible focus the week before Christmas when the HMS *Squirrel*, a square-rigged warship bearing twenty guns and a full complement of marines, sailed up the central passage between Aquidneck and Conanicut and dropped anchor in the mouth of the harbor at Newport. A week later, the Browns wrote to ask a friend there for an assessment. "Pray, what's the Man of War like to do in the sugar and melasses trade etc.?"

The brothers apparently believed the worst, and in the course of the next three weeks, they engaged with the rest of Governor Hopkins's political cohort to produce a cogent critique of the new trade policy. This was a singular act of temerity, a clutch of unschooled seafaring merchants addressing the ministers at Parliament as peers and not as subjects, speaking from a sense of autonomy bred of more than a century of self-rule.

January brought a great blizzard that cut off the land routes from Providence to the outside world. Snow drifted in the alleys leading off Towne Street, and sheeted ice encased the sloops lying silently at the wharves along the Great Salt River. But the committee didn't skip a beat, hashing out ideas and working over drafts around rough-hewn tables in the din of the Crown Coffee House facing Market Square, or in William Goddard's print shop, upstairs from the bookstore operated by Judge Jenckes, where the sign of Shakespeare's head hung out over an icy side street. They also had access to the warmth and privacy of the new statehouse, where the Providence Library was housed—each member of the cabal was included on the roster of the library proprietors.

The product of their efforts emerged in stages. The first draft appeared in the *Providence Gazette* of January 14 under the title "Essay on the Trade of the Northern Colonies," and was signed "P."—a pseudonym widely attributed to Stephen Hopkins. A second, more closely detailed document, produced as a working paper and never distributed publicly, provides a window on the group's method. Titled "State of the Trade," it consisted of a preamble, probably written by Silas Downer, followed by four distinct sections introduced as "a few pertinent remarks, as they come to hand from different persons." These sections, authored by individual members of the committee, offer firsthand accounts of the shipping business, each emphasizing the benefits to England of a thriving colonial trade. None are signed, but it seems apparent that at least one was penned by the Browns, the brothers serving as a sort of ad hoc sub-committee to the Providence group. Once compiled, "State of the Trade" was promptly forwarded to the merchants at Newport for their review.

The tone of these tracts remained strategically cordial: the old Molasses Act was due to expire, and if the trade ministry only understood the delicate na-ture of colonial trade, it might be relied upon to lift the duties, rather than en-force them. This courtly approach was based on the belief in New England that their real dispute lay not with the ministry, but with the rival colonies of the Caribbean, whose planters hoped to prop up the price of their molasses, and of their own rum. One writer in Boston typically called for unity to "defeat the iniquitous schemes of these over grown West Indians."

Still, "Essay on the Trade" was more than a simple prospectus. Silas Downer opened his preamble by asserting, "There are two things which En-glishmen always boast themselves upon, *Liberty* and *Property*," thus invoking the language of political rights that would become the foundation of the grow-ing dispute between England and her colonies.

Certainly the committee had provocation. The same week they were meeting to compile their arguments, John Temple, the new head of customs for New England, sailed up the icy waters of Narragansett Bay to pay an official visit to Providence. There he summoned all the deputized officers of customs and had them resworn to office. As reported in the *Gazette*, Temple "then, in a Dictatorial Manner, gave them his orders accordingly: And declared, even with an Oath, that in a few Days he would lock up all the Ports in this Colony, in such a manner, that not a Vessel should come in or go out." Goddard's anonymous correspondent—the story was signed "Publicola"—then offered his own sense of the scene: Temple "treated the Colony, and all its Officers, with the utmost Insolence and Contempt; and shewed every other Mark of an ignorant, haughty and illiberal mind."

John Temple was answered in kind when, after leaving Providence, he stopped in Newport to swear in the customs officials there. While in port Tem-ple personally ordered the seizure of a coasting sloop for smuggling foreign molasses. Two days later, under cover of darkness, the ship was "got under sail and carried off by persons unknown." The customs chief posted a reward for capture of the culprits, but the bounty went unclaimed.

In the meantime, Hopkins and his committee were ready to move. Just days before Temple's performance on the frozen docks of the Providence waterfront, the governor had issued warrants calling a special session of the assembly to consider a third and final draft of "State of the Trade," a "Remonstrance" addressed to the Lords of Trade in London. Several revisions were made, and the final draft approved on January 27.

The Remonstrance was historic in several respects. It represented the first official response offered by any colony to the new fiscal regime being considered at Parliament, thereby establishing Rhode Island at the center of the unrest beginning to spread across the young continent. It clearly demonstrated the leading role of merchants like the Browns in questioning the prerogatives of the home government. And it provided a theoretical framework for acts of disobedience that would soon proliferate in the face of royal authority.

Closely following the logic of Hopkins's answer to Pitt on illegal trade, the Remonstrance at once acknowledged and defended the routine violation of the Navigation Acts. The economy of Rhode Island, it said, was entirely dependent on molasses: converted to rum at the thirty-odd distilleries and reshipped to domestic markets and to the coast of Africa, it allowed merchants to earn the foreign exchange that enabled them to import British manufactures. The Remonstrance made plain that most of the molasses was imported illegally—of an average 14,000 barrels shipped each year, only 2,500 came from British islands. But it also asserted that, should that supply be cut off, British merchants would lose exports valued at more than one hundred thousand pounds.

Though the Rhode Island assembly was the first colonial legislature to protest the new sugar duties, the Remonstrance was stalled by internal politics, and by the time it arrived in London, the damage was already done. In March 1764, Parliament passed a new Sugar Act, designed explicitly to "defray the expenses of defending, protecting and securing" the colonies. The act cut the former duties on foreign molasses by half, but the three-pence charge still represented a quarter of the total value, enough by Stephen Hopkins's accounting to "operate as an absolute prohibition."

Hopkins and his brother Esek, like the Browns, had grown up British subjects, loyal to the king and to their Protestant heritage. But they had also grown up on the shores of Narragansett Bay, sailing south, dodging the British navy, and trading at any port that might accept their cargoes. The thought of separating from the home country had never entered their minds, but when they were faced with economic servitude—slavery, they often called it—there was never much question what they would choose.

～～

The Remonstrance was written in the spirit of conciliation, but with passage of the Sugar Act, matters turned for the worse. Aside from setting three-pence duties on foreign molasses, the Sugar Act expanded the jurisdiction of the admiralty courts, where illegal traders could be tried without juries, and informants awarded a share of the seized cargo. More disturbing, the House of Commons at the same legislative session warned that still more revenue was needed, and proposed charging new fees for an official stamp to be required for all documents used in colonial government or commerce, including newspapers and almanacs, as well as playing cards and dice. For the first time, the home government would raise revenue through a direct tax on the colonies of North America.

Once again, Hopkins answered back, penning an anonymous critique of Parliamentary taxation for the *Gazette*, and then a more polished, more expansive treatise titled "The Rights of the Colonies Examined." This was a powerful claim to autonomy that invoked the protections of England's "glorious constitution, the best that ever existed among men." That constitution was not a document but an agreement, a "compact," whereby a free people was governed only by its consent, and under laws written by its own representatives. As the colonists had no voice in Parliament, the Parliament had no jurisdiction over the colonial legislatures. The ministries in London might rightfully seek to manage the "general concerns" of empire, Hopkins conceded, even including measures to direct the flow and pace of trade, but levying taxes and writing laws for distant colonies clearly crossed the line. Those who submit to such encroachments, Hopkins averred, "are in the miserable condition of slaves."

At once forceful and elegant—it quoted Thucydides, Constantius, and other ancients to buttress the arguments put forward at the taverns in Providence—the pamphlet was published in December 1764 and reprinted throughout the colonies, marking Hopkins as among the earliest and most trenchant tribunes of American independence. The polemic afforded a singular satisfaction to John and Moses Brown, who saw their naked self-interest, in trade and in politics, elevated to the loftier plane of rights and constitutional privilege.

For the Brown brothers as for the colonies at large, *The Rights of the Colonies Examined* represented a turning point in the way they viewed England, and in the way they looked at themselves. Already the defiant spirit that Hopkins articulated in his essay was flaring up in acts of violence at Newport, the colony's cosmopolitan center. In June, sailors from the British revenue schooner *St. John* were accosted on the port's long wharf by a crowd that pelted the crew with paving stones. The sailors retreated to the shelter of a twenty-gun warship, but not before gunners at the harbor fort lofted several rounds of shot over their bow. The following spring, when a squad from the HMS *Maidstone* pressed into navy service the entire crew of a ship just returned from Africa, a mob of about five hundred men seized one of the *Maidstone*'s longboats and dragged it through the streets of town before setting it ablaze. Demands that colonial officials arrest the perpetrators were met with studied indifference.

Colonial relations with customs officers were strained as well. John Robinson, a career agent from England who assumed the post of chief collector for Rhode Island in May 1764, quickly learned the limits of his authority. He clashed with officials at every level of government, including the judge and chief attorney of the vice admiralty court, where his seizures had to be approved. In a letter the following year, Robinson complained of "the want of government to countenance our proceedings, and the general combination of the people against us." Witnesses disappeared on trial days, he said, and the admiralty court, though established as a counterweight to the colonial bench, was staffed by local men whose "connections with the people" led them to "favor the merchants to the prejudice of the crown." For his trouble, Robinson's complaint earned him a lawsuit for slander by the vice admiralty judge.

Passage of the Stamp Act, in March 1765, only inflamed the growing ranks of colonial patriots. The act wouldn't take effect until September, but in mid-August, riots broke out in Boston, where crowds of tradesmen and dockworkers streamed out of their taverns and laid waste to the home of Andrew Oliver, the stamp master appointed for Massachusetts. Two weeks later, a crew of Newport militants strung up a stuffed likeness of Rhode Island stamp master Howard Johnston alongside effigies of two prominent Tories. For three days a mob ruled the town, until two of the leading Tories sailed for England and Johnston, a longtime lieutenant in the Hopkins machine, retreated to the safety of a British warship. Johnston was welcomed ashore only upon his vow to ignore the edict of the Stamp Act.

While Newport churned, the political clique at Providence laid plans for a more systematic resistance to the decrees from London. The group had no formal name—at different times they were referred to as the Providence committee, or simply "a political clubb"—but by the summer of 1765 they had gone underground, adopting the name Sons of Liberty, in the fashion of Sam Adams and his rebels at Boston.

This was a curious role for men of means and property, and especially for the Browns, with their new homes and new wives, their ships and their candleworks, their coat of arms embossed on their wedding silver. The brothers were leery of the street violence breaking out in the larger towns; deriding the mobs in a letter to one of their ship captains, the Browns surmised "the whole town of Boston begin to be terrified as much by them as had before been of the Stamp Act." And yet, like the principal merchants of several other colonies, the Browns were fast making the transition from aggrieved citizens to leaders of a growing rebellion. They were the first to feel the impact of the new British trade policies, and they were the first to react.

Silas Downer was the most radical of the Providence group, but he was careful to take his cue from the merchants who made up its core. The Browns couldn't help but enjoy his fierce tirades against "the effects of this horrid policy. Men of War, Cutters, Marines with their bayonettes fixed, judges of admiralty, collectors, comptrollers, searchers, tide-waiters, land-waiters, with a whole catalog of pimps, are sent hither, not to protect our trade, but to destroy it." As for Stephen Hopkins, he was no longer governor—voters replaced him with Samuel Ward in 1765, apparently due to fears over his edgy rhetoric—but he remained the chief of the Providence club.

Their preeminence in Providence politics was conspicuous at a town meeting on August 7, called to develop a collective response to the Stamp Act. There Hopkins was named along with John Brown and several other Sons of Liberty to a committee that would issue express directions to the Providence delegates to the General Assembly. After another intense week of parleys, the committee endorsed two crucial measures: first, to send Rhode Island delegates to the Stamp Act Congress, proposed for New York that autumn, and second, to adopt a set of resolves authored by Virginia firebrand Patrick Henry. These resolves laid down in stark terms the positions Hopkins had first outlined in his *Rights of the Colonies Examined*. One, rejected by the Virginia burgesses but adopted in Providence, stated flatly: "The General Assembly of this colony"—and not Parliament—"have the only sole and exclusive right and power to levy taxes and impositions upon the inhabitants of this colony."

The Providence resolves were settled before the riots at Newport; they were taken up at the General Assembly in the days that followed. There Moses Brown, as a delegate from Providence, shepherded the resolves through committee. The assembly adopted the original five and tacked on one more, directing colonial officials to continue in their duties without regard to acts of Parliament. Most of the other colonies closed their courts and customs houses rather than issue stamps, but Rhode Island determined to do business as usual, rendering the Stamp Act a dead letter. As one historian observed later, "No other colony, not even Virginia, had gone that far in its protests or petitions."

Providence was never seized with the tumult witnessed in Boston and Newport. An effigy of Howard Johnston was hung over the Great Bridge and torched, but the atmosphere was that of a festival, not a riot. That was largely a measure of the town's political unanimity. No Tories swore allegiance to the crown in Providence; instead, the Browns and the other leading merchants rallied around Stephen Hopkins, who gave high expression to their traditions of ardent independence and illicit trade.

There was one brief moment when the unrest of the larger cities threatened to disturb the peace of Providence. On December 12, two weeks after the Stamp Act went into effect, word got out that John Foster, clerk of the county court, was refusing to do business without the required stamps. A large crowd, presumably fortified by rum from the Towne Street taverns, decided to confront the clerk at his home. As the mood turned ugly, someone thought to send for Moses Brown, whose status as a delegate to the General Assembly might sway Foster from his stance.

Moses was located, and promptly set out into the winter chill "to quiet the people," as he recalled later. Upon his arrival, Moses made his way through the crowd, and Foster let him in. Once inside, Moses reminded Foster of the assembly's guarantee to hold colonial officials harmless from any charges arising from their failure to deploy the British stamps. Thus reassured, and considering the alternative if Moses were to leave empty-handed, Foster penned an affidavit promising to "act and transact all kind of business consistent with my office the same as before."

This was peacemaking on a small scale, a bit of neighborliness that smoothed rough edges among friends, but it reflected a broader shift in sensibilities. The uprisings in the major cities, and the arguments pressed by Hopkins and others, had begun to take a toll. At Parliament, in January, William Pitt, the former prime minister, denounced the Stamp Act and startled his peers by declaring, "I rejoice that America hath resisted." The merchants of London organized to press for repeal of the Stamp Act and to restore good relations between England and the colonies. In March 1766, Parliament relented. The Stamp Act was repealed, and the duties on molasses reduced to a penny. At the same time, in a bid to save face, Parliament also passed the Declaratory Act, asserting its right to "bind the colonies and people of America . . . in all cases whatsoever."

The repeal was met in America with equal measures of shock, gratitude, and mistrust. For all the appeals to English rights and royal sympathies, the patriots never really believed that the imperious leaders of Great Britain might actually change their course. Yet few were ready to embrace an outright breach with the home country. While the Declaratory Act augured more trouble in the future, the suspension of the onerous revenue measures brought a huge sense of relief.

Providence joined the other cities of the colonial seaboard in celebration, but with a caveat: they waited, in a snub to Parliament, until June 4, the king's birthday. Dawn was greeted with a chorus of church bells and the boom of a cannonade echoing off Prospect Hill. The town militia marched down the main street, and ships moored in the Great Salt River showed off the skill of their crews, who ran their flags up the rigging in a coordinated display. After a pious Presbyterian sermon, the townsmen assembled for a great feast, followed by a drinking bout punctuated by still more rounds of cannon. As was their custom, the people of Providence distinguished themselves by drinking, knocking back thirty-four toasts, dedicated variously to the king, the queen, William Pitt, Benjamin Franklin, and Stephen Hopkins. For those still able to stand, the evening concluded with fireworks and a grand ball.

Certainly, the Brown brothers enjoyed the festivities along with their townsmen, but the truce with Parliament did little to stave off a growing sense of urgency in their business affairs. Even before the imposition of new sugar duties, the end of the Old French War stripped the steep profits from trade with the Caribbean, and with it the hard currency crucial for paying off debts to European creditors. The shortage of coin in turn shut down markets in the key ports of Boston, New York, and Philadelphia, and the colonies sank into a full-blown postwar depression. By May 1763, the Browns lamented to one of their shipping agents, "All business seems to wear a gloom not before seen in America." Their correspondent agreed that, in New York, business was "dull and extremely declined."

The family manufacturing interests were hurting as well. For reasons never mentioned in their correspondence, the Browns had dismantled their stills after Obadiah's death, and could no longer rely on the rum business. In the meantime, sales of candles were painfully slow, due both to increased competition and to the general weakness of commerce. Even as the Brown brothers sought to keep rival chandlers out of the market, they disdained an offer from Boston to purchase discounted equipment from a failed candle firm. As one dour letter explained, "The destruction of the works seems already accomplished by the business being so poor as barely worth pursuing."

The advent of the Sugar Act only deepened the economic doldrums. Gov. Samuel Ward detailed the malaise in a letter to the secretary of trade in 1765: "The merchants sustained very great losses in the late war; and the channels of that little commerce which they have left are so obstructed by regulations . . . that it is continually declining; the demand for the produce of the country, employ for laborers and other kinds of business, are proportionately decreased. . . . The lands within this colony, have also sunk nearly or quite one half in their value."

The Browns answered these dire conditions with their usual resourcefulness. The molasses trade remained a mainstay, and as the tariffs went up, the Browns systematically dodged them. The tone of the brothers' internal dialogue came clear in a letter from Nicholas to Moses dated the day after Christmas 1763. At issue was a homeward bound cargo of dubious origin in care of George Hopkins, brother to the governor and a regular captain in the Browns' employ. Rufus, mentioned later, is Governor Hopkins's son.

Brother John seems still to be of the opinion it's best for George to come direct home and pay the 2/3 pence (if his papers should be good) but seems to think we might get off as they do in Boston but can't be of his opinion to think it worthwhile. . . . Pray inform yourself as well as you can what the Man of War will do hereafter as it's certain she can stop all if they please and its also clear that the officers will admit these sort of papers as long as they can be justified by their conduct provided they are friends to the trade, otherwise they would follow their orders from home (if they have any) and permit no vessel to come up and unload without paying the duties. Doubtless you'll have heard that Bucklin got entered without any objection (except what made by that pussy William Mumford who said the papers was the same sort as C. Sheldon's). The captain of the Man of War was present with all the other officers—pray talk with old Mr. Mumford about this and some others as your prudence will direct. He (young Mumford) ain't out of the reach of wanting the favors of this town. Captain Cooke and others here resent it very much and say he must be taught better by some means or other. . . .

There was this difference between Bucklin's papers and Rufus',

Bucklin's certificate expressed his molasses to be the growth of the British Islands, Rufus' said his molasses was legally imported. . . . The collector asked Bucklin what was meant by the rates and duties but his pulling out his certificate without answering to the question quite sufficed and no more questions asked but swore to the manifest.

What is apparent is that while the Browns were unsure of the demeanor of the British authorities, they were always ready to engage in subterfuge. The question was not whether to break the law, but how. Still, the risks of seizure were high, and the profits more modest than during the Old French War. Clearly, the brothers needed to diversify.

One option they explored was a new manufacturing venture, a foundry to produce coarse, low-grade iron from deposits of bog ore found in the rural low country south and west of Providence. Early American iron production was centered in the middle colonies, particularly Pennsylvania, but there were several foundries in New England, and Joseph Jenckes, ancestor to Nicholas's wife, Rhoda, had made his fortune in the business. A new supply of ore was discovered near the Pawtuxet River around 1764, and the following year, the Browns established a foundry with Stephen Hopkins, who lent the project prestige and political muscle.

In time, the Hope Furnace would prove a resounding success, yielding anchors, cannon, foreign sales, and steady profits for decades. But at the outset it required patience and substantial capital. Before committing to such an ambitious undertaking, the Brown brothers decided to gamble on a quicker but far more risky venture. Following the course set by their father and uncle, entranced by the gaudy success of the leading merchants at Newport, they commissioned a voyage in the slave trade.

3

The *Sally*

IN SEPTEMBER 1764, as the heavy heat of the New England summer finally began to lift, John and Moses Brown sailed with their brother Joseph from Providence to Newport to supervise the final preparations for the voyage of the ship *Sally*. Usually the Browns put their vessels out from their own wharf at Providence, but in this case the primary cargo would be rum, and the quantity they were shipping made Newport the only logical point of departure. Besides, the *Sally* was putting out for Africa, and with so much at stake, the brothers wanted to be sure everything was in order.

Nicholas stayed behind, tending affairs at the countinghouse, as was his wont. John and Moses were the natural candidates for the assignment. A square-rigged brigantine, the *Sally* was larger than the sloops and schooners that made up the rest of the family fleet, and finalizing her inventory required all the deal-making acumen the young merchants could muster. Joseph's presence at Newport was a bit unusual, as he generally took a backseat in business affairs. But the *Sally* was being custom fitted for this expedition, with the chains and barracoon and other trappings of the slave trade, and Joseph may have been indulging his mechanical curiosity. More simply, Joseph may have taken the opportunity to visit Newport. It was the commercial capital of the colony and a jewel of a town, one of the great sights of the colonial seaboard.

Newport would fall during the course of the Revolution, and would rise again to become a summer resort for the rich and powerful, but this was its first heyday. The town was built around a quiet, deepwater harbor lying on the west-facing shore of Aquidneck Island, which stretched more than ten miles north and east, to the inland waters of Mount Hope Bay. The harbor was sheltered on three sides from Narragansett Bay, and by the rocky foot of Aquidneck from the angry gales of the Atlantic.

Within the harbor itself, the waterfront was sculpted for commerce, with scores of private wharves bisected by the Long Wharf, a public dock that jutted out two thousand feet, with a drawbridge leading to an inner mooring for smaller craft. The town itself stood close by, with brightly painted wood-frame houses clustered around an open cobblestone parade, dominated at the south side by a great stone marketplace and on the far end, to the east, by the Colony House, the model for Providence's own government seat. Farther back, windmills crowned the peaks of the rolling Aquidneck hills.

Larger and richer than Providence, Newport was more cosmopolitan, home to a handsome library—endowed by Quaker shipping magnate Abraham Redwood—and to the Touro Synagogue, the first of its kind in America. Newport was also home to the colonial slave trade, which had grown steadily since the early part of the century and drew the interest and engagement of all the great shipping families of the town—the Redwoods and the Malbones, the Vernons and the Ellerys, and the Browns' friends the Wantons.

Once their fortunes were secure, these merchant princes retired to elegant country estates encompassing thousands of acres in the dales and meadows on the outskirts of town. But there was no mistaking the influence of the Guinea trade on every facet of life in Newport. The very streets of the town were paved with proceeds from a duty on imported slaves. Aside from shipping, the leading industry was distilling rum from molasses, with at least a third of that product wheeled directly to the docks and loaded onto ships bound for Africa. Return cargoes of chained and miserable slaves were a common sight on the docks and at the main market, just off the waterfront. The early Quaker abolitionist John Woolman was shaken by the scenes from the waterfront during a visit to Newport in 1760, recording in his journal, "My appetite failed, and I grew outwardly weak."

The Brown brothers suffered no such revulsion during their visit to Newport. Years later, Moses proposed that it was John who "drew his brothers with him" into the expedition, driven by "his love of money and anxiety to acquire it." But there is no record of objections raised by any of the other brothers at the time. Indeed, unlike most of their joint enterprises, each signed on to this venture individually, and as equal partners.

The first evidence that the Browns were contemplating a move into the slave trade crops up in an exchange of letters with Carter Braxton, a Virginia slaveholder and petty customs official who raised tobacco at a plantation on the Pamunkey River. A shrewd businessman, Braxton traded in a wide variety of goods, and he wrote Nicholas Brown & Co. in February 1763 to offer his services and selling commodities at 5 percent commission. More intriguing, Braxton knew there was a "great traid carried on from Rhode Island to Guinea for Negroes," and he wondered if he could find a partner in that business.

The brothers answered that fall, when they sent another cargo southward down the coast. They would take him on as an agent, they said, but at half the rate he sought. As for slaves, they would entertain that collaboration as well. "It's very likely if its agreeable to you to be concerned that we may fitt a proper vessel for Guiney in the Spring, and as a considerable quantity of tobacco will answer there, you'll advise us in your next whether you could send a quantity of tobacco clear of duty by our vessel." Thus the brothers would acquire a part-ner and a key ingredient of the cargo in a single transaction.

Braxton answered promptly. He would accept the brothers' commission terms, and would sell their cargo of slaves to boot. "The prices of Negroes keep up amazingly," he enthused. Weeks after receiving that letter, the Browns sent another sloop to Virginia, this time with a slave aboard, perhaps as a test of Braxton's mettle, to be sold "for the most he would fetch." But here the trail dies out. Braxton, the plantation owner and aspiring slave trader, later turned up as a signer of the Declaration of Independence, but never again appears in the Browns' correspondence.

The loss of a possible partner set back the Browns' plans to enter the slave trade, but only temporarily. Young and ambitious as they were, and hemmed in by the postwar depression, their move to join such a profitable traffic seems almost inevitable.

Braxton was correct when he referenced a "great traid" between Rhode Is-land and Africa. In the years since James Brown had sent his brother Obadiah to Africa, few Providence merchants had followed his lead, but Newport had increased steadily in the trade, even as the shippers from the other colonial ports, primarily Boston and New York, had dropped out. By the time of the French and Indian War, vessels from Newport carried more than 70 percent of the American traffic in slaves; while colonial carriers remained a small frac-tion of the European ships bringing Africans to New World, the American trade was located almost exclusively at Newport. And with the end of hostili-ties with France, departures from Newport surged. From a low point of six clearances to Africa in 1759, the number of slavers setting out from Newport more than doubled in 1761, matching the prewar peak of fifteen. By the time the Browns dispatched the *Sally*, three years later, that figure would increase again, to twenty-seven.

Stephen Hopkins emphasized in his Remonstrance to the Board of Trade the crucial role played by rum and slaves in the fortunes of the colony:

This little colony, for more than thirty years past, have annually sent about eighteen sail of vessels to the [African] coast, which have carried about eighteen hundred hogsheads of rum, together with a small quantity of provisions and some other articles, which have been sold for slaves, gold dust, elephants' teeth, camwood, etc. The slaves have been sold in the English islands [of the Caribbean], in Carolina and Virginia, for bills of exchange . . . ; and by this trade alone, remittances have been made from this colony to Great Britain, to the value of about 40,000 pounds yearly. . . .

From this deduction of the course of our trade, which is founded in exact truth, it appears that the whole trading stock of this colony, in its beginning, progress and end, is uniformly directed to the payment of the debt contracted by the import of British goods; and it also clearly appears, that without this trade, it would have been and always will be, utterly impossible for the inhabitants of this colony to subsist themselves, or to pay for any considerable quantity of British goods.

While the logic of the colonial economy was driving the Browns to enter into the African trade, there was little in the way of moral stricture to hold them back. At that time, in the years before the Revolution, the idea that there was something wrong with trafficking in humankind was still just a glimmer on the ethical horizon. True, John Woolman and several other Quaker visionaries were just then beginning to raise their voices against slavery, but they were a tiny faction even within their sect, and had yet to be heard in the broader body politic. Among the Quakers themselves, the question was usually framed in terms of the treatment of slaves and their potential for conversion to Christian faith. Similarly, a few Protestant clerics, like Samuel Sewall in Boston, had spoken against human bondage, but they had been roundly denounced, in part on scriptural grounds.

More important, slavery was an accepted part of everyday life in the colony, and in the life of the Browns. James and Obadiah Brown each had slaves tending the kitchen and the nursery while the boys were growing up, and as the brothers established their own households, each included as his property Africans held in lifelong bondage. The best accounting that survives is the one for Moses; he had working for him in 1764 several African men, including Bonno, the oldest, aged about twenty-five years; Caesar, recently purchased at age twenty-three; and Cudjo, born in Rhode Island of African parents. In addition there was at least one woman slave in the household, named Eve. She had been bequeathed by Uncle Obadiah to his daughter Mary, the sister of Moses' wife; she lived with Anna and Moses at their home on Towne Street.

John offered some hint of his attitude toward his slaves in a summary of his ratable estate, a document filed with the town for tax purposes. In it, he accounted for two African servants: "One Negrow feller, also one negrow which I am uncertain is 14 years old or not." He would register his slaves as property, but disdained to mention them by name. As for Nicholas, he owned several slaves, and sold them on occasion, as in November 1763, when he recorded the sale of "one Negro girl named Desire" to the seafaring Abe Whipple.

In addition to the slaves they held at home, the brothers held several slaves in common. This was an unusual arrangement but not unique; several deeds of manumission, recorded in the mid-1770s, released an owner's partial interest in an individual slave. The Browns' practice was described years later by William J. Brown, whose grandfather grew up in bondage to the Brown brothers. "Grandfather Brown was born in Africa, and belonged to a firm consisting of four, named respectively, Joseph, John, Nicholas and Moses Brown," William wrote in a memoir. "They held slaves together, each brother selecting out such as they wished for house service; the rest of the slaves to perform outdoor labor."

The Browns' slaveholding was not exceptional. While the institution of slavery was always stronger and more advanced in the southern colonies, it was present throughout the British settlement, and especially in the seaports like Boston and New York, New London, and Newport, where most families of means kept black slaves. Slavery was more prevalent in Rhode Island than in most of New England, and it was stronger in the southern part of the colony than the north. By the middle of the eighteenth century, slaves made up more than 15 percent of the population at Newport, and in the Narragansett country, a district of fertile plantations on the coastal plain to the west, dozens of farms were tilled by teams of ten to twenty slaves.

In Providence, slaveholding was a mark of the elite. Slave auctions were held at the Crown Coffee House, just off Market Square. Many from the Browns' circle of friends owned slaves, including Stephen Hopkins, Jabez Bowen, and the Jenckeses. These personal slaves did chores around the house and on the country holdings of the leading families. If there wasn't enough work to keep the slaves busy, they were leased out. One 1763 letter to Moses asks the wages for his blacks, "that we may settle with his master."

The slaves of Providence became a part of the social life of the town, particularly in the mornings and evenings, when the blacks joined boys from other families in a headlong race across the Great Bridge to reach the town pump, or north on Towne Street to the banks of the Moshassuck, where they would draw water that they would tote back in buckets. This was the limit, however, of the town's tolerance for the Africans in their midst. Within the home, slaves lived out of sight, in attics or dank basements, or physically apart, in outbuildings and barns. In those churches that admitted blacks, they were consigned to balconies where they could not be seen. And after nightfall, a colony-wide curfew barred blacks from being abroad after 9 P.M.; transgressors were punished at the whipping post. In 1751, that law was amended "to prevent all persons keeping house within this colony from entertaining Indian, Negro or Mulatto servants or slaves . . . nor furnish any opportunities for dancing or gaming."

In the years after slavery was abolished in the north, chroniclers of New England history tended to soft-pedal the memory of slavery, assuring their readers that the institution of bondage was more gentle and more familial than the brutal mode prevailing to the south. References abound to "jolly darkies" and the "delightful experience of patriarchal manners." Yet in the north as in the south, slavery was always characterized by the tools of the trade, the manacle and the lash, and by mutual mistrust rooted in the master's arbitrary and total sway.

That fear lay at the base of the relationship between master and slave was made clear in an incident that took place at Newport, in 1707, and was remembered long after. In the spring of that year, the wife of a slaveholder was murdered, and one of the family slaves, a suspect in the crime, fled and threw himself into the sea, "by reason he would not be taken alive." Two weeks later, when the body of the anonymous slave was washed ashore, it was "brought into the harbor at Newport," where, upon order of the General Assembly, it was dismembered. The head, arms, legs, and torso were then "hung up in some public place, near to town, to public view . . . that it may, if it please God, be something of a terror to others."

The primary consideration for the Browns entering the slave trade was not moral, but logistical. Like their father before them, they would have to secure the substantial up-front capital needed to stage a voyage that would take a year to complete under the best of circumstances. They needed to assemble a cargo. And they needed to locate a captain they could rely on.

The brothers were already working on the first two tasks during their correspondence with Braxton. "We shall largely be concerned in the navigation this Fall which will bring molasses in the Spring and we living in a place where we can procure a large quantity of rum distilled amediately," they wrote in September 1763. A year later, they had secured 159 barrels, called hogsheads, which contained more than seventeen thousand gallons of high-proof rum. There were other items to locate and buy as the brothers sought

to adjust their wares to the tastes of the African coast. Tobacco was especially useful in helping to close a deal, and ten hogsheads of local leaf were
loaded on. Onions, produced in nearby Bristol, always traded well, and the
Browns obtained eighteen hundred bunches. Rounding out the cargo were
thirty boxes of candles, forty barrels of flour, ninety-six pounds of coffee, and
twenty-five casks of rice, presumably to feed the slaves on the trip across the
Atlantic.

In the meantime, the brothers wrestled with the crucial choice of who
would command their ship. During the months since the deal with Braxton
had fallen through, other merchants had stepped into the trade, glutting the
coast with rum and carrying off most of the available slaves. The Browns
needed a captain who could enter a thin and volatile market and still come
away with a successful venture. Their first choice was William Earl, the
helmsman on the *Wheel of Fortune*, Obadiah's last slaving venture, but Earl
was committed to Simeon Potter, a sometime privateer running slave ships
out of Bristol.

Word of the Browns' search for a captain reached their friend Joseph Wanton in Newport, and in August his son Joseph Jr. offered his services. "[I] flat-
ter my self that I can give you satisfaction . . . being well aquainted and well
experienced in the Ginea trade all down the coasts," he wrote. By then, however, the Browns had made their decision: they would enlist Esek Hopkins,
Stephen's brother and, when ashore, a colleague of the Browns in the Providence political scene, on various civic projects, and as a deputy to the General
Assembly during Moses' first term.

Then forty-six years old, Esek Hopkins was a handsome and headstrong
sailor, more than six feet tall, who had already lived a life of adventure on the
sea. His conquests in command of privateers, sometimes on ships commissioned by the Browns, were the stuff of legend, and had financed a farm of
more than two hundred acres and a retail shop on Towne Street. Not only was
he an able seaman, but Hopkins had proven a reliable supercargo, readily
moving cargoes at the cutthroat markets of the West Indies. True, Esek had yet
to try his hand on the coast of Africa, but then, neither had Uncle Obadiah,
and his voyage in the *Mary* had ended well.

Many images were rendered of Esek Hopkins, most in connection with his
later service during the American Revolution, but only one was made by
someone who actually saw Hopkins in person. This was a remarkable oil
painting, *Sea Captains Carousing in Surinam*, created by the portraitist John
Greenwood in 1755. The tableau does not convey much about Hopkins's vis-
age—there are twenty-two figures on a three-foot-by-six-foot canvas—but it

tells us much about his milieu. Set in the gloomy interior of a seaside tavern, the painting depicts the climax of a nightlong drinking bout. Hopkins is at the center, seated at a large round table wearing a tricorner hat, holding a glass of grog, and conversing with Nicholas Cooke, another Providence sea captain, who was later elected governor of the colony. Around them reel shipmasters and sailors in various stages of inebriation, some laughing, some dozing; a couple are dancing, and two are vomiting. The only women in the picture are two black slaves serving up still more libations. The painting confirms Hopkins's reputation as a popular figure in the maritime fraternity, at home in any port where the trade winds might take him.

When Joseph Wanton learned that the Browns had settled on Hopkins, he advised against the decision. "Depend on it," he warned in a letter on August 13, "such times as will be when your vessel gets there, never were before and having a stranger must make it worse." Wanton went so far as to suggest an experienced slaver as a substitute. "If Esek is willing to quit, don't believe you can better yourselves than by taking Croswel, which was it my case should do." But the Browns stuck with their friend, and Hopkins was on hand at Newport when John, Moses, and Joseph arrived.

The terms of his hire followed the custom of the African trade. Hopkins would earn 5 percent of all sales transacted during the voyage, but the lion's share of his profit would come in kind—he was to ship ten slaves as "captain's privilege" on his own account. In addition, Hopkins was to receive four slaves of his own for every hundred purchased. Hopkins was a part owner in the *Sally*, but this venture was underwritten exclusively by the Browns.

It was up to Hopkins to assemble his crew. Slave ships carried a larger complement than trading vessels of the same size, as seamen were required to guard their captives as well as handle the ship. At the time she set sail, the *Sally* had twelve men on board, including Hopkins, first mate James York, and Amos Hopkins, probably a nephew of Esek's, as he was listed just below the captain on the ship's roster.

Aside from detailing the captain's compensation, the sailing orders issued by the Browns afforded Hopkins full authority "to transact any and all business whatever," including sale of the vessel itself if that might be done for a profit. Aside from cash or "good bills of exchange," the Browns asked that Hopkins bring "four likely young slaves home for owners about 15 years old."

The orders were issued September 10, and Hopkins embarked soon after that, tacking north through the rocky embouchure at the mouth of the harbor and then south, through the main channel and out to sea. John, Moses, and Joseph were still in Newport, and certainly they stood at the docks to see Hop-

kins off. They were accustomed to striding the docks with the proprietary assurance of ship owners, but the brothers had cause for an added measure of
pride and trepidation as the crew loosed the mainsail and the *Sally* rounded
silently into the stream. John, the more sartorial of the three, may even have
sported a powdered wig to mark the event. This was, after all, the Browns'
entry into the rarefied caste of Newport slave traders, an order marked by
means, manners, and ambition.

   The voyage east went smoothly, and the *Sally* made landfall in early November near Bissau on the Windward Coast of Africa. Lying between the
Gambia River to the north and Cape Mount (in what is now Sierra Leone) to
the south, this was a region of heavy tides that surged against a low alluvial
plain. The shore was divided by a dozen major rivers and defined by great
stands of mangrove, which shaded the riverbanks and anchored the boggy
flats. Crocodiles and hippopotamus wallowed along the banks of the fast-
moving streams, while sharks cruised the Atlantic shallows between the coast
and the archipelago of the Bijagos Islands, which reached fifty miles out to sea.

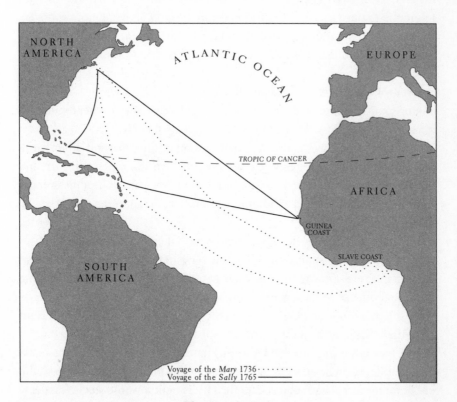

The Triangle Trade

This was the true Guinea Coast, a thousand miles north and west of the primary trading grounds of the Slave Coast, where Obadiah Brown had done business thirty years before. Hopkins may not have been a veteran of the slave trade, but his choice of destination was a bold one. The shorter route cut a good three weeks of sailing off each leg of the trip, and it allowed the *Sally* to avoid the postwar glut of sail, and rum, at the more established European trading forts. That region was already crowded: one contemporary report held that "trade, for these many months, has been miserable indeed"; another correspondent found at a single fort "17 sail . . . of Europeans & Rum Men & the latter could not get a slave at any price."

By trading farther to the west, Hopkins avoided some of the competition, but he was also forfeiting the convenience of European middlemen operating from their land-based slave marts. The Windward Coast in fact had a longer history with slavery, as the Portuguese had opened the Atlantic trade there as early as the fifteenth century. And after 1750, with the Slave Coast operating at capacity, slave exports from the Windward Coast surged. But instead of relying on caravans from the interior, the slave merchants of the Windward Coast found their quarry close by the shore; meaning supplies were more sporadic, and the slaves themselves were more rebellious. In choosing to work the well-watered Senegambia coast, Hopkins was committing to the vagaries of the black trade.

Control of the region between the Gambia and Sierra Leone was divided among scores of different tribes, most of which battled one another for dominion and for slaves to sell. The centuries of slaving had given rise to a state of constant insecurity, as tribal chiefs vied for liquor, firearms, and other European manufactures. Kings sometimes sold off even their own subjects, and travelers routinely carried firearms to fend off raiding parties. Traders or kings would advertise their wares by torching bonfires on the shore; a pillar of smoke signaled a going market.

To judge by the *Sally*'s log—among the most detailed documents that survive anywhere to illustrate daily life in the slave trade—Captain Hopkins was more than game. During the first week he made deals for provisions, trading small quantities of rum for wood, corn, yams, and fowl. Aboard ship, preparations were made for the long stay under the African sun; following the custom of the trade, the crew struck the yards and the topmasts and lashed them lengthwise between the masts to create a ridgepole above the center of the deck. Boards and more spars were used to set walls along the gunwales, and then the whole framework sheathed in sailcloth. This structure would shade the deck, and also serve as a daytime cage for the growing complement of slaves.

In the meantime, the crew was getting accustomed to the coast. For several, that meant enduring the crushing head and body aches and searing fever that was dubbed by sailors in the trade as "the malady of the land." This may or may not have been malaria, but it was debilitating and often fatal, contributing to a mortality rate among slave crews that was higher than it was for their cargo. Before the first month was out, Hopkins was seeking a doctor to minister to three ailing crew members.

Getting down to business, Hopkins made contact with Alkade, a local king. On November 13, he saluted him with three gallons of the legendary New England rum. This was the first of many palavers Hopkins would hold with Alkade and other royals; a month later he "went ashore to meet the king under the palaver tree. Carried 5 kegs 14 flask of rum and paid the king 75 gallons for his customs and received a cow as a present." The rest of the week was spent in daily fetes with Alkade and his entourage. Hopkins, perhaps accompanied by an officer or two, joined in drinking rum, eating roasted meat, and smoking fat spliffs of rolled tobacco. It was a macabre version of Christmas, with the fierce heat and the strange language, the potentates draped in brightly colored cotton, and the prospective slaves, naked and chained, huddled off to one side. But it was all part of the business.

This sort of flattery was standard for the black trade, a way to reassure the Africans that their white partners would not betray them. In years past, ill treatment and shipboard kidnappings by slavers had engendered fear and recrimination. In one notorious case, in 1732, local Africans overwhelmed the British slave ship *Dove*, killing the entire crew and destroying the vessel. Gaining the favor of the king was crucial to a successful venture.

Moreover, Hopkins had competition. The *Sally*'s log shows that other slave ships were a constant presence, some British, some French, and some Portuguese. Hopkins appears to have welcomed their company, and when business was slow on shore, he kept busy making deals with his ostensible rivals. On November 20, for example, he traded barrels of beef, ship's bread, flour, and sugar to a captain named Elliot, and received in return a supply of beads—for future trades—and "one garl slave." Onions were particularly popular with the crews of the European ships.

The consent of the king meant Hopkins had permission to deal, but he'd have to find his slaves where he could. While most of the trade was carried on by middlemen, primarily mulatto descendants of the early Portuguese adventurers, Hopkins also secured the services of slave hunters, who worked the low-lying coast for a retainer of a flask or two of rum. If they returned with captives for sale, the bargaining began anew. Sales took place on shore, where

Hopkins or one of his officers inspected their naked, exhausted quarry for signs of disease or other infirmity. The bargaining could take all day, as the slave merchant picked over the *Sally*'s trading goods. Some transactions were settled for a simple quantity of rum, but others were more elaborate—the price of one "small garle" was four kegs and four flasks of rum, seven sets of cotton clothes, one length of calico cloth, two large iron bars, one small cutlass, two English guns, one bunch of beads, a flask of gunpowder, and six knives. By early January Hopkins had secured thirty slaves—a rate of one every couple of days.

Once a purchase was made, the captive Africans were taken aboard. According to the custom of the trade, the slaves were kept on deck during the daytime, sequestered behind a barracoon that was hung with nets to keep the captives from diving overboard. Males were always shackled, but women and children were usually free to move about inside the compound. At night, as the stifling heat lifted, all the slaves were confined below decks, their quarters increasingly crowded as the tally of prisoners steadily mounted.

On some days, Hopkins ran a virtual bazaar on the *Sally*'s crowded deck. January 8 was especially busy, with canoes plying the waters from ship to shore and small boats ferrying officers and wares from other slave ships lying nearby. That day, a Captain James exchanged ten dozen knives for twenty-four bunches of onions, while a second captain sold two kegs of gunpowder for sixteen bunches more. Other trades brought a pistol, two pairs of handcuffs, "country clothes" favored by the slave dealers, two cases of blown-glass bottles, quantities of corn and yams, and one large cutlass, all for one or more flasks of rum. The following day, Hopkins traded the gunpowder, the country clothes, and the large cutlass, along with seventy-five gallons of rum, four guns, and two iron bars, for two slaves, one woman and one girl. Time was slipping by slowly.

By February, Hopkins was doing what he could to pick up the pace. He sent his first mate up the Geba River, whose broad tidal estuary ran forty miles into the interior of the tangled coastal forest. James York was gone a week and returned with mixed results. He procured one man, one boy, and one girl, along with three sets of country clothes and 165 pounds of beeswax, but the price was high: "He give and expended 328 galons rum, 28 bushels onyons many more wasted, 1 pr silk stockins 20 galons rum drunk and stole." Moreover, York fell ill on the expedition. The new slaves brought Hopkins's total to forty-nine.

There were other problems. In March, William Cookos, one of the sailors, died, presumably from the malaria. And some of the hogsheads of rum had begun to come apart—not surprising, considering that the barrels were made of fitted, rough-hewn oak bound by nothing more than hoops—creating a constant problem in ships covering the long distances involved in the slave trade. Hopkins estimated that he'd lost more than 10 percent of his rum to leakage, the rum adding a sour note to the *Sally*'s sloshing bilge.

As the months dragged by, Hopkins seems to have grown so enamored of the business of trades and palavers that he lost any sense of the urgency of his mission. He swapped slaves with other ship captains, sometimes to little effect. On one day in March, Hopkins bought two slaves on shore, then turned around and sold them to a Captain Patto for a trifling profit. And he enjoyed friendly relations with King Alkade, so friendly that he took to making advances of rum and other articles, presumably for aid in finding more slaves. Alkade proved his allegiance by returning to Hopkins a slave who had escaped from bondage on shore. Separately, Hopkins employed a number of Africans on the coast, including two boatmen to run canoes between ship and shore, and an interpreter named Antony.

By May, with the rainy season coming on, the slow pace of the trading began to take a toll on the slaves Hopkins was so busy procuring. May 1 brought the first, spare notation in the *Sally*'s trade book: "a boye slave died." Sweltering heat combined with despair to make life all but intolerable for the captives, and on June 8, a "woman slave hanged herself between decks."

From that day forward, Hopkins and the crew of the *Sally* found themselves in a grim race with mortality. On July 12, three slaves expired in a single day, bringing the total thus far to ten. That same day the captain recorded the purchase of two slaves, for a net loss of one. Two more slaves died the next day, but another ship captain sold Hopkins five women and two boys. That would have to pass for progress.

By this time, the *Sally* had completed the transition from oceangoing freighter to prison ship, with more than one hundred slaves crammed into the darkness below the main deck each night. Already, the crew was engaged in the daily, dirty process of bringing the fearful captives on deck to feed, and to stretch their cramped limbs while the stinking hold was scrubbed and flushed with seawater. The ship's log makes no indication of why the slaves were dying, but it does not appear to have been an outbreak of communicable disease, like measles, which could carry off half a slave cargo in a matter of days. More likely it was the combination of shock and heartbreak that afflicted each individual taken aboard ship. Olaudah Equiano offered a sense of that experience in his 1789 memoir, one of a handful of first-person narratives to survive from the slave era.

The first object which saluted my eyes when I arrived on the coast was the sea, and a slave ship, which was then riding at anchor, and awaiting its cargo. These filled me with astonishment, which soon converted into terror. . . . I was not long suffered to indulge my grief; I was soon put under the decks, and there I received such a salutation in my nostrils I had never experienced in my life; so that, with the loathsomeness of the stench, and crying together, I became so sick and low that I was not able to eat.

Hopkins did what he could to limit the damage. He sold off four elderly captives to another ship; on August 1, he managed a grisly exchange, trading "a man slave with his foot bitt off by a shark and goot a boy in his room." There is no hint of emotion in the cold accounting of the trade book, but this period had to tax the moral stamina even of a hardened Yankee slaving crew. Their spirits took another blow with the death of another of the sailors, Uriah Parker. The cause of death was not noted, but at the end of the journey, his widow received payment for nine months, eighteen days of service.

By late August, after ten months on the coast, Hopkins had achieved his target of 140 slaves—and more, hoping perhaps to answer for the extended duration of the trip by padding his profits, and the Browns'. He closed out his business on August 20 when he bought a woman slave, bringing the total crammed below decks to 167. In a final gesture, bidding once more to cut his losses, he handed over "1 woman all most dead" to Antony, the African interpreter. The next day, at long last, the *Sally* hoisted sail and headed south, seeking trade winds blowing west.

Back in Rhode Island, the Browns had no way of knowing Hopkins's progress, or the lack of it, in Africa. The brothers were busy with the business of their other ships, with the affairs of colonial government, and with the agitation against the British, but the fate of the *Sally* was constantly in mind. On December 30 the brothers wrote a chatty letter to Hopkins, reiterating that he was empowered to "dew as you shall think best for our interest," and belatedly reminding him, "It's an old proverb and we doubt not that you will verifye it, Dispatch is the life of Business." Also enclosed "for your amusement" was a copy of *The Rights of the Colony Examined*, by Esek's brother Stephen. Subscribed Nicholas Brown & Co. but written in Moses' hand, the letter was handed off to a captain of a late-sailing slaver in hopes it would find Hopkins in Africa.

The brothers' continuing concern with their captain and his cargo was evidenced by amended sets of sailing orders, sent July 4 to Barbados, and again July 15, on the chance Hopkins should touch there first after crossing back. The first advised that prices for slaves were strong in South Carolina; two weeks later they proposed Jamaica "if the slaves are in good health." The letter observed, "We have not received a line from you," and closed ominously, giving additional instructions "if Captain Hopkins should not be living and onbord the Brigg *Sally* when this reaches her."

The Browns had good reason to be pessimistic. Communications with ships at sea were necessarily spotty, and owners of vessels had to rely on rumor and unconfirmed reports for news. The first word of Hopkins to reach Rhode Island came in a letter from Benjamin Gardner, a Newport ship's captain, who'd seen a letter from his brother, yet another captain then on the coast of Africa. Gardner's brother "informs us of Capt. Hopkins' arrival on the coast." The *Sally* was "up the River Gamby . . . and they are all well on board." Underscoring the hazardous nature of the trade, Gardner closed by requesting that the Browns inquire of their captains after the fate of his brother, for Gardner had been told that his brother was dead.

The next report reached Rhode Island a month later. Benjamin Mason, a Newport merchant with his own ships in the trade, wrote the Browns with the news that Hopkins had lost all his hands in the river Basa and had taken refuge with "the Governor of Gambia," an apparent reference to the small and ineffectual garrison maintained by the British on an island in the river. This dismal tale was picked up and published as a shipping brief in the *Newport Mercury*, which lent credence to the report and sent a shudder of despair through Providence.

On June 26, with still no further word of Hopkins, Joseph and William Wanton sent a note of commiseration to the Browns. "We heartily condole with you the bad news from Hopkins," the Wantons wrote. They were generous enough to add that the Browns should not blame Hopkins for his decision to work the Windward Coast. "Had he proceeded down to Anamaboe [a primary trading fort on the Slave Coast] it would have been no better."

The Browns refused to give up on Hopkins, or on the fate of their venture. On July 15, they sent another dispatch, this to Barbados, hoping to reach him before he'd unloaded his cargo. It was addressed to Captain Esek Hopkins or the commanding officer of the brig *Sally* and began, "We have not received a line from you since you sailed." From there forward, it was strictly business. The market for slaves was soft in South Carolina, the brothers advised. He might try Barbados, but if he could not raise twenty-eight pounds sterling per head, "we advise your going to Jamaica if your slaves are in good health and there dispose of them for cash or good bills excepting only 30 hogsheads of rum 6 or 8 hogsheads sugar & 3 or 4 bags cotton all which you'll immediately bring home in the brig." The letter closed with a vote of confidence, and then a darker note. "If Capt. Hopkins is alive and in good health," he remained at liberty to proceed as he saw fit. But "if Capt. Hopkins should not be living," his stand-in should follow the detailed plan of action.

By the time that letter was sent, Moses Brown was no longer content to continue waiting for news. The next morning, he sailed for Newport, planning to alert captains then departing for Africa to seek out Hopkins and "take some method to supply the misfortune as much as possible." Upon his arrival, however, Moses was handed a letter from Hopkins himself, dated May 17. Hopkins reported that one crew member had succumbed to disease and three others were ill, but the rest were healthy and there were seventy-five slaves on board. The captain also related his problems with the rum.

Moses immediately wrote to his brothers, describing his "transports of joy to hear of [Hopkins] being in a state of health and the melancholy news before heard being in so great a degree contradicted he having lost only one of his hands." Moses then addressed the financial prospects for the venture still under way, sounding the first note of dissent on the general question of slaving. "As to the voyage, it is doubtless spoiled by the leakage if no other misfortune attended it, but however if Capt. Hopkins and people return safe with the brig I shan't be any great disappointed what else he brings, after engaging in so disagreeable a trade and being alarmed with so much loss of friends and interest."

Moses then wrote a note to Hopkins. After observing that, "Such a favorable account of your circumstance from what we had heard quite alleviates our misfortune," Moses went on to reiterate the news of the slave markets to the south. Two days later, Nicholas and John updated their advice to Hopkins yet again. Writing from Providence, the brothers again designated Jamaica as the most promising market for slaves, and then amended their request for a return cargo. "Bring with you five likely boys about 12 or 15 years old for our own use," they advised. "Take care to cloth them proper for the season." Apparently, naked and shackled would not do for the wharf at Providence.

There is nothing to indicate that Hopkins ever received any of the letters dispatched by the *Sally*'s owners from Providence or Newport. Not that they would have altered his course in any material way. During his stay on the coast of Africa, Hopkins had already lost twenty of his slaves to disease, despair, and suicide. And contrary to the rosy interpretation of Moses and his brothers,

Hopkins's crew remained in distress, several of them seriously ill with jungle fever. Now they faced the rigors of the middle passage.

Wooden sailing ships bearing human freight over the long haul from Africa to the Americas faced a series of daunting challenges. Fresh water was strictly rationed, and supplies were rarely sufficient. Conditions in the hold deteriorated rapidly, with a full complement of slaves locked down for long stretches, the miserable captives thrown about by the constant heaving and bucking of a ship on the high seas. Even under the best conditions, one slave in ten perished before reaching the docks of the West Indies, and often the total ran much higher.

Moreover, with the departure from land, the sense of desperation among the slaves increased sharply. On occasion, their fear and resentment led to outright rebellion—and such uprisings were far more frequent on the Windward Coast, where the slaves there were sold closer to home, and so less resigned to their fate. Ship captains dealt severely with these bloody, hopeless revolts. One favored method was to identify one or more of the ringleaders and bind them tightly around the chest, with the other end of the rope looped over the yardarm of the mainsail. Crew members then hauled the miscreants aloft, and as they dangled over the deck, a firing squad shot them dead.

Short of such terrifying exhibitions, wary ship captains limited slave revolts through strict vigilance. Male slaves were kept shackled in pairs day and night, despite the problems that created for sleeping and using the few latrines— buckets placed in the center of the slave decks. In fair weather, while the sun was up, the slaves were brought above decks to exercise, to eat their meals of mush and gruel and to breathe the fresh sea air. Even then, however, the men retained their manacles, which were chained together for added restraint. Women were allowed a modicum of freedom, but members of the crew kept a close watch.

Esek Hopkins was aware of these routines, but he relaxed them in the face of illness and fatigue among his crew. According to a newspaper report based on one of his letters to the Browns, "Soon after he left the coast, the number of his men being reduced by sickness, he was obliged to permit some of the slaves to come on deck to assist the people." In the nomenclature of the trade, "people" referred to members of a ship's crew—not the slaves between decks. It may be that Hopkins was accustomed to cordial relations with his slaves at home, who had become used to their lives in bondage, or that the captain assumed his experience with the hired blacks on the Guinea shore would translate to life on ship. In any event, he was pleased with his innovation, finding the four slaves he drafted into sailors' service "was become very helpful."

On August 28, after a week at sea, Hopkins paid the price for his leniency. As the *Newport Mercury* described it, "These slaves contrived to release the others, and the whole rose upon the people, and endeavored to get possession of the vessel." It was a slave revolt, just the sort of violent reaction to captivity that the white crews and captains feared most. The details of what transpired next can only be imagined—the slaves, scared but bold, massing on the deck by the main hatch leading to the hold; Hopkins at the quarterdeck rail, joined by the few crew members still able to stand, brandishing threats and weapons; the sea and sky forming a yawning backdrop of blue and green and gray. What is sure is that the crew of the *Sally* opened fire, with a swivel gun or with small arms, the lead shot cutting into the naked throng. The roar of the guns followed by anguished screams, and the blood running crimson on the polished deck.

Several slaves were slain on the spot. A few more jumped overboard, bobbing in the ocean swells as the ship cruised on. Several were sorely wounded, one with broken ribs, another with a broken leg. In all, eight died that day. Another died three weeks later, "of his wounds on the ribs when the slaves rose." The man whose leg was shattered in the volley of gunfire lingered for another month, his wound festering, his pain constant, until he too succumbed.

The chaotic melee of the uprising soon gave way to the slow-motion disaster that the *Sally's* Atlantic crossing became. As Hopkins wrote to his owners, the rebellion "made us confine the rest more close which gave them a bad turn in the head. Numbers starved themselves, all lost their spirits and became very sickly, and some died without being sick." The daily toll was entered on a special log Hopkins opened to track the status of his cargo. The somber ledger began August 21, the date of the first death while under sail. The entry read "1 garle slave dyed," and listed her as "No. 21," accounting for those who died on shore. Three more slaves had died even before the revolt.

The days thereafter proceed in numbing regularity. A boy and a girl died August 30. A woman died August 31. On September 1, two more slaves died, bringing the total to thirty-seven. That steady pace of near-daily mortality continued for the duration of the passage. An average crossing from Africa took fifty days, and Hopkins hit his mark, making landfall in the Leeward Islands at the entrance to the Caribbean in early October. A day before that, he entered in his roster, "1 man slave dyed." That brought his total mortality to eighty-eight.

When the *Sally* rounded the island of Antigua and sailed into the placid waters of Saint John's Bay, Esek Hopkins had to feel a sense of relief. He was, in a real sense, coming home: Antigua was a British colony, like Rhode Island, and home to the British naval squadron in the Caribbean. Saint John's had a familiar feel, with cobblestone streets, three hundred gaily painted homes, and, close by the water, a Georgian courthouse designed by Peter Harrison, the same architect who built the imposing stone market just off the docks at Newport. Hopkins knew the leading traders at Antigua, and he knew the taverns.

Yet Hopkins knew too that the business of his voyage was far from over. He had to dispose of his wretched slaves, and he had to assemble a cargo for the return trip to Providence. But first, he had to report the dismal state of the *Sally*'s affairs to the Browns. This he accomplished in a letter dated October 10. He described the uprising of the slaves on ship, and the subsequent, continuing loss of life. Those who survived were so dispirited, he said, that he could not follow the brothers' orders to seek out the best market. "I cannot carry them again to sea before I can get their spirits up," he wrote. "If I should I believe they should all dye."

Hopkins then set about selling his benighted captives for whatever profit he could raise. Antigua might not boast the thriving slave market of Jamaica, but it was home to more than 150 sugar plantations, all of them operated by enslaved gang labor. If the *Sally*'s cargo could not survive another stint on the ocean, they could be disposed of right there at Saint John's.

The usual custom for disposing of a slave cargo was to bring the captives on deck, bathe them and rub them down with oil to show off their physique, and then invite the leading traders of town to come aboard ship and bid against one another. There was no such auction on board the *Sally*, however. With the slaves weak, miserable, and many on the verge of death, Hopkins opted to get them on shore and into one of the warehouses commonly found in most Caribbean ports of the plantation era. There, he hoped, they might recuperate enough to bring a reasonable price at market.

That was wishful thinking. The warehouses were dark, squalid places notorious for filth and disease—not much better than the holds of the slave ships. One French official, after making an inspection at the nearby colony of Martinique, commented that the warehouse district "presented a revolting picture of the dead and dying thrown helter-skelter in the gutter."

The only evidence that survives of how the *Sally*'s slaves were handled on shore is a bill for storage from an Antigua slave merchant. But once they had been removed to shore, the die-off resumed its grim progression. On October 11, four more slaves perished.

The sales began soon after that. As it happened, Hopkins had landed at a strong market. In their sailing orders, the Browns had been hoping to find a price of at least twenty-eight pounds sterling per slave; at Antigua, healthy slaves could have commanded the sum of fifty pounds each. The *Sally*'s slaves were far from healthy, however, and the price fell accordingly. On October 17, six "sick slaves" were sold to a John Lynsey for a total of ninety pounds.

The first public auction was held that day, announced by a "cryer" who went through the streets of Saint John calling out the location of the event and, perhaps, the opportunity of buying slaves at discount prices. Liquor was provided to loosen the customers' wallets, but to little effect. Few buyers turned up, and those that did were unimpressed with the forlorn collection of sick and dying Africans. One man spent forty pounds for "3 sick men," according to notes made by Captain Hopkins. And Lynsey was back, apparently looking for bargains. He decided on adding to his purchase of two days before, buying "2 small garles & sick" for his wife. For all their misery and their dim future prospects, the two girls earned for Hopkins just nine pounds eighteen shillings.

The sales continued through the next month. A man named Caesar Roach, who may also have been proprietor of the warehouse, managed to sell eleven slaves, for which he charged a commission of 2½ percent. Hopkins sold a few on his own, including "2 prime slaves," apparently the only Africans to survive the voyage with their health intact, which brought the princely sum of one hundred pounds. Still another middleman, a merchant named Alexander Willock, managed to move twenty-four slaves for a total price of 486 pounds. Willock also bought some tobacco off Hopkins.

Looking to expand his circle of business contacts, Willock wrote to the Browns at Providence to pitch himself as a factor for their Caribbean interests. He anticipated a good sugar crop, he said, and promised "very reasonable" future prices for rum. As for the cargo delivered by the *Sally*, he apologized for the low price, but observed that the "slaves was very indifferent," and promised a better showing for any future ventures. "I am truly sorry for the bad voyage you must make had the Negroes been young and healthy I should have been able to sell them pritty well."

While the slave merchants were pushing their wares, Hopkins was attending to the ship and its crew. The sailors set about the task of converting the *Sally* back into a coasting freighter, breaking down the platforms between decks where the slaves had suffered and died, swabbing out the hold one last time. One of the sailors, Richard Smith, "went ashore and got drunk for 6 days and then came on board," according to the captain's log. It was his last binge. Smith, who had fallen ill on the African coast, died on the cruise back to Rhode Island.

The Browns remained ignorant of Hopkins and his travails through the summer and most of the fall of 1765. With no word from their captain since May, they could only speculate as to his progress; it appears they still expected to profit by their venture. In August, they wrote to a business partner in New York to request a loan. For surety, they proposed that "whatever sum you may be in advance for us" would be taken out of the *Sally's* "effects."

Their hopes were dashed by the receipt of Hopkins's October 9 letter, which arrived at Providence in the middle of November, at the height of the machinations against the Stamp Act. It was "a most disagreeable account," as the Browns described it in a letter to Esek's brother George Hopkins and two other captains who sailed vessels for the firm. As Esek had informed them, he had "lost 88 slaves and the rest on bord in very sickly & disordered manner." With the survivors selling at depressed prices, the best the brothers could expect was to break even; more likely, they would take a loss.

The setback came at a difficult juncture for the Browns, who had been counting on the *Sally*, along with several other shipping ventures, to finance their stake in the new Hope Furnace. But they allowed no umbrage to color their communications with Hopkins. Writing November 16, the brothers assured him, "We need not mention how disagreeable the news of your losing 3 of your hands and 88 slaves is to us and all your friends, but yourself continuing in health is of so great satisfaction to us, that we remain cheerful under the heavy loss of our interest." The letter went on to give the same advice as previously regarding various slave markets and the best return cargo, and warning that the price of salt had fallen in Rhode Island. But as before, they closed with a vote of confidence. "We knowing your capacity submit the whole management of the voyage to your judgment . . . and notwithstanding your misfortune in this voyage, we well on your arrival at home employ you in any business you may chuse."

Once again, the dispatch was sent in vain. Hopkins continued to pursue the original plan to purchase a cargo of salt. He made his last recorded sale of slaves on November 23, when he sold four weakened men for forty-five pounds. He left Antigua soon thereafter, sailing west, to the Turks Islands, at the southernmost reach of the Bermudas, where he took on a load of salt. Finally, he headed north, heavily laden and carrying as well the last five surviving Africans. During the trip, the *Sally* began to leak, and Hopkins ordered the crew to stand regular shifts working the bilge pump. His orders were ignored, however, and much of the salt was spoiled, prompting him to deduct wages from five crew members, and himself, for the overnight. On December 20, as the *Sally* slogged northward, one of the remaining slaves died. Hopkins noted the event in his ledger, closing his morbid accounting at 109 deaths, well over half the slaves he had purchased on the Gambia shore.

Hopkins arrived at Rhode Island in February 1766, hunched down in the folds of a woolen greatcoat that had hung useless on a peg in the captain's cabin during more than a year in the tropical climes of Africa and the Caribbean. The icy breeze blowing off the frozen shores of Narragansett Bay chafed against his sunburned face. And while he was once again sailing familiar waters, his mood was tempered by the anguish that would attend his landing at Providence, where the wives and families of his crew were waiting anxiously to learn the fate of husbands, sons, and fathers.

But Hopkins was a veteran captain, and so was accustomed to the mixed emotions of a homecoming from the sea. His owners and friends, as the Browns signed their letters to their captains, knew from the outset that their entry into the slave trade was an especially risky venture. And besides, the brothers might take some solace from the fact that Hopkins had fulfilled one express wish. Despite all the death and woe that had attended his efforts, Hopkins would deliver four "likely boys," as the Browns had requested.

4

Success

WHAT IS ABSENT from all of the Brown brothers' correspondence relating to the *Sally*, and from any of the letters and journals written by Esek Hopkins, is any reference to the plight and ghastly demise of the captive Africans. Their suffering is tallied but not described, their agonies presumed but not the subject of contemplation.

To modern eyes this appears an unconscionable oversight, evidence of Hopkins's callous indifference to human suffering close at hand, and of the Browns' willful disregard for the consequences of their business decisions. But that interpretation fails to account for the manners and emotional tenor of the time. Radical as they were in their politics, Americans in the eighteenth century were painfully circumspect in making judgments or critiques of the social fabric around them. Education was limited, and usually confined to readings of the classics and the Bible. Within the circles of family and community, colonial men and women were deeply conservative, and loath to question the status quo.

Conformity started at home. The historian Arthur M. Schlesinger wrote of colonial children, "For them life was implacably real and earnest. Their first and last duty was to walk in the ways of their elders, supplying obedience without question or delay. . . ." As with the children, so with their parents. The institutions of men—Parliament, the customs office—might be torn down and rebuilt, but the state of man, his lot in life, was all but sacred, the work of an obscure but infallible God.

This inclination to quiet submission was a measure of the culture, but it was also a consequence of the difficult lives that people lived in the eighteenth century. Privation was constant, as were hunger, hard labor, illness, and, in the winter, bitter cold. Suffering was taken as a matter of course. Medicine was rudimentary, and death came randomly and often suddenly. Sailors routinely failed to return from the sea. Even families of the elite frequently lost half or more of their offspring before they reached maturity. In that environment, fate was accepted as part of a grand design, beyond the ken of ordinary men.

Such reticence is reflected in the letters of the time, which survive as studies in form and decorum. Salutation and subscription were elaborate, and often made up the bulk of the text. Feelings were expressed in the most stilted form, when they were expressed at all. When anecdotes were offered, the accounts of episodes and events were painfully spare, including perhaps the names of people and a word or two about the weather, but rarely delving into description or emotional content. There were a handful of writers whose works transcended the era—John and Abigail Adams were remarkable for their candid exposition of how they felt and what they thought—but they were a rare exception.

Against this backdrop of restraint, the Browns' failure to remark on the calamity that attended the *Sally* seems less strange. If there was any ruminating over the destruction of so many slaves, or the moral culpability of their captors, it took place in close company, between friends and over a bowl of punch, and certainly not in writing. Life returned to its normal rhythm. Three months after his return, Hopkins was again at sea under orders from the Browns, sailing this time to Surinam, where he traded tobacco for molasses and spent a full month on a tropical sickbed.

Still, while the Brown brothers accepted the human disaster of their African voyage in stony silence, they could not ignore the financial setback it represented for their joint enterprise. It's hard to say just how much damage the Browns sustained. It was not a total loss—Hopkins bought his slaves in Africa at prices ranging from five to ten pounds apiece, and sold the survivors for as much as twenty pounds or more, leaving a net gain on the slave transactions. But that did not cover the cost to the Browns of having one of their finest ships tied up for more than a year on a single venture, or the payroll due to Hopkins and his crew. In December, before the *Sally*'s return from Antigua, the brothers estimated their loss at two thousand pounds sterling. That was before they knew the final proceeds from sales of the slaves and Hopkins's Caribbean cargo, but all told, the voyage of the *Sally* was taxing to the firm at a time when the Browns were scrambling to raise investment capital.

It may have been the simple result of so heavy a blow to the brothers' fortunes, or it may have been the added weight of unspoken guilt, but in the years following the return of the *Sally*, the family firm fell subject to increasing internal dissent. The strife signaled the first rift among siblings who had grown close through the loss of their father and then the uncle who replaced him, and through the maturation of their thriving enterprise. In time, the brothers found their differences irreconcilable.

The first indication of strain came in the spring of 1768, when Moses began absenting himself from the family firm's countinghouse. That February, his wife, Anna, had suffered the loss of a daughter—the second child born to the young couple—who expired two hours after she was born. Not long after, Moses found himself beset with sleepless nights, headaches, and recurrent bouts of depression. It was the first manifestation of a nameless but sometimes debilitating malaise that would dog him for the rest of his years. He consulted doctors and experimented with a variety of folk remedies, but while he became something of an authority on the healing arts, he was never able to answer his own persistent complaint.

During the same period, the family firm moved into new fields of business, launching a series of whaling ventures, commencing production of iron at the Hope Furnace, and opening direct trade to London—another giant step for a firm based at a secondary port like Providence. These interests had to be juggled with the continuing operations of the candle works, the still house, a rope walk where they produced ship's rigging, and the coastal and Caribbean voyages of scores of ships and sloops. The diversification meant growing demands on the individual partners—more than Moses was ready to take on.

Writing to his brothers that July, Moses acknowledged his truancy, and blamed it on a "state of health so impaired as to be much injured by a close attention to any kind of business." His only course, Moses wrote, was to resume a "regular course of living," free from the stress of the family firm. He would take a hiatus, for the summer and possibly into autumn, to see if he could find "satisfactory relief." In the meantime, his brothers would have to manage without him.

While Moses was feeling overwhelmed, John was chafing at the constraints of the family partnership. He agitated constantly to expand the business, pressing his brothers to paper over losses by taking on debt. And he continued to believe that the course to true wealth lay through Africa. As a group, the brothers apparently opted to leave the slave trade—but in the winter of 1769, John set about outfitting another Guinea expedition. This was undertaken by the ship *Sultan*, a larger vessel carrying a larger crew than the *Sally*. Determined to avoid the mistakes of his earlier venture, John beefed up the ship's armament, loading the *Sultan* with two cannon, six swivels, and four blunderbusses, as well as the usual small arms. He also sought insurance for slave mortality, but his request was rejected by his agents in London.

The arm's-length relationship between John and the family firm was apparent in a letter from Nicholas Brown & Co. to Benjamin Mason, a Newport merchant who staged a number of slaving ventures of his own. "Our Jno. Brown is concerned in a vessel bound for Guiney will sail in 15 or 16 days," the brothers wrote to Mason. "He will want about 2000 gallons of rum more than can be got here within time, please advise us, lowest price this quantity may be had. . . ." The letter concludes with a postscript: "If it suits you to recommend the gentlemen in the West Indies who sold your last cargo of slaves, please to give us their names."

Moses returned to the family firm around the time John was outfitting the *Sultan*. He'd spent the intervening months exploring his interests in science and mathematics, attending to political affairs, and developing a farm he had inherited on the lowlands to the west of the Salt River. He removed his family to the farm during the warm summer months, and resided in Obadiah's old house near Market Square in the winter. The variety of his pursuits suggest that it was the strife and anxiety of business affairs, more than any physical ailment, that Moses found so taxing.

Soon after his return, Moses was again butting heads with John over the direction of business affairs. Nicholas remained the titular head of the firm, but it appears he spent much of his time running interference between his younger brothers, seeking at once to rein John in and to placate Moses' sense of propriety. John would not be headed; profits should be plowed back into enterprise, he insisted, and not allowed to gather dust in the countinghouse.

To Moses, this course appeared risky in the extreme. He might be the youngest of the four brothers, but he was thirty-one years old, a man of fortune and gravity, and he was more than ready to challenge his headstrong brother. He laid out his agenda in a detailed memo presented to the firm in 1770. At issue was a bill of eight thousand dollars due for interest on outstanding debt. Until those obligations were retired, Moses insisted, all plans to expand the business should be deferred. Moses then declared his opposition to John's scheme for reinvestment, asserting, "I conceive if duly examined [it] will not hold either prudent or advantageous."

This cautious approach contradicted the entrepreneurial impulse that helped distance the firm from the other merchants in Providence, but it fit with Moses' view of the world. Moses saw John as a reckless gambler, always ready to double his bet. "Who ever plays any game the rubbers, or plays for the last value of the whole gain of the preceding many, will sooner or later lose the whole at one throw," Moses cautioned. "The same is applicable in trade, the business of which is truly to get something to lay by in safety. . . ."

Aside from risk, Moses felt that John's aggressive style took too great a toll on the personal lives of the principals. "It appears to me most rational that the laws of society or the injoyment of our selves by no means will extend any man's business beyond what he can attend with due care and leave time to injoy his family and connections." This was a clash of values more than strategy, rooted in sharply differing views of the world. John was restless and enterprising, impatient with setbacks, disdainful of obstacles, and always looking forward. Moses was more pessimistic. He couched his outlook in a sort of homily that seemed to derive from some ancient parable. "Fortune is a round stone that easily turns every way," Moses wrote, "and when once removed from the long rested successful past may not again revolve in the same place."

John did not take kindly to this sort of chiding, and before the year was out, he had determined to set out on his own. He divided the shipping interests with his brothers, retaining his warehouse on Towne Street and access to the wharves left to the brothers by Obadiah and by James before him. Nicholas, Moses, and Joseph continued as the family firm, and formalized the new configuration in a written partnership. They would pool their several warehouses and raise a new, two-story building downtown, with a shop facing Towne Street and a counting room upstairs.

The division was reasonably amicable, as evidenced by the decision that all four brothers would continue to hold the candle works and their interest in the Hope Furnace in common. It was the shipping ventures that broke up the family firm. And while the stated reasons were limited to strategies of risk and investment, it seems inescapable, in hindsight anyway, to include as a factor the growing but still-unspoken moral rift over engaging in the slave trade. The question did not arise in any of their correspondence of the time, but Nicholas, Moses, and Joseph stayed out of the business, while John pursued it vigorously.

If the split generated any bad feelings, John and Moses each took pains to get past them. The two might differ on questions of policy, but they respected each other's acumen, and they made sure to preserve their family connection. Throughout the division of their interests, the brothers continued to correspond, and Moses made a point of offering John counsel and assistance. Writing in January 1772 to acknowledge one such overture, John made sure to emphasize the bond between them. "I am much obliged to you," John wrote, "and really hope to have all our future connections conducted in the most brotherly manner it's possible to conceive of, by which it will not only be satisfactory to us and our families, but a beautiful example for all our acquaintances to follow."

While the affairs of business were working to drive the Browns apart, community affairs helped keep them close. As with so many families, they kept their internal squabbles to themselves and presented a united front to the outside world. And after their trying experience in the slave trade, rallying around a campaign for hometown good works was the sort of balm the brothers could use.

The issue that brought them together was public education. For more than a century, children in neighboring Massachusetts had been required to attend schools conducted by the Puritan ministers who ran the social and political life of the colony. But Rhode Island kept church and state strictly separate, and while Newport had fostered several well-regarded schools, in Providence neither local government nor any of the several churches had developed to the point of providing education. Schools were built privately, and piecemeal, with instruction reserved to children whose parents could pay for it. During the middle of the 1760s, new private schoolhouses were built at the north end of town and on the rapidly developing west side of the river, but none stood in the downtown district.

This was just the kind of public-spirited enterprise that could provide common ground for John and Moses. Both had early embraced the communitarian ethic that had helped raise towns and cities from the American wilderness. Both still smarted at the remembrance of their own rudimentary schooling. And in joining together, each might reassure the other that shared goals superseded their growing differences. In 1767, in the months following the return of the *Sally*, the two brothers joined in a personal campaign to organize an educational establishment in Providence. By May, Moses had produced a memorandum citing the demands of the town's growing business establishment, and calling for a property tax to support universal public education. The plan was controversial, particularly among those who had already laid out funds to build private schoolhouses.

John followed his brother's lead and presented a comprehensive plan to a town meeting on December 2. His argument rested on principle. Lack of a public school meant many children in Providence had "been obliged to go unlarnt," John worried. "It would be a very easy matter to raise money by subscription from a very few persons to be proprietors to build a school house to their own private use," he acknowledged, but that would "not be of service to hundreds there is in this town who is not able to build a house to school their children in."

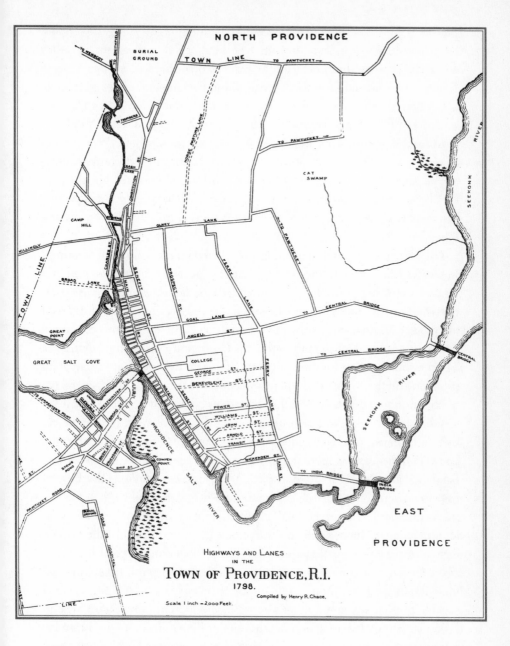

HIGHWAYS AND LANES
IN THE
TOWN OF PROVIDENCE, R.I.
1798.
Scale 1 inch = 2,000 Feet.
Compiled by Henry R. Chace.

Within the close confines of the meeting, John was forceful and persuasive as ever, and his proposal carried the day. At a second meeting a week later, John was appointed, along with John Jenckes, to a committee that would select locations for three elementary schools, to be made of wood, and one high school, to be built of brick. At the same session, Moses was named with Jabez

Bowen to draw up ordinances for a public tax and for governing the schools. Even as the Browns were falling out over questions of business strategy, they could congratulate themselves for their good works.

But in the days that followed, the coalition backing the school plan broke down, and at still another town meeting, convened on New Year's Day, the freemen of Providence rescinded their support for a school tax. Opposition arose from the proprietors of those schools already standing and, more vexing to Moses, from lower-class voters. Moses recorded his frustration in a memorial he penned years later. "What is most surprising and remarkable, the plan for a Free School, supported by a tax, was rejected by the poorer sort of people, being strangely led away not to see their own as well as the public interest therein."

Once the vote failed, the meeting adopted a fallback position of erecting a single, two-story brick schoolhouse, free to the public, with funds raised by a tax and a matching private subscription. By February, however, it was apparent that even this fund could not be raised. But the Browns moved ahead with the project on their own, securing use of the lot where the ruins of the old courthouse lay, and raising funds from the family and a small group of friends. The new building was finished two years later, with the downstairs used for instruction and the second floor for private offices. That spring, the General Assembly authorized a charter for the proprietors of the Town School House.

John and Moses teamed up in the political arena as well, but the object there was power, not redemption. The campaign of 1767 marked a turning point in the annual gubernatorial contest between Stephen Hopkins and Samuel Ward. Ward having prevailed at the last two elections, the Browns were determined to return their mentor to office. Their political clique was much the same as in previous years, with Hopkins at the helm, closely attended by Silas Downer, Jabez Bowen, and the other Sons of Liberty. The biggest change was the departure of William Goddard, editor of the *Providence Gazette*, who went on to continue a turbulent publishing career in Philadelphia and Baltimore. Goddard was succeeded by his mother, Sarah, a capable printer and editor in her own right, and then by John Carter, who in 1766 had completed an apprenticeship under Benjamin Franklin. From his print shop over the bookstore at the sign of Shakespeare's Head, Carter kept his readers versed in the polemics raised in the other colonies, and in the current debates at Parliament. He also maintained the *Gazette*'s standing as a virtual house organ for the Hopkins machine.

As the campaign of 1767 swung into gear, the Brown brothers resumed their position as Hopkins's leading strategists and primary financial backers.

With the votes of Providence secure, the brothers dispatched cash in hundred-dollar lots to the provincial seats of Greenwich, North Kingston, and Coventry, to be spent either in securing support or to ensure that "persons that is stranius for Mr. Ward who may be agreed with for a small sum to lay still." In a letter sent with one such disbursement, John proclaimed his "Great expectation of giving our Inemys a good drubbing." Mud was slung along with money; a Providence reverend aligned with the Newport faction complained that their foes "don't stick to perjure, or be perjured, and I begin to suspect they will succeed."

The results bore out the prognostications: Hopkins won by a majority of more than four hundred votes, the widest margin yet in his campaigns against Ward. Elisha Brown, the incumbent deputy governor, fared even worse, falling to Joseph Wanton Jr. Washed out by a landslide, Uncle Elisha found himself "obliged to quet the feeld"; the trouncing concluded his career in public office.

As had become something of a local convention through the years of contentious rivalry, the onset of the spring elections occasioned widespread denunciation of the whole messy business of machine politics, which all agreed cost more in ill feelings than they yielded in sagacious leadership. And as had become the corollary to the annual vituperation, the side in power proffered a peace plan of sorts. These parleys were mainly for show, with the victors magnanimously suggesting that the opposing camp accept the role of second fiddle. In 1764, for example, Hopkins offered to appoint Ward to the post of deputy governor. Ward responded "that no peace could be expected while Governor Hopkins was in the chair."

But as the political season of '68 approached, the Hopkins camp felt secure enough to pursue a genuine compromise. The twist on the old formula was a subtle one: the leaders of each faction would select state officers from the other party's camp. Thus Hopkins's people would name a Ward ally, presumably from Newport, for governor; Ward and his allies would then select a Providence man for deputy governor, and so on through the list of "assistants," the ten delegates that constituted the upper house of the legislature.

This was not democracy, of course, but backroom deal making of the first order. Key members of both factions—particularly Elisha Brown, Ward's man in the north, and the Wantons, Hopkins's allies at Newport—defected. But the recurrent political wars had exhausted the electorate, and the compromise carried. Hopkins and the Providence clique settled on Josias Lyndon, a Newport Baptist and clerk of the lower house, as governor, while the Ward people designated Providence sea captain Nicholas Cooke for deputy. The slate won handily, defeating the protest candidacy of the senior Joseph Wanton by better than three to one.

The peace did not hold. Lyndon was soon compromised by the Ward allies in the assembly, who succeeded in throwing judgeships and other appointments to their Newport cronies and challenging tax rates set under the Hopkins regime. Lyndon, never a force in politics before, appealed to Moses Brown, who was then leading the Hopkins faction in the assembly, but Moses sternly held Lyndon to account. By the spring of 1769, the coalition was in shambles.

Here the Browns were divided as well. John and Joseph continued to stand with Lyndon and the coalition, but Moses, who had carried on an extensive correspondence with the beleaguered governor, saw a chance for a more decisive victory. Joining with his close friend Joseph Wanton Jr., Moses threw his weight behind Wanton's father, whose protest of the year before would now become a genuine challenge. Stephen Hopkins himself stayed in the background, as did Ward, but it soon became clear that Wanton would serve as his proxy.

On Election Day, the Hopkins faction won in a rout, carrying twenty of the colony's twenty-eight towns, including Newport as well as Providence. This was a stark show of force, matching the unprecedented majority of the prior year, but without the trappings of a consensus slate. Instead of burying the hatchet, the Hopkins forces had wielded it to devastating effect. Though Joseph Wanton was a Newport man, political power in Rhode Island now rested securely in Providence. And while Stephen Hopkins remained the titular head of his faction—after he bowed out of the statehouse, his backers named him chief judge of the superior court—Moses served as the party whip, its leading strategist, and primary conduit to the Newport combine, through Joseph Wanton Jr. Indeed, in the course of the senior Wanton's first term as governor, his son reminded Moses of their "sole reliance" on him to "steer the lower house" in the assembly.

The political triumph of the Providence faction was matched during this period with a parallel achievement, accomplished by the same coalition arrayed against the same familiar foes, but in an ad hoc forum and yielding more tangible and lasting benefits than any governmental post. The contest was over where to establish the permanent seat of a new college, the first in the colony and the third institution of higher learning in all of New England. Here the Browns and Stephen Hopkins saw the chance to elevate the stature of their community and to boost their own prospects at the same time. They did not let the opportunity escape them.

The idea of founding a college in Rhode Island first arose in Philadelphia, where the leaders of an association of twenty-nine Baptist churches agreed that a "seminary of polite literature" should be established to provide learned pastors for the pulpit. This in itself represented a new step for the Baptists, who in early years had shunned book learning, along with tithes to the ministry and singing in church, as worldly trappings that served only to interfere with a true and unvarnished communing with scripture. The Baptists of Pennsylvania and New Jersey, especially, were more modern than that, and more aspiring.

Though they could boast more numerous congregations, the Baptists of the middle states recognized Rhode Island as the first home to their faith in America, and as a citadel of religious freedom. Consequently, in the summer of 1763, they dispatched James Manning, twenty-four years of age and a recent graduate of Princeton, to treat with the Rhode Island legislature and seek a charter for a college. The young scholar settled in the small port village of Warren, south of Providence on the eastern shore of Narragansett Bay, where he opened a Latin school and organized a church under his direction. The townspeople answered by building a new wood structure on a lot by the main road, a proper Baptist meetinghouse with plain lines and a simple four-sided tower. For the next several years, his congregation grew steadily.

While Manning toiled quietly in Warren, his bid to charter the colony's first college sparked immediate partisan dispute, as different factions and denominations vied to lay claim to the still-speculative venture. Manning unveiled his proposition at a meeting of leading Baptists in Newport, including several legislators and Josias Lyndon, then clerk of the lower house. For all their skills and experience, none of those on hand felt competent to draw up the necessary petition to the assembly, and so they turned to Ezra Stiles, the Presbyterian minister who would later serve as president of Yale. Stiles, who always took religious distinctions seriously, consented to serve, but in drafting the document he inserted a clause reserving control of the board of fellows to his own denomination.

When the charter was presented to the legislature, Daniel Jenckes, deputy from Providence, recognized the ruse and denounced it. That night he took the charter home, showed it to several friends, and in the course of a few days, the document simply disappeared. Court charges were filed and speeches made, all of which demonstrated the central role assumed by the college in the long-running dispute between north and south.

A new charter, ensuring Baptist predominance but also nondenomina-

tional policies of admission and matriculation, was soon adopted. In the spirit
of conciliation, Stephen Hopkins, the colony's gray eminence, was named
chancellor, and Samuel Ward, his persistent nemesis, as vice chancellor.
Manning took on his first undergraduates, and in September 1769, a class of
seven students stepped forward to accept baccalaureate degrees. The event
won the applause of the legislature, which declared the first official holiday in
the history of the colony. Dignitaries from all around Narragansett Bay, and
Baptists from across New England and as far as Georgia, traveled to Warren to
observe the daylong commencement exercises.

The ceremony apparently rekindled a sense of mission on the part of the
college trustees, for they agreed that fall to raise a new building to house
the growing school. Warren was presumed to be the site of the project, but the
more astute trustees soon hit upon a more ambitious scheme. The college
would settle, the board declared, in whichever county raised the largest fund
toward establishing a new campus. Now the crafty schemers and ready warriors
from the colony's long-running sectional dispute had a real prize to vie for.

Here the Browns played a central role. Working with Stephen Hopkins,
who set aside any pretense to neutrality, the principals of Nicholas Brown &
Co. threw their weight into the college campaign just as they did the annual
gubernatorial contests, writing pamphlets, debating strategy, pressing their
friends for donations, and making the largest contributions themselves.

Nicholas, the eldest brother and titular head of the family firm, had been a
trustee of the college from the outset, but as the campaign heated up, it was
John and Moses who took the lead, setting their growing differences aside as
they had in pursuing the Providence schoolhouse. In the campaign for the
college, however, the brothers confronted the determined hopes of leaders
from across Rhode Island, all seeking to crown their aspirations for stature
with so durable a legacy.

Newport was a natural choice. It was the colony's "metropolis," as Joseph
Wanton termed it, with twice the population of Providence; home to the celebrated Redwood Library, to several magnificent churches, and to a chartered
chapter of the American Philosophical Society, the oldest learned organization to be founded on the young continent. Samuel Ward, Ezra Stiles, the
trading magnate William Ellery, and Abraham Redwood, benefactor of the library, all contributed to the college bid, and Newport soon had raised an imposing subscription of several thousand pounds. The citizens of Warren also
entered a bid, as did East Greenwich, a town on the west side of the bay, home
to the influential Greene family. Both were little more than country hamlets,
far smaller than Newport or Providence, but they argued that "institutions of

this kind have been found by experience not to prosper in popular towns" and would better thrive in a rural setting.

The bid from Providence was authored by Moses Brown, in collaboration with John Cole, the town postmaster and a member of the Hopkins machine with a seat in the General Assembly. Providence could offer a central location, they argued, was home to a wider range of religious faiths—a dubious assertion, as all Rhode Island embraced religious diversity—and could secure building materials more cheaply than Newport. Moreover, Providence would produce a larger building fund.

The last claim was critical, and a bit speculative. By the time set for a final tally—January 1, 1770—the sum raised by Newport had escalated steadily, to more than three thousand pounds. With subscriptions from Providence already tapped out, the Browns, with Stephen Hopkins, wrote to the neighboring towns of Glocester and Scituate, pressing them to consider "that the building of the college here will be a means of bringing great quantities of money into the place . . . and of increasing the value of all estates to which this town is a market." The letter went on to warn that "the people in Newport . . . are very diligently using every method in their power to carry the prize from us." If financial self-interest were not sufficient, perhaps the fervor of sectional rivalry would rouse them.

Daunting as the challenge from Newport must have been, John and Moses were apparently convinced they would prevail, and made elaborate preparations for the new institution. The college, they agreed, should be set upon the summit of Prospect Hill, with the town of Providence laid out below, and all the broad reach of Narragansett Bay in view to the south. As it happened, this enchanting spot was encompassed by the original home lot assigned to Chad Brown, the brothers' great-grandfather, when the ground that became Providence was granted Roger Williams by the native inhabitants. Parts of the lot had been sold off, by James Brown, one of Chad's sons, and most of it devoted to pasture in the generations since. John and Moses repurchased the property and presented it for sale at cost to the college corporation. The trustees could not ignore the symbolism that the college would rest on land cleared and settled by the first elder of the Baptist church in America; in equal measure, the Browns were seeking to confirm an enduring connection between their family and the school.

The brothers' optimism proved slightly premature. The deadline of January 1 came and went, but only because President Manning refused to call the meeting. This prompted something of an uprising against Manning, and two weeks later, three Newport trustees, including Henry Ward, brother and political adviser to the erstwhile governor, published a notice in the *Providence Gazette* and the *Newport Mercury* announcing that "the County of Newport hath raised a larger sum than has yet been offered . . . to be paid on condition that the college edifice be erected in the town of Newport." As a Baptist, President Manning strongly supported the choice of Providence, but he was bound to accept the largest fund that might be produced, and he could not see a way to block a final hearing on the Newport bid. The notice called for a meeting of the college corporation in Warren on Wednesday, February 7.

This announcement prompted a "great noise and high tumulto," as one contemporary described it, stirring rallies in all four of the towns vying for the college. In Providence, a town meeting was called by a handbill proclaiming "a matter of the greatest consequence," and took place at the statehouse Monday afternoon. Stephen Hopkins presided, and John Cole was named with Moses to present their case. Manning, who feared the worst, sent an anonymous communication to the Browns proposing a twofold strategy: the Providence faction should offer an advanced schedule for erecting the college building, and if the vote failed on the first ballot, Providence should throw its support to East Greenwich, presuming that a subsequent vote might then turn back to Providence. Manning may have been a divine, but he was something of a parliamentarian as well.

When the meeting convened at Warren, all the factions turned out in force, the men in their ruffled shirts and greatcoats crowding into the clapboard meetinghouse or retreating to caucus outside in the snow. Hopkins, as chancellor, offered a statement presuming to clear the air, but as usual, his partisan voice only stoked the dispute. "Some gentlemen of Newport, perceiving a probability that the college might be erected at Providence, were moved by their unreasonable enmity to that town, to do that which the good of the institution itself could never induce them to do," Hopkins alleged. Manning, describing the proceedings in his careful prose, noted that, "in the course of the debates there was sometimes undue warmth."

Aspersions aside, the question still turned on the matter of who had raised the largest fund. And that, with all the veteran merchants and traders on hand, took a full two days to resolve.

Moses Brown recorded a detailed account soon after the meeting. As he described it, the Newport contingent delayed showing their hand all through the first day's meeting "until well after candle light, and after we insisted they should lay these subscriptions on the table." The delegation from Newport finally produced a bond for thirty-one hundred pounds—a first bid, as it turned out. This figure was quickly dismissed—Providence had already put up nearly that sum, and attached a parcel of land to boot. Moses continued: "We insisted then that as it did not amount to so much as ours, with the land, that they should give up their claim." But the Newporters stalled again, and at ten o'clock, the meeting was adjourned to nine the next morning. The disputants then retired to the taverns and boardinghouses—there could not have been an empty bed in Warren that night.

The next morning, the Newport men touted two new commitments, wielding the paper bonds before the house but refusing to reveal their value until Providence offered a final bid. "At length," as Moses recounted, "Henry Ward took me out towards the door, and declared that was all they had, and that they had no orders to go any higher, and proposed if we would not lodge any further subscriptions, they would lay down their papers and proceed to trial accordingly. We agreed."

Providence and Newport—the smaller towns had by now been eclipsed—made their final bids. Each side had scrounged up a few new shards of coin or scrip, and when all the paper was counted, Providence held a lead of 225 pounds. But Newport was not through. "Hereupon they delayed by many evasions proceeding to business, and insisted for adjournment to dinner," Moses groused. When parties convened again, Samuel and Henry Ward announced they would kick in another thousand pounds, though no bonded commitments were produced, "they alleging they had left them at home." This latest, final tally exceeded the Providence sum by close to four hundred pounds, even allowing for a generous appraisal of the land part of the package.

Moses presented the closing calculation for Providence. He offered one last subscription, for 226 pounds, and urged the trustees to take into account the savings they could expect in building costs by locating at Providence, which he estimated at more than five hundred pounds. This claim might be debated, but it allowed the contingent of eight Baptist ministers who sat on the board to throw the decision to their spiritual home. "The vote came on after long litigation and argument," Moses reported with satisfaction. The final tally was twenty-one to fourteen. The college would reside in Providence.

Newport could not accept the verdict, but they could not find a way around it either. They tried, a week after the vote at Warren, launching a bill in the General Assembly to authorize a second charter for a college, this one at Newport. Moses Brown led the floor fight against the bill, but it passed the lower house. The battle then moved to Newport, for the May meeting of the legislature, where Samuel Ward was staging his last gubernatorial bid. There, the

Providence coalition swept the field, placing Joseph Wanton in the governor's chair and rejecting the Newport college charter. The northern faction had prevailed: Ward and his cohort would never again hold sway in Rhode Island.

The Browns savored their conquest at a ceremony atop Prospect Hill a week later, where laborers had spent a month excavating a foundation for the building that would house Rhode Island College. Chancellor Hopkins, President Manning, and a score of trustees and ministers gathered around, their spirits leavened by a generous serving of rum-based punch, but this was largely a family affair. Joseph Brown had designed the structure, after first traveling to Boston to study the buildings there. His plans were expansive: it would be the largest building in Rhode Island, with dimensions of 150 by 46 feet, five stories high, and all enclosed in brick. Nicholas Brown & Company had been awarded the contract for all construction, and John and Moses had brought the trophy home. At the culmination of the ceremony, John Brown clambered down into the imposing hole that had been opened in the rich turf first staked out by his ancestors, and laid the granite cornerstone, the first block in the southwest cellar wall.

If the crowd stuck to custom, they drank a long, hearty toast to John's efforts. It was the first of many draughts that would be drunk as the edifice rose, steadily, through the summer of 1770. Ledgers of expenses for the building record the purchase of rum to entice a crowd to lend a hand in raising each floor in succession—the quantities growing as the building mounted higher. One gallon was on hand for laying the first floor; two gallons, with two pounds of sugar, for the second; four gallons, "very good and old," for the third floor; the same for the fourth; and seven and three quarter gallons of "old West Indian rum," with two pounds of sugar, for the fifth. As the large number of subscriptions demonstrated, and as the community floor raisings emphasized, this was a group enterprise, establishing another bond between the Browns and the people of Providence.

The premier position afforded John in the groundbreaking ceremony comes as no surprise. He was, after all, a primary force in establishing the college in Providence, and would assume, for more than twenty years, the post of treasurer of the college corporation. He would also become the majordomo of the annual commencement, closing the exercises and festivities with lavish balls at his Towne Street home, rum-soaked dinner parties that helped advance his reputation as a toastmaster and something of a sybarite.

The first commencement at Providence took place that year and set the tone for those that followed. All the eminent families of the colony were on hand, including Samuel Ward and his brother Henry, along with William Greene of Warwick and his distant cousin Nathanael, the Quaker who would rise to second in command of the Continental Army under George Washington. Gov. Joseph Wanton led the trustees of the college in a procession across the Weybosset bridge, impressing the townspeople with his Newport airs: "The governor's wig, which had been made in England, was of the pattern and size of that of the Speaker of the House of Commons, and so large that his shallow crowned hat could not be placed on his head without disturbing the curls," according to one contemporary account. "He, therefore, placed it under his left arm, and held his umbrella in his right hand. This was the first umbrella ever seen carried by a gentleman in Providence." That the commencement was a raucous affair is evidenced by the vote of the corporation, later that year, to "repair all damages that were occasioned by the throng."

The ceremonies that year, and for several years thereafter, were held at a Congregational church on the west side of the river, as it was the only building in town large enough to handle the crowd. That circumstance chafed with the Baptist trustees, however, and as they had led the drive to move the college to Providence, so the Brown brothers moved to put their stamp on the church itself. For close to fifty years, the Baptists at Providence had worshiped on hard benches in a squat building of rough-hewn oak, forty feet square. With the new college under construction, the Baptists, led by the Browns, determined to raise a new church as well, one that would also serve as a proper forum for the annual commencement exercises.

In April 1774, a new Baptist Benevolent Society was convened, and set as its first task the construction of the new church. John Brown was put in charge, and a committee of eleven men, including Nicholas and Joseph Brown, was named to "assist and advice" in the project. Joseph, who was becoming an accomplished architect, was sent to Boston once again to view possible models for the church. This would be a large and striking edifice, marking a clean break from the plain buildings by which Baptists signaled their piety. The final plans, adapted from drawings Joseph found in a book by the British architect James Gibbs, called for a ground floor eighty feet square, with a tower rising in four stages to a steeple two hundred feet high and a spire visible from well out on Narragansett Bay, all painted a virginal white. The General Assembly approved a lottery to finance the project in June 1774; Nicholas, Joseph, and John Brown were the first three names on the petition requesting the lottery.

More surprising than John's grandstanding was the reticence displayed by

Moses. He had played, if anything, a more central role even than John in bringing the college to Providence; he kept minutes of the key meetings and wrote the drafts and amendments to the motions that finally won the day. But when Moses was asked to join the board of trustees, he declined, and when he was elected to the post, he refused. This may have been a result of the quest for a "regular course of living" that led to his brief retirement in 1768. But the continuing pace of his engagements in the years that followed, and particularly the vigor he showed in pursuit of the college itself, suggests that his malaise was rooted more in the nature of his obligations than in his physique.

In fact, Moses felt conflicted about the whole college enterprise. The arrival of James Manning at Providence provoked a split in the church that went to the root of what the Baptists were all about. The denomination presided over by Chad Brown and his sons was an austere one, grounded in individual spiritual discovery and skeptical of the material world. Churches were spare, ministers were unschooled and unpaid, and worldly erudition was regarded with suspicion. The venerable Roger Williams, founder of Providence and a pioneering Baptist, made the notion explicit, writing that "the title of scholar appointed to the ministry is a sacrilegious and thievish title, robbing all believers and saints."

Manning was cut from more contemporary cloth. He believed in education, of course, and assiduously raised funds for the college. At his services in Warren, he introduced the collection of tithes and the practice of singing in church, which caused great consternation among the Rhode Island elders. When the college was removed to Providence, Manning brought his preaching and his modern ideas with him.

Moses Brown understood the boon a college could mean for his hometown—that's why he worked so hard to obtain it—but he had trouble accepting the drift Manning brought to the doctrine of the church. Moses described his feelings in a letter he wrote late in his life, which memorialized the early years of the college but also delved into a critique of church itself. "The difference is marked between the old church of the Baptists in this town and after Elder Manning," Moses recalled. Manning was "a worthy godly," but "in diverse respects, however, his practice was different from the church here, and much difficulty was in the meeting upon the subject of singing and the contribution box, these being never before known. To give a vote of the church in favor of the first, more particular, the female members were called upon to vote, though not usual, and my mother and sister attended accordingly. This occasioned a serious division with the old deacons and members." The opposition was led by the pastor of the Providence church at the time, Samuel G. Winsor, who pronounced that "singing in public worship was very disgustful to him."

In a time when people took grave interest in their religious practice, such disputes were enough to divide a congregation, and that is what happened in Providence. Within a year of Manning's arrival, the congregation agreed to split, and Winsor took his flock to a new, simple church in Johnston, a village due west of Providence. Moses remained in town but grew uncomfortable with the new tenor of worship. He put the matter delicately in his letter years later. "My brother Joseph was a member of the church, and when he brought his contribution box to my mother's pew, I now remember my reluctant feelings for him, our family and the church never having seen the like in the meeting, though often in the Congregational and other churches." More pious than his brothers, more deliberate and more introspective, Moses' thirst for spiritual peace would only grow as the years went by.

The Brown brothers' partnership with Stephen Hopkins helped shape the political and civic life of the town and the colony, but that was not the extent of their collaboration. The Browns and their mentor also shared an entrepreneurial vision: they understood that they lived in times of growth and change, and were always ready to invest in new avenues of enterprise. Both Hopkins and the Browns found early success launching ventures at sea, but it was at the Hope Furnace, smelting green-tinged ore from the rural backwoods, that they partnered to establish a franchise that became a mainstay for the two dominant families of Providence.

Unlike its policy toward most other kinds of manufactures, Britain laid no impediments on iron making, because home production was handicapped by the lack of fuel. From nominal output at the beginning of the century, iron production in America grew into a primary colonial manufacture, and by 1775, the British colonies produced 15 percent of the total world output. In Rhode Island, the Greenes of Warwick and the Jenckes family had both made early starts in digging and smelting iron, and their steady growth induced the Browns to follow. As with Uncle Obadiah's move into candle making, the Brown brothers' foray into this new industry renewed their position at the leading edge of colonial economic development.

Yet this was more than a reprise of their elders' inclination to experiment in new and different fields of business. Erecting and operating a blast furnace was a major undertaking, requiring resources, influence, and ingenuity. The

Browns knew little of the market for iron, and less about metallurgy, but they trusted their instincts and bet on their capacity to learn. In launching an enterprise of such scope, the brothers demonstrated the foresight, technological know-how, and sheer audacity that distinguished them as venture capitalists in their own right, and economic pioneers of the first order.

Where the major foundries in Pennsylvania were situated on huge estates with wood, ore, and water close at hand, the Browns had to carve out space and resources on closely settled land, terrain already exploited for the same purpose by the Greenes. The brothers and Hopkins agreed on their business plan early on, but kept their first moves quiet, securing contracts on the cheap. The first step was taken by an intermediary, Israel Wilkinson, an "ingenious mechanic" of wide repute and a partner in the furnace for its first two years.

Wilkinson secured the rights to a new deposit of iron ore recently discovered in the boggy lowlands of Cranston, a rural district fronting the Pawtuxet River southwest of Providence. The price was a bargain, consisting of a down payment of three pounds, which bought Wilkinson the right to dig and test a first batch of ore, and then sixpence per ton extracted, in perpetuity. A week later, Moses made a score of his own, landing a contract with two brothers in Glocester, about twenty miles north of Cranston, guaranteeing all the ore he could haul. The terms were even better than those secured by Wilkinson: twenty shillings up front, and sixpence per ton.

Wilkinson and Moses Brown brought their leases to the table when the founders of the Hope Furnace incorporated on July 9, 1765. Governor Hopkins claimed a quarter interest, the four Brown brothers were assigned one-eighth each—for a family share of 50 percent—and two subordinate partners split the final quarter. Separately, Moses and Wilkinson retained an eighth share of any ore pulled from the deposits they had secured. Moses might be more cautious than John, but he could strike just as smart a bargain.

Stephen Hopkins and the Browns were able to trade on their reputations as business pioneers to secure another set of remarkably favorable contracts for fuel and for the site of the furnace itself. Once the group had settled on a location—on a bend in the Pawtuxet, in Scituate, seven miles west of Providence—they enticed nearby landowners with the prospect of improving their property by hosting a new growth industry. In August 1765, a farmer named Joseph Remington took the bait, leasing three acres of riverfront property for consideration of "one mill'd dollar in hand." How else Remington stood to profit is unclear, but he granted "free priviledge of the river" along with the land. A less credulous neighbor of Remington's held out for one hundred dollars plus annual rents, but the Browns passed him by.

While those talks were proceeding the Browns contacted more than thirty landowners nearby, asking them to provide wood for free, in return for "incouraging so useful an undertaking and more particularly to induce Hopkins & Associates to erect said works at the place aforesaid." The only benefit to the landowners would be fees for cutting and carting wood, and proximity to the project. But the farmers of Scituate knew that the Greene's forge in nearby Coventry provided employment for most of the people in that town, and were ready to stake their woodlots on the future success of a new furnace.

Stephen Hopkins and Moses Brown also threw their political weight into service of the new ironworks. The advance of basic manufactures that used dams for power—mainly gristmills and sawmills—had already earned the resentment of farmers and other country folk who counted on river fish as a staple of their diet. The dams blocked spawning runs of salmon, shad, and alewives, and fish populations were slipping into decline. As still another crucial step in launching the foundry, Hopkins and the Browns petitioned the General Assembly for an exemption to the Fish Act, which required that all dams incorporate fish ladders and release water to maintain downstream flows during the dry summer months. The bill easily passed the assembly, though the upper house balked, insisting that a fishway be included. Four years later, during Hopkins's final term as governor, a similar petition was granted without amendment, and the Hope Furnace enjoyed all the power the river could supply.

The furnace was a massive operation. The physical plant consisted of a two-room house for the manager, a boardinghouse for twenty men, a bellows house, several other outbuildings, and the blast furnace itself, built of stone laid into the side of a small hill. The furnace consumed cords of wood by the thousands and employed more than thirty full-time woodcutters to keep the fire stoked. At the outset, Hopkins and the Browns relied on veteran ironworkers hired from forges in Connecticut, but the resident managers proved hard to trust and hard to keep. In the second year of operations Stephen Hopkins's eldest son, Rufus, was installed as manager at the forge. Putting his brief career at sea behind him, Rufus Hopkins stayed on for close to forty years.

The Browns never made a formal division of responsibilities in the operations of the furnace, but as in their other joint interests, the brothers worked as a team. It's apparent that Moses played a central role, securing contracts and schooling Rufus in the arts of administration. His letters show Moses to be savvy, and sometimes a little stern. "We are sorry to see in you a diffidence, and too much dependence on the approbation of the owners before you close agreements with the employees or contract for what is wanted as thereby time is delayed and the business consequently postponed," he scolded on one occasion. "Use your best judgment," he told the young manager, "and put the same into immediate execution."

John demonstrated little of Moses' tenacity or patience in building up the business. As was his wont, John's primary contribution came in the form of capital, and in seizing opportunity wherever his business travels might take him. He hobnobbed with merchant princes like John Hancock in Boston and Thomas Willing in Philadelphia, and picked up tips on prices and markets for iron from his wide range of acquaintances. John's main assist to the early operations of the furnace came in 1767, when the owners were casting about for an experienced ironmaster. Rufus Hopkins did well enough handling the various labor teams, but he knew next to nothing about smelting ore.

June of that year found John in Philadelphia, arranging shipments of oil and candles, and seeking, but failing, to secure insurance for new shipping ventures. Before heading home, he planned to proceed "to westward," where he would canvass the dozen-odd foundries of Pennsylvania looking for skilled workers. That expedition, combined "with my disappointment about the insurance, will make my journey long and tedious," he wrote in a letter home.

John found his man a week later in Elizabeth Township, west of Lancaster, and secured his services with a twenty-pound advance. Jacob Shower reported for duty a month later, but his Rhode Island crew found him imperious and arrogant. After a summer and autumn of mixed results, nerves began to fray. In December, with snow on the ground and the furnace operating at half capacity, Shower stepped out to enjoy the warmth and grog of a neighbor's hearth. Tramping back to the furnace that evening, he became a little too free in his estimation of the skills of the foundry operator, and the two "got to blows," as Rufus Hopkins described it. Shower was relieved of his duties soon after.

Still, after an erratic start, production at the furnace began to climb, and the quality of the iron began to reach manufacturing standards. On a good week, the furnace turned out eighteen tons of pig iron, which was carted to forges around New England and New York for refining into bar iron, which could be rolled and split into nails and barrel hoops, or cast into kettles and other implements. By 1768, the Browns were handling orders for more than a hundred tons a year from a single New York ironmonger.

Even better, the brothers incorporated the iron produced at Scituate into their cargo manifests, using the new commodity to open important new markets. After the Browns divided their shipping interests, both Nicholas Brown & Company and John Brown carried iron by the ton to ports on the east coast, and to London, where they brought European manufactures and crucial hard currency. The brothers also supplied the heavy iron "pigs" to Newport merchant Aaron Lopez, who shipped to London and the Caribbean.

The success of the Hope Furnace, added to the continued operations of the candle works, thrust the Browns to the forefront of the small circle of early New England manufacturers. And with their continuing status as the leading deep-sea shipping firm in Providence, their close partnership with the governor of the colony, and their own political advances, Nicholas Brown & Company now assumed the stature of a powerhouse, a firm with diversified interests and deep reservoirs of capital that could withstand all the shifting currents of the erratic colonial economy.

The Brown brothers were growing apace with their town and their colony, reaching a level of stature and sophistication their forebears could hardly have imagined. More particular, they were realizing their dream of achieving real parity with the haughty and aristocratic trading barons of Newport. They were genuine trading rivals to the most prosperous colonials, they commanded the statehouse, and they had secured for their town the establishment of a college that would pay dividends in culture and prestige for generations to come. As they approached middle age, John and Moses both could anticipate a quiet future of dignified ease. What they didn't anticipate, but what loomed ever larger in the years after the sailing of the *Sally*, was a conflict with the home country that would shatter their close, comfortable world and confront them with new challenges, from within as well as from without.

The peace that prevailed after Parliament rescinded the Stamp Tax lasted only long enough for the ministry in London to reform, and regroup. George Grenville, author of the Stamp Tax, was replaced as chief minister in 1765 by William Pitt, a friend to the American colonies and critic of any internal taxes there, but too old and infirm to enforce his will. Under Pitt, Chancellor of the Exchequer Charles Townsend promptly offered up another colonial revenue scheme, this time by import duties levied on glass, lead, paper, paints, and tea, and established new admiralty courts to enforce their collection.

These measures appeared relatively innocuous—they respected the distinction, made by Stephen Hopkins and other early patriots, between internal taxes and regulation of trade—and the funds to be raised were dedicated exclusively to the costs of military defense of the colonies and to payment of colonial governors and other officials. But they were taxes nonetheless, and rekindled the dormant passions of the Sons of Liberty.

Boston, as became the pattern, answered first. On October 28, 1767, three weeks before the new duties were to take effect, a Boston town meeting adopted a "nonconsumption agreement," pledging individuals to boycott European imports and buy colonial manufactures instead. On December 2 a town meeting at Providence went a step further, pledging not only to shun purchases of, but also not to import the fruits of British industry. John and Moses were on hand for the decision; at the same meeting, the freemen endorsed—albeit temporarily—their plan for a public school.

Newport followed suit two days after the Providence meeting, but warily, endorsing only the consumer boycott. As the months went by, merchants there continued to import and trade in British goods.

In February, seeking to capitalize on popular outrage, Sam Adams persuaded Massachusetts lawmakers to issue a circular letter calling on merchants throughout North America to join in opposition to Parliament's "illegal" measures. The other colonies applauded the request, but London did not; the newly appointed secretary of state for the colonies ordered the Massachusetts legislature dissolved and dispatched several regiments of troops to Boston.

The British reaction only confirmed the dire scenarios drawn by the patriots, and nonimport was soon embraced as the most viable means to assert the rights of the colonists. The merchants of Boston adopted the measure in August 1768, followed quickly by New York and Philadelphia. The movement soon spread to the south, and by the fall of 1769, only Rhode Island and New Hampshire had failed to adopt nonimport as official colonial policy. Frustrated merchants in rival ports angrily denounced Rhode Island for sabotaging the boycott.

Unaccustomed to lagging behind in the American challenge to Parliament, the people of Providence gathered in October 1769 to reiterate their support for nonimport. But when Parliament, shaken by the boycott, repealed most of the Townsend duties—except for the tax on tea—the merchants of Providence and Newport, the Browns included, rushed out a new set of orders on London, prompting another round of protests by those merchants still honoring nonimport. Boston and New York threatened their own boycott of all Rhode Island goods.

The freemen of Providence convened again and voted, in May 1770, to censure the recalcitrant merchants and appoint committees to inspect cargoes and warehouses to ensure that no imports be landed there. And while the record is silent on the Brown brothers' role in the debate, Nicholas and John were both named, along with Stephen Hopkins and Jabez Bowen, to the committees of inspection. Clearly, the Browns were torn between their inclination to do business and their standing among the patriots of Providence. But when called to account, they accepted the direction of the town meeting and confirmed their standing as Sons of Liberty.

While some Rhode Island merchants faltered in maintaining an official challenge to nonimport, there was no mistaking the sentiment of its citizens. In May 1769, at the height of the controversy, the Board of Customs dispatched an armed sloop, sailing under the unfortunate name *Liberty*, to enforce the revenue laws. William Reid, the *Liberty*'s captain, wasted little time, seizing a Providence sloop the day after his arrival. A month later, Jessie Saville, a "tidewaiter," or assistant customs officer, was assaulted on the Providence waterfront. Saville had taken his job far too seriously, the story went, boarding a ship at night, while he was off duty, to search for contraband. Branded a spy, Saville was jumped by a gang of men, stripped of his clothes, slathered with tar and feathers, and beaten "unmercifully to the point of death." His assailants were never identified, but John Carter gave them only encouragement in the *Gazette*, suggesting that Saville "was treated with more Tenderness and Lenity than is perhaps due an *Informer*." Finally, in July, after Captain Reid had seized two Connecticut vessels, and with his crew on shore, a Newport mob commandeered the *Liberty* and ran it aground. Still not finished, they dismasted and scuttled the ship, then seized both her lifeboats, dragged them clattering through the center of town, and torched them.

These violent incidents only complicated an already delicate task being handled by Moses Brown. As one of his duties at the General Assembly, Moses had been named to a committee, along with Henry Ward and two other ranking officials, to consider pleas for reparations made by two principal Tories who had lost property in the last round of Newport riots, in 1765. Those Tories had since fled to London, where they appealed to Parliament for restitution; the colonial ministry there had demanded an accounting from the governor of Rhode Island, and would hold up long-delayed payments due to the colony if satisfaction were not obtained.

The report produced by Moses' committee mixed unctuous tone and rigid intransigence in a strained style that typified the colony's correspondence with the home country—today it might be termed passive-aggressive. "It is with pleasure we acknowledge the obligations we are under to Your Lordship for the attention you have pleased to give the demands of the colony," the letter began. Yet, "Your Lordship will excuse our saying, that the credit which hath been given in Great Britain to representations made to the prejudice of His Majesty's faithful subjects in America, by persons on this side of the water, hath been the principal cause of the unhappy jealousy subsisting between the parent state and the colonies."

Moses' report went on to belittle the losses sustained by the two former res-idents of Newport, who fled after their homes were ransacked by a mob in-cited by the Stamp Act. Their furniture, books, and other belongings "had been saved; a considerable part of which rested in the hands of their attor-neys," and their losses "had been estimated at a most extravagant rate." As to their demand to be compensated for the cost of their passage to England, the decision to emigrate was "a voluntary act . . . not occasioned by any kind of danger to their persons from remaining in Newport, but from a resolution taken to proceed to London, with the pleasing views and hopes of making their fortunes by representing themselves as sufferers on account of their zeal for the power of the British Parliament."

This jaundiced view of the Tories contradicted the vivid memory of three days of mob rule at Newport, but Moses may actually have believed it. He wasn't on hand for the violence, and there were plenty of people to attest—falsely, in this case—to the idea that the Tory complaints were trumped up. Moses was, then and in the years after, a true believer. He always felt com-pelled to act from a morally righteous position, to the point that he would bend the facts if they didn't agree. Not surprising, the committee report failed to settle the dispute; the colony never paid the reparations, and it never re-ceived the sequestered funds from Parliament.

The bitter resentments persisting between England and her northern colonies flared next in March 1770, in Boston, when a squad of red-jacketed British troops opened fire on a crowd of heckling street ruffians outside the customhouse. Five people were killed, and while John Adams took up the sol-diers' defense and managed to get them acquitted at trial, the Boston Massacre came to symbolize for all of America the arrogance and brutish contempt that the king and his ministers reserved for their subjects across the sea.

Moses echoed the sense of rising indignation in his correspondence with Joseph Sherwood, the colonial agent in London, who carried the Rhode Is-land petitions to the king and Parliament. Writing in June 1770, in his capac-ity as the leader of the lower house, Moses informed Sherwood that he had "nothing to advise you only the resolution of the colonies to continue their non-importation agreements until the duty on tea be repealed, which they consider as a design of the ministry to continue as a test of their right to tax the colonies. We are sensible that article comes cheaper now than before but are not thereby to be induced to receive the bait. . . . I wish to hear of the matter being some way settled . . . and that there may be that harmony as heretofore subsisted take place between Britain and the colonies who are now very jeal-ous even to the lowest peasants."

For all Moses' bravura, the partial repeal of the Townsend duties had the desired effect. Despite the imposition of the new admiralty courts, and despite the continuing tax on tea, the colonial nonimport movement collapsed in the fall of 1770. What ensued was a brief period described in some texts as one of "material prosperity and political calm." Yet in Rhode Island, at least, stepped-up customs activity, against smugglers of tea and molasses and for other violations of the Navigation Acts, gave rise to fierce antagonism.

5

The *Gaspee*

DURING THE COLDEST WEEKS of winter in 1772, William Dudingston sailed from Cape Ann, north of Boston, to Newport, where he joined the small naval squadron patrolling Narragansett Bay. A stout Scot raised near Edinburgh, Dudingston was a lieutenant in the Royal Navy, pursuing a lifelong career at sea. His ship was a swift, two-masted schooner named the *Gaspee*, one of a new generation of small, lightly armed ships commissioned by the Royal Navy to enforce the revenue laws along the American coast—"the original coast guard cutters," as a naval historian dubbed them later. The eight-gun *Gaspee* was Dudingston's first command.

Even before his arrival, Dudingston knew of the mutual suspicion that lay between British officers and the colonial officials in Rhode Island. He had been in Newport the day, three years before, when a dockside mob had trashed the *Liberty*, though his own ship and his command were not directly involved. He attributed the incident to lack of rigor on the part of the officers involved, and deplored the desultory investigation staged by Governor Wanton. Dudingston was stern, he was confident, and like so many in the king's armed forces, he held the colonists in contempt.

The next morning, the first full day at his new station, Dudingston found his ship constrained to port by a cold northeast wind. Putting his time ashore to use, the lieutenant made his way across the icy cobblestones of Queen Street to meet Governor Wanton in person. Perhaps he sought to forge a more useful relationship with the governor, or perhaps he believed he might intimidate the ranking official in the colony. What Dudingston did not seem to realize was how much he might have learned from the elderly patrician. Joseph Wanton was a true Brahmin, given to wigs, walking sticks, and imported silks. But he was also a seafarer and a statesman whose father and uncle had both served in the governor's office before him, whose ships were engaged across the globe in whaling, slaving, trading, and, in times of war, privateering, and whose personal estate was rated second only to that of Aaron Lopez in all of Newport. A former customs collector himself, Wanton knew the pitfalls of the revenue system, and as the southern standard-bearer for the Hopkins political machine, he could pull strings in the legislature and the courts.

Dudingston made a careful reconstruction of his encounter with the governor in a letter to his commanding officer in Boston. It appears that Wanton, then sixty-six years old and more than twice the age of his visitor, handled the meeting adroitly. Once the lieutenant introduced himself, Wanton made the dry observation, "We have had many different schooners here lately," and proceeded to name several of the royal revenue ships. The talk turned to the unfortunate case of the *Liberty*, and Wanton gently suggested of Captain Reid and his officers "that it was in their power to have saved her before she had received much damage." If there was a message there, Dudingston brushed it off: "I said I had heard it otherwise mentioned," the lieutenant recorded.

Dudingston then came to the point of his visit. "I hope I should meet with no difficulty in the execution of my duty," he told Wanton. "You may depend on my support and assistance," the governor answered blandly. Dudingston pressed the point, observing, "It was not clear to me, if I made a seizure, it would be safe" at Newport. Wanton repeated his Cheshire-cat response: "I will do all in my power." Not satisfied, Dudingston recounted to the governor how one confiscated vessel had recently gone missing while under colonial custody; when he made a seizure, the lieutenant asserted, "I did not think I should put it to the trial"—the implication being that Dudingston would post his own guard.

The elderly governor smiled graciously. "I suppose you will be much here. I shall always be glad to see you." Realizing, perhaps, that this was not quite the assurance he was seeking, Dudingston replied stiffly, "I shall be where I find I can best execute the service." The interview was over.

Over the next couple of weeks, once the weather had cleared and the *Gaspee* had got under sail, Dudingston displayed his firm commitment to "the service." Not satisfied with inspecting seagoing ships as they arrived at port, he began stopping coastal vessels, local packets, and even the ferries plying the channel between Newport and Bristol. This was smart, as contraband was often offloaded at night and moved locally in small boats, but it was an aggressive new approach at a time when the colonists were already leery of British intervention. In addition, where other naval officers had confined their cruises to the southern, deepwater reaches of Narragansett Bay, Dudingston contracted a local pilot and extended his patrols northward, to rivers, inlets, and tidal estuaries that had long served as sanctuary for smugglers.

Often, the skippers of the coasting freighters and inland packets simply ignored the peremptory commands shouted from the officers on the little revenue cutter. But Dudingston brought them up short, firing a blast from a cannon or a swivel, and sending a boatload of sailors to perform a close inspection of the offending vessel. To the hardy mariners of Rhode Island, Dudingston was clearly taking matters too far.

Dudingston made his first seizure on February 17 off North Kingston, to the west of Conanicut Island. His quarry was the coasting sloop *Fortune*, belonging to the Greene clan of Coventry, and captained by Rufus Greene, then twenty-three years old. Finding the sloop at anchor, Dudingston put out one of his boats with a boarding party under command of an officer named Dundas. Climbing aboard, Dundas ordered Greene to open the hatches of the *Fortune* for a search. When Greene objected, Dundas drew his sword, shoved the young sailor into the cabin, "jammed the companion leaf upon his head, knocked him down upon a chest and confined him there." A quick inspection found twelve hogsheads of undeclared rum, enough to warrant seizure of the vessel. Greene was taken prisoner aboard the *Gaspee* and released the next day; in the meantime, Dudingston towed the *Fortune* to Newport.

Dudingston could not leave the sloop and her cargo there, however, as the customs officials warned him that "no seizure could be safe with them." Determined to enforce his confiscation, he elected to send the sloop up to Boston, despite the fact that, as he wrote later, "I was not ignorant of the statute to the contrary." He was not willing, as he had warned the governor, to be tied down guarding his prize, but it was a mistake to ignore the law. Removal of seized vessels to distant courts of admiralty had provided colonial patriots with one of their most potent arguments against the crown, and the courts in Rhode Island and elsewhere had routinely awarded damages against customs agents for just such maneuvers. In the case of the *Fortune*, the Greenes promptly sued Dudingston in the local superior courts, and for the next several months, the lieutenant could not go ashore for fear of arrest.

Stymied by the conflicts between the law and his commission, Dudingston shifted into what became a personal campaign against the smugglers of Rhode Island. Having no safe depot for his captures, the lieutenant stopped making formal seizures altogether, but he continued his inspections, plying the waters of Narragansett Bay, stopping every vessel he could hail, and confiscating merchandise at will. The *Newport Mercury* gleefully reported the depredations of "this piratical schooner," prompting Dudingston to complain that "every invention of infamous lies calculated to inflaim the country is put in the News Papers."

By inciting the traders and the colonial officials at Newport, Dudingston was following a trail blazed by the coterie of royal revenue men who preceded him. But his initiative and his persistence won him an unusual degree of personal notoriety. Moreover, his efforts to press his inspections to the northward alarmed the merchant leaders at Providence, who were accustomed to observing such official imbroglios at a safe distance.

John Brown, in particular, was determined not to accept Dudingston's incursion without a challenge. After huddling with the other primary merchants in town, Brown composed a formal complaint against the *Gaspee* and presented it to Darius Sessions, a Providence lawyer recently elected deputy governor on Joseph Wanton's slate. Sessions, in turn, met with Stephen Hopkins, then sitting as chief judge of the superior court, who was always glad to find a new venue for testing the reach of British authority. Hopkins answered with a dissection of Dudingston's rights based on the strict reservation of police powers prescribed in the colony's royal charter. "No commander of any vessel has a right to use any authority in the body of the colony, without previously applying to the Governor," Hopkins opined, ". . . and also being sworn to a due exercise of his office."

This was a novel theory that had yet to be invoked in any of the occasional altercations between Rhode Island and the king's officers. But it carried the force of logic—the charter did, after all, grant full powers of internal law enforcement to the colony and the authority of the local courts. Sessions relayed it to Wanton at Newport along with John's petition, who seized upon them immediately. On March 22, the day he received the letter from Sessions, the governor wrote to notify Dudingston of complaints by "a considerable number of the inhabitants of this colony . . . of your having, in a most illegal and unwarrantable manner, interrupted their trade." He closed with the demand that Dudingston produce his official orders, "As I know not by what authority you assume this power." Wanton handed the terse directive to the sheriff of Newport County, who delivered it in person to Dudingston's ship.

Dudingston was stunned at Wanton's change of tone. He had, of course, presented himself to the governor a month before, and his "authority" was manifest by the epaulettes of his uniform and the sword that hung at his side. Rather than continue what had to appear a ludicrous charade, Dudingston referred the entire matter to Adm. John Montagu, commander of His Majesty's fleet at Boston. Montagu responded with an indignant letter to Wanton on April 8, denouncing the governor's position as "insolent" and insisting that "it is your duty, as governor, to give [Dudingston] your assistance, and not to endeavor to distress the King's officers for strictly complying with my orders."

Montagu went on to deliver a warning. "I am also informed, the people of Newport talk of fitting out an armed vessel to rescue any vessel the King's schooner may take carrying on an illicit trade. Let them be cautious what they do; for as sure as they attempt it, and any of them are taken, I will hang them as pirates." Finally, he added with unvarnished scorn, "I would advise you not to send your sheriff on board the King's ship again, on such ridiculous errands."

Sharp as was Montagu's missive, Wanton didn't flinch. In a defiant reply, the governor assured the admiral that he never intended to offend any of the king's officers, but since Dudingston had still not presented any formal papers, "it was altogether out of my power to know, whether he came hither to protect us from pirates, or was a pirate himself." Wanton was equally firm in answering Montagu's admonishment regarding the sheriff. "Please to know," the governor wrote, "that I will send the sheriff of this colony at any time, and to any place, within the body of it, as I shall think fit."

This was a remarkable escalation of hostilities. Governor Wanton may have been raised on Rhode Island's bracing notions of political freedom, but there was never any question of his allegiance to the crown. For all their long tradition of governorship and other high office, his family's proudest moment came in 1702, when Wanton's father and uncle were honored at the royal court in London for their service as privateers in defense of British shipping. The mark of distinction was preserved on the Wanton family coat of arms. Yet Joseph's identification with the monarchy didn't translate into obedience to the edicts of his ministers. Rather, as with Stephen Hopkins and other radical patriots, it emboldened him to assert prerogatives on a par with any other royal subject—or in this case, royal officials.

The haughty exchange between the governor and the admiral quickly exceeded the bounds of courtly civility that characterized most official communications. And the loose talk of piracy couldn't mask the gravity of the accusations: as Montagu emphasized, the charge carried a death sentence. In any case, the correspondence failed to settle the dispute. Each was convinced he was in the right, and both Montagu and Wanton sent copies of their letters to the Earl of Hillsborough, the secretary of state for the British colonies in North America. But as with so many colonial quarrels, the appeal home was a futile gesture. This would not be settled by ministers an ocean away.

On June 8, 1772, Captain Benjamin Lindsey arrived at Newport at the helm of the sloop *Hannah*, a small coastal packet carrying passengers and merchandise from New York. Lindsey duly filed his cargo manifest at the customshouse, and spent the night in the harbor. About noon the next day, a Tuesday, Lindsey sailed north for Providence. As he passed by the head of Conanicut Island, Lindsey was hailed by the *Gaspee*, which was lying in the mouth of the west passage, close by the HMS *Beaver*, another of the swift new revenue cutters. When Lindsey ignored the signal and continued on his course, Lieutenant Dudingston left the *Beaver* at her station and set out in pursuit.

With the wind blowing from the north, the two small ships tacked their way up the bay. The twin-masted *Gaspee* could mount more sail, but Lindsey had a better knowledge of the currents and the tides, having spent ten years at the helm of a packet that sailed between Providence and Newport. Besides, Dudingston was without his local pilot—he had recently been transferred to the *Beaver*.

Around three o'clock that afternoon, the *Hannah* and the *Gaspee* passed Warwick, where the Narragansett Bay narrows from three miles across to just over a mile. Tacking northwest, Captain Lindsey sailed into the shallows off Namquit Point, a spit of sand and scrub formed by tidal currents and extending into the bay about two miles below the Pawtuxet River. It may have been a ploy, or Lindsey may have simply been trying to gain all the ground he could from his tack, but as Dudingston attempted the same maneuver, the *Gaspee* caught fast on a shallow sandbar. Lindsey promptly recognized her predicament, as the *Gaspee*'s mainsail luffed and the cutter suddenly began to recede in the distance. The British warship was stuck, with the tide running out. Within minutes, the *Gaspee* was practically beached; one of her seamen said later the water was a foot deep on one side of the ship and two feet on the other, and that the crew spent the afternoon scraping down the exposed hull.

Lindsey continued north without further incident, pulling into Providence at about sunset. Once ashore, he set out to find John Brown. He knew that Brown was the town's most vocal critic of Dudingston and his depredations; he knew Brown would be glad to hear of the lieutenant's plight. It was not recorded where John was when Lindsey located him that evening—one version posits that John was a passenger on the *Hannah* when she sailed from Newport—but find him he did, and Lindsey related the news that John's hated nemesis was stranded and helpless just a few miles south of town.

John well understood the situation confronting Dudingston. He himself had been stranded off Namquit Point, twelve years before, at the outset of a trip he took with Moses to Philadelphia, and their vessel had grounded on the bar until the tide lifted them off early the next morning. John had every reason to believe Dudingston would stay put as well, and according to the most authoritative account of what happened that night, John "immediately resolved on [the] destruction" of the *Gaspee.*

John quickly formed a plan. He would round up the captains of his ships that were in port, row out in open longboats, and surprise the British mariners in their slumber. It would be, simply put, a pirate raid, with a desperate charge over the rail and the enemy subdued in hand-to-hand fighting. To raise a raiding party, he drafted a drummer boy, who paraded up Towne Street, beating his drum and calling out an alarm. It was a pleasant night, lit by a waxing moon, and over the course of the next couple of hours, most of the men in the harbor area—by one report as many as five hundred—were crowded into the taverns and milling in the street at the southern end of town. One gathering place was "a place of resort" operated by Joseph Bucklin, a blacksmith and merchant who'd recently had a cargo confiscated by the *Beaver.* Nearby stood an unfinished three-story house. On the ground floor was a tavern and inn operated by James Sabin. This became the headquarters for the raid.

John Brown held court inside Sabin's main room, flanked by several of his saltwater captains. The most prominent was Abe Whipple, distinguished for his success capturing merchant ships in the sea lanes of the Caribbean. Also on hand was John B. Hopkins, Esek's son, and a captain who occasionally sailed for the Browns. Mixed in with these prominent men were the usual harborside collection of sailors and stevedores, many of them in their teens or early twenties. John's proposition—to overwhelm the crew of the *Gaspee* and then to destroy the ship—was bold to the point of absurdity, an act of sheer vengeance that would invite sure retribution from the Royal Navy. Yet his was an audience of hardy seafarers and fierce privateers, men who reviled the haughty swagger of uniformed sailors and of William Dudingston in particular. Nobody spoke in opposition. Instead, off to one side, hovering about the stove in Sabin's kitchen, a clutch of men busied themselves in melting lead to pour into molds for use as bullets. Several of the raiders carried firearms; the rest collected barrel staves and paving stones for use in close combat.

Around 10 P.M., after giving the men time to quaff enough rum for courage, John Brown gave the order to move down to the docks. There were other men more experienced in the business of staging assaults against armed vessels, but John made it clear this was his operation. John dubbed himself the captain of the expedition and, partly in jest, named Abe Whipple the sheriff of Kent, the county that encompassed Namquit Point. Together they selected about sixty men, warned them to be sure to keep all identities secret, and deployed to eight of the largest longboats in the harbor, stout craft built with seats and locks for five oarsmen apiece. The oars were wrapped in canvas to muffle the sound, and the boats set out, each with one of John's ship's captains at the rudder.

The little flotilla made its way smoothly down the bay and came up on the silent silhouette of the *Gaspee* around midnight, just as the moon began to slip below the horizon. At Whipple's whispered command, the boats fanned out, forming a line, and slowly approached the stranded ship. At about sixty yards' distance they were hailed by a sentinel. Nobody moved. The sentinel called again, and then left the rail. After about a minute, a new figure appeared. "Who comes there?" It was Lieutenant Dudingston, in his shirt-sleeves, a sword in one hand and a pistol in the other, peering into the darkness. Whipple decided to answer. "I am the sheriff of Kent, and I want to come aboard."

Still uncertain what he was facing, Dudingston replied that no sheriff would be admitted aboard at that hour of night. Whipple roared back his answer, his voice echoing across the water: "I am the Sheriff of the county of Kent, God damn you! I have got a warrant to apprehend you, God damn you! So surrender, God damn you!" With that, the oarsmen pulled in unison, the longboats leapt forward, and the raiders were under the bows of the *Gaspee*. Dudingston sounded the alarm and ordered his men on deck with their weapons, but events were moving too quickly. As his crew of about twenty men stumbled half awake from belowdecks, the raiders were swarming over the gunwales. Dudingston, alone at the starboard bow, fired his pistol and raised his sword to strike the closest boarder, but his shot was answered by one from the boats. The marksman's aim was true; the musket ball slashed Dudingston's left arm and penetrated his groin. The lieutenant fell, bleeding profusely.

No more shots were fired—the raiders did the rest of the work with their barrel staves. "They used us very ill," one of the crew members said later, "by beating and knocking down the people." At the center of the melee stood John Brown, barking orders and directing traffic. For all the privateers and slave ships he had sent to sea, this was his first experience of close combat, and he appears to have maintained a cool head amid the exhilaration. It was also the occasion for the single firsthand description of John to survive from this period, offered by the *Gaspee*'s midshipman during a deposition a year later. "The captain, who was called the captain of the gang, was a well-set man, of a swarthy complexion, full face, hoarse voice, and wore a white cap, was well-dressed, and appeared rather above the common rank of mankind." The reference to a hoarse voice would be remarked upon again years later—along with his growing girth, it was one of John's distinguishing features.

While Captain Whipple made sure the ship was secured, John located Dudingston lying on his side on the deck. According to the midshipman's account, John was in a rage, and raised a club over the lieutenant's head. "Stand aside," he shouted; "let me dispatch the piratical dog." But John relented. Rather than slay him, he demanded that Dudingston order his men to surrender, and the officer complied. John then called for John Mawney, a young Providence man who had studied in medicine. When Mawney answered, addressing John as "Mr. Brown," John reminded him, "Don't call names," and then sent him below with Dudingston to attend to his wounds.

Mawney had little experience, but he performed well under the pressure, stanching the severe gunshot wound to Dudingston's groin with a compress. Despite his pain, Dudingston was able to survey the chaotic scene while the surgeon attended to him. The cabin was invaded by a dozen men, apparently including both John Brown and Abe Whipple, who went immediately to Dudingston's desk and began rifling the ship's books and log, and inspecting the lieutenant's official commission. "They appeared to me to be merchants or masters of vessels, who were at my bureau reading and examining my papers," Dudingston later recalled.

Back on deck, the chaos began to subside, as the raiders shoved the British seamen into the longboats, their hands bound at the wrist behind their backs. Soon their captors clambered in after them. Several of the longboats struck out north, heading back to Providence, while those with prisoners veered west, to the sandy point above the mouth of the Pawtuxet River, where they put the navy men ashore. Sitting on the beach and looking back through the gloom, they saw the first flicker of flames from inside the captain's cabin, at the rear of the ship. After about an hour, the fire caught the rigging and leaped into the shrouds. At about half past four in the morning, with the first light of dawn spreading from the east, the last three longboats pulled away from the burning hulk. Not long after, the powder in the magazine exploded, sending up a boom that reverberated across the bay.

Years later, John Brown told the story of his attack on the British revenue ship to his grandson. As his grandson recounted it, John "was the last man to leave the deck, being determined that no one should carry from the vessel anything which might lead to the identification and detection of the parties. By doing so he narrowly escaped with his life, in consequence of the falling timbers and spars." At least one souvenir escaped his scrutiny, however, and made it back to Providence. The morning after, Justin Jacobs, one of the youngest members of the raiding party, was seen cavorting at the center of the Weybosset Bridge wearing Lieutenant Dudingston's gold-embroidered beaver hat. Jacobs drew a small crowd, until he was warned off by some more heedful passerby. It would be decades before anyone else from Providence would publicly admit any connection to the *Gaspee* affair.

By the time the sun reached its zenith on June 10, there was hardly a soul in Rhode Island who did not know what had happened the night before on the placid waters of Narragansett Bay. Even those who slept through the echoing blast of the *Gaspee*'s magazine could see, in the morning light, the plume of smoke that rose from the smoldering ruins of the vessel, still stranded on the shallow sandbar. News of the episode traveled fast, into the hinterlands of Connecticut and Massachusetts, and quickly to the major seaports beyond. No longer was Boston the primary miscreant in the colonies' struggle against royal authority.

In Providence, of course, the details of the story were known firsthand. For every man who embarked on the expedition that night, there were many more who attended the gathering at Sabin's Tavern and lined the wharves as the longboats pulled away. The gossip about so dramatic an event could not have taken long to make the rounds. And yet, for all the fame and notoriety the perpetrators of the raid must have enjoyed, the fact ramained that the attack on the king's armed cruiser was a high crime, and the initial response throughout the colony was tinged with fear.

Deputy Gov. Darius Sessions understood instantly the grave threat the burning of the *Gaspee* represented to the autonomy of the government in Rhode Island, and even to the colonial charter, which might be revoked at any time by the king. Recognizing that officials in the colonial government would be called to account, he set out that day to Patuxet, a hamlet resting between the Pawtuxet River and the bay, to see what he might be able to learn, and to proffer his services to the wounded lieutenant. He traveled on horseback with John Andrews, a Providence resident who served as judge at the vice admiralty court in Rhode Island.

The two colonial officials located Dudingston and several members of his crew at "a small house by the shore" that the sailors had managed to locate in the early hours of the morning. They found the lieutenant "in dangerous circumstances," lying on a blanket, despondent and in pain, the bullet still lodged in his body. Leaning over him, Sessions asked if he needed any money, or doctors, or help removing "to a place more convenient."

Dudingston declined any assistance for himself, but asked that his men be collected and sent either to the admiral at Boston or to Newport. Sessions then asked Dudingston if he would make a deposition describing the attack on his ship, "that the perpetrators might be brought to justice." Dudingston was skeptical. He did not feel physically capable of making a statement, and furthermore, he was obliged to offer his first full account of the action to his superior officers, at a court-martial, which was required of any officer who lost a ship under his command. If he were to die, Dudingston added, "he desired it all might die with him." Here Dudingston was being a bit dramatic—he had already dispatched his midshipman, William Dickinson, to report to Admiral Montagu at Boston.

Reluctant to leave empty-handed, Sessions asked Dudingston for permission to interview the crew members present. Dudingston at first declined, but finally, exhausted, he relented. Sessions then interviewed seven members of the crew, and took brief statements from two of them. Both recounted in broad strokes the story of the attack on the ship, accounts that Sessions dutifully transcribed into two separate statements, each marked with an X by the illiterate seaman. Then he asked each the key question: could either identify any of their assailants? Both answered no.

After one last effort to obtain a statement from Dudingston, and after securing a promise from the owner of the house to look after the injured officer, Sessions and Andrews returned to Providence. Sessions had little to show for his efforts that day—two thin statements signed with an X—but much had been accomplished on two important fronts. First, he had established a record of official concern and action in response to the outrage perpetrated on the waters of the bay the night before. Second, he had obtained news that would bring a huge sigh of relief in Providence: the identity of the attackers appeared to be safely obscure. Nobody had been recognized.

Lieutenant Dudingston did not die, but it was some time before he could be moved. And if he was persuaded by the visit of the deputy governor that his conflict with the people of Rhode Island would be suspended during his convalescence, he soon learned otherwise. The next day, June 12, a sheriff rode out from Providence and arrested Dudingston on charges of theft stemming from the seizure of the *Fortune.* Close behind, having heard of the sheriff's mission, rode William Checkley, head of the Providence customs office, as he feared "the sheriff will use great severity with him." Arriving at the little house where Dudingston lay, Checkley found the sheriff had just departed; he had served the lieutenant with a summons to court, but had let him remain where he was on the advice of his doctors. Checkley did what he could, offering to post bail for his freedom, but Dudingston waved him off. "Dudingston told me he should not ask any person to be security, as he did not expect to live long, and the sheriff might do as he pleased."

Dudingston did manage to avoid spending time in jail. By July, he was safely aboard a British warship, though still in pain, and in fear for his life. "I cannot help telling you," he wrote to Admiral Montagu, "without I was able to retire to a ship, I should not exist one night on shore." But the hated lieutenant did make at least one shore visit, on the third Monday in July, where he entered a plea of not guilty at the handsome white-clapboard courthouse in East Greenwich. Two days later, a jury found against him, awarding three hundred pounds damages to the Greenes for the confiscated cargo of the *Fortune*. Dudingston's attorney filed two appeals, but the cases were heard in the colony, and the result remained the same. In the end, the damages were paid by Checkley from the customs office account.

~~~~~

While Dudingston was occupied in fending off the claims of the Greene clan, the colonial government at Rhode Island was engaged in a much more elaborate game of damage control. The first move was made by Deputy Governor Sessions the day after his ride to Patuxet. He mapped out his strategy in a June 11 letter to Governor Wanton that would set the tone for all the official inquiries that followed. The letter opened stern and somber—as if Wanton had yet to hear the news. "A very disagreeable affair has lately happened within this part of the colony," Sessions wrote. He described his urgent visit to see Dudingston at Patuxet, and his diligent striving "that the perpetrators might be brought to justice."

Sessions then made his thinking explicit to Wanton. "The dangerous tendency of this transaction [a curious phrase to describe an attack on a navy ship] is too obvious, to pass it over with the least appearance of neglect; and therefore, I doubt not Your Honor will give it due attention," he wrote. Sessions showed the way by lauding the feigned outrage of his circle of friends in Providence. "It is the prevailing opinion of the gentlemen in this quarter, that a proclamation, with a large reward, be issued, for apprehending the persons who have thus offended."

The next day, gaining confidence in his strategy, Sessions wrote again. "I have received the advice of all the civil authority in this town, as well as an application in writing, by a great number of the most reputable inhabitants, who are unanimously of the opinion, and earnestly desire that Your Honor forthwith issue a proclamation, with proper reward, for the apprehending and bringing to justice any and every person that was concerned in destroying the schooner Gaspee, or in assaulting and wounding William Dudingston." Sessions knew full well, of course, that "a great number of the most reputable inhabitants" had in fact conceived and executed the raid. From the outset, and as became more obvious as the months went by, Sessions was engaged in a cover-up.

Whatever suspicions Wanton may have harbored regarding the "gentlemen" of Providence, he embraced Sessions's strategy, and on June 12, the same day the sheriff served papers on Dudingston, the governor issued a proclamation calling on "all His Majesty's officers, within the colony . . . to exert themselves with the utmost vigilance, to discover and apprehend the persons guilty of the aforesaid atrocious crime." To that end, Wanton further offered a reward of one hundred pounds sterling. The proclamation was posted in all the towns ringing Narragansett Bay, and published in Newport and Providence.

The same day, Governor Wanton received a terse note from Admiral Montagu, objecting to "the piratical proceedings of the people of Providence," and enclosing a detailed deposition from midshipman Dickinson. The statement included several intriguing new details; Dickinson observed that the raiders "appeared like men of credit and tradesmen, and but few like common men," and he had learned that "they beat a drum around Providence, in the evening, to raise a mob." The professed outrage of the "most reputable inhabitants" of the town was beginning to ring hollow.

Wanton wrote back to describe the reward he'd posted, and to commiserate over "this daring insult to authority." Montagu answered promptly, adopting a collegial tone, but still pressing for results. Word of the true source of the action was spreading: "It will not bear a dispute that [the raiders] belonged to Providence," Montagu wrote, "as they were heard by four or five gentlemen that were in that town, and are now here, beating the drum to arms, to raise a body of people to destroy the King's schooner."

At the same time they were exchanging letters, both the admiral and the governor were composing dispatches to Lord Hillsborough. In this case, Montagu's communication was charged with umbrage. He denounced "the lawless and piratical people of Rhode Island," and singled out Providence as "a nest of daring smugglers." Governor Wanton struck a more nuanced pose. Confessing his dismay that "I am now reduced to the necessity of addressing your Lordship upon a most disagreeable subject," he related the story of the attack, and then detailed the good works of the deputy governor. "Your Lordship may be assured, that the utmost vigilance of the civil authority will not be wanting," Wanton vowed.

Then the governor changed tone, expounding at great length on the "unprecedented and oppressive" measures taken by Dudingston and the other naval officers enforcing the revenue laws. Wanton was doing all he could to temper British reaction to the attack with reminders of "the complaints of [the] much abused and injured people" of Rhode Island.

However well conceived, Wanton's pleadings had little effect. The attack on a ship and a uniformed officer of His Majesty's Navy shocked the British authorities, exciting even the personal attention of the monarch, King George III. The news traveled slowly, but the incident seemed to grow in infamy as the weeks went by. In August, Alexander Wedderburn, the attorney general for Great Britain, pronounced the *Gaspee* affair to be a crime of "five times the magnitude of the Stamp Act" riots. The Earl of Dartmouth, who had replaced Hillsborough as secretary of state for the colonies, termed it "an offense of much deeper dye" than piracy, "considered in no other light, than as an act of high treason, vis: levying war against the king."

On August 26, King George himself weighed in, issuing a royal proclamation offering a reward of five hundred pounds for information leading to the capture of any of "the persons who plundered and burnt the Gaspee schooner, and barbarously wounded and ill-treated Lieutenant William Dudingston." The proclamation went into some surprising particulars, offering an added five-hundred-pound bounty for capture of the individuals "who acted as, or called themselves . . . the head sheriff, or the captain." If the informant were a member of the raiding party, he would be pardoned. A thousand pounds sterling—a tidy fortune—vouched by the king himself, for the capture of Abe Whipple or John Brown.

We can only surmise John's state of mind regarding the bounty that hung over his head. In all of his surviving correspondence, John never mentioned the *Gaspee* by name. His sole statement on the matter comes from his grandson, who recalled in his brief account that John "deeply regretted this affair, as foolhardy in itself, and resulting in so much needless apprehension for himself and for his family. For a long time he was accustomed to sleep away from home, lest he be arrested during the night." But it wasn't just guilty knowledge that kept John on the move. By early July, John had been named as a ringleader in the attack.

The accusation came from Aaron Briggs, a black indentured servant who lived on a farm on Prudence Island, a long, low stretch of pasture that lay in the center of Narragansett Bay. About a month after the *Gaspee* was burned, Briggs stole a boat and rowed out to the *Beaver*, which had anchored near Prudence. Once on board, he claimed he had been on hand during the raid, and offered himself as a witness.

He had not been at Providence the night of the crime, Briggs said, but rowing a skiff off Prudence, where he encountered men in a longboat rowing from Bristol, on the east shore of the bay, and heading out to join the raiders from Providence. Their alleged leader was Simeon Potter, a well-known sea rover and privateer from Bristol, who pressed Briggs into service. After joining with Potter and rowing another half hour, Briggs said, they encountered a fleet of seventeen boats, led by none other than John Brown. It was Brown who fired the shot that felled Dudingston, Briggs said, and Brown who steered the boat that landed the lieutenant ashore.

Briggs's story had some immediate problems. This was the first mention anywhere of a launch from Bristol joining the Providence boats, and presumed an exceptional degree of coordination, considering the pace of events. Moreover, he said he joined the attack under duress, though he could have simply rowed on that night.

And, Briggs was black, or, more accurate, mulatto, which led to rough handling by the British, which compromised any subsequent testimony. The son of a black father and a Narragansett Indian mother, Briggs was abandoned at an early age, and as was common with children of color left to the charge of a town in colonial Rhode Island, he was placed in indenture, to be freed at the age of twenty-four. Briggs was not yet twenty when he put himself in the hands of the British navy; the afternoon he presented himself on ship, he was deemed a runaway, and shackled belowdecks. The next day, the captain planned to have him flogged as a matter of course, but then he struck on a better plan: Briggs could avoid his whipping if he would serve as a witness in the *Gaspee* investigation. When Briggs complied, two seamen agreed to swear they had seen Briggs the night of the raid, and the investigation had new life.

The named suspects attributed to Briggs, then, were selected purposefully, probably by the British themselves: Simeon Potter, already notorious, and John Brown, apparently the victim of his spreading fame. Not surprising, the British were zealous in protecting their star witness. Briggs remained aboard the *Beaver* after making his statement, and his story relayed to Admiral Montagu in Boston. Montagu immediately wrote to Governor Wanton, advising him to arrest the two suspects, "that they may be examined before you, in the presence of Lieutenant Dudingston, who . . . may possibly recollect the persons of Potter and Brown."

That procedure likely would have meant a quick conviction for John— after all, Dudingston got a good look at him rifling the ship's papers in the captain's cabin. But Governor Wanton chose to keep John out of the picture, and focus instead on the veracity of the witness. Fortunately for John, Briggs was easily discredited. Within two days, Wanton had personally taken depositions from the owners of the farm where Briggs lived, and from two other indentured servants on the farm, all contending that Briggs had not left the island that night. Their story was that Briggs had heard talk of the attack, and of the reward, and turned informant as a means to gain his freedom.

The tangle over the witness quickly became a test of wills between the British authorities and the colonial government. On July 11, Wanton moved to assert his prerogatives, issuing a warrant for Briggs's arrest on charges of helping to burn the ship. When it was presented to John Linzee, captain of the *Beaver,* Linzee summarily rejected it. Briggs's owner thereupon swore out a warrant for the arrest of Captain Linzee, on charges of stealing his servant, and Admiral Montagu was forced to post bail to keep Linzee out of jail. The investigation had fallen into a stalemate, and the matter lay quiet through the rest of the summer and through the autumn that followed. In the meantime, Montagu dispatched five men-of-war to assert his authority on the waters of Narragansett Bay.

The next move came from King George. On September 2, a week after posting his reward, the king announced the formation of a special commission of inquiry, charged with taking evidence in the case, with reviewing the inquiry mounted by the colonial officials on the scene, and more important, with sending prime suspects, and the witnesses against them, back to England for trial. Admiral Montagu was ordered to attend the hearings, and to take personal custody of any indicted suspects. If local citizens tried to obstruct the proceedings, regiments of troops would be dispatched to maintain order. Named to the commission were Governor Wanton, Judge Robert Auchmuty of the vice admiralty court at Boston, and the chief justices from the colonies of New Jersey, New York, and Massachusetts. This was the first such panel ever assembled to adjudicate a criminal case in America, and the first royal edict to ship prisoners to trial in England.

News of the extraordinary commission reached Rhode Island in October, via Admiral Montagu, who again called for the arrest of John Brown and Simeon Potter. Governor Wanton again ignored Montagu's directive to make arrests, but he had the king's proclamation published and distributed throughout the colony.

The reaction in Providence was one of spiteful defiance. According to one early, unsourced account, "The King's proclamation was posted on the pillar of the hay scales which then stood near the northeast corner of the market square. . . . It had not been there more than fifteen or twenty minutes when Mr. Joseph Aplin, a distinguished lawyer, came up to see what had collected the crowd. Lifting his cane he struck it down and it soon mingled with the filth of the street."

Stephen Hopkins penned a direct attack on the royal provocation. Writing under the name Americanus, Hopkins denounced the commission as "a court of inquisition, more horrid than that of Spain or Portugal," an "alarming star chamber." Hopkins's article, published in the papers at Providence and Newport, and in the *Virginia Gazette*, focused on the challenge the commission posed to the principle of trial by a jury of one's peers, "the greatest privilege a subject can wish for . . . the grand barrier of our lives, liberties and estates." Hopkins called for the colonies to stand in open resistance to the commission. "To be, or not to be, that's the question: whether our unalienable rights are any longer worth contending for, is now to be determined."

As Rhode Island's chief justice, however, Hopkins could not simply issue diatribes. When the General Assembly sat at Providence in January, Hopkins asked for direction in responding to the commission. A motion to deny its jurisdiction and stand upon the rights guaranteed in the colonial charter was rejected in favor of a more cautious posture, though Hopkins himself vowed not to cooperate in making arrests or summoning witnesses.

Once the question turned political, Moses Brown became involved as well. Still pursuing his ideal of a "regular course of living," Moses had quit his seat in the General Assembly and moved with his family, that summer, to Elmgrove, a two-hundred-acre farm on the back side of Prospect Hill. Yet he remained a central figure in the Sons of Liberty, and this was a challenge that demanded their response. The same week Americanus was published, Moses sat down with Hopkins, Deputy Governor Sessions, and Judge John Cole, and together they composed a letter alerting "several gentlemen in North America" to the threat now looming over the colony.

One of those gentlemen was Samuel Adams, the Massachusetts patriot organizer, who immediately seized upon it as a crisis to "awaken the American colonies, which have been too long dozing upon the brink of ruin." In his prompt reply, Adams revealed himself as more than a firebrand, but an acute legal mind. Establishing such an ad hoc commission of inquiry "is against the first Principles of Government and the English Constitution, Magna Carta and many other Acts of Parliament," Adams surmised, citing specifically "the Act of Parliament of the 25th of Edward III (in the true sense of the words the best of Kings)," which had abolished "that accursed court called the Star Chamber" in favor of British common law. Like Hopkins, Adams saw the commission as a fundamental challenge to American liberties.

For his part, John Brown adopted a more practical approach. He may have been heartened to see patriots rallying to his side, and he was certainly pleased to see that two members of the commission were personal friends—Governor Wanton, of course, and Peter Oliver, chief justice of the Massachusetts court, who owned a forge and had contracted with the Browns to fabricate nails and hoops from Hope Furnace pigs. But the fact remained John had been named as the leader of the raid, and the king had posted a thousand-pound bounty for his head. This was "the time of terror," as one contemporary described it.

Never one quietly to await his fate, John set about building a defense. On the second week in January, he introduced a new witness into the fray, Daniel Vaughan, a Newport resident who worked on a cargo sloop. Vaughan had been retained to haul scrap from the wreck of the *Gaspee* down to the *Beaver*, and claimed that he was on board the *Beaver* when Aaron Briggs first turned himself in. According to Vaughan, Briggs told him then that he knew nothing about what happened on the *Gaspee*, and that he had come to the British seeking protection from his master. Three days later, Vaughan said, he was again on board the *Beaver*, and he happened to see Briggs being lashed to the mast for a flogging. This ordeal Briggs avoided at the last minute by naming Brown, Potter, and several other suspects, all within earshot of Vaughan.

This set of coincidences was unlikely enough; Vaughan's credibility was further undermined by the fact that he was the commander of the Goat Island gun crew that had opened fire, eight years before, on the revenue cutter *St. John*. But Vaughan was willing to swear to his story, and when he turned up in Providence, John Brown presented him to Deputy Governor Sessions, who obliged by taking a deposition.

These maneuverings took place against a backdrop of grave and growing threats. The *Providence Gazette* published a letter from England warning of plans to vacate the colony's charter, one from Boston predicting an armed occupation of Newport and a repeat of the Boston Massacre, and another letter from Boston asserting that Admiral Montagu "swore by God that he would burn the town of Providence to ashes." With the harbor at Newport crowded with British warships, all Rhode Island was on edge.

⁓

The first two out-of-town judges named to the commission, Frederick Smythe of New Jersey and Daniel Horsmanden of New York, arrived at Newport on

December 31, Horsmanden making a great commotion as he traversed the half mile from the wharves to his lodgings in a carriage drawn by two horses that he had shipped along with him. Together with Governor Wanton, the judges constituted a quorum of the commission, and might have commenced proceedings at once. But for all the fear and trembling of the patriots, it was the commissioners who seemed cowed by the controversy. Admiral Montagu also showed little zeal for the business. The king's proclamation directed him to attend the opening session, but in a letter to Wanton dated January 2, the admiral demurred, contending that "the season of the year does not admit of my coming," and offering the services of a captain already stationed at Newport in his stead. It is true that, after a mild start, the winter of 1772 had turned unusually severe, but cold weather seemed a flimsy excuse for a British admiral to shirk an order from the king. More likely it was Montagu's intimate knowledge of the shaky standing of Aaron Briggs, the key witness for the prosecution, that dampened his enthusiasm.

The commission sat for the first time on January 5, after a procession through town, in bitter cold, behind a phalanx of British marines. Commencing in closed session on the second floor of the Colony House, their first order of business was to write Montagu, insisting that he make the trip to Newport in person. Next, after taking oaths of fealty to the king, they heard from Darius Sessions and Stephen Hopkins, who both pledged to render every possible assistance. Despite Hopkins's militant stance before the General Assembly, he had settled on a more moderate course, "that so the commissioners may not seem necessitated to usurp an executive jurisdiction within the colony."

The commissioned played their hand carefully as well. They were not, after all, ministers from across the water, but colonists themselves, albeit members of the elite, and of unquestioned allegiance to the crown. Some were confirmed Tories, but all of them, except Governor Wanton, were jurists, and they took seriously the questions of law and jurisdiction posed in formation of the commission itself. This resulted in an early compromise: they made clear, in their first interview with Hopkins and Sessions, that they would not make arrests on their own, but only in concert with, and through the offices of, the local officials and the colonial courts. Moreover, pursuant to their mandate to report on the "circumstances" that gave rise to the crime, the commissioners said they would take testimony on the conduct of Dudingston and other revenue officers, as well as the band that attacked the *Gaspee*.

This was "very unexpected," according to the diarist Ezra Stiles, who was able to track the secret proceedings through dinner conversations with the principals as the hearings progressed. "By this the Tory bellowing and insouciance was hushed," Stiles wrote.

Instead of tangling with the colonial authorities, the commission found it-self wrestling for primacy with Admiral Montagu. Loath as he was to take or-ders from civil authorities, the admiral delayed his departure for Newport as long as he dared, then decided, curiously, to make the trip overland. Choosing an easterly route—not to burn Providence, but to bypass it—he arrived on the eastern shore of Narragansett Bay on January 12. From there he embarked on the HMS *Lizard*, a schooner stationed at Newport, and sailed into the harbor with his pennant flying. The other warships in the harbor fired cannons to mark his approach, but no salute sounded from the fort on Goat Island, an in-tentional affront that laid bare the tensions between the admiral and the com-mission. With all the bickering and the strained efforts at cooperation, the inquiry was turning into a farce.

Still, hanging over the proceedings was the specter of a ravaged warship, and the commission had yet to hear evidence. On January 14, a day of snow and freezing rain, Aaron Briggs finally appeared in person to make his state-ment. After all the threats against him, and despite his status as a virtual pris-oner on board the *Beaver*, Briggs told his story "with much plausibility," as Judge Horsmanden wrote soon after. Admiral Montagu also presented a peti-tion taken in July from a *Gaspee* seaman who swore Briggs was among the boatmen who rowed him to shore the night the schooner was destroyed.

The examination fell to Deputy Governor Sessions. He countered with Vaughan's deposition, never mentioning to the commission Vaughan's history of overt hostility to British authority. Sessions then proffered his own deposi-tion, given in Providence two days after Vaughan's, in which the deputy gover-nor sought to establish that it was simply too dark on the *Gaspee* for any sailor to identify Briggs positively as being on board. Should the commissioners begin to wonder if Sessions had become an advocate for the defense, the deputy governor offered an explanation. "I look upon it as my duty to protect the innocent, as well as punish the guilty," Sessions averred.

While the commission weighed the conflicting accounts regarding his key witness, Admiral Montagu could only fume. He had left Boston against his will, and had been insulted upon his arrival. Now he was forced to watch as the prosecution drifted. On the fifteenth, the weather was so stormy the com-mission didn't even sit. The next day, Montagu put his last cards on the table. He submitted a list of prominent people from Providence, men who, Mon-tagu apparently believed, might know what happened the night the *Gaspee* was burned and might be willing to tell what they knew. At the same time, Montagu announced that he would leave Newport within the week. The ad-miral had seen enough.

If Montagu was playing a hunch, it promptly backfired. Each of his witnesses, including vice admiralty judge John Andrews and attorney John Cole, both close associates of Stephen Hopkins and Darius Sessions, declined making the trip to Newport, and instead submitted affidavits clearly designed to kill the inquiry. They had indeed been in Providence the night in question, and had even been at Sabin's Tavern. They heard, too, the drummer beating through the street. But they saw no gathering of men, and could not discover what all the commotion was about. They were "surprised," they testified, to learn the next morning that a ship had been burned on the bay. James Sabin himself closed the circle, swearing that each man on Montagu's list had "supped at my house, and stayed there until two of the clock, in the morning," but that nothing of note had transpired.

With their inquiries stymied, and with Montagu leaving town, the commission was at a standstill. Rather than admit defeat, the commissioners decided to cite "the rigors of the season" and adjourn until May. It was a simple matter of saving face, they must have assumed, and preserving some shred of their dignity. But it proved a serious mistake, for rather than end the crisis that the sitting of the commission represented, they prolonged it.

Quiet as the commission was in performing its duties, its appointment represented an escalation in the efforts by the crown to assert its authority in the colonies. It was created in answer to a glaring provocation, of course, but to the patriots of North America, that was beside the point. The Reverend John Allen, a minister recently arrived from England, voiced the popular reaction to the commission as early as December 3, in a fiery sermon delivered at the Second Baptist Church in Boston. The sermon was framed as an address to Lord Dartmouth, and spoke directly to the question of the *Gaspee*. "Have not the Rhode Islanders as much right to the privileges of their own laws, as the King of England to the crown?" Allen asked. "Sure they have! . . . If there is any law broke here, it is this, that the *Gaspee* schooner, by the power of the English ministry and admiralty, have broke the laws and taken away the rights of the Americans."

Allen described in grave terms the ire being raised by the royal inquiry. "For violating the people's rights, Charles Stuart, King of England, lost his head, and if another king . . . should tread in the same steps, what can he expect?" He had the same message for the Lords of Trade. "Should this be the bloody intent of the ministry, to make the Americans subject to their slavery, then let blood for blood, life for life, and death for death decide the contention." To the colonists themselves, Allen issued a call to arms. "Stand alarmed! See your danger, death is near, destruction is at your door."

More angry and more violent than any of the rhetoric issued during the Stamp Act protests, Allen's sermon created a sensation, and in the weeks that followed, while the *Gaspee* commission sat at Newport, it was published in five successive editions, becoming the best-selling pamphlet of its time.

By February, the fevered locution of Allen's address, along with Hopkins's Americanus essay and the appeals of the Providence committee, had generated fear and concern throughout the eastern seaboard. In particular, Richard Henry Lee, an aristocratic orator and a member of the House of Burgesses in Virginia, wrote to Samuel Adams at Boston requesting more detailed information on the proceedings at Rhode Island. Based on what he'd heard so far, Lee was ready to denounce the commission as "so unreasonable, and so unconstitutional a stretch of power, that I hope it will never be permitted to take place while a spark of virtue or manly sentiment remains in America." More important, Lee saw the commission as a "powerful cause of union" among the colonists.

American patriots throughout the colonies understood political union to be a prerequisite for any real challenge to Parliament, but ever since Franklin's plan for union had been rebuffed at Albany, it had seemed impossible. The divisions between the colonies, rooted in sectional pride and cultural difference, appeared too broad. The Stamp Act Congress raised hopes again, but Parliament was smart enough to back off. For Lee, as for Sam Adams and Stephen Hopkins, this latest encroachment by Parliament promised to break the impasse at last.

Lee raised this prospect weeks later during the spring session of the House of Burgesses at Williamsburg, while the *Gaspee* commission was in recess. It was a measure to be considered carefully, but the logic was inescapable. Thomas Jefferson described the caucusing in his autobiography:

A court of inquiry held in Rhode Island in 1772 with a power to send persons to England to be tried for offenses committed here was . . . demanding attention. Not thinking our old and leading members up to the point of forwardness and zeal which the times required, [Patrick] Henry, R. H. Lee, [his brother] Francis Lee, [Jefferson's brother-in-law Dabney] Carr, and myself agreed to meet in the evening in a private room [at the hulking old Raleigh Tavern, a favorite redoubt of the Virginia radicals]. We were all sensible that the most urgent of all measures was that of coming to an understanding with all the other colonies to consider the British claims as a common cause to all, and to produce a unity of action: and for this purpose a committee of correspondence in each colony would be the best instrument.

Underlying all their thinking was the hope that such committees would give rise to "a meeting of deputies from every colony at some central place," as Jefferson called it, or as it soon came to be known, a congress. That goal was still too chimerical to name, but on March 11, Dabney Carr moved that the House create a committee of correspondence, and for all the presumed backwardness of the older members, the measure passed handily. Eleven delegates were named, including Carr, Richard Henry Lee, Jefferson, and the speaker of the House, Peyton Randolph. Within days, the first circular letter had been dispatched, consisting mainly of the House resolution "to keep up and maintain a correspondence and communication with our sister colonies" and "that they do, without delay, inform themselves more particularly on the principles and authority, on which was constituted a court of inquiry, said to have been lately held in Rhode Island."

Reaction to the Virginia letter was electric. In Boston, so long isolated as the seat of rebellion, the patriot minister Samuel Cooper wrote in relief to Benjamin Franklin, "Virginia has led the way." Franklin, then in London, immediately grasped the import. "It is natural to suppose," he wrote in June, "that, if the aggressions continue, a congress may grow out of that correspondence. Nothing would more alarm our ministers."

Not surprising, Rhode Island was the first to answer. The Virginia resolutions were published in Newport and Providence in April, and when the General Assembly sat on May 8, a committee of correspondence was immediately appointed, with Stephen Hopkins, Moses Brown, and John Cole named from Providence. The committee stayed busy through the rest of the year, fielding inquiries from as far as the Carolinas, and by December, ten colonies had established standing committees of correspondence.

By the time the royal commission returned to Newport, the justices on the panel were painfully aware of the movement building against them. They sat for three weeks, taking more testimony from *Gaspee* crew members and from several tight-lipped residents of Providence, but these were just formalities. By June 22, the commission closed its inquiry with a report to Lord Dartmouth. It found that the destruction of the *Gaspee* had been accomplished "suddenly and secretly," that the colonial officials of Rhode Island had responded "very properly," and that Aaron Briggs's testimony had to be dismissed because it had been coerced through "illegal threats" by Captain Linzee. As to the causes of the incident, the commission adopted a neutral stance, citing "the great impatience of some people, in this colony, under any restraint of trade, however illicit," and charging, on the other hand, that "in some instances Lieutenant Dudingston, from an intemperate, if not a reprehensible zeal to aid the revenue service, exceeded the bounds of his duty."

No arrests were made, no culprits apprehended, and the fearsome prospect of royal retribution had simply evaporated. The might of England, one Tory complained, "sat down silently under the affront, laughed at by Rhode Islanders." More important, as William Checkley noted, failure to find the offenders meant "an end to collecting a revenue and enforcing the acts of trade." It was, by any measure, a complete victory for the colony, and more particularly, for John Brown.

In private communications afterward, the commissioners were less politic. Judge Horsmanden damned Rhode Island as "a downright democracy," while Smythe of New Jersey condemned the "egregious excess" of the Narragansett Bay smugglers and surmised that "without all doubt the actors must be known to some hundreds of inhabitants," but that "to keep this matter secret is now become common cause."

To observers on the scene, it was apparent the commission wanted to push harder for answers, but feared the consequences. "I apprehend something severe would have been done," Ezra Stiles noted, "had not the commission given an extensive alarm to all the assemblies on the continent." Peter Oliver provided confirmation in his memoirs, albeit in hindsight. "The whole continent was alarmed," Oliver wrote, and should suspects have been arrested and sent to England for trial, "they would have rushed into rebellion three years before they did."

John Brown may indeed have slept "away from home," as he told his grandson, during the weeks that the commission was in session, but he was never very hard to find. In the fall and winter of 1772, he was frequently at Newport, attending meetings with the association of spermaceti manufacturers. And John was on hand in the spring of 1773 when he was appointed by a town meeting to help out in the latest civic improvement project for Providence, the erection of a brick market house at the foot of market square. John's task was to build a stone retaining wall, ten feet high and more than one hundred feet long, extending south from the foot of Weybosset Bridge, along the eastern shore of the Great Salt River. John probably did no heavy lifting, but purchasing the stone and supervising the crews would have kept him constantly about town.

What is apparent is that John felt secure in the confidence that the fellow freemen of Providence would keep his identity secret. They closed ranks from the highest tier, including Stephen Hopkins, who did all he could do to bamboozle the royal commission, and Deputy Gov. Darius Sessions and Judge John Andrews, who clearly perjured themselves in their descriptions of the quiet streets of Providence the night the raiders set out. The sailors and stevedores, the servants and boys and drunks who crowded around Sabin's Tavern that night, followed their leaders and kept their mouths shut.

Before the year was out, John was being hailed as a hero, his exploits touted in a drinking song sung in smoky seaside taverns. The last stanza had to be especially gratifying—after alluding to the reward posted by King George, the song concluded:

> But let him try his utmost skill
> I'm apt to think he never will
> Find out any of those hearts of gold,
> Though he should offer fifty fold.

John had to be gratified as well to find the royal commission checked by an upwelling of principled, patriotic sentiment against the minions of the king. He could not have expected, at the moment Lieutenant Dudingston was shot, or during the melee on the decks of the *Gaspee*, that his brazen attack would be hailed as an act of courage and a blow for American liberty.

John was never a theorist of liberty and freedom like his friends Stephen Hopkins and Darius Sessions, or even like his brother Moses. But he readily adopted the language of rebellion; and the committees of correspondence, formed to challenge the royal edict for punishment of the *Gaspee* raiders, remained in place until Parliament passed the Tea Act, and Boston staged its Tea Party, and the American patriots finally assembled together at the first Continental Congress. For John, revolution was an expedient, a means to keep his ships and his cargoes moving. Indeed, John might serve as proof of the observation, made by an American merchant in London in February 1775, that the elusive union of the British colonies in North America had finally been accomplished "from no object of a more respectable cast than that of a successful practice in illicit trade, I say contrived, prompted and promoted by a confederacy of smugglers in Boston, Rhode Island, and other seaport towns on that coast."

6

Anna

DURING THE EVENTFUL YEAR OF 1772, when John Brown burnt the *Gaspee* and spent the ensuing months dodging British authorities, Moses Brown underwent an ordeal that was just as revolutionary, and more profoundly transformational. It marked the end of his course in the footsteps of a father whose life was devoted to commerce, and culminated in a moral awakening and a spiritual rebirth. This dramatic change of direction had been building for years and unfolded over a period of several months, but it began one afternoon in September, when Moses and his wife, Anna, were visiting friends in Boston. That day, Anna suffered some sort of overwhelming physical breakdown. She collapsed, and spent the rest of her days confined to a sickbed.

Anna had long been unwell. As early as 1765, just a year after their marriage, Moses received reports of his wife being subject to "several fitts," and before the death of her stillborn daughter, in 1768, Moses had been forced to curtail his travels due to the "circumstances" of his wife. She succeeded, in July 1771, in giving birth to a boy, whom the couple named Obadiah, in memory of Anna's father and Moses' uncle. But like their mother, young Obadiah and his sister, Sarah, were both often ill, and Obadiah was all but lame, with swollen knees and frail limbs that Moses termed "rickety."

These family infirmities may have derived from the Browns' practice of intermarriage. Anna's mother and father were cousins—Obadiah had married his first cousin Mary Harris—and of their eight children, four, all boys, failed to survive infancy. Likewise, Anna was first cousin to Moses. And Joseph Brown, Moses' brother, had married his first cousin Elizabeth, daughter of Nicholas Power. Such intrafamilial unions were fairly common in that time, and subject to none of the stigma they carry today. Instead, they reflected the intensity of the family connection. Moses' business and political interests ranged far and wide, but he always operated from within the redoubt he built of his close relations—his brothers, who were his partners in business, and his household. In later years, after they had separated their business concerns, Moses and John both kept their financial affairs within the family circle; with a single exception, when they engaged in partnerships, their counterparts were sons-in-law. And while the passing years drove them further apart on questions of politics and morality, Moses and John always honored their bonds of familial loyalty.

Still, of all the four Brown brothers, Moses was the one who stood closest to the core of their ancestral heritage. He provided a home to both his mother, Hope, and his uncle Obadiah's widow, Mary. Moses' widowed sister, Mary Vanderlight, and Anna's sister, also named Mary, lived with Moses and Anna as well. These women, all kin, comprised Moses' inner sanctum.

The summer of 1772 was a time of great promise for Moses and his family. Anna had suffered through a difficult pregnancy with Obadiah, and he was a sickly infant, but both he and his mother had survived the parturition. Moses had adopted the practice of shuttling his growing brood between the family farm on Weybosset Neck in the summer and the Main Street house in the winter, but the accommodations were never satisfactory. In the spring, a perfect solution was presented by the demise of William Merit, "an English gentleman of fortune," who left a grand three-story mansion with several outbuildings and two hundred acres of pasture on the back side of Prospect Hill. Elmgrove, as the estate was called, looked out to the east, over the Seekonk River, a broad tidal flow that was swifter and deeper than the Great Salt River, which fronted Providence. Across the Seekonk stood the small farming town of Barrington and the little port of Warren; Narragansett Bay lay to the south, and the plains of Massachusetts to the northeast, all visible from a seat beneath the Doric columns that framed the porch at Elmgrove. Providence was less than two miles distant, but separated by the hill where the new college was being built. This was a retreat that would allow Moses to pursue his pacific interests in horticulture and raise his family in the peace of the countryside, while allowing easy communication with business and political affairs in town.

Moses bought Elmgrove at auction, in the spring, and by June he'd moved in. This was not rustic living; or at least, it was rustic splendor. His furniture was lustrous, hand-rubbed mahogany, crafted at Newport, and his plate was silver, wrought at Boston. The fields, consisting of the two hundred acres purchased of the Merit estate and another hundred acres adjacent, previously held by Moses, were tilled by slaves, who lived in a barn near the mansion house. Slaves worked in the kitchen as well, and helped raise the children and serve the meals. For the whites at Elmgrove, life was an easy course of polite manners, with regular visitors from town, tutors for the children, and tea served at five.

This country idyll was shattered when Anna was stricken, at age twenty-eight. Upon her return to Elmgrove, she retired to bed, and lingered through the fall and winter, attended by her sister Mary, by their slaves Eve and Pegg, and by a nurse, Audrey Greene. Doctors could not diagnose Anna's condition, and her health failed steadily. Moses continued to attend to his civic obligations—he was chairman of the lottery to build the market house, which was designed, like University Hall, by his brother Joseph, and he was engaged with Stephen Hopkins in organizing the political resistance to the *Gaspee* commission. But these activities couldn't allay his grief. Moses expressed his dismay in a letter to his brothers: "Nature must be dissolved and all our joys come to an end!" he wrote in September. "Providence unerring Providence determines these events, not only to be sensible to this but be prepared by the kind premonitions is our best comfort."

As his letter implied, during Anna's last days, Moses turned to God. But it was not the religion of his forefathers that answered his yearnings. Late in her life, Anna had begun to attend Quaker services, along with her sister Mary and John Brown's wife, Sarah. The meetinghouse was in Providence, though the services were conducted under the auspices of Smithfield, a small town to the east that was home to the Monthly Meeting. With Anna bedridden and declining, Moses began attending there as well.

This was a profound shift in allegiance, the repudiation of a family religious tradition that followed in a direct line to Chad Brown and his revered role as the first Baptist pastor on the continent. Yet Moses' shift of allegiance was fundamentally conservative in nature. Since the arrival of James Manning, the Baptists had been changing, with more formal services and the introduction of singing as the most obvious outward signs. Gone were the days when, as in the early years, the services were comprised of the congregation sitting in the silence of a plain and simple church until, one by one, each of the elders felt moved to rise and speak his mind, closing his soliloquy with the invitation: "There is time and space left if anyone has further to offer." This format survived unadulterated at the Quaker meetings, where silence, reflection, and declamation were the centerpiece of the service.

In leaving the family church, Moses was painfully aware that he was making a public break with "the people, my brothers, mother and only sister among them, with whom I heretofore attended in their worship." But he was hewing more closely to the faith of his forebears, and he never doubted his decision.

Anna died on February 5, 1773, and for the next several months, Moses was utterly distraught. Sitting at his polished writing desk, as the breezes blowing off the Seekonk turned from icy cold to humid and hot, Moses composed a skein of rambling, tortured letters. Most were addressed to the new acquaintances he met at Friends meetings in Providence and at the New England Yearly Meeting, held at Newport in June. A letter he wrote in August, to a Philadelphia Quaker he'd met in Newport, captures the temper of his anguish. "I have at times, unworthily partook of the extended branches of the divine fountain, alas how often they are absorbed in the dry and barren earth and I left to wander as in the deserts till the gentle rain is again distilled and raises the dry traces to a union with the more enlarged streams, which as they increase to flow overwhelm and bear down all opposition. These are happy moments . . . and when I have been enabled to compare the greatest outward comforts and enjoyments with these they dwindle down to nothing."

In the same letter, Moses pleaded for guidance. "I have need of every aid in my intended travel through the wilderness. . . . Use me rather as a child, indeed I have much need of pruning to be worthy of that appellation, since to become a little child, is a truly honorable state."

Yet for all his supplication, Moses was already moving past conversion, and onto a course of conviction. God might be mysterious, but Moses believed that there was a reason for every occurrence, and that calamity was rooted in retribution. This was standard fare at the time; ever since the days of Cotton Mather, and especially since the Great Awakening, the religious revival that swept America in the 1740s, Protestant preachers had warned that God would exercise his wrath in the form of plagues or famine until sinners returned to the fold. Moses was convinced that Anna was taken as punishment for his sins.

He believed, too, that he knew the nature of that sin. According to lore, the revelation came to him in a flash, upon "returning from the grave of his wife, and medidating upon the Lord's mercies and favors, and seeking to know what the Divine will was concerning him." Moses is quoted relating a vision that came to him: "I saw my slaves with my spiritual eyes plainly as I see you now, and it was given to me as clearly to understand that the sacrifice that was called for of my hand was to give them their liberty." From that day forward, Moses committed himself to the eradication of slavery.

There is little doubt that the roots of this spiritual encounter reached back to Moses' engagement in the disastrous voyage of the *Sally*. Moses said as much on repeated occasions in the years that followed. More mysterious is the lapse of eight years between the return of that doomed ship and the moment Moses moved to acknowledge the imperatives of his conscience. During that interim period, Moses never expressed any gnawing doubts, never hinted at any sense of guilt. That absence may suggest the strength of the social conventions that buttressed the institutions of slavery, or conversely, the depth of the inner dialogue that led Moses to his conversion. But the protracted delay did not diminish the degree of his commitment once Moses came around.

Of course, Moses' share in the *Sally* was not his only encounter with the institution of slavery. More immediate, he had faced in his everyday life the moral dilemmas that accrued to anyone who held Africans in bondage in colonial America.

In September 1770, Moses learned during a stay at Newport that his slave Pero, a boy in his teens, was assaulted while walking down a street in Providence. Pero was hit in the back of the head by a paving stone thrown by an Irish immigrant. Knocked unconscious, he was "taken up for dead," but under a doctor's care he revived. Racism against blacks was widespread, and slaves were always vulnerable to assault from the general population, as well as from their owners.

Moses felt obliged to look out for the welfare of his slaves, but found that even in his own household he had to be vigilant. The story of one sobering incident was passed down by one of the slaves on his farm to his grandson, who later published it in a memoir. Noah Brown, the father, was born in Providence, the son of an African imported on a Brown family ship—most likely, one of the four boys delivered by the *Sally*. Noah and his two brothers worked the fields at Elmgrove, or were hired out to other farms, with Moses collecting their wages. The tale told by Noah's son provides a rare, intimate glimpse at the operations of Moses' farm, and relations in his family.

> My father during his youth worked on the farm belonging to Moses Brown, and at one time he had occasion to find fault with his food, which displeased [Anna] Brown very much. She was accustomed to save all their turkey carcasses until they were musty, and then make soup for the men. So every morning they were treated to some musty soup for breakfast. Week after week this was continued, and nobody dared say anything for fear of offending someone. One morning after the horn had been blown for breakfast, father came in advance of the men, and looking on the table beheld the soup and exclaimed, "Musty soup again—damn the musty soup." Then to his surprise he saw Mr. Brown partly behind the door wiping his hands. "What did thee say, my boy?" said Mr. Brown. "I said musty soup," said

father. "Is that soup musty?" said Mr. Brown. "Yes sir," said father. Mr. Brown ordered a spoon, and tasted of the soup, which he ordered to be put in the swill. By this time the field hands had come in. Mr. Brown asked them how long they had been eating musty soup. They replied, "Several weeks in succession." Mr. Brown sent for his wife to come into the kitchen, and said to her in the presence of the men, "Is not my house able to give good victuals? Here you have been feeding them week after week on musty soup. I have tasted it; it is fit for nothing but hogs. I don't wish you to give them any more such stuff; they work hard and should have good victuals, and I am able to give it to them." Then to the men he said: "Why did you not speak to me about your victuals? You have been going on week after week and said not a word, until this boy had to speak for you. Hereafter, if everything is not right, come to me." After Mr. Brown's departure, his wife called my father a black devil, and said he should not sleep with the men any longer, but should have his lodgings in the attic room. This was quite a severe punishment to my father, as he was compelled to retire soon after eight o'clock. Mr. Brown was very particular that his men should not be overworked, and allowed no punishment on his farm. He was always willing to grant his men leave of absence whenever they desired. This made them more willing to work. . . .

Moses probably never learned that Anna had punished Noah, but he certainly felt the gulf between master and servant, and the mixture of tension, resentment, and fear that attended the lives of even the best-kept slaves.

Whether Moses concluded suddenly to sever his ties to slavery, or over the course of months, his decision came as part of a wholesale revision of his priorities in life. In August, Moses decided to make a final break with the family firm. "After the most deliberate consideration," he wrote in a letter to his brothers, "I verily believe my business and ingagements in the world has been a principal means of preventing my injoying any increase of that better part that has a foundation and will indure when all things here below will vanish and be no more." Moses withheld that letter in order to contemplate even further; a month later, after a brief journey with a new Quaker acquaintance, he wrote once again, proposing detailed terms for dissolution of the shipping business, the candle works, and the Hope Furnace. "Dear Brothers," he wrote, "this looks to me and feels like separating bone from marrow . . . but that brother love may continue . . . is the desire of your affectionate brother." The family accepted his decision in good spirit, Nicholas explaining to his firm's London agent that Moses "has removed to his seat out of town where he may enjoy himself and his friends consistent with a serious contemplative mind."

Finally, in November 1773, Moses turned his attention to his slaves. On the fourth day of that month, Mary Brown, Anna's sister, freed her slave Eve, along with Eve's daughter. The preamble to her deed of manumission stated Mary's thinking: "I am sensible that the holding of Negroes in slavery, however kindly used by their masters and mistresses, has a tendency to encourage the iniquitous practice of importing them from their native country. . . ."

Six days later, a Tuesday, Moses followed suit. He was hosting several visitors from out of town, and called them together, along with everyone in the household, and all of his slaves, to mark the occasion. After leading the group in silent prayer, Moses turned to his slaves and read to them from a prepared statement. "Whereas I am clearly convinced that buying and selling of men of what color soever as slaves is contrary to the Divine Mind manifest in the consciences of all men however some may smother and neglect its reprovings . . . I do therefore by these presents for myself, my heirs etc. manumit and set free the following Negroes being all I am possessed of or any ways interested in."

Moses named six slaves—Bonno, Caesar, Cudjo, Prime, the boy Pero, and Pegg, aged from eighteen to thirty-four years. He then renounced his claim to three slaves whom he held in common with his brothers, Yarrow, Tom, and Newport, though they would remain in bondage to the family enterprises. Lastly, Moses named the child Phyllis, "aged about two years born in my family."

Moses went on in his papers of manumission to detail at some length the parameters of his new relations with his former slaves, and the efforts he would make to help them get on their feet. He offered as his "direction and advice" that the freed workers should deposit with Moses their surplus wages, for which he would provide interest and a receipt, and which they might use in case of illness, "or to be applied to the use of your children (if free), and if not, to the purchasing of their freedom." Further, to encourage "sober prudence and industry," Moses offered "the use of one acre of land as marked off on my farm as long as you improve it to good purpose.

"I no longer consider you as slaves, or myself as your master but your friend," Moses explained, warning them to "use not the liberty thereby to go into or practice lusts of the flesh, the lusts of the eye or pride or any occasion for temptation, but be more cautious than heretofore."

The tract Moses wrote granting freedom to his slaves also provided insight into the degree to which Moses had embraced the tenets of the Quakers. His former slaves might not be able to read, and thus might plead ignorance of the scriptures, "But there is a book within you that is not confined to the English or any language," Moses wrote. "And as you silently and reverently wait for its openings and instantly it will teach you and you will be able to understand its language and as you are careful to be obedient thereto and often silently read it, you will be able to speak its language with African as well as English tongues. . . ."

It's hard to say what the assembled slaves might have made of this admonition, but it was a clear statement of a central tenet of the Quakers, who, almost alone among Protestant sects, regarded the Bible as a guide but not the word of God. Rather, the Quakers believed that each individual had his or her own intimate connection with God, who revealed himself through the workings of conscience. This distinction was made explicit in *Barclay's Apology*, a treatise with wide circulation in the colonies: "We cannot go the length of those Protestants who derive their authority from the virtue and power that is in the writings themselves. We desire to ascribe everything to the Spirit from which it came." Moses was convinced that by looking within, his former slaves would be able to discern naturally right from wrong. It was a simple enough precept but it set Moses apart; many Quakers opposed slavery but only a few—John Woolman and Anthony Benezet among them—acknowledged Africans as their spiritual equals.

As obvious a moral affront as slavery appears today, there was no consensus on the evils inherent to slavery at the time Moses freed his slaves in 1773. Opposition to slavery was, in fact, espoused by a tiny minority, controversial even among the Quakers, and considered heretical by theologians and political thinkers on both sides of the Atlantic. In the West Indies in particular, but also in North and South America, slavery was the engine that drove the mercantile empires of Europe. The institution was as old as time—finding explicit sanction in the Bible, and in the glory days of Greece and Rome—and had flourished, in its modern form, for two hundred years. It appeared, in the eighteenth century, as universal and as immutable as human nature.

The facts of slavery were there for all to see—the cruel business of capturing and chaining the people of Africa, the grim conditions of the middle passage and plantation agriculture, the high rates of slave mortality, and the inescapable injustice of lifelong servitude. But it stands as an enduring testament to the influence of social convention that these conditions were rarely questioned, and when they were, the dissidents themselves were castigated.

The early protest against slavery raised by Samuel Sewall serves as a case in point. Scion of a wealthy merchant family, a jurist and member of the governing council in Massachusetts, Sewall demonstrated his propensity for painful introspection when he recanted, in 1697, the guilty verdicts he'd pronounced at the Salem witch trials. Three years later, Sewall voiced his conscience again, this time as author of a tract against slavery titled *The Selling of Joseph.*

Sewall owned slaves himself, but he was roused to act by a legal claim for freedom filed on behalf of a slave owned by John Saffin, another prosperous Boston merchant. Leaving the facts of that case aside, Sewall looked to the Bible in expounding on the questions of servitude and freedom. "All men, as they are sons of Adam, have equal right unto liberty," Sewall held. "God hath said, He that stealeth a man and selleth him, or if he be found in his hand, he shall surely be put to death." If the Bible weren't authority enough, Sewall called upon a common sense of decency. "How horrible is the uncleanness, mortality, if not murder, that the ships are guilty of that bring great crowds of these miserable men and women."

Despite his umbrage, Sewall was not ready to acknowledge blacks as equal to whites. "They can never use their freedom well," he offered; "they can never embody with us, and grow up into orderly families." But they were people nonetheless, and Sewall worked out an elaborate defense against the usual arguments supporting slavery. To those who believed slaves to be lawful prisoners of war, Sewall pointed out that "every war is upon one side unjust," and that "unlawful war can't make lawful captives." To the argument that heathen slaves were blessed by exposure to Christianity, he said simply, "Evil must not be done, that good may come out of it." More troubling was the ambiguity in the Bible itself. In particular, the scriptures relate the story of Abraham, who kept slaves. All Sewall could add was that "until the circumstances of Abraham's purchase be recorded, no argument can be drawn from it."

If Sewall believed his mock argument would satisfy his critics, he was soon disappointed. A year later, John Saffin published a biting rejoinder. Central to his case was an argument against the very idea of equality. The proposition of equal rights "seems to invert the order that God hath set in the world, who hath ordained different degrees and orders of men, some to be high and honorable, others to be low and despicable." It wasn't just slavery Saffin was defending, but the system of indentured servitude as well, whereby proprietors "deprive our brethren, of our own or other Christian nations of the liberty, (though but for a time) by binding them to serve some seven, ten, fifteen, and some twenty years, which oft times proves their whole life." Ending slavery, Saffin suggested, would undermine the entire social order.

With that, Saffin presented a vicious ditty called "The Negroes Character":

Cowardly and cruel are those blacks innate,
Prone to revenge, imp of inveterate hate . . .
Libidinous, deceitful, false and rude,
The spume issue of ingratitude.

That Saffin enjoyed the weight of public opinion is evident from Sewall's lament, as he put it in a letter to a friend, that his agitation against slavery had earned him "frowns and hard words." In any event, public challenges to slavery remained exceedingly rare for the next fifty years. When controversy did arise, it usually turned on the question of how slaves should be treated, and whether they were candidates for ecclesiastic instruction. Similarly, efforts to limit or ban the slave trade were widespread, but they were usually based on the conviction that slavery was detrimental to white society, and not out of concern for the slaves themselves. At any rate, such measures were routinely vetoed by the crown, which saw the African trade as an economic mainstay. It was not until the Stamp Act and its perceived threats to colonial liberties that Americans again stopped to examine the moral implications of human chattel.

But while mainstream writers and thinkers were largely silent on the question of slavery, the Society of Friends was not. Alone among the constellation of Protestant faiths to seek freedom of worship in the New World, Quakers were continually troubled by the institution of human bondage, and resolved, in growing numbers as the years went by, to rid themselves of the practice. It was not, however, a stand arrived at suddenly or quickly, but haltingly, and by degrees.

In the beginning, at a time when when Quakers were being persecuted in England as well as in Boston, Friends were deeply involved in slavery, especially on the island of Barbados, where Friends operated sugar plantations, and at Newport, where Quakers Abraham Redwood and the senior Joseph Wanton were pioneers in the African trade. By 1671, George Fox, the founder of the church and architect of its westward expansion, visited Barbados to find hundreds of Africans toiling and dying under the tropical sun. Fox held services on the island for slaves as well as their masters, and felt moved to admonish the slaveholders: "Christ died for all . . . for the tawnies and the blacks as well as for you the whites."

Following on this maxim, Fox advised the plantation owners to raise their slaves as Christians, and even "to let them go free after a considerable term of years, if they have served faithfully. . . . This, I say, will be very acceptable to the lord." But Fox went no further; when the non-Quaker slaveholders of Barbados accused him of encouraging slave revolt, Fox demurred, rejecting the accusation as a "most egregious and abominable untruth." Four years later,

Barbados passed a law barring Quakers from holding services for their slaves. Soon after, when William Penn established his Quaker colony on the Delaware, slavery was instituted as a matter of course.

Yet Fox's early doubts set the pattern for sporadic challenges to slaveholding from within the sect. William Edmundson, a traveling companion of Fox's, issued a circular letter from Newport in 1676, which proclaimed that "perpetual slavery is an aggravation, and an oppression upon the mind." Twelve years later, a group of German and Dutch Quakers in Pennsylvania posed the question at their Monthly Meeting: "Have these Negroes not as much right to fight for their freedom as you do to have them as slaves?" As it was raised in formal session, the appeal could not be ignored; the Germantown petition was referred to the Quarterly Meeting, and finally the Yearly Meeting, which concluded feebly that "it was adjudged not to be proper for this meeting to give a positive judgment in the case, it having so general a relation to many other parts; and therefore at present they forebear it."

The Quakers of Germantown remained the exception; Quaker merchants in Philadelphia showed just as much enthusiasm for the slave trade as merchants in other colonial ports. Yet as the years went by, voices of protest arose everywhere Quakers had settled: John Hepburn in New Jersey in 1715, William Burling in New York in 1718, Ralph Sandiford in Philadelphia, Elihu Coleman in Nantucket in 1731. The high-water mark for the early abolitionists was reached in 1711, when the Pennsylvania assembly voted a prohibitive tax on imported slaves, but the scheme failed when it was vetoed on the higher authority of the Privy Council. The Friends' leadership in England was little help, as Quakers there were fearful of offending the royal court, but the London Meeting did recommend against participation in the slave trade.

In the 1730s, the crank and visionary Benjamin Lay, an itinerant hunchback who lived for many years in a cave outside Philadelphia, refused to settle for the polite modes of petitions and pleadings. After publishing his tract *All Slave-Keepers: Apostates*, Lay took to the road, traveling throughout Pennsylvania and New Jersey to harangue ministers and church elders as hypocrites, and to be forcibly ejected from a score of quiet meetings. Still he refused to be ignored: on one occasion, he kidnapped some Friends' children to force their parents to feel the pain of the Africans. On another, he secreted a bladder of fake blood in a hollowed-out Bible, then raised it during the course of a New Jersey meeting, and stabbed it with a sword, splattering the shocked worshipers nearby and declaring that slave masters might just as well "thrust a sword through their hearts as I do with this book!" In 1738, Lay was publicly disowned by the Philadelphia Meeting.

The accumulated incidents of Quaker protest raise the question of why the Society of Friends would prove so susceptible to a moral quandary that other faiths successfully avoided. The answer appears to lie in the unique nature of Quaker worship. Instead of following the dictates of scripture, as interpreted by ordained authority, Quakers insisted that spiritual insight came from within, and that "truth," as revealed by "inner light," was their guiding principle. Meetings, then and now, were marked by silence and introspection, and by individual statements of faith and conviction. Shorn of attachments to convention or institution, the Quaker conscience fixed on the inescapable conflict between the practice of slavery and the simple logic of the Golden Rule.

Even so, the Quakers were a church as well as a method. For all their emphasis on individual insight, they sought consensus in their meetings, and imposed "discipline" by ostracizing or banishing dissidents. Moreover, as outsiders who prized the freedom to pursue their beliefs, they were leery of challenging the established social order. Like Benjamin Lay, many of the most aggressive early critics of slavery were disowned, and it took a century for the Friends to move from intuition to policy.

Still, it was among the Quakers that the question of slavery refused to rest easy. If the heyday of the slave system can be considered a dark age, the persistent challenge raised by the Quaker dissidents appears as the light of a torch on a windy night, blazing and then sinking into darkness, then flaring again.

As the seat of the colonial slave trade, Newport also became the site for some of the most forward Quaker protests against slavery. In 1714 and again in 1717, the New England Yearly Meeting was confronted with fervent appeals on behalf of slaves, which it answered by posing the question "to Friends everywhere, to wait for the wisdom of God how to discharge themselves of that weighty affair"; in the meantime, Quakers were asked "to write to their correspondents in the islands . . . to discourage their sending any more [slaves] in order to be sold by any Friends here." In 1744, that admonition was expanded to proscribe buying slaves from non-Quaker importers.

But it was not until the latter part of the 1750s that American Quakers moved from questioning slavery to actively challenging it. The catalyst was John Woolman, a clerk and tailor from New Jersey who developed convictions against slavery in his youth, and then devoted his time to sojourns through the South and the mid-Atlantic colonies, where slavery was deeply entrenched. "I saw in these southern provinces so many vices and corruptions increased by this trade and this way of life, that it appeared to me as a dark gloominess hanging over the land," Woolman wrote later. "Though many now willingly run into it, yet in the future the consequences will be grievous to posterity."

With his convictions thus "fixed on my mind," Woolman made his way to Pennsylvania, and in collaboration with the prolific pamphleteer Anthony Benezet, set about composing his critique of slavery for a broad audience. His *Considerations on the Keeping of Negroes* was published by the Philadelphia Yearly Meeting and distributed to every Quaker meeting in America, and to England as well. The response was electric: in 1758, the Friends in London at last issued an unequivocal denunciation of the slave trade, and later that year, the Philadelphia Meeting moved past its warning against trading in slaves, now proposing that Friends who held slaves should set them free. Further, they issued an edict that Quakers who bought or sold slaves should be barred from holding positions in the church, and deputized Woolman and four others to visit slaveholders and exhort them "towards obtaining that purity which it is evidently our duty to press after."

This was a resounding achievement after twenty years of patient persuasion, but Woolman didn't relax his efforts. In 1760 he traveled to Newport, where he found the waterfront crowded with the spoils of the slave trade — hogsheads of rum and molasses, distilleries on every alley, and human cargo for sale in the market. Despite the vested interests of some of the members, he prevailed on the New England Yearly Meeting to issue its strongest directive against the trade to date: "We fervently warn all in profession with us that they be careful to avoid being in any way concerned in reaping the unrighteous profits of that iniquitous practice in dealing with Negroes." On the same trip north, Woolman visited the slave plantations of Narragansett country, where he held several general meetings and conducted "deep exercises" with a number of slaveholding families.

It was another five years before Woolman accomplished on a personal level the sort of institutional success he'd achieved in the Quaker meetings. Continuing in his lifelong mission, he traveled on foot through slave districts of Delaware and the Eastern Shore of Maryland, trekking across tidal flats and tobacco plantations to meet with families and individual slaveholders. Here his efforts yielded more incremental but more tangible results than any of his writing and lobbying: a spate of manumissions, beginning with two in 1767. The following year, one Sarah Powell freed four slaves; a man named Benjamin Berry freed nine. These acts of manumission represented substantial sacrifice: the relinquishment of a valuable personal estate that took years to acquire.

More important, they marked a signal breakthrough for the idea that appeals to conscience might actually succeed in subverting the iron economic logic of slavery. There are scattered reports of Quaker manumissions prior to the 1760s, but most cases involved posthumous grants of freedom that slave owners entered in their wills. The manumissions induced by Woolman in Delaware and Maryland were virtually unprecedented. Moreover, the practice continued in the years after Woolman departed eastern Maryland, spurred by the Nicholites, disciples of a maverick preacher named Joseph Nichols.

The Quaker manumissions movement arrived at Rhode Island shortly before Moses Brown granted his slaves their freedom. The first to act were the Quakers of South Kingston, in the heart of the slave-laden Narragansett country. Here Tom Hazard, son of the largest slaveholder in the region, refused to accept possession of any of that legacy upon his father's demise in 1762. As a delegate to the Quarterly Meeting, Hazard delivered the query from South Kingston, in 1769, which proposed that all Friends be "clear" of holding slaves. The answer came in stages: in 1770, the Yearly Meeting directed that Friends should grant liberty to any slaves "that are of age, capacity, and ability suitable for freedom." Finally, in 1773, the language was simplified, and the New England Yearly Meeting became the first Quaker council to require that all Friends free all their slaves.

Still, most Quakers who actually held slaves remained unconvinced. As one writer observed, progress "on the slavery question was made . . . not by convincing so many slave-owners, as by turning out those who were unconvinced." Thus Moses Brown's manumission of seven slaves was virtually unprecedented in Rhode Island, and created something of a sensation in the Quaker councils of New England. Four months later, in March 1774, Moses formally applied for admission into the Society of Friends. He was admitted April 24, 1774, and from that time forward he adopted the Quaker practice of wearing simple clothes and a broad-brimmed hat that he removed only in the meetinghouse.

The question arises: did Moses join the Quakers in answer to his guilty association with slavery, or did he renounce slavery in order to gain the acceptance of the Quakers? From the time of the French and Indian War, the Quakers had turned inward, disavowing members who married "out of meeting" and cutting off much of their contact with the world at large. Moses may have believed that he needed to make some grand public gesture to pave his way into the good graces of the Friends. But whatever his motives, Moses wholly embraced his new role. In joining the Quakers, and in his act of manumission, Moses took his place at the forefront of a movement against slavery that was just emerging as a genuine threat to property interests, and a challenge to the ideals of liberty, throughout the British colonies of North America.

The Quakers took the lead in the moral struggle against slavery, but by the time Moses made his momentous conversion in 1773, the Friends were no longer alone. In Europe, the advent of the Enlightenment had given rise to a humanist critique of slavery, articulated by voices as disparate as the baron de Montesquieu in France and the Scot jurist George Wallace. Yet the capitals of Europe never countenanced slavery at home—just in their colonies—and the leaders of the Enlightenment remained divided on the question, with writers like John Locke giving the institution explicit endorsement. It was left to the Americans to formulate their own response to their more immediate confrontation with slavery. They did so around the time of the Stamp Act, when Americans first began to enunciate their ideas of liberty and natural rights.

In Massachusetts, the contradiction between the language of liberty and the fact of slavery was impossible to ignore, as was pointed out by slaves themselves in a raft of petitions filed with the General Court. "We have in common with all other men a natural right to our freedoms," one asserted. And in Philadelphia, the physician Benjamin Rush, who would play such a prominent role in the coming Revolution, observed in 1773 that "Anthony Benezet stood alone a few years ago in opposing slavery in Philadelphia; and now three-fourths of the province, as well as of the city, cry out against it."

But if the idea of slavery was losing public sway, the institution of slavery remained entrenched. In Boston, the freedom petitions filed by slaves and free blacks were summarily rejected. And in Rhode Island, slavery was still deeply enmeshed in daily life—especially for the elite. In Providence, that meant more than one hundred of the most prominent families kept Africans slaves to cook in their kitchens and mind their horses and carriages. According to a census taken in 1774, the slaveholders included each of Moses' brothers—John claimed two, Nicholas two, and Joseph four—along with such family friends as Daniel Jenckes, who owned four slaves, Jabez Bowen, who had one, *Providence Gazette* editor John Carter, who had at least one, and Esek Hopkins, who kept four.

It was true as well, as the early provincial chroniclers liked to point out, that slavery was often more intimate, and less severe, in New England than on the plantations of the Southern colonies and the Caribbean. The distinction is reflected in the will of a sea captain who bequeathed for "my Negro man Jeffrey

. . . that he chall chuse which of my children or my grand children he shall think proper to live with . . . or any other person as he thinks proper to take him . . . and in case any of my children shall see cause not to accept of said Negro then he shall be kept and maintained by my executor." Jeffrey might have been a slave, but his was not the sort of subjugation that so moved Benjamin Lay and the Quaker activists in Philadelphia.

This more nuanced state of servitude made some aspects of New England slavery less painful to endure, but all the more difficult to eradicate. The paradox was brought into stark relief in Providence at the very moment that Moses stepped to the forefront of the Quaker campaign. During the same year, as part of their "testimony against slaveholding," the Quaker meeting at Smithfield demanded that Stephen Hopkins set free his household slave. And Stephen Hopkins, early Son of Liberty, former governor, then serving as chief justice of the superior court and Providence deputy to the General Assembly, refused.

The details of the case are puzzling, as the 1774 census showed six Africans living in the Hopkins household, and no formal papers of manumission were filed for any of them. But the Quaker challenge concerned only one, "a Negroe woman," as recorded in the minutes of the Smithfield Monthly Meeting. But regardless of the circumstances of the other five, the status of this single slave gave rise to the impasse.

The confrontation began with a visit by two delegates from the meeting, who reported on January 28, 1773, that Hopkins "desires Friends not to act hastily." Two months later, the minutes show that Hopkins "still refuses to set her at liberty tho often requested." The Quakers responded with deliberate determination. Moses Farnum, the clerk of the meeting, was assigned with an associate to draw up a "Paper of Denial" that would expel Hopkins from the meeting if he continued to resist. The document was presented on April 29, and consideration deferred until June. Farnum was busy that month; it was he who interviewed Moses Brown, reviewed his credentials, and recommended his admission to the meeting.

Finally, on June 24, "the matter concerning the Testimony of Stephen Hopkins' Denial was considered, and said Testimony was approved of." A month after Moses was taken into the meeting, his mentor Stephen Hopkins was disowned. It was a wrenching decision, though not so extreme as it might appear; Hopkins assented without protest, and while he was barred from attending the business sessions of the meeting, he continued to worship at the Providence meetinghouse.

Moses Brown never recorded his reaction to the meeting's move against

Hopkins, but it appears to have had little impact on their personal relationship. Nor, surprisingly, did his disownment steel Hopkins against the growing abolition movement. In fact, at the very time that Hopkins was defying his fellow Quakers' demand that he free his slave, Hopkins teamed with Moses to author the most advanced legislation against the slave trade yet to be presented to a government body in America. The occasion was the surging, even revolutionary, resentment against Great Britain. Colonial anger at Parliament had given rise, in December 1773, to the Boston Tea Party, and the British reaction had precipitated a full-blown crisis.

Providence responded to the events at Boston with a town meeting, called by warrant January 19 to consider measures that might "contribute towards escaping the dreadful train of evils which must be the consequence of a tame submission to any invasions of American Freedom." Jabez Bowen was the moderator, and John Brown, now notorious as a patriot firebrand, played a prominent role.

Many colonists considered the sudden deterioration of relations with England a fearful prospect, but the mood in Providence was distinctly belligerent. The duties on tea represented a tax, the meeting resolved, and any tax by Parliament "has a direct tendency to render [colonial] assemblies useless, and to introduce arbitrary government and slavery." Regarding tea in particular, the meeting appointed a committee, including Bowen and John Brown, to ensure that no new shipments be ordered, and to correspond with other towns and colonies on any affairs "thought to affect the liberties of America."

The reference to slavery was commonplace for the colonial protests against Britain: back in 1764, in his *Rights of the Colonies Examined*, Stephen Hopkins had proclaimed that "those who are governed at the will of another, and whose property may be taken from them by taxes . . . without their own consent . . . are in the miserable condition of slaves." In the years since, the metaphor had become ubiquitous: the acts of Parliament would end in "perpetual slavery," "unmerited slavery," "vile ignominious slavery." The obvious connection to the actual practice of slavery by those same liberty-loving colonists was rarely mentioned. But in May 1774, Moses Brown saw a chance to make that link explicit.

The opportunity arose from the death of Jacob Schoemaker, an elderly landowner from the Caribbean island of Antigua who lived in Providence off the rented labor of his slave Tom. As Shoemaker died intestate, Tom, his wife, and their four young children became property of the town. Moses seized on their plight, petitioning the town meeting to set Tom and his family free.

The case was heard May 17, at an emergency meeting called to answer the latest outrage from England—the Boston Port Bill, which closed that harbor to all shipping except food and fuel until the East India Company was paid for its lost cargo of tea. The patriots at Providence, never patient with the provocations from Parliament, now moved to the forefront of the radical movement. Gathered together at the statehouse, the freemen endorsed the first formal call issued anywhere on the continent "for promoting a congress, as soon as may be, of the representatives of the General Assemblies of the several colonies and provinces of North America, for establishing the firmest union." The resolution went on to propose what that congress would eventually adopt as its primary economic weapon, a "universal stoppage of all trade with Great Britain, Ireland, Africa and the West Indies."

The next clause of that same groundbreaking resolution shows how Moses was able to capitalize on the revolutionary fervor at the meeting. It cites the case of Schoemaker and his slaves, and asserted "that it is unbecoming the character of freemen to enslave the said Negroes; and they do hereby give up all claim of right or property in them."

That was not all. "Whereas the inhabitants of America are engaged in the preservation of their rights and liberties; and as personal liberty is an essential part of the natural rights of mankind, the deputies of the town are directed to use their endeavors to obtain an act of the General Assembly prohibiting the importation of Negro slaves into this colony; and that all Negroes born in the colony, should be free, after obtaining to a certain age." In May 1774, in Providence, the ardor for liberty had spilled over to include even the degraded Africans.

This was a heady moment for Moses. As a new Quaker and by his personal inclination, Moses was dubious of the rising ire against England and opposed to any resort to arms. Yet his new mission to seek justice for the Africans in America seemed to be rapidly gaining ground. Much as Benjamin Rush had observed in Philadelphia, Moses' brother Nicholas commented in a letter on "the present disposition of people in New England against slavery."

Following the directive of the town meeting, Moses sat down with Stephen Hopkins to compose a bill banning the slave trade in the colony—the more difficult question of emancipation was left to a later date. The language was simple, and couched in the rhetoric of the rebellion against England. "Whereas the inhabitants of America are generally engaged in the preservation of their own rights and liberties," the preamble read, and "as those who are desirous of enjoying all the advantages of liberty themselves, should be willing to extend personal liberty to others; Therefore, be it enacted . . . that for the future, no Negro or mulatto slave shall be brought into this colony; and in case any slave shall hereafter be brought in, he or she shall be, and are hereby, rendered immediately free."

In June, Moses traveled with Hopkins to Newport to push the bill. Hopkins was a Providence delegate to the assembly, Moses served as his scribe and his conscience. It was a time of anticipation, and great aspiration. The New England Yearly Meeting was gathering in Newport at the same time, with its own campaign against slaveholding at the top of the agenda. Moses had also opened a correspondence with Anthony Benezet, the leading abolitionist in Philadelphia (John Woolman having died, in 1772, on a visit to England). Benezet forwarded a letter from Patrick Henry, the Virginia patriot, who denounced the slave trade as "repugnant to the first impressions of right and wrong." Henry held slaves himself, but admitted in his letter, "I am drawn along by the general inconvenience of living without them; I will not, I cannot, justify it." It appeared the whole edifice of slavery was on the verge of collapse.

As the assembly convened, prospects for the slave-trade bill were bright. Moses and Stephen Hopkins had obtained the support of Henry Ward, brother of Hopkins's longtime rival, and so both sides of the colony's enduring political divide were on board. Once the bill was introduced, Moses departed the Colony House confident of success.

To his dismay, he found afterward he had left too soon. Upon "the solicitation of some Guinea and West Indies merchants," Moses learned later, the assembly attached a series of riders that all but gutted the bill. They included exceptions for nonresidents who moved into the colony with their slaves and, crucially, for any Africans imported by slave traders who could not dispose of their cargo in the West Indies. Such traders were explicitly granted a full year to re-export their slaves. Lastly, as if to underscore the defeat of the bill's original sensibility, the act provided penalties of one hundred pounds "to prevent any slave or slaves from being clandestinely brought into this colony, in order that they may be free."

All the bill achieved, then, was to end the importation of slaves for sale within the colony. Since most Newport slave traders already disposed of their captives outside the colony, and since the number of slaves residing in Rhode Island was already in decline, the practical impact of the final act was nil.

There is no record of Stephen Hopkins's efforts in behalf of the bill, but he had other pressing matters to attend to. Following the lead of Providence, and of the Virginia House of Burgesses, the assembly endorsed a "firm and inviolable union of all the colonies." And even before Philadelphia had been settled on as the site of the first congress, Rhode Island named its delegates: Stephen Hopkins and Samuel Ward. Thus the colony united behind the leaders of its two great factions to face off against the august, and angry, British empire. Hopkins and Ward had the honor of being the first delegates named to attend the historic congress; their failure to extend the spirit of liberty to the slave trade was all but forgotten.

Still, Moses Brown had embarked on what he surely recognized would be a protracted crusade against slavery. After making a formal break with his past, he had adopted a course of atonement and spiritual development, and he pursued it with stubborn determination.

In the months after his defeat at Newport, Moses pressed his campaign on several fronts. Within the Society of Friends, he lobbied others to follow the example he set in freeing his slaves. The results were sometimes ambiguous, as in the case of Caleb Greene, a devout Quaker who lived in New Bedford, Massachusetts, and attended the Smithfield meeting. Greene agreed, toward the end of the year, to release his interest in two slaves, citing "a desire to remove as far as may be the evil practice [of slavery] by complying with the manifestations of that divine light that has shined and is shining in the minds of men." Yet Greene could release only a third interest in one slave and a half interest in another; neither Greene nor Moses was able to convince James Lovett, a Providence businessman who owned the balance of interest in both slaves, to renounce his stake in the bondsmen.

Moses also found that emancipation could be a fearfully transitory state. That fall, creditors from Antigua moved to claim the slaves of Jacob Schoemaker—the same ones freed by decree of the Providence town meeting. The claim was made via John, who handed off the papers to Nicholas; who consulted with Moses before responding. The claimants had apparently gotten hold of Schoemaker's Antigua's slaves, and were demanding the return of Tom and his family. Nicholas advised that "there is no getting possession of them without an expensive [law]suit," and suggested that a New England jury would likely find in favor of the children, especially. Moreover, he wrote, "I have a brother (Moses Brown) a person of influence in this colony, who is so deeply impressed with a sense of duty, to use his influence against keeping or making slaves . . . that he told me lately, he would be at the expense of a lawsuit himself before they should be carried away to the West Indies as slaves."

Nicholas added that "Brother John Brown [was] much of the same way of thinking."

Beyond his personal exertions in specific cases, Moses did what he could to promote his cause in print. He prevailed on John Carter at the *Gazette* to publish several articles criticizing the slave trade, and sent antislavery tracts to correspondents in several colonies. Aware that Quaker writers were often dismissed as zealots, Moses emphasized the writings of non-Quakers like John Wesley, the founder of the Methodist Church, who came out against slavery around that time, and the London abolitionist Granville Sharp, who was publicly skeptical of Quakers. Moses was devoted to his new faith, but he remained a practical and savvy advocate.

These various activities were important, but politics remained Moses' primary focus. That fall he did all he could to recapture the momentum of the Providence town meeting, and with the issue of the slave trade effectively preempted by the Newport slaving interests, he returned to the question of emancipation. Anticipating the next meeting of the General Assembly, set for East Greenwich in October, Moses directed a petition drive that registered signatures from "all the lawyers of principal note in the colony" endorsing a plan to grant freedom to all slaves born in Rhode Island upon their arriving at the age of twenty-one. This scheme for incremental emancipation was less than a pure abolition, but was calculated to sidestep the difficult question of confiscating the property of slaveholders. It would bring freedom slowly but surely.

It was a sign of the waning public support for slavery that two of the signators to the petition were Nicholas and John Brown. But their endorsement also serves to show the gulf between public support and private interest. Whatever they said publicly about slavery, and whatever they told Moses, Nicholas and John both continued to deal in slaves as part of their stock in trade. That October, Nicholas included "a Negro boy" in partial payment for a shipment of pearl ash. The boy was sent off to live with a new master in Massachusetts. As for John, he continued buying and selling Africans, but took steps to conceal it. One artifice he adopted suggests a sense of irony; in shipping orders to one of his sea captains, John advised securing "Orin Briggs" as part of a return cargo from the West Indies. This was a sly reference to Aaron Briggs, the unfortunate would-be informant from the *Gaspee* affair. "Orin Briggs" was John's code word for "slave."

The petition for a gradual abolition bill was tabled by the General Assembly in October. But Moses was buoyed by news from Philadelphia, where the members of the Continental Congress, the first conclave of delegates from twelve of the British colonies of North America—Georgia was not represented—deliberated on how to answer the latest escalation from Parliament. Joseph Galloway of Pennsylvania proposed a conciliatory scheme for an American legislature that would serve under a president general appointed by the king, but that was narrowly defeated. Instead, the Congress agreed to a sweeping economic boycott that would end all imports from Great Britain beginning December 1, and if relations did not soon improve, an additional ban on exports from America, to begin in September 1775.

Moses followed the progress of the Congress through correspondence with Thomas Arnold, a young Friend and nephew of Stephen Hopkins, who attended his uncle in Philadelphia. Arnold wrote to Moses in September that he was not allowed into the debates, but that he was "informed in confidence" of what transpired. "I am not without hope that they will take the slavery of Negroes under consideration, at least in so far as to endeavor to remove the obstructions to passing acts of assembly for eradicating this evil," Arnold wrote, a reference to Parliamentary vetoes of bills to stop the slave trade.

In fact, after intense lobbying by Anthony Benezet and the other Quakers in Philadelphia, the Congress went further. The second article of the Continental Association, as the agreement to ban imports was called, said explicitly, "We will neither import nor purchase, any slave imported after the first of December next; after which time we will wholly discontinue the slave trade, and will neither be concerned in it ourselves, nor will we hire our vessels, nor sell our commodities or manufactures to those who are concerned in it." The new Congress had achieved what the Rhode Island legislature could not.

Flush with this news, Moses in November hosted a visit by a group of Quakers from Philadelphia, who were guiding Friends from London on a religious tour of America. Among them was John Pemberton, one of the leaders of the Philadelphia Meeting. Like Moses, Pemberton was partner with two brothers, Israel and James, in a merchant firm that found great success trading with the West Indies and had once been active in the slave trade. Unlike the Browns, however, the Pembertons had renounced the slave trade as a group, and underwent a shared political conversion that left them vigorous critics of slavery. Working closely with Benezet, they had pushed the movement against slavery at the Pennsylvania Meeting; in 1774, the Philadelphia Meeting agreed to disown any member found selling or transferring slaves. This was not so advanced as the standard against slaveholding adopted by New England, but it was a strong and unequivocal policy.

Moses spent two weeks on the road with Pemberton and several New England Friends, including Anna's sister Mary and Mary Olney. The troupe visited Taunton, Salem, and Boston, moving briskly until John Pemberton fell ill near Lynn, Massachusetts. There Moses "tarryed with him 5 days," during which Pemberton recovered and formed a lasting bond with the converted Baptist. First John and then his brother James became important correspondents with Moses, sharing their thoughts on the successive crises that confronted Quakers during the war years, and reporting on their respective efforts on behalf of "the poor Africans."

These new friends came to supplant Moses' old ones as his primary points of reference. He never had an overt break with Stephen Hopkins and the Sons of Liberty, or with John Brown and the other members of his family. But on matters of conscience and questions of practice, Moses came to rely on James Pemberton and the Quaker elders of New England and Philadelphia as his counselors and confidants. By the time the colonists declared their independence from England, Moses' conversion was complete.

7

Capture and Release

IN THE WEEK after American patriots took up arms against Britain, John Brown traveled from Providence to Newport in the service of the rebel cause. He set out early in the morning of April 26, 1775, directing two small freighters, the *Diana* and the *Abigail*, down the channel from Providence, past grazing herds on Prudence Island, in the heart of the bay, and across open water to the shelter of Newport's elegant harbor. John had made this trip a hundred times before, but never with such excitement, and never with so much at stake.

Just six days before, the simmering discord between England and her colonies had finally flared into open conflict. Shooting had broken out at Lexington, Massachusetts, and during a headlong retreat to Boston, British regular troops had suffered a humiliating and painful defeat. Like a thunderclap heralding a break in the weather, the battle marked the end of long years of escalating disputation. Now the American colonies faced the prospect of outright war.

Events moved quickly in the days that followed. News of the battle reached Rhode Island that same afternoon; on Saturday, three days later, the General Assembly met in emergency session in Providence and voted to raise an Army of Observation of fifteen hundred men, with orders either to defend the towns of the colony or to march north and join forces with the rebels assembling outside Boston. It was a daring position to take. For individual deputies, voting to raise arms against the king meant treason, a capital offense; for the colony, it meant siding with Massachusetts in a showdown with the mightiest military force on the globe. Too daring a position, in fact, for Joseph Wanton.

The Brown brothers' old ally had just been elected to his sixth consecutive term as governor. As the consensus choice for compromise between the Hopkins and Ward factions, Wanton had done his best to preserve Rhode Island's independence in the face of the British revenue acts and, more recently, the commission inquiring into the *Gaspee* affair. Yet Wanton remained loyal to his king and joined with Deputy Governor Darius Sessions in a formal protest against the resort to arms. "Such a measure will be attended with the most fatal consequences to our charter privileges," the governor and his deputy wrote in a formal dissent, and "involve the country in all the horrors of a civil war." But in Rhode Island, where the leading families had built their fortunes in open defiance of the British empire's laws, the decades of official insult and mutinous retort had taken their toll. Already, several towns in the colony had raised their own militias, and in Providence, a company of seventy-five cadets dressed in scarlet-and-yellow uniforms had drilled for months in a pasture near the new college. Sitting again in Providence on April 25, the assembly rejected Wanton's dissent, voting instead to distribute arms and gunpowder in each of the colony's towns, and to proceed with enlistments. The army was called up, and a week later, Wanton was barred from the legislature, with Nicholas Cooke, a retired sea captain and distiller who occasionally sailed at the helm of the Brown brothers' ships, taking his place. In Providence as in Boston, the Revolution was under way.

At the close of the same legislative session, John Brown met in secret with the Committee of Safety, created to coordinate the war effort. There he received the secret commission that sent him, the next morning, to Newport, where he was directed to secure enough flour to provision the new army in its first expedition. It was a natural assignment: John was nobody's idea of a soldier, but he was brazen and zealous, a proven enemy of the British; and as the master of his own commercial fleet, he had the perfect excuse to be shopping for foodstuffs in quantity.

John was never an articulate advocate of American independence, but he was always ready for a fight. The shifting fortunes of war, the maddening uncertainty, the long odds and moments of desperation, matched his disposition, his inclination to snap judgment, and his easy acceptance of loss and reversal. Even in peacetime John built his fortune as a smuggler and a privateer; the turmoil of war only increased his advantage. Moreover, in the commission to supply the new rebel army, John recognized the unique opportunity to conflate his own interest with that of the government. In the years to come, John made government contracts for supplies and munitions to the American war effort a primary—and lucrative—line of business.

Still, even for a risk taker like John, this assignment was a gamble. Newport was home to the strongest British force between Boston and New York, a Royal Navy squadron under the command of Capt. James Wallace. His flagship was the *Rose*, a square-rigged, twenty-gun frigate capable of destroying any ship the colony could muster or reducing to rubble any town within range of its guns, Newport in particular. Wallace also had at his disposal the fourteen-gun sloop *Swan*, as well as a smaller armed sloop, and commanded altogether a force of more than five hundred sailors and soldiers. A career naval officer and son-in-law to the royal governor of Georgia, Wallace shared with the British ruling class a haughty disregard for the colonial rebels. As the contemptuous Lord Sandwich declared at Parliament, "Believe me, My Lords, the very sound of cannon would carry them off."

Posted to Newport in November 1774, Wallace immediately adopted the posture of the reviled Lieutenant Dudingston, stopping every vessel he could hail to search for contraband, especially articles of war. Suspect ships that did not heave to were promptly fired upon. Fully aware of the fate of his predecessor, Wallace made little pretense in his dealings with the colonials. In December, after a drunken mob made a raucous parade through the streets of town, Wallace wrote Governor Wanton with the curt rhetorical demand, "Is it war or peace?"

Also like Dudingston, Wallace had a special disdain for John Brown. While the royal commission had been unable to produce indictments in the torching of the *Gaspee* and the assault on its commander, Newport's Tories were quick to share the rumors—truthful, after all—of John's central role. John was also named as the author of another act of piracy, this of more immediate concern to Wallace. Weeks after arriving at Newport, Wallace had put to sea for a quick, weeklong tour of Long Island Sound. During his absence, a band of volunteers from Providence descended on Goat Island, a chunk of rock lying a quarter mile off the mouth of Newport harbor, where they made off with all the armament from the colonial fort. The haul included six twenty-four-pound cannon, eighteen eighteen-pounders, fourteen six-pounders, and six four-pounders.

It was the last set of cannon that tended to incriminate John Brown; they happened to be guns that had formerly served as the armament of the *Katy*, a sturdy sixty-foot sloop that John originally fitted out as a privateer with ports for six cannon. Brown had retired the guns—and stored them at the fort—when he converted the *Katy* to whaling, but soon after the Goat Island raid, the *Katy* once again flaunted the four-pounders at her gun ports. Wallace took note of the coincidence in a bulletin to his commander.

Wallace had one more bit of intelligence that helped draw his attention to Brown. Upon assuming the patrol of Narragansett Bay, Wallace had inherited primary contact with a well-placed spy—a wealthy Portsmouth farmer and merchant named Metcalfe Bowler. Born in London and brought to Rhode

Island as a boy, Bowler was an early leader in the colony's struggle with Parliament, and in 1765 was named one of two delegates to the Stamp Act Congress in New York. Ten years later he was speaker of the house and, as such, a member of the Committee of Safety, which secretly dispatched John Brown to Newport.

Like Governor Wanton, Bowler was loath to join the revolt against the king. But where Wanton sought neutral ground by quitting his office, Bowler chose sides. For months, as the colonies slid toward war, Bowler provided detailed reports on the activities of the insurgents to the top British military authorities in New England—Vice Adm. Samuel Graves, Wallace's direct superior, and Gen. Thomas Gage, the military governor of Massachusetts and commander of all British forces in North America. When John Brown arrived at Newport that morning in April, Captain Wallace knew just why he was there.

John, of course, had no idea his cover was blown. The *Rose* lay at anchor just off the harbor, the better to train its guns on the town; John and his two ships had to glide close by on their way into port. Most likely he headed first to Malbone's Wharf, one of more than forty commercial piers that helped secure Newport's prewar status as one of the great colonial entrepots. John Malbone was a Tory, but he was a close friend and sometime business partner of the Browns, and Malbone's Wharf offered close access to one of Newport's capacious stone market houses.

Even before they reached the tarred timbers of the dock, John and his captains could hear turmoil on the wharves and see traffic snarled in the streets. When the General Assembly had authorized its new army, Captain Wallace threatened to bombard the city if any sons of Newport answered the call, and the prospect threw the town into panic. The confusion focused on the waterfront, the commercial heart of the island town and its primary means of egress. Merchants scrambled to get their ships out to the safety of the open sea, while scores of longtime residents piled their possessions on carts and jostled for berths on ships headed to Philadelphia and elsewhere. It was the beginning of a wartime exodus that would reduce the town's population by half and allow Providence to supplant Newport as the colony's leading port.

The crush on the wharves and the confusion in the streets would have made ordinary business untenable, but for John the chaos came as a blessing. His business was secret and—considering the late developments at Lexington—patently treasonous. His best strategy was to get lost in the crowd. Making his way against the flow on Thames Street, the main commercial thoroughfare, John headed up Queen Street to Colony House, where he obtained clearance for his cargo from the royal customs authorities. Normally he would shun such registration and thereby avoid paying impost duties, but for this shipment he wanted official sanction. Returning to the wharf, he attended to the loading of the two sloops with three hundred barrels of flour.

His chores over, his documents in order, John boarded the *Diana* and set sail for Providence. His two freighters were still in the harbor and just getting under way when they were hailed by Captain Wallace from the quarterdeck of the *Rose*. Sitting under the shadow of the *Rose*'s ten-gun broadside, John had no choice but to heave to. A boat was put out and the *Diana* occupied by an officer and ten men. John produced his papers and asserted the flour was his own, but his protests were brushed aside. He was transferred to the *Swan* and held belowdecks in the ship's brig.

News of John's arrest reached shore immediately, and sparked frantic efforts to secure his freedom. One Newport merchant even won permission to visit him aboard the *Swan*, but Wallace granted no further favors. The friend wrote to Nicholas Brown the next day, "I was from four o'clock in the morning till 10 or 11 in soliciting [his release], but in vain." The following day, despite his break with the assembly over taking up arms, Governor Wanton joined in the protest. He wrote Wallace to press for John's discharge, citing John's extensive business affairs, his prominence in the colony, and the official papers showing that duties had been paid for the seized cargo. Wallace ignored the petition, confident that the man locked in his hold was a prisoner of war and not some errant merchant. As the captain recorded in his log, the seized sloops were laden with stores "bound to Providence for the rebel army." Accordingly, Wallace seized the ships as well as the flour, pressing the *Diana* into service as an armed tender to the *Rose* and dispatching the *Abigail* to Boston, under Royal Navy command and with John Brown on board as its prisoner.

Wallace's action had an immediate impact. Though the confusion of the moment prevented Rhode Island from raising its full complement of fifteen hundred, by April 28 more than six hundred stood armed and ready to set out for Boston under command of James Angell, appointed brigadier general by the assembly. Without the flour from Newport, however, Angell decided that "it will be impossible for our forces immediately to proceed." The army at Boston would have to wait.

On May 1, the *Newport Mercury* reported the arrest with partisan outrage. "Mr. Brown was sent off in one of the Packets, to be carried to Admiral Graves, at Boston, without having a single reason given for his being thus violently

seized and carried out of this colony, contrary to all law, equity and justice."
But for Brown himself, shackled belowdecks as the *Abigail* rounded Cape
Cod and pointed north, indignation had to be tempered with genuine concern. America's uprising against the crown was just a week old and already he
was a prisoner facing charges on two potential counts—for leading an armed
raid on one of His Majesty's ships and, now, for ferrying supplies to the insur-
gent army. Under new regulations issued by Parliament—dubbed by patriots
the Intolerable Acts—either charge could result in his being sent to England
for trial on capital charges. And as John well knew, he was guilty of both.

On the same day that John Brown traveled to Newport to help launch the
American Revolution, Moses Brown was doing what he could to head it off.
With the General Assembly in recess, the Providence town council met to
consider erecting a fort with a battery of artillery to defend the upper reaches
of the harbor. Moses stepped forward to counsel restraint.

While not so bold as John's secret mission, Moses' appearance also tested
the new boundaries of conduct during wartime. In a town swept up in the passion of the first days of open conflict, Moses risked being branded—as he was
in some circles—a British sympathizer. As one observer put it at the time,
"Moses is meek and recommends moderation but his advice is ridiculed by
the warm partisans." As well, Moses was risking reproach by the strict arbiters
of his adopted religion. Quakers were adamantly neutral, on the question of
war in general and on the challenge posed by the Revolution. In the heated
controversies over American rights and British rule, the usual position for
Quakers was to abstain. To take sides in the conflict, especially in a public
forum, was to risk censure and possible expulsion.

And Moses certainly appeared to be choosing sides. Stepping to the burnished mahogany rail on the floor of the statehouse during a packed session of
the town council, Moses presented a circular letter from Lord Dartmouth,
secretary of state for the colonies of North America. Dartmouth advised that
the Parliament was offering new terms, and a more accommodating tone, on
the divisive question of taxation. Since the colonists objected so strongly to
taxes imposed from England, Dartmouth proposed that the colonies tax
themselves, by whatever means they might choose, and simply forward to England the funds required to maintain the British land and sea forces stationed
in America, and to pay for the colonial governments. Such a scheme might
prompt "a reconciliation of the unhappy differences" between Britain and its
dominions.

It was a belated compromise, already far outpaced by the onset of hostilities, and was quickly dismissed up and down the Atlantic seaboard as a clumsy bid to divide the colonies. But it appealed to Moses' instinct for accommodation, and he entreated the council to weigh the dispatch with "candor and moderation, a spirit much wanting in these times of hurry and commotion." As to the artillery emplacement, Moses asked that the decision be referred to the General Assembly, along with Dartmouth's letter. Remarkably, and in a measure of Moses' stature in Providence, the council agreed on both counts.

The next morning, an express rider from Newport brought word that John had been seized and was now under arrest. The news was startling, suggesting by its timing that the fighting outside Boston would quickly spread to a wider arena. Within hours, Stephen Hopkins, home on leave from the Continental Congress in Philadelphia, dashed off a dispatch to the provincial congress in Massachusetts, terming John's capture "the first struggle which hath happened in our Colony." Hopkins understood immediately that John had been betrayed, and he warned his colleagues in Massachusetts of the risk to patriots from within their own ranks. Brown's arrest "could not have come to pass," Hopkins wrote, "but by the Faithlessness of some of the Members of our Assembly, who must have revealed their Proceedings, although the Oath of GOD was upon them to Secrecy." That faithless member was Metcalfe Bowler, but his duplicity remained obscure for the duration of the conflict.

The legislators in Massachusetts replied to Hopkins promptly, offering to trade several British prisoners of war "for obtaining the liberty of said Mr. Brown." A similar proposition came from as far as the Canadian frontier, where Ethan Allen wrote from Fort Ticonderoga to donate "a Present of a Major a Captain and two Lieuts" who "may serve as ransoms."

Word of John's predicament inspired another venture to win his freedom, this closer to home, led by Elkanah Watson, an indentured servant of John's then just eighteen years old. "Mr. Brown had occupied a father's place to me," Watson wrote in a memoir more than forty years later. "I felt grateful, and in common with the whole community, indignant and exasperated at his seizure." With abundant fervor, though perhaps not much sense, Watson strapped a musket on his back, mounted a fast horse and rode to his native Plymouth. He arrived at two o'clock in the morning and woke the town by crying "Fire" in the streets. Thus alerted, the town's Committee of Safety authorized an expedition to snatch John Brown back from the British. The next day, a crew of between thirty and forty men outfitted two dilapidated fishing schooners, each with a pair of old cannon lashed to their bows. "Thus equipped, we plunged into the ocean, reckless of every consequence, determined to rescue Mr. Brown," Watson wrote. The ragtag squadron cruised for ten days east of Cape Cod, but never caught sight of John or the *Abigail*.

But if the surprise and outrage at John Brown's arrest spurred militant reaction in patriots throughout New England, his brothers, in Providence, were inclined to less radical measures. Moses in particular was encouraged by the reception Dartmouth's compromise received at the Providence town meeting, and was convinced he could find a diplomatic path to John's release. Believing John still to be in custody at Newport, Moses quickly composed a letter asking for a "speedy, but cool and dispassionate meeting" of the town council there. That session might consider both Dartmouth's overture and "conciliating measures for the liberation of the colony's agent now on board the man of war" — a not so veiled reference to John.

Moses went further, proposing that the leaders of Rhode Island "enter into a mediation between the inhabitants of Massachusetts and General Gage, and under the direction of divine wisdom bring about a suspension of hostilities in that colony." In other words, Moses hoped to effect his brother's release by ending the war. And while it sounds absurd in hindsight—the fighting would continue for another seven years—British authorities at the time proved surprisingly receptive to Moses' peace initiative.

Moses hastily gathered endorsements from Nicholas and Joseph and from several influential friends, and promptly set sail for Newport. He arrived to find the same scenes of chaos that had greeted his brother, and quickly realized there would be no "speedy but cool" consideration of Parliament's new tax plan. Nor would there be any "liberation of the colony's agent" — John was already at sea.

Moses did make one stop before leaving Newport, to meet with the governor. Joseph Wanton was by then seventy years old, and his son Joseph Jr., Moses' close friend, had lost his seat at the assembly the year before after being pilloried as an unregenerate Tory. But Wanton Senior also felt the fraternal bonds of the colonial elite, and had chafed, like the Browns, at Captain Wallace's arrogance. The governor told Moses that he'd already petitioned Wallace for John's release; at Moses' urging, Wanton followed up by sending a strong protest to General Gage at Boston.

⌇⌇⌇

By the time Moses returned to Providence later that same day, his brothers had gathered letters from a dozen town leaders addressed to various entities at Boston, including several officers in the British garrison there, demanding John's release. Armed with those dispatches, Moses set out with his brother

Joseph the morning of Friday, April 28, and headed overland, on horseback, to Roxbury, south of Boston, where they stayed at the home of a friend. On Monday the brothers parted ways; Joseph headed west, to Concord, to confer with members of the provincial congress, while Moses continued north. He arrived at Boston shortly before nightfall, to find the port city fearful and under siege.

Boston in the colonial era was practically an island, its wharves and taverns and churches crowded onto a handful of hills surrounded by water and tidal marsh, and attached to the mainland by a single narrow isthmus called the Neck. Now the approaches to the Neck were occupied by a patriot force of six or seven hundred soldiers; facing them, defending the entrance to the city, was an entrenched British battery. In the week since the fighting at Lexington, the two positions were stalemated.

Inside Boston, the situation was delicate. After their defeat at the hands of the minutemen, General Gage had pulled all of his three thousand troops into the city and barred any civilian transit in or out. Basic provisions were scarce, soldiers and citizens alike subsisting on salt pork and hardtack bread. Several days later, recognizing the distress of the inhabitants and the danger of an uprising, Gage proposed a truce of sorts: if the town residents would surrender their arms, he would allow passage across the Neck to the relative safety of the countryside. Accordingly, on April 27, more than two thousand firearms were collected at Faneuil Hall, and hundreds of families prepared to leave the city.

When Moses attempted to enter Boston on Monday, no arrangements had yet been made for passage into town. But Moses was pragmatic by nature and simply ignored what must have seemed an intractable impasse. He first located the officers in charge of the rebel army, explained his business, and obtained a permit to pass through the lines. At dusk, leading his horse by the reins, Moses ventured into the no-man's-land between the opposing forces on the Neck. Before him stood elaborate earthworks, burnished brass cannon, and scowling, red-coated sentries. Stepping toward the British position, he "sent in some of my letters and got the promise of return from some of the officers," as he recalled the episode in a letter years later.

As the minutes passed, darkness fell on the Neck, and Moses realized he could no longer wait for an answer. He saw an officer decked out in gold braid and approached him from behind. It was a rash step, Moses recounted. "When he turned and saw me near he was so angry that he gave me such a blast as I never had or heard before." But Moses answered with an exercise of Quaker principles that seems borrowed from the annals of some Oriental martial discipline. "I stood and felt in a humble state of mind and as soon as he had left room for a word I replied to him in such a manner and with information of my message that he came down in mind as low as he was high before and in a very kind and gentle manner offered and did take a message." This was certainly an unusual adaptation of Quaker orthodoxy, but also a deliberate one. As Moses put it to Nicholas a week later, "I have seldom seen a patient, humble mind more needed nor more useful and as in proportion I have found this to be my state way was made for success." Indeed, moments after calming the officer he had startled at the fortified gate, Moses was escorted to a meeting with General Gage, becoming "the first man that entered Boston after the Lexington battle."

Portly and courteous, a career officer dubbed Honest Tom by his friends, Gage was as much an envoy as he was a soldier. He had taken an American wife and spent the last ten years as a colonial administrator in New York, and while he counseled stern measures against Sam Adams and the radical patriots, he felt that war would be a tragic mistake for England and for her colonies. As the crisis in Massachusetts reached its peak, beset by partisans and by the frustration of his own soldiers, Gage was glad to encounter a prominent colonist who showed as much enthusiasm as Moses did for Dartmouth's last-ditch compromise.

Accordingly, in their meeting at Province House, the stately brick compound that served as headquarters for the British high command in Boston, Gage surprised Moses by welcoming him warmly. The general listened with full attention as Moses described his brother's detention, and his own efforts to persuade Rhode Island to intercede with the angry patriots. Gage assured Moses that he too would follow whatever path might lead to peace, and then introduced several of his officers. Among them was Maj. John Pitcairn, the commander who led the advance party of British infantry into Lexington. Tall, lean, and earnest, a professional soldier and the son of a parson, Pitcairn importuned Moses in a thick Scottish brogue: the Americans had fired the first shots on the green that day, initiating the bloodshed that followed. The partisan colonial press berated the British as warmongers eager to spill American blood, but during his visit to their Boston redoubt, Moses found the British commanders solicitous, almost contrite.

In fact, Gage was being less than candid with Moses. The general had already decided to release John Brown, and wrote that day in a reply to Governor Wanton that "I don't . . . see any reason for his detention." But he didn't mention that to Moses just yet, apparently hoping to use John's arrest as leverage to guarantee his cooperation. Instead, Gage scheduled another meeting for the next morning and dispatched a guard as an escort. Moses rode through the iron gates of Province House that night feeling optimistic for his brother's release, and for his peace plan as well.

Moses returned the next day to find that John's ship had arrived at Boston harbor but that he remained a prisoner. Moses met with Gage, who regaled him with insights into the proceedings of the first Continental Congress, still in session at Philadelphia. Gage was clearly toying with him—possibly to better gauge his political leanings—for he still did not divulge his plans for John, and sent Moses to speak with Adm. Samuel Graves, where he got "a rather cool reception."

As cantankerous as Gage was courtly, derided in the colonial press as a "surly old admiral," Graves outlined the serious nature of the case and said John was being held on suspicion of taking part in burning the *Gaspee*. Now it was Moses' turn to be coy. He insisted to Graves that he had no knowledge of John's even being accused, though considering the notoriety of the raid, and Moses own role on the committee corresponding with the other colonies over the proceedings of the commission of inquiry, that seems highly implausible. His professed ignorance swayed Graves, however, and the admiral finally relented so far as to allow Moses to visit his brother.

The admiral sent Moses under escort onto a flat skiff that rowed out into the harbor and up to the imposing hulk of Graves's flagship, the new fifty-gun frigate *Preston*. Once aboard, Moses was led between decks, where he found his brother tearful and distraught. John had heard no good news and seen no friendly faces since his arrest six days before. Whatever distance there was between the brothers was erased in that instant. "He was glad to see me as he ever was," Moses wrote later.

Once the shock of recognition had passed, John explained to Moses his defense. He showed him the documents, which Captain Wallace hadn't bothered to confiscate, warranting that the suspect flour had been purchased to supply John's merchant ships. As for the *Gaspee*, John informed Moses—if he didn't already know—that one member of the commission that exonerated him was Peter Oliver, a prominent Boston Tory who sat as chief justice of the Massachusetts Superior Court.

Moses took John's papers, returned to shore to present them to Admiral Graves, and then headed off to meet with Oliver. The judge had much on his mind: several of his children were outside Boston and he'd been unable to reach them; his home and a foundry he owned were likewise exposed to the depredations of the rebels. But Oliver knew the Brown family through the iron business, and he greeted Moses warmly. When Moses described John's predicament, the judge cut him off, saying, "Mr. Brown, the admiral can do nothing with your brother." He then recounted to Moses the *Gaspee* commission's failure to reach a verdict, and offered to personally vouch for John's innocence with Admiral Graves.

Armed with Oliver's statement, Moses hurried back through the besieged city for a return visit to Graves. "When I went next to the admiral he appeared in quite a different state," Moses recounted, "and very kindly sent an officer with me to his barge to bring my brother on shore." Before John's release, however, there was a final audience with General Gage. There, Gage and Moses executed a scheme the two had apparently devised in the course of their meetings: as a condition of John's release, both the Brown brothers were to sign a pledge that they would lobby the General Assembly in Rhode Island to intercede between the patriots in Massachusetts and the British forces in Boston.

This, of course, contradicted John's clear record as rebel activist and his strong inclination to resist the mandates of the crown. But it fit nicely with Moses' effort to derail a revolution that was still just gathering steam, and he was glad to enlist Gage in forcing John to speak for moderation. For John, forced to choose between freedom and a trial for treason, this was an easy decision: he signed without protest.

General Gage closed the deal with a flourish. He ordered that John's flour be returned to him along with an award for damages, that the *Abigail* and the *Diana* both be released from navy custody, and that Captain Wallace receive an official reprimand for arresting John Brown. Admiral Graves added a cheerful note, encouraging John to meet with Wallace personally to settle their differences, and the brothers were released that evening.

After spending the night with Joseph at Roxbury, John and Moses set out for home the morning of May 3. They traveled together on the back of a single horse—John in the saddle, Moses perched to the rear, as their size would dictate. Was there bonding going on during that long trek across the New England countryside, wet and green with the spring? We know they didn't tarry along the way—they set out in the morning and arrived in Providence before midnight. And we know both of the brothers had much to celebrate.

John had to be thankful just to be at liberty. His luck had held, his brother had come through for him; he even had the saddle for the journey home. His stretch in custody was a harrowing one, shadowed by the prospect of an English jail or a noose. He'd spent a week at sea in irons, been forced to taste the hell that the new slaves experienced in the holds of his own Africa-trade ships.

Now all that was behind him. He was back on his feet, with a full pardon in his pocket.

Moses, too, had reason to rejoice. He'd sprung his brother from dire circumstances, and done so on his own terms. There was no resort to arms, no exchanging prisoners of war. One of the tenets that had drawn Moses to the Quaker faith was its clear conviction that reason and truth would always reveal the proper course of action. Moses felt that America was being "Drove and Hurried with the Spirit of these Unhappy Times" and felt the only safe course was to resort to reasoned dialogue. In freeing John, he'd deployed his convictions like weapons, and slipped through enemy lines like a spirit. More than that, he'd won John's sworn pledge to join him on the side of moderation, and support an intervention that Moses believed could break the impasse at Boston and head off the insurrection. The calamity of war might yet be avoided.

How much they shared, and how much they kept to themselves, the brothers did not record, but their spirits were high when they arrived in the gloomy streets of Providence around eleven o'clock that night. They were greeted by the huzzahs of a crowd that spilled out into the cool of the evening from the Golden Ball, Sabin's Tavern, and the other haunts along Main Street. As word spread of John's pardon and the reprimand to Wallace—though not of the oath signed by the brothers—they were hailed as patriot heroes. Writing the next day, patriot diarist Ezra Stiles exulted, "A humbling stroke for the Tories!"

John made good on his pledge the following Thursday, May 5, in an address to the General Assembly, then in session at Providence. It was a remarkable oration, with John obviously torn between his inclinations and his obligations. Reasoned argument was always a strain for John, whose preferred approach was to plunge ahead, answering impulse with action and leaving rationales for later. Forced to lay out a considered strategy, he couldn't help but meander.

John opened his address on "the unnatural and unhappy contest between Britain and America" by declaring his "clear opinion . . . that every colony on the continent are by the ties of honor justice and humanity obliged to stand and support each other in their just rights and privileges." Still, he argued for peace: "Although the sword has been drawn and the scabbard as yet seems to be lost, I am not out of hopes that the latter may be found and the former returned to its usual rest and quiet."

Pressing on, John picked a tortuous path around his own warlike disposition. "Although many are of the opinion that if this dispute must be determined by might and not by right that America can wish for no better time than the present, that we are united and have it in our power to blockade Boston in such a manner as the regular troops cannot march from thence to the country and that their situation there, living wholly on salt provisions, will be rendered so disagreeable, that better terms of peace may be obtained now than at any future time, but in my humble opinion we ought at the same time we are preparing for defense, to spare no pains in our endeavors for conciliating measures." To that end, John proposed sending a delegation to General Gage to plead for a truce that would "effectually put a total stop to any hostilities till the Continental Congress and each colony can consider an answer" to Lord Dartmouth's proposal on colonial taxation. Considering the time involved in orchestrating a full debate among the colonies, let alone getting word to England, John's scheme was patently ludicrous. But at least he was trying.

In closing, John asked the assembly, "Pray excuse this imperfect scrawl." But more important than the weakness of his argument was the fact that John Brown had made it at all. As the wealthiest merchant in Providence John enjoyed the stature of a British lord, and he was already a hero of the days-old Revolution. After heated debate, and despite the bellicose mood of the assembly, John's appeal for peace carried the lower house, with Metcalfe Bowler casting the deciding vote. Moses went home that night satisfied that John had upheld his end of the bargain, but events soon eclipsed the brother's fragile truce. The upper house and Nicholas Cooke, the patriot who had replaced Governor Wanton, rejected any suggestion of intervening with Gage.

The leaders of the colony were spoiling for a fight, and with the king's forces isolated behind the barricades at Boston, Newport emerged as the next likely flashpoint. The town was home to a strong contingent of loyalists, but also to a vigorous chapter of the Sons of Liberty, the secret society that was spearheading the revolution. The tensions spilled over in early June, when a crowd of at least three hundred men—some estimates ran as high as seven hundred—fell upon a train of wagons carrying supplies to Captain Wallace's ships. Having ransacked the wagons, the mob jammed into the narrow streets of the town, armed with muskets, sticks, and cobblestones and roaring with threats to kill the leading Tories. Wallace quickly assembled a force of a hundred marines brandishing long steel bayonets, marched them in formation from the docks up into town, and suppressed the riot with a threat to "put every man to the sword" and to bombard the town from his ships.

Wallace maintained his aggressive position at sea as well. Far from returning the *Diana* and the *Abigail* to their owners in Providence, the British commander fitted both the packets with all the guns they could carry and used them to expand his patrols to every passage in or out of Narragansett Bay.

This use of the packets presented a special threat to Rhode Island's merchants, as their captains, returning from weeks at sea, would have no way to know the familiar freighters had been impressed for customs duty, and thus would not think to evade them. As the weeks went by, with his shipping threatened and the emotions of the conflict ratcheting higher, John abandoned any pretense to neutrality.

John took his first step in defiance of his oath on June 6, when he filed a lawsuit seeking ten thousand pounds' damages against Captain Wallace. It was a meaningless gesture, as Wallace's commission held him immune to any civil action—not to mention the soldiers and guns that stood between Wallace and the Newport County sheriff—but John could no longer contain his fury at his arrest. Besides, as John explained in a letter to Moses, "my not prosecuting him was on argument made use of against me and indeed all the [Brown] brothers that we are Tories, and that we were in league with General Gage and consequently with Capt. Wallace and others under him." Passions were cresting all around him, and John simply would not stay quiet.

With his legal avenues closed, John settled on a more drastic course. He determined to confront the enemy at sea. This would be more audacious than any surprise attack on a stranded schooner; the idea was to seek out and overpower the armed British patrols. His vehicle would be the *Katy*. She was smaller than the *Rose* but sported a gaffe-rigged mainsail and shallow draft that made her faster and far more maneuverable than Wallace's flagship. And once equipped for war, she would easily outgun either of John's converted packets. The captain would be Abraham Whipple, the cagey privateer who helped John burn the *Gaspee*.

But if John was rash he wasn't foolhardy; this would be a colonial venture. John laid out his plan in a June 12 letter to Governor Cooke. His ship was sailing to Newport the next day, where it could take on soldiers from the colony's new army; if the assembly so wished, John would be willing to sell or lease her to stage an expedition against the British patrols. Nor would John repeat the mistake of accepting direct commission as the colony's agent. "If the sloop *Katy* goes out as my property it will make me so much more obnoxious than any other person to Capt. Wallace that my vessels and cargo will be all taken as they come in, and I now having ten sail out, that it's unreasonable that the public should desire me to sacrifice all my interest for the benefit of the common cause." He emphasized caution again in a postscript: "As I fared so badly by means of undertaking to purchase the flour for the government, I choose that you should keep my name concealed from the house."

Cooke presented the plan that day, and the assembly promptly signed on. Its resolution, authorizing a force of eighty men, ten cannon, and fourteen swivel guns for the *Katy*, and thirty men for a second, smaller sloop, the six-gun *Washington*, represented the first navy ever commissioned by a British colony. Rhode Island might be the smallest colony in America, but it never lacked in gumption.

In deference to John, the assembly resolution made no direct mention of the *Katy*, but Abraham Whipple was named commander and given the rank of commodore. Whipple's little force saw its first action three days later. Sailing at the helm of the *Katy* with a full crew and trailed by the *Washington*, Whipple encountered the *Diana* around 6 P.M. off of Jamestown, a village on Connanicut, the island that sits across from Newport at the mouth of Narragansett Bay. With Wallace's *Rose* anchored in plain view across the channel, the *Diana* sailed forth to perform its customary cargo inspection, but her commander soon found the tables had been turned. "She hailed us and told us to bring her to or she would sink us immediately," the captain recorded. Whipple's soldiers fired an opening blast, and after a half hour of "smart fire on both sides," the *Diana*'s powder chest exploded. Clearly overmatched, the British patrol made for Jamestown's north shore and ran the ship aground. When Whipple sent longboats in pursuit, the sailors fled into the woods. Whipple then claimed the *Diana*, put his own crew aboard, and the three ships headed north to Providence, their sails aglow in the setting sun.

Captain Wallace had already learned from the spy Bowler that the assembly had authorized a naval force, but he was reluctant to pursue the *Katy* into the shallow waters lying below Providence. Seething, he dispatched a curt address to Whipple. "You, Abraham Whipple, on the 10th June, 1772, burned His Majesty's vessel, the *Gaspee*, and I will hang you at the yard-arm." Whipple's reply was equally succinct: "Sir—Always catch a man before you hang him."

For John Brown and the other patriots in Providence, Whipple's adventure and his tart retort to Wallace were something to celebrate, the stuff of toasts and guffaws in taverns and coffeehouses. But for Moses, the news his brother had underwritten an armed expedition against the British was mortifying. Moses had been at Newport the week after the riots, there to attend the founding of the New England Meeting for Sufferings, convened as the Quakers sought to fashion their own response to the rising conflict. He was on the island when he received John's letter informing him of the lawsuit; when he returned to Providence a week later he "heard of a vessel or two being armed and fitted and gone out to cruise," and immediately suspected that John was involved.

John's resumption of patriot activity distressed Moses on several levels. Obviously, he was disappointed at the short duration of his brother's vow, but that didn't surprise him. He was skeptical from the beginning, enough that, on the night John was writing his peace address to the assembly, Moses had laid before him a copy of the agreement they had signed with General Gage, the better to guide his brother's strained argument. More important, Moses had signed that document as well; now he feared that the British would come to regard him, along with John, as a "deceiver and a hypocrite."

But there was more at stake than reputation. During his stay at Newport, Moses had attempted to intercede once more with British authorities, this time with regard to the storied whaling and fishing village on Nantucket, a sandy spit of an island thirty miles south of Cape Cod. Nantucket was populated almost exclusively by Quakers, and became entangled early on in the policy disputes between England and the colonies. Determined to maintain a neutral stance, the town government there had refused to abide by the nonimportation agreement imposed by the first Continental Congress. As a result, Parliament exempted Nantucket from the Fisheries Act, which barred American ships from the fertile Grand Banks off Newfoundland. Fearing Nantucket would become a supply base for the British fleet, the Continental Congress answered by banning colonial exports to the island, leaving the Quakers there isolated and increasingly desperate. Their plight generated concern in the Quaker strongholds of Pennsylvania, New Jersey, and London.

On June 6, the same day John filed his suit, Captain Wallace had seized a ship carrying provisions to the island. Ironically, the cargo violated American edict, not British, but Wallace was stopping any shipping carrying stores that might benefit the enemy, and he didn't bother with the details. Moses pleaded for release of the Nantucket schooner, but the British would have none of it. Moses blamed John and his lawsuit for Wallace's intransigence, as "the officers must consider me at least consenting if not aiding in ye writ." That Moses had squandered his moral capital only to see his brother renege on their deal was especially galling.

Moses challenged John's new course in a long letter written the day after Whipple captured the *Diana*. John's lawsuit, Moses wrote, "would increase instead of lessening thy difficulties," as "thy vessels wherever found will be particularly marked and detained to thy great loss." And Moses' own guilt by association would undermine his standing as a neutral Quaker, "at this time when we as a people cannot expect to stand between the violence of two parties except by our faithfulness to the leadings of that divine principle of truth which we profess to follow." Moreover, Moses pointed out, John had placed in jeopardy any future negotiations with the British. "If all confidence is once lost by solemn engagements being violated how will future innocences suffer if there is no ransom complied with?"

Moses took pains to explain to John that he had "as great regard for my country's rights and liberties and happiness as the most sanguine Whig," but that he was convinced that war was no solution. "I am clear of having entered into any engagements but such as if pursued by all would be like to effect the happiness of both countries."

And yet, for all his protest against John's decision, Moses never accused him of betrayal. Instead, he suggested that John had succumbed to the "torrents of censure so prevalent against considerate moderate men that don't run with the tides." Consequently, Moses wrote, "I am induced to believe that thou art led aside from that standard of resignation to thy alotment which I was pleased to find thee in a degree possessed of at Boston." John might be mistaken, and John might be wrong, but he was family, and Moses refused to accept that his brother had acted in bad faith.

Still, Moses was not above trying again, as he had in Boston, to pressure John into submission. "I have for some time back thought it would be more agreeable to me to go before the Committee of Correspondence of ye town and lay before them every transaction respecting thee getting thy liberty from the admiral's ship and unless matters are restored as far as may be that violates or is said to violate our engagements I must in justice to my self, family and friends make known the part that I acted for thy relief." If that wasn't enough, Moses threatened to take his case to the British as well. "I am not yet clear whether it may not become my duty to lay before the admiral my entire disaprobation of such conduct for the clearing of myself but I hope there may be no necessity for this."

Moses' obvious distress prompted a friendly but obstinate reply. Addressing each of Moses' points blithely and without rancor, John argued that his lawsuit was the only measure that might force Captain Wallace "to alter his tyrannical measures." Then, in a remarkable display of self-interested logic, John suggested that even the British high command would approve. "I have not the least doubt but that the admiral expected I should have made a demand of Wallace for his unprecedented conduct towards me, or he would not have desired me in so particular a manner as he did on our parting to meet Capt. Wallace in the most friendly manner."

On the question of Nantucket, John doubted "whether anything you could have said to so savage a person as Wallace would have been of advantage"; and, "As to ransoms in wartime I am apt to think they are of a different nature by law from an obligation given in my situation when on board the man of war, but let this be as it may, if our estates are all to be forfeited in case of conquest it matters not so much." John treated Moses' threat to expose him in the same cavalier tenor. "I do not think it to be necessary but if you think otherwise I will cheerfully submit to your judgment." More broadly, answering Moses' lament that John had strayed from the path of peace, John was simply defiant. "I am so clear in my opinion that the measures now taking to force America are wrong that it's out of my power to restrain myself from wishing success to the country in which I was born."

But if John was brusque in dispensing with Moses' appeals, he was effusive in embracing his fealty. "I am really sorry that my taking out a writ against Capt. Wallace should be so disagreeable to your sentiments," John wrote at the top of his letter. Toward the end, he continued in the same vein: "I am sure I never ought to forget your friendship and goodness in what you did for my redemption and am so much obliged and indebted to you therefore, that I may never have it in my power to discharge the least part of said debt. And I assure you it gives me pain that you should suppose that either your character or fortune may in the least suffer on my account." Once again, in closing, John asserted, "I am much obliged to you for your advice in every particular and shall take it kind at all times when you or any of your Friends are in town that you'll make as free at my house as though at your own."

These were not empty terms of endearment; they were terms of engagement. John and Moses had each accepted early on that they were not just members of their community but leaders of it, and both had learned that their divergent instincts would lead them to dissent, if not outright contention. But this war threatened to change everything. The sudden rush to arms, led by radicals who took to the streets with mobs at their backs, posed the most serious challenge the family had ever faced. Already, the brothers had adopted clashing identities—John was a fighting patriot; Moses, though not a Tory, was a conscientious objector who opposed the fighting on principled grounds. John wanted to make it clear that for him, despite the extraordinary times, the bonds of family stood entirely outside the range of their strategic and philosophic differences. And he could be confident Moses would be receptive. Ever since the loss of their father the two youngest Browns had been especially close, and of all the brothers, Moses was the one who had braved the enemy lines to bargain for John's freedom. For all his misgivings, Moses had come through for him at Boston, and while the gulf between the brothers' beliefs would only widen, Moses would do so again.

Liberty, 1775

IN THE SUMMER AND FALL OF 1775, Moses Brown returned once more to press the General Assembly for an end to slavery in Rhode Island. Excitement over the pitched battle between British redcoats and patriot minutemen at Bunker Hill, in June, had pushed the finer questions of liberty and freedom into the background, but Moses couldn't, or wouldn't, accept that the debate was over. His bill against the slave trade had been gutted; Moses was determined to erase the amendments to that bill, and to revive the provisions for emancipation of all children born to slaves within the colony. The Continental Congress had issued a ban on slave trading, but Moses understood it was an ad hoc measure, and he wanted to effect a broader and more lasting prohibition in his home colony.

Crucially, Moses pursued this remedial legislation against slavery without the assistance of his fellow Quakers. The New England Yearly Meeting had appointed a committee in 1774 to lobby for any laws that might "tend to the abolition of slavery"; its members included Tom Hazard of South Kingston and Moses Farnum and Thomas Lapham of Smithfield, all friends of Moses in other contexts, but here he labored alone. This may have been a strategic error, as the Quaker leaders, especially Tom Hazard, carried genuine weight in the legislature. But Moses was confident of his own political connections and his own powers of persuasion. Besides, this was a personal mission.

Moses deployed new weapons for his new campaign. When he first raised the issue of slavery at the Providence town meeting, he referred his fellow freemen to their own rhetoric of rights and liberty. Now he adopted the tactics of Anthony Benezet, drawing on a variety of sources to illuminate the cruelty and inhumanity that attended the slave system in Africa and the West Indies. If an appeal to the higher ideals of common humanity did not suffice, then perhaps Moses could shame the deputies at the General Assembly into submission.

To that end, Moses composed a lengthy treatise, "Observations and Historical Remarks upon the Slave Trade," which he posted to each of the deputies then holding office. The compilation begins with a description of the Guinea Coast, derided by slave traders as a virtual wasteland, but described by a French correspondent to the Royal Academy of Sciences, who traveled to Africa in 1749, as a verdant paradise. "Far from being an horrid, dreary barren country, [Guinea] is one of the most fruitful as well as the most pleasant countries in the known world, and tho unhealthy to strangers is very healthy to the native inhabitants," this traveler reported. Considering "the ease and quietness of the Negroes," the correspondent advised, "there ought to be considerable abatement made in the accounts we have of the savage character of the Africans."

From there Moses portrayed the wars of conquest by which the Africans were enslaved, and the trials of the Middle Passage. "Where is the justice of inflicting the severest evils, on those that have done us no wrong?" Moses demanded. "Of murdering thousands of them in their own land . . . many thousands year after year on ship board, and then casting them like dung into the sea." Thence to the West Indies; Moses quoted a correspondent from Jamaica, where "the most trivial error is punished with the most terrible whipping."

"I have seen their bodies all in a gore of blood," the Jamaican writer testified. "Their skin torn off their backs with the cruel whip, beaten pepper and salt rubbed in the wound, and a long stick of sealing wax dripped leisurely upon them." Moses was making sure that, should the deputies of the General Assembly continue to reject his plea, at least they could not profess ignorance.

Returning to argument, Moses ventured so far as to "enquire whether these things can be defended, on the principles even on heathen honesty? Whether they can be reconciled (setting the Bible out of the question) with any degree of either justice or mercy." This section was crossed out in Moses' draft— eschewing the Bible to appeal to "heathen honesty" was apparently too radical a notion—but he closed with a reference to the equally secular rhetoric of the Revolution. He quoted Stephen Hopkins's maxim from *The Rights of the Colonies Examined* that "Liberty is the greatest blessing that men enjoy, and slavery is the heaviest curse that human nature is capable of." A seasoned lobbyist, Moses understood that the legislature could not be browbeaten with Bible citations, but they might listen to their own logic.

Moses understood, as well, that freedom for slaves posed more thorny practical problems than did abolition of the trade. His plan for gradual emancipation called for all children born to slave parents after a certain date to be free by right, but required that those children serve a lengthy period of indenture to compensate masters for the cost of raising them. This was a feature of most early abolition schemes, conforming to standard practice for the offspring of indigent whites. Freedom would not mean special treatment for blacks, just the end of lifelong bondage.

More troubling was the prospect that freed slaves—especially those too old to find gainful employment—might soon find their way to the poorhouse, or to jail. Already in colonial New England, care and feeding of the indigent was the single highest cost borne by the towns; civic works were funded by lottery and judges, and courts were funded through fees. In a separate position paper, Moses acknowledged the concern among Rhode Island freemen that a slave set at liberty might fall on hard times and become "chargeable to the town." This Moses answered in uncharacteristically blunt terms. "Carry it still further," Moses argued. "Suppose it come to pass bad or imprudent conduct, can liberty and the rights of man be restored without expense? . . . Nay what are we spending not only our treasure but our blood for, but liberty?" Here again, Moses closed by quoting Stephen Hopkins.

Anticipating a hearing before the General Assembly, Moses in August petitioned the Providence town meeting to direct its delegates to support his new slave-trade and abolition bill. A year before, with Stephen Hopkins at his side, Moses had won a full endorsement. This time, however, Hopkins was in Philadelphia attending the Continental Congress, and the townspeople were more concerned with news of the armies encamped at Boston than the ethical dilemmas raised by slavery. They voted that "as the act contains matters of great importance, and will materially affect the property of individuals," the question should be tabled until the next meeting, and would be called by warrant "to warn the freemen of the town" that the controversial abolition bill would be considered. There is no record of the debate that ensued, but on September 12, the town voted "that no instructions be given to the representatives of this town regarding the slave import bill."

Moses' legislation was finally heard by the General Assembly in November, after news arrived from England that King George had declared the colonies in a state of rebellion and had withdrawn the protection of their sovereign. With the assembly thus provoked, the gradual emancipation bill received short shrift. It was tabled once again, this time not to be revived. Instead, in another slap at the abolitionists, the assembly voted that anyone setting free his slaves would be required to post one thousand pounds bond against their becoming "chargeable."

It was a resounding defeat, replicated throughout the colonies: on the eve of a Revolution fought in the name of freedom and liberty, the popular movement against slavery crested, then collapsed. The legislature in Massachusetts considered several abolition bills, but with British troops and ships massing in Boston harbor, the representatives passed the question on to the new Congress, where it languished; John Adams, among others, considered it too "divisive" to pursue. Quakers in New Jersey presented "a flood" of petitions in 1774 seeking abolition and an end to the slave trade, but as in Rhode Island, the resulting bills were riven with amendments; before the abolitionists could demand reconsideration, the government there had collapsed. In Philadelphia in 1775, the immigrant polemicist Thomas Paine made his American debut by publishing an acerbic attack on slavery, and Anthony Benezet organized the world's first abolition society, the Society for the Relief of Free Negroes, Unlawfully Held in Bondage. But the society shut down after only four meetings, its legislative agenda abandoned for another five years.

The early years of the rebellion proved a critical juncture, as well, in the thinking of Thomas Jefferson, whose maxim on man's universal rights became the touchstone of the Revolution. In 1774, enumerating the "Rights of British America," Jefferson pronounced the abolition of slavery as "the great object of desire in those colonies where it was unhappily introduced." That goal had been thwarted when King George and his ministers vetoed colonial laws taxing imports of new slaves, leaving the rights of human nature "deeply wounded," Jefferson wrote. This was artful phrasing: as Jefferson well knew, the limits proposed on the slave trade were means to manage the traffic, but not to stop slavery. Duties on slaves were a reliable means of raising state revenues. And large planters with large stocks of slaves—like Jefferson himself—sought to limit the prospects of smaller landowners by keeping the price of new slaves high. But in his attacks on King George, Jefferson was happy to capitalize on popular attachment to human rights, and even to include slaves in the equation.

Jefferson made the same charge in 1776, when he enumerated the crimes of the king in his first draft of the Declaration of Independence. But when the slave clause was excised by Congress, the author silently assented. And upon his return to Virginia that fall, when Jefferson embarked on a revision of the laws of the state, he set aside that "great object of desire," leaving the task of ending slavery to future generations. Even on the more limited matter of manumission, Jefferson ignored the rhetoric of liberty; he proposed making the practice legal—slaveholders in colonial Virginia could free their slaves only after obtaining permission from the legislature—but required that freed blacks immediately leave the state. Later, he proposed a diabolical scheme for emancipation that required separating free children from their slave parents, raising them in compulsory education camps, and then expelling them from the United States. In the years that followed, Jefferson never did reconcile his commitment to freedom with the glaring exception of slavery.

In fact, it was the British, not the rebels, who dangled the prospect of freedom to win the allegiance of black American slaves in 1775. In November, the same month that Rhode Island lawmakers rejected Moses' second plea for abolition, Lord Dunmore, the royal governor of Virginia, proclaimed that any slaves who joined the British ranks would win their freedom, and a thousand blacks promptly answered the call. Later, as the fighting moved southward, more than fifty thousand slaves deserted their masters and crossed the line. The irony of the American conundrum was not lost on critics of the rebel cause; in 1775 the avid Tory Samuel Johnson asked the pointed question, "How is it that we hear the loudest *yelps* for liberty from the drivers of the Negroes?"

Moses Brown felt deeply the sting of that jibe, but by the close of the legislative session in November, it was clear that the high ideals espoused by the patriots extended only so far as personal interest would apply. Moses was pained as well, as the prospect of war loomed larger, to find himself further alienated from Stephen Hopkins. Their relationship survived Hopkins's resistance to manumission, but their friendship soon was tested again on another heartfelt issue: Moses' growing opposition to an open breach with England. In December 1775, he wrote Hopkins an impassioned letter denouncing the belligerent stance of the patriot radicals. Hopkins, in Philadelphia, ignored the pleadings of his erstwhile protégé and the teachings of his adoptive faith. "The gun and bayonet alone will finish the contest in which we are engaged," Hopkins famously declared.

Disillusioned, certainly, and probably disgusted with his fellow freemen, Moses retired from the public forum for the duration of the struggle with England. He was a skilled politician, veteran of scores of town meetings, elected seven times as a Providence delegate to the General Assembly; he had served on committees of correspondence and for several years was the primary contact with the colony's agent in England. But as the patriots rallied in assemblies throughout the colonies, and soldiers marched to join Washington's army outside Boston, Moses retreated to the councils of the Quaker church. He would not ignore the conflict that raged all around him, but he would contest it on his own terms.

8

Moses at War

ON THE FROSTY MORNING of December 13, 1775, Moses Brown rode north from Providence with David Buffum, a longtime Quaker minister from Smithfield. Clad in the broad-brimmed hats and plain dark clothes favored by their sect, they made slow headway, their horses stepping carefully along the rutted, icy roads of the New England countryside. The pair arrived outside Boston that evening, met with three other Quakers from the Smithfield Monthly Meeting, and spent the night at Roxbury. The next day the small band of Quakers rode on to Cambridge to meet with George Washington, commander of the sixteen thousand soldiers then laying siege to the British garrison at Boston.

Their mission, they explained to the general, was to distribute alms to poverty-stricken families dispossessed by the fighting and the British occupation. Between them, the Quakers carried more than four thousand dollars, mostly in gold coin; they wished to issue their donations in person, evaluating need on a case-by-case basis. There would be no distinction made for religious or political affiliation.

Then forty-three years of age, Washington was five years Moses' senior, and possessed of the grave reserve that distinguished him ever after. He received the Quakers "kindly," as Moses put it, but declined to suspend policy and grant them permission to enter the city. Further, the general advised that several hundred of Boston's poorest residents had recently evacuated from the town, and that a lethal outbreak of smallpox had flared up behind the British fortifications.

Thus began a round of delicate negotiations, similar to those attending Moses' last visit to Boston. The Quakers proposed making contact with Gen. William Howe, the British commander. Washington agreed, but required that the scheme first be presented to his subordinate commander, Nathanael Greene. A Rhode Island native who knew Moses through his family's iron business, Greene readily endorsed the aid project. It was decided to submit a letter to Howe for delivery the next day. In the meantime, General Greene invited the Quakers to dinner.

Gathered around a rough-hewn table in a room illuminated by flickering candles and firelight from a stone hearth, Moses and his fellow travelers fell into conversation with Greene, several members of his staff, and James Mitchell Varnum, another soldier-statesman, who was among the early graduates of Rhode Island College. Stocky and plain-spoken, an autodidact like Stephen Hopkins, Greene was born a Quaker himself, but had been disowned for his engagement in the war effort. Still, Greene made clear over the course of the meal that he sympathized with the Quaker principles, and advised that if they "meddled not in the dispute . . . they would meet with protection from both sides."

When the talk turned to politics, Varnum espoused the still-controversial notion of American independence. Moses countered that "we ought to keep an eye to a peaceable union and not think of Independency." Moses went on to lament the forward sentiments of John Adams, whose pronouncements in favor of a division from England had recently aroused indignation on both sides of the Atlantic. Then, perhaps surprisingly for a general already fighting the British, "Greene joined and said he believed in the beginning of this unhappy war no one entertained such an unhappy idea, but if the war continued he could not promise for the consequence." A vigorous patriot, Greene was probably just being polite, but the exchange underscores the uncertainty that prevailed at the time. Even after combat had commenced, to most Americans a full break with the mother country remained unthinkable.

After a long day in conference with the high command of the Continental Army, the Quakers finally retired. With so many troops and refugees in Cambridge, there were no beds to be had, but Moses and his friends found a host who allowed them to lie down by his fireplace. They slept in their clothes, wrapped in riding cloaks and a single spare blanket, some lying on the hard wood floor, some on a thin layer of straw. Moses slept fitfully, but reflected that "this trial seemed necessary to fit us for our journey, by giving us a sympathy with those we had to visit who had not the comforts of life."

When negotiations resumed the next day, Moses took the lead, in part due to his acquaintance with several British officers from his earlier journey on behalf of his brother. Riding out from Cambridge soon after sunrise, the Quakers reached the approaches to Boston and the vast encampment of the Continental Army. There had been no fighting here, but the conflict had already taken a toll. Volunteer soldiers from all over New England were straggling out of their tents to squat around the scores of campfires that sent thin plumes of smoke wafting over the frozen field. Orchards, fences, and buildings had all been taken for fuel. It was, Moses noted, "a scene of desolation."

By nine o'clock that morning, the Quakers arrived for a parley at the fortified gate on Boston Neck. Flanked by a colonial colonel, a drummer, and a third officer bearing a white flag hoisted on a staff, the Quaker expedition crossed the line. General Howe would not meet with them and denied them permission to enter the city, but he sent as an emissary the sheriff of Boston, a well-known Tory. Unsure whom they could trust, the Quakers delivered a promissory note for one hundred pounds, which the sheriff agreed to deliver to Quakers inside the town. This was not quite what Moses and his friends had in mind, but it was a start.

~~~

The outbreak of war with the British placed American Quakers in a delicate, even dangerous, position. From the time it was founded, the Society of Friends had sought to avoid any connection with armed conflict, following the maxim of Quaker founder George Fox: "Whatever bustlings or troubles or tumults or outrages should rise in the world, keep out of them." More particular, Fox counseled that Friends should maintain quiet allegiance to whatever government might be in place: "The setting up and putting down kings and governments is God's peculiar prerogative, for causes best known to himself."

The Quakers of Philadelphia upheld that policy through the French and Indian War when they elected in 1755 to resign their posts in the colonial government rather than prosecute war on the frontier. The Revolution, however, did not allow such a clear-cut solution. Patriots in the colonial assemblies were demanding oaths of allegiance to the American cause, and those who professed neutrality or, worse, maintained allegiance to the king, were denounced and persecuted. Beginning in 1775, there would be no middle ground.

As a new convert to the Quaker faith, Moses Brown embraced the Society's orthodoxy. He abhorred the rebels' resort to arms as the product of "vain imaginations," and he demonstrated on his mission to Boston to free his brother the lengths to which he would go in seeking reconciliation with Britain. Yet Moses understood the Quakers could not simply ignore the conflict that raged in Massachusetts and threatened to spread down the colonial seaboard. They needed to illustrate, by some concrete act, the content and the meaning of their faith. They might remain neutral, but they should not remain passive.

The strategy Moses settled on, to establish the Quakers' role in the conflict and to answer their patriot critics, was the relief mission to Boston. It was not a novel idea; since the British blockade had sealed off the port in 1774, town councils and colonial assemblies throughout New England had taken up subscriptions and sent alms to Boston. In fact, in July 1775, the Second Continental Congress explicitly recommended that conscientious objectors make amends by staging relief efforts "in this time of universal calamity." By acting to aid the victims of war, the Quakers could demonstrate solidarity with their fellow colonists while preserving a principled neutrality.

The vehicle would be a Meeting for Sufferings, an adjunct to the Yearly Meeting that would direct fund-raising and distribution, as well as coordinate policy with other Quaker meetings. This was a new formation for New England; Meetings for Sufferings had been convened previously in New York and Pennsylvania to answer the crisis of the French and Indian War. Crucially, and in contrast to those earlier efforts, Moses advocated distributing aid to all victims of the conflict, Quaker and non-Quaker alike.

It was not an easy strategy to sell. For many Quakers, any affirmative response to the war was tantamount to an endorsement of the fighting. And in Philadelphia, where most American Quakers lived and where most of the relief funds would be raised, Boston and its radicals were simply anathema. The Pemberton brothers were especially leery of working through Boston's overseers for the poor, whom they suspected as partisans. But Moses and the other leaders of the Meeting for Sufferings were persistent. They wrote a series of letters to Philadelphia, soliciting funds and emphasizing that such an aid effort would "stop the mouths of the censorious."

By June, the Quakers at Philadelphia had begun to come around, and by November, the Philadelphia Meeting had forwarded two thousand pounds for distribution by the New England Meeting. Moses added another five hundred pounds of his own funds, and in December, he was appointed with David Buffum personally to conduct the distribution. The aid project represented a major departure for the Quakers, a break from their separatist leanings that helped establish a new tradition of humanitarian relief. For Moses it afforded a bracing view of the human cost of war that only reinforced his convictions.

On December 18, frustrated in their bid to enter Boston itself, Moses and his Quaker cohort decided to shift their focus to the towns nearby, many of them overrun by refugees from the city. Riding north and east to Marblehead, they found what they had come for: children dressed in rags and running out to the windswept road to beg for coins or a crust of bread. Within town, destitution was everywhere. Most men of fighting age were gone, leaving wives, widows, and orphans to fend for themselves. Food was in short supply, and what fuel there was had to be carted from woodlots more than two miles distant. Moses and his friends spent the day meting out cash donations to more than sixty families, their alms greeted with tears and prayers.

Heading farther east, Moses and his companions reached Cape Ann, a fishing village on a rocky headland thrust into the Atlantic. There the Quakers split up, each joining with a selectman from the village to tour the cottages and rural hovels where destitute families sought shelter from the bitter cold. "The general state of the poor here exceeded Marblehead . . . having been poor before when the fishery was carried on, which now being wholly stopted," Moses recorded. "Some families with no other bread but potatoes for some time, with Checkerberry tea was seen the only food for a woman with a suckling child at her breast. . . . I may say it hath been a sort of school to us, for we never saw poverty to compare with about 100 families in this time."

Moses and his fellow Quakers returned to Providence on December 29 and composed a detailed report for the Meeting for Sufferings. They were satisfied that they had made a difference, providing relief to hopeless people in desperate circumstances. At the same time, they had made a start toward repairing the reputation of the Quakers and their pacifist beliefs. "The name Quaker though little known in these parts, will be remembered, and perhaps none may no more think it reproach," Moses wrote in a letter to one of the Quaker donors. Ever tactful, he made sure to share credit with his sponsors. "May a sense of favors be upon us that we have had it in our power and been possessed of a heart to administer to the distressed. I mean the donors among you with our selves here."

Moses headed a second delegation to Boston in 1776, distributing cash grants to 160 families. More funds were sent to independent committees in Salem and Lynn. Along with coin, Israel Pemberton sent personal praise, pleased to find that accounts of the aid project had been published in several newspapers. The success of the effort established Moses as a leader among New England Quakers just two years after he joined the Society, and cemented his bonds to the most prominent Quakers in Philadelphia.

Fighting between American rebels and British redcoats never reached the northern shores of Narragansett Bay, but the war became an inescapable presence in Providence soon after the battle of Bunker Hill. By April 1776, town clerk Theodore Foster recorded in his diary more than three thousand troops quartered in Providence, at a time when the civilian population numbered just over four thousand. Many of the soldiers were in transit, but many more took up residence in town, and the four-story structure raised by the Browns as the primary edifice for Rhode Island College was converted to a barracks.

The presence of so many men under arms brought dramatic changes in everyday life. The number of licensed taverns and liquor stores doubled in the year 1776 alone and continued to rise, peaking at fifty in 1778. Drinking and carousing was not limited to soldiers alone; military authorities lodged an official protest with the town council seeking "some method to be taken to suppress the progress of so many Tipling Houses and Grogg Shops in town which are so fatal, not only to many of the inhabitants but to the soldiery in general." Separately, Gen. John Sullivan, the ranking army commander in Rhode Island, denounced the "inconsiderate and riotous . . . residents of this town who make it a constant practice to revel in the night, insult sentries, raise tumults in the streets and commit outrages: which disgrace human nature and of course destroy that tranquility of mind which every peaceable inhabitant in a garrison town has a right to expect."

The war's impact on public mores was marked as well by James Manning, the Baptist pastor. News of the fighting at Boston came "like an electric stroke, filled every mind with horror and confusion," Manning wrote to a clergyman in England. But, "Strange to tell, everyone would have thought it would have promoted seriousness among us, [but it] operated the very reverse, for since that fatal day, langor and abatement of zeal for God, seem greatly to have obtained: and instances of conversion and addition to the church, but rare." Manning's church recorded 114 new members in 1775, thirteen in 1776, and just four in 1777.

While it was eroding civic institutions and manners, the war brought unprecedented hardship to Providence and the rural areas around it. Shortages of basic provisions cropped up in the markets, and prices soared. Representatives of the four New England states met in Providence as early as December 1776 to confer on the rising cost of commodities; price controls were proposed but never enacted. "The universal cry for bread is very alarming in our streets," one correspondent wrote to Jabez Bowen, elected deputy governor in 1778.

Removed from town at his Elmgrove estate, surrounded by rolling pasture and neighboring farms, Moses Brown was insulated from the privation of Providence, but it reached him through an incessant stream of appeals. Moses already owned a reputation for altruism; as early as 1770, a supplicant reminded him that "you have often been the means of helping those in distress." His work with the Quakers only confirmed that standing, and as the sufferings crowded in, Moses made benevolence a primary occupation.

Moses' debtors were well aware of his philanthropy, and on occasion invoked it. One plea, from Ezekiel Burr in 1777, was especially poignant. "Whilst thou are, I hope, usefully employed in collecting relief for the distressed, forget not the unhappy subject who is confined by sickness—and a large family to provide for," Burr began. After detailing the other demands on his limited resources, Burr advised, "May the same spirit dictate that humanity and kindness towards me, which thou hast often extended others—and that thou mayest enjoy the comforts arising from well-doing."

In the winter of 1778, with conditions approaching the stage of outright famine, Moses did what he could to help. As the bakers of Providence were required to consign all their flour to the troops quartered there, Moses forwarded a shipment of corn to his uncle Elisha, and requested that he make it available "to supply poor women who have nobody to look out provisions for them. . . . I should have thee spare to those that come and have no meal or bread today, taking money of such as appears able to pay, letting those who are not have without."

The next winter proved especially severe, even for New England. The entire Narragansett Bay was frozen over, and wood, grain, and other necessities were fearfully scarce. An inventory conducted by the town council found 275 families with no grain or flour, and another 177 with less than a bushel. By that measure, well over half the residents of Providence were in need. The crisis was finally relieved when authorities in Connecticut suspended an emergency embargo and sent a shipment of grain to their eastern neighbors.

The situation in Newport was even more dire than in Providence; sailors and soldiers from the British warships based there stripped the town of wood and livestock, and boats bearing fish and other provisions were routinely commandeered. In the year 1775 about half the residents of Aquidneck abandoned the island, including four hundred who fled to Providence that December; those who remained faced outright starvation.

Moses was made painfully aware of the crisis in Newport by letters from Philip Wanton, son of his friend Joseph, and from a Quaker, Mary Callender. Both wrote to Moses on January 24, 1776. Wanton was concise: "The great distress of the poor in this town is much greater than persons at a distance can conceive." Callender offered more detail: "Many hundreds, if not thousands, are not able to provide for themselves . . . reduced to live many days together on bran and water boiled together and a bit of bread, and some have hardly

Moses Brown came to embrace the Quaker mode, including the broad-brimmed hat and the uncombed hair. This portrait was made around 1898.

This is the sole surviving image of John Brown, painted late in his life by the celebrated Rhode Island miniaturist Edward Greene Malbone.

Maritime commerce was the mainstay of the Brown family fortune; the *George Washington* was one of the last and largest ships in John's mercantile fleet.

The Landing of Roger Williams offers a fanciful version of the founder's arrival at Providence. Williams established Rhode Island as a haven of religious and political freedom.

Stephen Hopkins was a homegrown Rhode Island intellect, a visionary American patriot, and a mentor to the Brown brothers.

5

Hopkins lived in this modest house, which he built himself and which stands today in Providence.

7

John Greenwood's 1755 painting *Sea Captains Carousing in Surinam* captures a tavern scene from the sometimes ribald life of the merchant/captains who sailed for the Browns. Esek Hopkins is pictured at the center of the round table, with a reveler slumbering to his left. He is conversing with Nicholas Cooke, who served as governor during the Revolution. The second man to Hopkins's left, oblivious as he is doused with punch and vomit, is reputed to be another future governor, Joseph Wanton, Jr. Nicholas Power, a cousin of the Brown brothers, hoists a decanter at the right.

8

Detail: Esek Hopkins: Adventurer, slave trader, first commodore of the American Navy.

Abe Whipple was an able and irascible seaman who joined John Brown's raid on the *Gaspee.*

9

10

Elmgrove was Moses
Brown's country home
overlooking the
Seekonk River.

This conference room in
the old State House in
Providence is preserved
unchanged from the days
when John and Moses
Brown took turns at
the podium.

11

David Howell was one of the few
political figures in Providence
who collaborated with both John
and Moses.

12

13

John Brown's house was among the largest and most opulent of its time. It is now a museum.

14

John Brown's chariot was a source of pride and a mark of distinction.

John's calling card (shown front and reverse) marks him as a sociable and humorous host.

15

Mr. JOHN BROWN, requests the Favour of Miss Cortori Company to a Dance, at his House on the Hill, on *Friday* Evening next, Seven o'Clock. *January* 2, 1788.

16

17

College Hall, the
first building at
Brown University,
then and now.

18

Courtesy Rhode Island Historical Socie

This painting of Providence toward the
end of the eighteenth century displays
the cobbled streets and handsome
homes of the town overlooking the
Great Salt Cove.

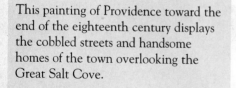

The slave trade was a source of windfall profits but also of constant moral friction throughout the Revolutionary era.

Roger Sherman of Connecticut, described as "grotesque" but also "extremely artful," helped ensure the preservation of slavery in the Constitution.

Gouverneur Morris of Pennsylvania denounced the "dirty compromise" over slavery, but to no avail.

23

Slater Mill, financed by
Moses Brown, sparked the
industrial revolution in
New England.

The First Baptist Church was
a Brown family project.

The first building raised at
Moses Brown School. The
institution is part of Moses'
enduring legacy.

24

2.

that to eat." Callender was active in the Newport Meeting and a correspondent with John Pemberton; she pleaded that Moses add Newport to those receiving aid from the Meeting for Sufferings.

Such an amendment to the close directives from Philadelphia was apparently outside Moses' authority, particularly on such short notice, but he proposed an alternative: upon a vote of the town council, Moses would make a loan of one hundred pounds for relief of the poor. This plan Callender embraced as a "generous offer," and on February 29, the deal was struck. Other patrons pitched in with grants of wood and foodstuffs, and the prospect of famine was averted. The woes on Aquidneck resumed the next winter, however; in December 1776, a British fleet landed six thousand troops at Newport and took possession of Aquidneck Island. Before the British force evacuated the town three years later, as many as half the homes had been demolished, some of them shipped to New York, where they were rebuilt to house Tory sympathizers.

Moses might have been excused for exhibiting some degree of resentment at the steady stream of demands on his charity. After all, he was already devoting time and energy—and funds—to relief efforts through the Meeting for Sufferings. But he shouldered the burden without complaint, confirming by his actions the testimony and piety that he espoused. If there was a selfish motive at work, it does not appear to have been a craving for approbation so much as a drive to answer some inexorable sense of guilt. He described that sensibility in a letter to William Wilson, whom Moses regarded as a confidant. "I am at times jealous over myself that I'm instrumental to these calamities, for want of that purity of life which a freedom from punishment for neglected mercies implies and have therefore to expect a share in the general calamity," Moses wrote in 1776. "And tho a renewed engagement after purity and peace is necessary at all times, yet it is peculiarly so at this time of almost general depravity, when darkness seems to cover the land."

Aside from his private efforts to assist those dispossessed in the conflict with Britain, Moses continued in his personal campaign on behalf of former slaves and those still held captive. Here as well, his reputation for generosity and compassion brought constant demands on his time and attention. And as his correspondence shows, the war for American rights brought little improvement in the circumstance of American blacks. Even for free blacks, liberty was a transitory state, always subject to encroachment and sudden reversal.

A typical entreaty was one he received from Newport resident Joseph Aplin in July 1775. Aplin described the plight of a free black man jailed at Newport on the claim of one John Smith. "Debt is the pretended occasion of his commitment, but a wicked design of enslaving him appears to be the real motive," Aplin reported. The jailed black man was well known in Newport for his work in Surinam to effect a peace treaty with runaway slaves. He had moved north, finally settling in Rhode Island, where he scratched out a living by working as a laborer. "This poor man is without money, and therefore without friends," Aplin wrote; he was appealing to Moses because "the man, methinks, who absolved his own slaves from bondage, cannot withhold his hand from one that is free, to prevent his being reduced again to that debasing and humiliating state." Aplin asked Moses to intercede with Smith.

It was a tricky request. The John Smith involved was a prominent privateer and merchant, a close associate of John Brown and likely related to the Brown family through John's wife, Sarah, and Uncle Elisha Brown's wife, Martha. How Moses handled the affair was not recorded, but the following May, Moses received another urgent appeal, this from Thomas Robinson, a Newport lawyer and Quaker who was a regular correspondent on slavery and church affairs. After spending close to a year in jail, Robinson wrote, the black from Suriname had recently been moved on Smith's order to Providence. Smith planned to sell the black to a broker from North Carolina. "Smith's still holding him is illegal," Robinson wrote; "if thou could prevent his being sold away til I see thee here at our yearly meeting or until the sitting of the Assembly, I think it may finally be prevented."

Robinson collaborated with Moses on another case that year, successfully preventing the sale of a woman named Binah to a "Carolina man." Most New Englanders believed the conditions of slaves in the South were especially barbaric, and considered sales to that region reprehensible. In 1779 the General Assembly in Rhode Island made it illegal to sell slaves out of state without their consent. The new law represented a modest interim victory for the abolitionists.

The limits of such provincial legislation were soon made apparent in the case of Priamus, a slave raised in South Kingston. Like most men who grew up on the shores of Narragansett Bay, Priamus was an able sailor, and around 1777, at just over twenty years of age, he shipped out from Providence on a privateer cruising against the British. Priamus's owner, William Barden, was to collect Priamus's wages and promised that, after his third voyage, he would set Priamus free. But on his last tour his ship was captured by the Royal Navy, and Priamus was landed as a prisoner at Philadelphia during the British occupation there. Before the enemy departed, in June 1778, Priamus had been sold back into slavery.

For the next two years, Priamus never stopped asserting his right to liberty, but all his protest earned him was harsh treatment and shipment to the countryside, as his owners were "doubtful of their right to detain him." Priamus finally escaped in March 1780 and made a fifty-mile barefoot trek over icy roads into Philadelphia, where he found his way to the Quaker meetinghouse. In May, John Pemberton wrote to Thomas Hazard to ask his assistance in documenting Priamus's agreement with Barden; Hazard referred the case to Thomas Robinson and Moses Brown.

Moses acted promptly, obtaining an audience with Gov. William Greene, who certified an affidavit from a witness to verify Barden's deal with his slave. During the interim, Priamus attended Quaker meetings in Philadelphia and won the affection of abolitionists there, but the Pennsylvania courts rejected the Rhode Island affidavit, and in August 1781, Priamus was again seized by his purported owners. After another letter from Pemberton, Moses obtained a second deposition, this with certification that Barden had been served notice of the case, while Robinson took a statement from a soldier on the privateer who corroborated Priamus's account. This time, Priamus was vindicated.

Not all the blacks who turned to Moses for help had sponsors. Late in the summer of 1778, two slaves slipped away from their owners and made their way to Elmgrove to ask Moses' help in claiming their freedom. The pair said they had been living as freemen in another state, and had been kidnapped by slave traders who brought them to Providence for shipment south. Moses described their case in a letter to Theodore Foster, the former town clerk, then sitting as a judge of the superior court. Moses argued that, since "by nature all men are free," the slaves needed only to assert their liberty; the burden fell on the slaveholders to prove their claim to the two men. Moreover, Moses cited the legislative ban he had authored against the slave trade. The bill had been much amended, but its basic provision remained intact; any slaves imported to Rhode Island "by land or water" were automatically free. Moses left the matter to Foster, "with reliance on thy integrity and knowledge of the unalterable Rights of Man."

Moses' continuing engagement in the affairs of slaves in Rhode Island earned him the warm regard of blacks throughout the colony, expressed in a letter from John Quamine, a free black in Newport. "Having some late understandings of your noble and distinguished character, and boundless benevolent engagements, with regard to unforfeited rights, of the poor unhappy Africans in this province . . . has [prompted] one of that nation, though an utter stranger, to present thee with gratitude and thanks."

During this period, Moses continued to proselytize for manumission, traveling as far as New Hampshire to exhort and then to witness individual acts of emancipation. At the same time, Moses developed a close familiarity with the travails of blacks wrestling with life after freedom. As he had promised, he looked after the savings of his freed slaves, maintaining their accounts with interest or investing them in public securities, and he intervened with their employers—sometimes at enterprises operated by his brothers—to ensure they were paid fair wages.

Despite his continuing engagement in the lives of Africans in Rhode Island, Moses' removal from public life placed him on the sidelines for one of the great experiments with emancipation in all of Revolutionary America: the formation of a Rhode Island army regiment comprising liberated slaves. The decision came after the grim winter of 1777, when George Washington saw his tattered army depleted by disease, starvation, and desertion at its winter camp in Valley Forge. With the Continental Congress clamoring for new recruits, James Varnum, by now a brigadier general, proposed that his colony answer its quota by offering slaves their freedom in return for military service. Until then, Washington had restricted enlistments to free blacks, a policy capitalized on by the British, who wooed thousands of Southern slaves to flee their masters and fight for England.

Varnum's plan won grudging approval from Washington, and in February 1778, despite opposition from slaveholding interests, the Rhode Island General Assembly called upon "every able-bodied Negro, Mulatto, or Indian Man slave" to sign up. The slaves would receive their freedom, and their masters would be compensated. The measure was controversial, and the assembly revoked it three months later, but more than two hundred soldiers were enlisted, and they fought with distinction for the duration of the war.

Moses made no record of his reaction to this episode, but it had to be equivocal. Certainly he endorsed any course toward emancipation—but just as certainly he opposed any engagement by blacks on the field of battle. At the same time, Moses likely was aware of the uneven application of the law, as evidenced in the case of Prince, a slave owned in common by Moses' brother Joseph and his cousin Nicholas Power. Prince was kept by his masters in Grafton, Massachusetts, where he worked on a farm. When the call for a black regiment was announced, Prince made his way to Providence and was duly enrolled. But Joseph Brown and Nicholas Power wanted Prince, not the bounty promised by the army, and they petitioned the assembly to reclaim their slave. Upon a vote of the legislature, the disappointed Prince was discharged from his regiment and returned to bondage.

On one occasion toward the end of the war, Moses learned more than he probably wanted about the mixed blessings that attended freedom. Prime Brown, one of Moses' former slaves, had befriended Cesar Lyndon, the free son of a well-educated Newport slave. Prime had invited Cesar to stay with him at his home in Providence, and over time, Cesar became romantically involved with Prime's common-law wife. They finally ran off together, leaving Prime to write an angry letter to Cesar's father. "Under the mark of friendship, he persuaded my wife to leave me. . . . He had better not marry her," Prime warned. "His life will be in danger."

Cesar Senior was apparently little perturbed by his son's romantic adventures, and composed a wry letter in answer, addressed not to Prime, but to his former master. "I think the female sex about which he is so anxious had none, or but little, regard for him," Cesar wrote Moses, "or she would not keep another's company, while he was alive." Besides, Moses was informed, the Providence couple was not legally married. "As far as I can learn, the woman is no wife to Mr. Prime—they have only kept each other's company, for so long a time as they could agree; which time now seems to be at an end." How Moses handled this bit of insouciance is not recorded, but we can surmise that Prime was admonished by his former master on the price of living in sin.

As for his own home life, Moses appears to have recovered from the loss of his beloved Anna, at least enough that he was able, by the close of 1778, to propose a new marriage. His bride was Mary Olney, a Quaker activist and clerk of the Smithfield Women's Meeting. Moses knew her from childhood; in his early twenties, he had courted her cousin, Polly Olney, who decided to marry a Boston merchant. Moses renewed his acquaintance with Mary after Anna's death, and Mary stayed at his home, along with several other Quaker visitors, in November 1774.

At the same time Moses was kindling his romance with Mary Olney, Moses' friend Thomas Arnold was courting Mary Brown, the daughter of Obadiah and sister of Moses' late wife. The son of an industrious Baptist farmer, Arnold was one of the first graduates of Rhode Island College, and was, like Moses, a disciple of Stephen Hopkins—it was Arnold who traveled with Hopkins to attend the first session of the Continental Congress. In the few years since, Arnold had worked closely with Moses in the campaign against slavery. As Mary resided with Moses at Elmgrove, Arnold was able to combine business and romance during his frequent visits there.

Arnold and Mary Brown were wed at a Quaker meeting in January 1779, but only after Arnold had converted from his Baptist faith and renounced the practice of law to which he had been trained. Arnold's decision caused a lasting breach in his own family, as he had been selected as the only child his father could afford to send to college. For years after, his brother Welcome Arnold, a successful merchant and occasional partner with John Brown, so resented Thomas for spurning his birthright that Welcome bought Thomas's law library and began his own amateur practice. But Thomas's betrothal appears to have inspired Moses. During the January meeting where Arnold's wedding was held, Moses and Mary Olney announced nuptials of their own. They were married two months later, at a sober Quaker ceremony attended by seventy guests. The dual weddings introduced two key new figures to the Quaker leadership in the persons of Moses Brown and Thomas Arnold, and cemented a lasting bond between the two men.

The arrival of Mary Olney in place of Mary Brown restored a sense of domestic balance, but Moses' household at Elmgrove had remained a busy place through his widowerhood. Moses always welcomed guests, sometimes as many as a dozen, as Friends made their way to the monthly or yearly meetings, or stopped in Providence on religious tours of New England. As well, beginning in the winter of 1773, the melancholy season after Anna's death, Moses took on a young boarder named Job Scott. A Providence native in his early twenties, Scott was a devout Quaker who made a living as a schoolmaster in town. Scott tutored Moses' children and resided, along with his wife, for several years at Elmgrove.

Moses and Job Scott formed a friendship that quickly grew into an abiding spiritual connection. Scott was something of a mystic, grave and solemn, distinguished by painful introspection and by pious application of Quaker discipline. In his youth he indulged in "music, gaming, pleasure," until, around age nineteen, God "disturbed my carnal satisfaction, and blasted all my joys," as he recorded in a journal. Thereafter, by "illuminations, and openings of divine light in my mind," Scott underwent a conversion and "gave up to the holy requirings of God." At Quaker meetings Scott was a model of quietude, often maintaining his silence throughout.

Moses found Scott's devout certainty and moral rigor enormously appealing. Moses was no divine, but with the death of his wife he had become a seeker, and he gravitated to Scott as an authentic instance of true religion. Or as Moses put it in a letter to a friend, "I find his company very agreeable . . . we are sometimes favored to feel the living springs that has closely united us." When Scott moved off Moses' estate later in the war, taking up residence in the hamlet of Springfield and winning renown as a traveling preacher, Moses remained his friend and sponsor, writing letters of introduction and helping to look after Scott's children.

Moses' quest for meaning drew him to another homegrown mystic during the early days of the war, a tall, striking woman named Jemima Wilkinson. As deep and stoic as was Job Scott, Wilkinson was extravagant. She called herself "the Public Universal Friend," and mesmerized audiences for hours by proclaiming moral convictions she said were acquired by revelation, or simply by delivering from memory lengthy quotations from the Bible. Some of her contemporaries considered her a charlatan, but she had genuine charisma, and won a following among powerful people in Rhode Island, including several prominent judges.

Moses knew Wilkinson from her youth. Her father, a Quaker farmer, was a cousin to Israel Wilkinson, the ironworker long associated with the Browns, and also to Stephen and Esek Hopkins, connections that ensured her entrée to the elite families of Rhode Island. Jemima was intrigued early on by a variety of religious doctrines, including those of the New Light Baptists and the Quakers, but her transformation took place in 1776, when she contracted a case of typhus. Beset with fever and delirium, she was pronounced dead, but she arose after thirty-six hours, and proclaimed her own resurrection.

In the following months, Jemima Wilkinson renounced her former worldly identity and began holding ad hoc prayer meetings in country glades or borrowed meetinghouses. She preached a sort of radical strain of Quakerism, damning war, slavery, and matrimony in sermons that often ran over two hours. Her traveling services evolved into a sort of religious circus, featuring appearances by devotees who dubbed themselves Prophet Daniel and Prophet Elijah and who mimicked Wilkinson by professing visions and delivering messages from on high.

Moses was intrigued by Wilkinson and attended several of her meetings. He was impressed with her knowledge of the Bible, but more than that, Moses was drawn to her story of divine inspiration. From the time of his own revelation, while walking home from Anna's grave, Moses looked for similar signs of God's active hand. Another adherent was Moses' uncle Elisha Brown, who attended several of her meetings and, convinced "that she was a messenger from God," invited her to his home, where they spent several evenings discussing her message and the controversy she had caused among Rhode Island Quakers. Fortunately for Moses, however, he could not accept her as a prophet, and when the New England Meeting formally ostracized Wilkinson and barred attendance at her meetings, Moses was able to watch the proceedings with a sense of bemused detachment.

These religious meanderings were more than diversions for Moses. Like his philanthropy and his efforts on behalf of Africans in America, these were exercises in an awakened faith, the outward expression of his inner life. Whereas in his early years Moses had been concerned with the affairs of family and politics, now he was absorbed in exploring the meaning of spiritual inclinations, to which he had decided to give full vent. But as much as he sought inspiration, Moses could not escape his allegiance to reason. What attracted him to the Quakers was not their mystery but their logic, their adherence to "truth," which derived from strict application of Christian principle.

At his core, Moses remained more a man of action than of contemplation. Try as he might to separate himself from the affairs of the world, he felt drawn to the arena where ideas were hammered into policy, and where policy was translated into doctrine. Even as he removed himself from the committees of business and politics, he migrated into the councils and institutions of the Society of Friends. He engaged in endless committee and general meetings, wrote scores of letters, and traveled extensively to attend quarterly and yearly meetings at Newport, around New England, and on several occasions in Philadelphia, devoting most of his energy to the questions of policy and practice, of war and peace.

In Rhode Island as throughout the colonies, the Quakers were appalled at the outbreak of armed rebellion against Great Britain. In Providence they refused to comply with official requisitions of small arms, refused to answer a call for enlistments and a subsequent military draft, and protested "that their worship is disturbed by the parading of the troops on Sundays and Thursdays." But in their testimony against war and their allegiance to King George, the Quakers were simply out of step. From the outset of the fighting at Boston, Rhode Island established itself as the most forward of any of the colonies in its opposition to the British. On the first of May 1776, two months before the Continental Congress issued the Declaration of Independence, the Rhode Island legislature sat at Newport and voted to renounce allegiance to the king. It was not called independence, but it severed the last remaining ties to England. It made Rhode Island the first free state on the American continent.

Moses Brown took no part in this phase of the movement for rebellion—his days as a Son of Liberty were behind him. But as in his official connection with the Meeting for Sufferings, he was closely engaged in negotiating the terms of Quaker resistance, both within and without the sect.

The most fundamental question that occupied his attention was the Quakers' principled objection to taking up arms. This axiom was honored at the outset in Massachusetts, and especially in Rhode Island, where, in 1673, a Quaker governor had endorsed the first law on the continent to establish a noncombatant status for conscientious objectors. As the conflict deepened and both colonies instituted military drafts, Quakers remained exempt, but patriot legislators began to regard their peace principles more skeptically.

The truce was broken in 1777, after the British occupation of Newport. Frustrated at the slow pace of enlistments, the Rhode Island General Assembly ordered that townships should hire soldiers to replace any Quakers exempted from military service, and recover the cost by taxing or seizing goods from the dissenters themselves. The Quakers, through the Meeting for Sufferings, answered with outright noncompliance, ceasing to issue the certificates of membership that the military required for religious exemptions. A confrontation was inevitable.

The dispute came to a head in June 1778, when two brothers were arrested by Gen. John Sullivan for refusing military service. When the case was brought before the colony's Council of War, the Quaker leadership announced they could not comply with the law or endorse any certificates. Jabez Bowen, then deputy governor and chairman of the council, was outraged. He ordered the brothers back to the custody of the army, and wrote a stern letter to Moses: "I call upon you Moses and the whole Society of Friends . . . to show the shadow of injustice or inequity in the law."

Bowen went on to challenge the whole construct of Quaker neutrality. "I am afraid that unperceived by some, others of your body have let politics creep in and mingle with your religion." Their apparent allegiance to the king, Bowen wrote, had raised popular enmity against Quakers. "You must be sensible that the body of your society are reputed to be against the American cause. . . . I must bear my witness against them as holding fast the shadow and losing the substance" of their testimony for peace. Bowen made it clear this was a painful breach for him, as it must have been for Moses. "We have been good friends from our earliest childhood to this day, and for my part I am very desirous it should continue to the end of our lives," Bowen wrote, "but if we disagree for the sake of politics, fare you well."

Bowen and Moses apparently made amends, as their correspondence resumed toward the end of the war. But the Quakers remained intransigent in refusing military service, and were forced to pay thousands of pounds in fines and confiscations through the balance of the conflict. Some of these charges were defrayed through the Meeting for Sufferings, which kept the accounts and reported to the Yearly Meeting in New England and London.

Moses engaged in the defense of Quaker neutrality in Massachusetts as well, but with better success, perhaps because the scene of the fighting soon moved south from Boston. In several instances Quakers were jailed for declining enlistment, but the judiciary and the legislature there generally honored the Friends' peace testimony. Their exception was challenged in 1778, and Moses with other New England Quakers drafted a new exemption and submitted it to the state legislature. When it stalled there, Moses composed a florid discourse to John Hancock, recently returned from the Continental Congress. Addressing him by his preferred title of "general," Moses requested an "additional instance of the indulgence you have shown to persons of tender conscience," and promised that "the honors of applause in this life will be exchanged for a crown immortal with our blessed Lord for ever more." It was the right tone to strike with Hancock, as the Quaker exemption was preserved.

Though the Quakers' refusal to bear arms earned them the disdain of America's patriot rebels, it was a relatively easy stance for the society to uphold. Opposition to warfare was a central tenet of the sect from its early beginnings, and Quakers embraced the fines and derision—and occasional jail terms—that they sustained as sufferings that confirmed their faith. More vexing was the question of whether to pay taxes that might help support the war effort. This dilemma offered no easy answers, and gave rise to an internal debate that resulted in dangerous divisions within the Society of Friends itself.

The debate was opened at the very outset of the war when the Quakers in Philadelphia, at the urging of the Pemberton brothers, issued a general statement against paying taxes or even using paper currency issued by the rebel governments. This generated widespread dissent, as many Friends were reluctant to side with Britain against their fellow colonists. A challenge was raised in July 1775 by an anonymous pamphlet addressed to Moses Brown, who duly presented it to the Meeting for Sufferings. The nameless author denounced the Philadelphia policy as betraying any pretense to neutrality, and observed that in the past, both in England and in the colonies, Quakers had willingly submitted to charges for civil defense. Further, the author observed that while Christ forbade taking up arms, he himself had paid war taxes under the resounding dictum "Render unto Caesar the things that are his." Thus, the pamphlet argued, "Let a man be under any form of government that he can imagine to himself, where he receives any advantage by it, and while he remains under it, he ought to bear his proportion of the charge of it."

The statement generated consternation in a body already uncertain how to answer the unique circumstances of the Revolution. The Quaker's principle of quiet submission to worldly authority had allowed them to stand aside through the turnings of royal succession in England, but offered no guidance when two warring regimes vied for allegiance. The policy against paying taxes was a facile reaction, and now its contradictions were being exposed within the meeting.

The secret of the author's identity was the subject of speculation and accusation for months, until April 1776 Timothy Davis, a member of the Sandwich Monthly Meeting on Cape Cod and a regular delegate to the New England Yearly Meeting, admitted authorship. Moses knew and liked Davis, and was moved by Davis's explanation that he had kept his identity secret out of simple humility—as Davis put it, "I fear a desire to be taken notice of." Moreover, Moses shared Davis's misgivings about the Philadelphia policy. He subscribed to a more nuanced position, that Quakers should pay civil taxes but not those expressly devoted to warfare. He acknowledged, however, that it was often impossible to distinguish between the two.

Moses was more troubled by Davis's method than by his argument. Davis had published his pamphlet outside the authority of the Meeting for Sufferings, which was charged with censoring any Quaker writings that deviated from official policy. In acting on his own, Moses observed, Davis had threatened Quaker unity "in a time of tryal." This exposed still another fundamental contradiction in Quaker practice: the sect was founded on the precept that adherents were guided by conscience informed by an inner light, yet they were organized in strict hierarchical formations and governed through firm application of "discipline." On this question, Moses came down solidly on the side of organization; Tim Davis must conform or be disowned.

Moses rode overland to Davis's home at Dartmouth, in southeastern Massachusetts, to ask that Davis either recant his essay or appear at the next Yearly Meeting to defend it in person. Davis did neither, and at the next Meeting for Sufferings, Moses and the other Quaker committeemen issued a formal request that the Sandwich Monthly Meeting rein in its maverick leader. The Quakers at Sandwich balked, however, reporting that they could find no violation of society discipline. The question was referred to the Quarterly Meeting, which reached the same conclusion; finally, in 1778, it was referred back to the New England Yearly Meeting. Their patience exhausted, the central body now ordered that Davis be disowned. He was, along with more than thirty Quakers who stood by him. Others, including Moses' friend Caleb Greene, supported Davis but reluctantly submitted to the will of the church leaders.

Davis did not accept this judgment quietly. He began holding meetings on his own, and petitioned the Massachusetts legislature to assert his rights over the meetinghouse in Dartmouth. Davis and his followers, by now dubbed Free Quakers, had split from the main group.

This was just the sort of division Moses most feared, and with the war now raging to the south and west, he did what he could to shore up Quaker unity. He traveled again to meet with Davis, imploring him to forget whatever offense he may have endured, to acknowledge his errors, and to return to the fold. At the same time, Moses kept up a steady correspondence with James Pemberton and Anthony Benezet, reporting on Davis's intransigence and lamenting the factions threatening the Friends. As in New England, the Quakers in Pennsylvania were wrestling with their own dissenters—a parallel Free Quaker movement, as well as hundreds of "Fighting Quakers" who joined Washington's army—and in 1782, Davis himself traveled to Philadelphia to preach among the dissidents. In letters exchanged through the rest of the war, Moses and the leadership in Philadelphia gossiped and complained about the separatists, whom James Pemberton in particular denounced as "evil."

These fissures in the society were deeply distressing to Moses. He had joined the Quakers just a few years before, impressed by the simplicity and consistency of their practice; now he was forced to choose sides between people he respected and, in the case of Davis, to ostracize a man whose faith and devotion Moses considered as strong as his own. At the same time, Moses was beset at home by the constant presence of illness in his family. Mary Olney proved just as frail as Anna had been, and his son and daughter continued to suffer the effects of childhood ailments.

By the winter of 1779, Moses himself suffered a recurrence of the illness that had prompted his temporary retirement from business a decade before, a "palsy and apoplexy," as he termed it. This episode was more extended—and apparently more serious—attended by chills, fatigue, and vertigo, and rendered him incapable of work or study for weeks at a time. It's hard to ascribe causes for such a vague complaint, but Moses himself believed it derived from the combined stress of illness in his family, the death of a longtime friend, "and added to these the cares of the Church was not the least."

Moses sought opinions from friends and doctors, and received advice from all over, including a physician in Philadelphia, who considered the symptoms Moses described in a letter to John Pemberton. Dr. Abraham Choock rendered a diagnosis of "atonia, or relaxation of the nerves that enter the composition of the coats of the blood vessels of the head to direct vital actions, probably from too great an attention of the mind." Choock prescribed "a

proper course of antispasmodic and tonic medicines," which included powdered rhubarb, "cinnaber of antimony," "volatile salts of hartshorn," and other
curious potions, concocted as pills or as a tonic. Credulous by nature, Moses
accepted and applied the remedy, and recorded in a note that it "proved
highly useful for me." But the condition persisted. As late as April 1783, Moses
complained of his "oft and indeed almost constant infirmities of writing . . .
by reason of the weakness of my nerves and it affecting me with pain in the
back of my neck."

Yet for all his infirmities, Moses drove himself to attend all the monthly, regional, and annual gatherings of Quakers, to sit on committees, to lobby and
wrangle over questions of policy, and to counsel all comers on proper deport-
ment. This was more than a compulsion; Moses never accepted the role of
gadfly, hovering on the fringe of crowds and assemblies just to feel the press of
humanity. In any conference, any forum, Moses made himself a formidable
presence, helping to establish the parameters of debate and pushing to codify
the outcome in clear and meaningful terms. He was effective in large part out
of his deep conviction that rules mattered, that human nature was malleable,
and that society could be shaped and reformed by law. In this, Moses appears
to conform to the old Roman notion that *nomen est omen*—that name fore-
tells fate. Of course there are as many exceptions to that theory as confirma-
tions, but throughout his life, Moses embraced the role of his biblical
namesake, consulting his conscience and writing laws to answer it.

In the dispute that divided the Quakers, Moses was convinced that the sep-
aration of Tim Davis and his followers derived not so much from Davis's short-
comings as from a weakness in the organization of the church itself. The
Society of Friends was giving too much latitude to the Monthly Meetings and
was too lax in enforcing unity and discipline. Consequently, in the waning
days of the war, and for months after the peace was signed with Britain, Moses
devised a plan for a "Uniform Conduct," which he promoted at the Meeting
for Sufferings, at the New England Yearly Meeting, and in letters to James
Pemberton and other Quakers in Philadelphia. The idea gained some currency, but even so rigid a thinker as Pemberton finally demurred, recognizing
that no single set of rules would find favor with Quaker leaders from the Carolinas to New England. Pemberton recognized, as well, that "some Friends
entertain a fear introducing a reliance on written rules to the lessening of the
exercise of their spiritual gifts."

Moses had more success on his home turf. There he helped steer the Meeting for Sufferings in a thorough revision of the New England discipline,
which melded doctrine from London, Philadelphia, and New York. Moses

found this work enormously satisfying, and personally rewarding: in January 1783, with the fighting over but the peace with Britain not yet official, he was afforded the post of elder at the Smithfield Monthly Meeting.

That august title, which he shared with lifelong Quakers like David Buffum, confirmed the principal role that Moses had come to play in the New England Meeting. But Moses never became a religious leader within the Society of Friends, like John Woolman or Job Scott. Rather, the church became his vehicle for projecting his social vision, his sense of order and equity. His spiritual concerns always led to a critique of the community at large, and an overtly political agenda. In that sense, Moses belonged not to New England's venerable ecclesiastic heritage, but to the more modern cadre of American social reformers, antecedent to the likes of John Dewey and Jane Addams or, later, Martin Luther King and Betty Friedan. In throwing off the bonds of monarchy, the American patriots had engaged in the project of building a wholly new society. In the aftermath of the Revolution, Moses and the Quakers would engage in that project as well, working to ensure that law was subject to principle, that liberty was attended by justice.

9

John at War

As much as Moses abhorred the outbreak of hostilities with Britain, as much as he feared the prospect of bloodshed and the human toll that would ensue, John Brown reveled in it. Having survived his close call in the clutches of the British military authorities, having endured the brief tenure of moderation imposed on him by his brother, John threw himself into the war effort, saluting the soldiers, cajoling their officers, and pursuing every opening that promised to augment his personal fortune.

John had plenty of company in his enthusiasm. Under direct orders to "scourge the rebels whenever the opportunity presents itself," Capt. James Wallace kept His Majesty's three men-of-war and several smaller vessels busy raiding for provisions and attacking any patriots who opposed him. On Conanicut Island his troops burned homes and shot the occupants as they fled; at Bristol, when townspeople responded too slowly to a demand for livestock, Wallace drew his warships into battle formation and turned loose an hourlong cannonade, flattening several buildings and sending a shock throughout the colony. As long as John's nemesis provided that sort of backdrop, Quaker appeals for calm could generate little sympathy.

With Newport neutralized by the presence of Wallace's squadron, as well as the leaders of the Rhode Island's Tory faction, Providence became the center of patriot action. John's brothers Joseph and Nicholas, and his sea captains, including Abe Whipple, Nicholas Power, Esek Hopkins, and Ambrose Page, were all engaged in the business of assembling armaments or, in Whipple's case, in commanding the colony's fledgling navy. Nicholas Cooke, the patriot replacement of Gov. Joseph Wanton, was an old chum. As thousands of uniformed militiamen and backcountry volunteers made their way through town, John and his friends drank to their valor; in the afternoons they huddled under the sign of Shakespeare's Head at John Carter's print shop, to catch the latest news of the enemy.

What may have been the highlight of those heady days came in late June of 1775, when the Kentish Guards of East Greenwich marched into town under command of James Mitchell Varnum. Distinguished for their close drill formations and their own fife and drum corps, clad in serge woolen uniforms with scarlet facings and tricorner hats, the Kentish Guards were the pride of Rhode Island's patriot militias. John Brown invited the entire regiment to observe Sunday services at the new Baptist church, and to his lasting satisfaction, they obliged.

At the Providence town council, John was appointed to direct the placement and construction of several guardhouses around town, with the actual construction assigned to Zephaniah Andrews, a master carpenter and mason who supervised the work at the college and the other major construction projects undertaken by the Browns. In August, Esek Hopkins was named to command a new battery erected on Fox Hill, just south of town, and in the months that followed, Esek and Joseph Brown were dispatched to tour the coast of Narragansett Bay to inspect colonial fortifications. As the autumn waned and the British settled into their garrison at Boston, John, his brothers, and their erstwhile commanders mulled over mock battles and plotted cannon placements like children with tin soldiers.

Along with gossip and pipe dreams, the war opened entire new fields of economic opportunity. Here John and Nicholas both proved adept at pursuing their financial interests while attending the needs of the forces in the field. The first crisis to draw their attention was the shortage of gunpowder. There had been plenty available when the fighting began, but the raw troops burned through it heedlessly, and by the time George Washington assumed command during the siege of Boston in July 1775, he found the magazines nearly empty. By Christmas, Washington lamented, "Our want of powder is inconceivable."

John and Nicholas both directed their captains to secure cargoes of gunpowder that fall, from either Europe or the West Indies. Most of their efforts failed, but in November John landed one shipment, from Suriname, of more than a ton of high-grade pistol powder. He promptly offered it to General Washington, but at six shillings per pound, a price 50 percent higher than the going rate. Washington termed the rate "most exorbitant," but having no choice, he placed the order. John immediately dispatched the faithful Elkanah Watson with a covered wagon and a guard of six men to deliver the crucial payload to Cambridge. At the same time, John capitalized on a recent amendment to the Continental Association providing that any merchant importing gunpowder was then allowed to export a cargo of equivalent value. Thus he profited twice, from the sale of powder to Washington and by securing permission to stage another trading venture.

More broadly, the powder deal alerted John to the unique possibilities that arose when the overriding imperatives of the military collided with bottlenecks for critical supplies. Most of his trading business had been shut down by the combination of the Continental Association embargo and Capt. James Wallace, whose cruisers were stopping every ocean-bound vessel. But here was a new avenue for profit. The war was still not declared, but already John had sold a ship to the new Rhode Island navy, and a cargo of gunpowder at a premium price. Practically overnight, John had become what is called in modern parlance a defense contractor. And if he fell into the role by accident, he was sagacious enough to see there was much more business to be done.

Early in December, John set out for Philadelphia, where the Continental Congress was charting the course of the nascent Revolution. Their debate involved high-flown ideals and delicate questions of diplomacy, as fervent patriots wrestled with conservative loyalists over the still-fearsome prospect of separating with Mother England. But it also involved the brass-tacks business of establishing and outfitting the American armed forces. That was the part that concerned John Brown.

Philadelphia in 1775 was the largest city in America, more than ten times the size of Providence, with wharves that stretched two miles along the shore of the Delaware River. Its broad streets were crowded with throngs of people and scores of farm wagons that rolled into town for the twice-weekly market days, but John was spared the disorienting confusion of the first-time visitor. He'd stopped at the Quaker capital several times in his early trading days, and could rely on a close friendship with Tench Francis, a wealthy merchant and former business agent for the family firm, for contacts at the highest levels of Philadelphia society. He could also count on a warm reception from Rhode Island's delegates to Congress—Stephen Hopkins, whom John had served as a political lieutenant, and who was still an active partner at the Hope Furnace, and Samuel Ward.

Hopkins and Ward were both aged and increasingly infirm, having spent their best years fighting each other in the Rhode Island gubernatorial wars. But now they were partners, leading patriots in the Continental Congress, and together they had laid the groundwork for the business that called John to the city. From the time it first met, in September 1774, the Congress moved carefully, still hoping to find some path to rapprochement with Britain. But in June 1775, after the fighting at Lexington and Concord, it authorized formation of an army. That October, returning from a summer recess, Hopkins and Ward presented a resolution from the Rhode Island General Assembly calling for creation of a Continental Navy.

The plan was roundly denounced, especially by the southern delegates, "as the most wild, visionary, mad project that has ever been imagined"—and perhaps it was, considering the primacy of the Royal Navy and the time and expense that would be necessary to build and outfit a fleet. But its sponsors were widely respected—his peers elected Ward chairman of the Committee of the Whole—and the delegates could not ignore continued depredations by the likes of Captain Wallace. By the end of October, the Congress agreed to build four ships and established a Naval Committee to supervise the effort. The roster included John Adams, whose ardor for the navy became a lifelong passion, John Langdon, a merchant and former sea captain from Portsmouth, New Hampshire, and Stephen Hopkins.

It was on the committee that Hopkins made his influence felt, charming his colleagues with his wisdom and his homespun intellect. Business was conducted after hours in the warmth of a waterfront tavern, where Hopkins held court from under the broad brim of his Quaker hat. "Governor Hopkins . . . kept us all alive," Adams memorialized in his diary. "He kept us in conversation till eleven and sometimes twelve o'clock. His custom was to drink nothing all day nor til eight o'clock . . . and then his beverage was Jamaica spirit and water. It gave him wit, humor, anecdotes, science and learning. He had read Greek, Roman and British history . . . and the flow of his soul made all his reading our own."

Tellingly, on November 5, the Congress named Hopkins's brother Esek as the first commodore of the still-hypothetical Continental Navy. It was a high honor, but also a heavy responsibility to bestow on a man who had spent most of his fifty-seven years on the sea. More impetuous and less sophisticated than his brother, Esek struck one Continental commander as "an antiquated figure, shrewd and sensible. . . . I might have mistaken him for an angel, only he swore now and then." Esek might have been a bit old for the task—George Washington, his army counterpart, was fourteen years his junior—but Esek certainly knew the ways of the sea, and after receiving notice from his brother, he set sail from Providence, arriving in Philadelphia soon after John Brown. In a burst of enthusiasm, the Rhode Island General Assembly sent along as well John's old sloop *Katy*, with Captain Abe Whipple and a complement of volunteer seamen, to help augment the new force. The colony was giving up its flagship, but it now had a favorite son at the helm of the Continental fleet.

A week later, spurred by the success of patriot schooners harassing the British off Boston, the Naval Committee expanded its shipbuilding plan to add thirteen new frigates, two of them from Rhode Island. Critically for John Brown, those ships were to be built by local men chosen by the committee members themselves. With John close at hand, Hopkins selected a group of prominent Providence merchants, including John and Nicholas Brown. The deal meant John and his brother would coordinate and disburse contracts estimated at one hundred thirty thousand dollars, though in the two years it took to complete the job, the actual figure would increase to several times that amount.

With the Congress sitting in daily session, John made his way through the biting winter wind blowing off the Delaware to a second public house, the three-story, century-old Tun Tavern, where still another committee had rented a room to conduct after-hours sessions. This was the Secret Committee, charged with securing gunpowder and other critical supplies for the Continental Army and, now, the new navy. Such prominent figures as Benjamin Franklin and Samuel Ward sat on the committee, but its leader and chairman was Robert Morris, a delegate to Congress who, like the Brown brothers, had made a fortune in the West Indies trade.

A successful and savvy entrepreneur, Morris was dedicated to the American cause, and several times risked his own fortune to supply Washington's forces in the field. But he believed that the only way to provision an ad hoc army on short notice was to offer guaranteed commissions to the most prominent shipping firms in the colonies. He spoke often of duty and patriotism, but he spoke just as often of percentages and profits. He mingled those motives on his own account; his mercantile house, Willing & Morris, was the single largest contractor with the Secret Committee.

John Brown may have established contact with Morris through Samuel Ward, or he may have used his personal connections: Thomas Willing, Morris's business partner, had formerly been a partner of Tench Francis. Whatever the avenue, the contact was made, and before he left Philadelphia John had joined the team of merchants importing munitions and supplies for Morris and the Secret Committee. Upon receipt of a twenty-thousand-dollar advance, John agreed to send out cargoes from Providence to Europe or the West Indies, his ships returning with gunpowder and small arms or, just as necessary, lead for bullets or cloth for uniforms and sails. Except for the misfortune of shipwreck, the risk was to be borne by the united colonies, including capture by the enemy. John was to collect lease fees for his vessels, commissions of 5 percent on the outward cargoes, and 2.5 percent on sales and purchases at the ports of destination. It wasn't specified in the contract, but John could expect to stock the outward voyage from his own stores of candles, of which he had a surfeit, or other trading goods. At a time when trade was stifled by embargoes and risk of capture, this was an excellent way to keep his mercantile fleet employed.

There was one last piece of business John looked after in Philadelphia. It was possibly the most prosaic of his efforts, but it highlights his uncanny knack for sales. His business agent in Pennsylvania, Joseph Hewes, was sitting on scores of crates of whale-oil candles that he couldn't unload. In better days, candles were used in quantity to illuminate ballrooms for plays and dances, but such assemblies had been forgone as the prospect of war settled over the city. Household budgets were tight as well; Hewes wrote to Providence that he had tried "every means to sell them"—even soliciting members of Congress— "but to no purpose." All of that changed once John arrived in town. John prevailed on the Secret Committee to include the candles in the outbound inventories of their trading ventures, and promptly secured orders for all the stock he had with Hewes. Even better, John obtained a premium price. "A lucky affair, this," Hewes declared.

Sailing back to Providence after two weeks of negotiations, his ship nosing through ice floes that would soon close the Delaware for a month, John could finally afford to relax. He had liquidated a stagnant inventory and had negotiated a firm partnership with the new government of the united colonies of America. War might be looming, but at least for John, that might not be such a bad thing.

⁓

The first meeting of the committee named by Stephen Hopkins to build frigates for the Continental Navy convened on January 8 at a tavern on Towne Street in Providence. It was a convivial group, consisting of the Browns, their in-laws John Smith and Jabez Bowen, a cousin named Daniel Tillinghast, and the leaders of two other prominent shipping firms—the brothers Joseph and William Russell, and John Innes Clarke and Joseph Nightingale, of the firm Clarke & Nightingale. Gov. Nicholas Cooke's presence lent the group the authority of the local government. As so often happened in Providence, this junto of the town's elite shared social ties along with their business connections. Clarke, Smith, Bowen, the Russell brothers, and Governor Cooke all sat with John Brown on the board of trustees at Rhode Island College, and Tillinghast and Joseph Russell were both related by marriage to Stephen Hopkins. When the initial session convened, John Brown picked up the tab for "refreshments."

From the outset, the committee was full of purpose, meeting after work four and five times a week, drafting teams of carpenters and caulkers, and issuing requisitions for plank, masts, spars, and rigging. The plan was to build two square-rigged warships, the *Warren* and the *Providence*, each more than 120 feet long by 30 feet wide, and to carry an armament of thirty-two and twenty-eight guns, respectively. Within a week, two saw pits were working "constantly."

John moved with the same alacrity to pursue other wartime opportunities on several fronts. With his brothers Nicholas and Joseph, he ordered a thorough retrofit of the Hope Furnace, raising an air furnace to allow for casting of cannon. This was a perfect match for the low-grade ore available in the bogs around Scituate, allowing the Browns for the first time to produce finished goods instead of the raw pig iron they had been shipping to other manufacturers. And the orders came pouring in—sixty cannon for the Continental frigates; twenty-seven for the Rhode Island General Assembly, which was busy fortifying the harbor towns against Captain Wallace and his raiders; and soon after, an order for another twenty-six carriage guns from John Langdon in New Hampshire, to equip the frigate he was building there. It was a seller's market: in the deal they struck with the assembly, the Browns stipulated that the colony would accept delivery "whether the war should continue or not." And the brothers set a price higher than that then prevailing in Pennsylvania, the closest viable competitor.

John also brought Nicholas in to join the Secret Committee contract. This was something of a reunion for the two brothers, one that must have pleased Nicholas. His fortunes had stagnated during his partnership with Moses; doing business with John was always exciting, and usually more profitable. On January 20, in return for a cash advance, John made Nicholas a minority partner in his original deal with Congress; two weeks later, after an exchange of letters with Samuel Ward in Philadelphia, the brothers entered into a second contract, this for $24,000. By mid-February they had received a cash advance from the Congress, and in April, the Browns sent the first of three trading vessels to Europe to trade for stocks of powder and canvas.

Yet even as they juggled these various enterprises, the Brown brothers couldn't help but lunge at one new and even more enticing endeavor. As early as December 1775, Nicholas had written John suggesting that privateering might be the "most profitable business" that the brothers might explore, and little more was needed to convince John. He well remembered the bounties shared among owners and crews during the old French War, and he had half a dozen veteran sea raiders still sailing for him on the quarterdecks of his commercial fleet. In January, the brothers snapped up yet another ship, the six-gun sloop *Washington*, which the General Assembly had decommissioned when they sent the *Katy* to Philadelphia. But without letters of marque from some government body authorizing raids against noncombatant shipping, privateering was still just piracy.

Massachusetts presented the first opening in February when it established a Naval Board to authorize attacks on ships supplying the British garrison at Boston. Impatient to get under way, John and Nicholas applied for permission to send the *Washington* to Boston harbor; rather than booty, the Browns cited as their motivation "the cause of our bleeding country." The Naval Board was unmoved, and informed the Browns that they could commission only vessels owned in Massachusetts. But the brothers were stymied only briefly; on March 18, the General Assembly in Rhode Island passed a bill authorizing the governor to issue "letters of marque and reprisal" and send private ships to "attack, take and bring into this colony . . . all vessels offending or employed by the enemy."

By April, Nicholas and John Brown had carted twenty-four new six-pound cannon and close to that number of four- and three-pounders, away from the Hope Furnace. These guns they sold to a variety of privateers, but some they reserved to outfit their own maiden venture, the *Diamond*, which set sail in July with William Chace in command. The *Diamond* was a small vessel, less than sixty feet in length, and carried just six four-pound cannon. But Chace fitted her for close combat, with ten swivel guns, and crammed her deck with forty sailors armed with muskets, blunderbusses, cutlasses, and pistols. The idea was not to blast their quarry to pieces but to swarm lightly defended merchant ships and take their crews captive. In his sailing orders to Chace, John assured him that "three grand prizes" had recently been captured off Boston by ships just as small as the *Diamond* and urged that "no time ought to be lost before you get on the ground for prizes."

Not long after the departure of the *Diamond*, news arrived from Philadelphia that Congress had approved the Declaration of Independence. At long last, the war with Great Britain had become official. Providence celebrated the final breach with an elaborate ceremony—a parade to the statehouse, where Governor Cooke read the text of the declaration, followed by a military pageant. The colonial light infantry fired off thirteen musket volleys, and the artillery company thirteen charges from their field pieces. Then John Brown took a turn, arranging thirteen new cannon just arrived from the Hope Furnace along the south-facing rail of the Great Bridge and firing them in a volley, bathing the town in the acrid smell of gunsmoke. The revelry continued into the night, with public feasts at several taverns punctuated by toasts—thirteen, naturally—to the independent colonies, to the army and navy, and, perhaps at John's urging, to the commerce of the United States. Toward midnight, a crowd gathered in Market Square, just doors up from John's home, where they tore down the gold-painted sign hanging in front of the Crown Coffeehouse and torched it in a bonfire.

Over the first few weeks the news was all good. After the British evacuated Boston, John enjoyed a sweet taste of revenge when he obtained and rode back to Providence in the elegant state carriage used by Thomas Gage, the military commander who had briefly held him prisoner. To the south, General Washington's force was securely entrenched at New York, and a British assault had been repulsed at Charleston, South Carolina.

The *Diamond* was finding success as well. Within a week William Chace had sent his first victim into port; after a month cruising the sea lanes off Bermuda, he'd captured five British vessels, each time putting aboard a few sailors from his own to steer the prize back to Providence. Beyond the value of the ships themselves, the *Diamond*'s haul included a thousand hogsheads of sugar, twelve thousand gallons of rum, and thirty tons of coffee. Even after splitting the proceeds with the government, there was bounty enough to enrich the Browns, Captain Chace, and all of the *Diamond*'s crew.

Nobody expected an easy victory, but in those early months, the war was starting to look like a lark. The spirit of privateering reached a fever pitch on the wharves at Providence and throughout New England, as shipowners outfitted even fishing vessels with cannon and sent them out to sea, enticing sailors with newly minted sea chanties:

Come all you young fellows with currage so bold
Come enter on bord and we'll cloth you with gold!

The gold rush at sea in the early months of the Revolution soon began to tax the maritime resources of New England. Gunpowder was already scarce; shortages soon began to crop up in materiel, in seamen, and especially in armament. For John and Nicholas Brown, that meant choosing between the competing demands of the privateers and the new Continental fleet they were charged with helping to build. It soon became apparent that, despite their avowed concern for "our bleeding country," the Browns heeded their private interest first.

The Browns were not alone in their conflict of interest: the roster of the frigate committee encompassed the leading sponsors of privateers in Providence. Beside the Browns, the Russell brothers, Clarke & Nightengale, and the governor himself sent out privateers, sometimes singly, but often in combination with the others. After all the energy demonstrated by the frigate committee in January and February, the pace of construction began to lag as skilled craftsmen and the best building materials were diverted to help raise fast new ships to sail as privateers. Accident was also a factor: in May, when the *Warren* was first floated from drydock, she keeled over and smashed her foremast and mainmast against a pier, which, as the committee reported in its minutes, "must greatly retard compleating said ship." But graft may have played a role here as well. One expert who reviewed the committee files concluded that the crash "could only be attributed to rotten rigging supplied by John Brown at exorbitant prices."

The *Warren* and the *Providence* were among the first of the thirteen frigates to float, but there they languished, awaiting topmasts, spars, rigging, and sails. At first the delays were simply a local problem, as the work on the frigates gradually began to fall behind schedule. But the ramifications were broader than that; as the frigate projects in Boston, Connecticut, and New Hampshire neared completion, their masters began to clamor for the sailcloth, and especially the guns, that had been assigned to the frigates at Providence. The bottleneck led to a direct confrontation between John Langdon in New Hampshire and the Browns of Providence.

Langdon was a proud and forceful character, in some ways as headstrong as John Brown himself. On the eve of the war, Langdon had led four hundred men on a raid against the British armory at Portsmouth, and later he led a company of volunteers to join with the Continental Army in upstate New York. And like John and Nicholas Brown, Langdon sponsored several privateers. But Langdon was a more principled patriot than his counterparts in Rhode Island. As a member of the Naval Committee of Congress, he understood the critical nature of the frigate project. He left Philadelphia early in 1776 to attend personally to construction of the New Hampshire warship *Raleigh*, and always gave it priority over his own maritime interests.

By May, Langdon was proud to report that his frigate was finished, the first of those ordered by Congress, and "the compleatest piece of work ever done in this part of the world." The *Raleigh* could set out to challenge the British as soon as she was armed, but that proved a sticking point, as the forges at Pennsylvania, expected to outfit the entire fleet, had reached capacity. "We can launch at any time," Langdon lamented in a letter to Congress. "O! the Guns, the Guns," he wrote.

The obvious solution to Langdon's problem lay in Rhode Island, where the Hope Furnace was turning out cannon by the dozen. The guns Langdon needed were available, he learned in correspondence with the Browns, but they were already assigned to the warships being built there. Those frigates were nearly ready for launch, John and Nicholas asserted, and there was no surplus armament available. Langdon was skeptical, and in June visited Providence personally. There he found the hulls of the *Warren* and the *Providence* lashed to the pier, but without masts and far from seaworthy. The cannon he coveted were there as well, lying peacefully on the dock nearby.

Langdon was astonished. The cannon he so desperately needed were ready and waiting, but the Providence committee was holding them back out of petty jealousy. As the stalemate dragged into July, Nicholas Brown informed Langdon that the hearth at the furnace had collapsed, and that it would take another six weeks to complete repairs and resume casting cannon. Langdon knew better; he was aware that the Browns were making and selling guns to outfit privateers. But he did his best to stay diplomatic, proposing that, rather than wait for a new set of guns, the Providence committee forward those already made, "as it will most certainly serve us all to get this ship out." Langdon wasn't the only one becoming impatient. In Boston especially, word of the delays in launching the frigates fostered skepticism of the Congress and "disgust" among officers of the new navy.

By the end of August no progress had been made. The Browns were still projecting two months before they could deliver cannon, and now the price was going up. More aggravating, the committee had yet to consider Langdon's plea for a loan of the finished guns. And Langdon knew full well the laggard state of the Rhode Island frigates—the Browns were coming to *him* to find still another new set of spars and masts. In frustration, Langdon turned to the Naval Committee at Congress and persuaded Stephen Hopkins to approve the loan of the Providence guns.

This order finally prevailed—after all, Hopkins was not just a member of Congress, but was a partner in the Hope Furnace—but with the proviso that Langdon strike an agreement with the owners of the forge. The Browns, as usual, drove a hard bargain, advancing the price of the cannon to one hundred pounds per ton, double the initial price. Langdon agreed to the deal despite misgivings—"an unheard of sum," he termed it—and made the long ride to Providence to close the deal. It was his third trip there in as many months.

Langdon met in conference with the frigate committee on a late-summer afternoon at one of the taverns on Towne Street, where the light filtered in through thick panes of glass and pungent clouds of tobacco smoke. The committee counted a dozen members, but it was the Brown brothers who held the floor. The deal had changed again: not only would Langdon have to pay the new, higher price, but he would have to personally guarantee payment. They might all be working for the government, but a congressional I.O.U. simply wouldn't suffice. Moreover, the Browns insisted that Landgon advance half the total in cash. Outraged, Langdon reminded the Browns of his authority as an agent of the Congress, and of their shared duty to get warships out to sea, but John and Nicholas just glowered. Langdon might hold sway at Portsmouth and in Philadelphia, but he couldn't dictate terms in Providence. John and Nicholas knew just what those guns were worth, and they weren't going to forfeit a premium price just to help Langdon win laurels as the first to get his frigate to sea.

Langdon returned to Portsmouth empty-handed, where he drafted a letter to the Naval Committee and to its new chairman, John Hancock. His angry protest marked what one historian described as "perhaps the first time in American history [that] a demand was made for a Congressional investigation of a war contractor." The complaint prompted stern letters to the committee at Providence and to Stephen Hopkins, denouncing the "extravagant demands" made by the Browns, and asserting that "no consideration shall induce us to submit to such extortion as was attempted with Mr. Langdon." More practical, the committee was ordered to deliver the finished guns to Langdon immediately.

A week later, however, the Naval Committee changed course. The frigates at Providence, they learned, were nearer completion than expected, and "very near fit for sea." In that case, the guns should stay at Providence, as the Congress's sole priority was "to get such of the frigates as are ready into action." For all his troubles, Langdon would just have to find his guns elsewhere.

It's hard to blame the Naval Committee at Philadelphia for this reversal. They had many other problems to deal with, and were at too far a remove from New England to referee the disputes of their subordinates there. But the upshot was that the *Raleigh* would lie dockside for another long year, her sails furled and her gun deck vacant. The frigates at Providence stayed in port as well, idled by still another conflict between the private interests of the Browns and the needs of the Revolutionary navy. This time, their antagonist was not a brahmin from another colony but an old friend.

Esek Hopkins returned to the familiar waters of Narragansett Bay in May 1776, sailing at the head of his little fleet after four months at sea. He had led a raid against a British fort in the Bahamas and fought several engagements with enemy ships, but his tenure as commodore was already in trouble. Accustomed to the prerogatives of a ship's captain, Hopkins had set his own course, several times ignoring direct sailing orders from Congress. Within the navy itself, he had little feel for the incessant politicking of his captains, who jockeyed for promotion and complained when they were passed over. And his crews had been swept by typhus, forcing Hopkins to put into port at New London. When he learned that Captain Wallace and his squadron had departed Newport, Hopkins set off for home seeking a safe harbor to regroup.

In June, Esek was called back to Philadelphia to answer for his conduct and for the slow progress of building the frigates. Fortunately for the commodore, he still had the support of John Adams, who "exerted all the talents and eloquence I had" in mounting a defense. Those efforts won Hopkins a compromise: he was censured for violating orders, but retained his commission and received new orders calling for an expedition against the British fishing fleet off Newfoundland. Congress anticipated easy pickings, and included detailed instructions on how to handle prisoners and captured prizes.

Returning again to Providence, it quickly became clear to Hopkins that no such expedition would be launched. The frigates *Warren* and *Providence* were finally armed and ready to sail, but now their operations were crippled by a shortage of enlistments. No seaman wanted to sign up for the navy and take his pay in Continental scrip while privateers were sending loot into port. Those sailors who did enlist deserted their ships soon after collecting their first paychecks. Frustrated on the wharves and pressured by Congress, Esek pleaded with his friends on the frigate committee for help getting his ships manned and out to sea. He fared no better than Langdon, as the Browns and their friends continued sending vessels to sea crammed with arms and men.

By October, Hopkins was getting desperate. He addressed a letter to the Naval Committee at Philadelphia complaining of the conduct of the frigate committee, and citing John Brown in particular for diverting so much manpower and materiel to private use that the frigates "cost twice as much as the contract price." Coming on the heels of John Langdon's complaint, Hopkins's letter prompted another stern inquiry by the Naval Committee. This was too much for the Browns and their friends on the Providence committee. Stung by criticism, which "bears hard on the characters of the committee, as merchants and gentlemen," the entire group resigned, leaving a single agent to answer any future orders from Congress.

That same month, Hopkins tried a more practical approach, traveling down the bay to address the General Assembly, in session at South Kingstown.

There Hopkins asked for an embargo on commissions for privateers until he could get crews for the new frigates and the other ships in his fleet. Esek had reason to expect compliance—he remained a popular figure in the colony, and carried all the prestige of his rank as commodore. Besides, as the delegates well knew, the war was going badly, with Washington's army in retreat from New York. But an embargo would suspend the one profitable enterprise in a state that was quickly sinking into wartime privation. At the assembly as on the frigate committee, John Brown led the opposition against his former captain. John had been selected a delegate to the assembly in May, and he rallied the mercantile interests against the bill, defeating it by a slim two-vote margin.

Hopkins shared his dismay with the members of the Naval Committee. "I thought I had some influence in the state I have lived in so long but find now that private interest bears more sway than I wish it did," he wrote. "I am at a loss as to how I shall get the ships manned as I think near one third of the men . . . have been one way or another carried to the privateers."

By December, the *Warren* and the *Providence* were finally complete, though still short of men, and Hopkins had the pleasure of guiding the new frigates on their first exercises, the decks gleaming with new paint, the new sails snapping in the wintry breeze. If Hopkins had any illusions of his beefed-up fleet punishing the Royal Navy, however, they vanished the afternoon of December 7, when Adm. Peter Parker sailed up the channel between Aquidneck and Conanicut. Trailing him were seven ships of the line and four frigates, each more powerful than any of Hopkins's ships. Behind them sailed seventy troop transports, carrying a force of more than six thousand British troops. Parker's fleet sailed in stately procession past Goat Island and halfway up the Aquidneck shore to Middletown, where it anchored. The next day, the troops landed without opposition, occupying Newport and sealing the American fleet off from the sea.

Clearly outgunned, Hopkins retreated back up the bay to the shallow and relatively safe waters off Providence. With the British now close at hand, Gov. Nicholas Cooke agreed to Hopkins's plan, issuing an embargo on new privateers and ordering the sheriff to help round up deserters. But if the governor and the General Assembly had come around, John Brown had not. John believed Hopkins had betrayed him in his reports to the Naval Committee, and he was determined to exact retribution.

John found his foil in Richard Marvin, one of the carpenters who had worked for the frigate committee, and whom the committee appointed to serve as a lieutenant aboard Hopkins's flagship, the *Warren*. Early in February 1777, with the fleet stymied and half its seamen ready to desert, Marvin began circulating a petition denouncing Hopkins for "such crimes as render him quite unfit for command," including, primarily, that the commodore "speak[s] in the most disrepectful manner concerning the honorable Continental Congress." At a time when decorum carried as much weight as actual conduct, this was a grave charge.

Marvin obtained ten signatures for his petition, and toward the end of the month one of the signers, a captain with the *Warren's* infantry, slipped off the ship and rode to Philadelphia to present his complaint to the Naval Committee. In the interim, Hopkins learned of the plot when three other signers confessed their intrigues and recanted their allegations. Hopkins promptly called Marvin before a court-martial and discharged him from the service. But a week later word arrived from Philadelphia that Hopkins himself had been suspended from command; already impatient with the travails of the fleet, the Naval Committee had seized on Marvin's petition and dismissed Hopkins without a hearing.

Hopkins took the decision in stride—he was old and tired of the backstabbing. But he couldn't abide the slur against his reputation, and filed suit for defamation against the complainants who refused to recant their charges against him. When the plotters were jailed, John Brown finally showed his hand in the whole affair, appearing personally before the sheriff to post bond for Richard Marvin.

John's attack on Esek Hopkins marks him as a man of calculation and influence, and of overweening pride. With the frigate committee disbanded and his privateers returning a stream of riches, John might have contented himself to count his loot and enjoy the mounting problems confounding his grizzled old shipmaster. Instead he plotted, patiently, until he finally had the pieces in place to sabotage the one man in Rhode Island who had dared to cross him.

But John was more than the arrogant, vindictive merchant prince that he appears from his dealings with Esek Hopkins and John Langdon. In his own mind, and within the circle of his family, John was caring and compassionate, a father who doted over his children and shared their smallest concerns. John showed his sensitivity in recording the death of his second son, Benjamin, who died in July 1773, at ten years of age. Seized by an intestinal "mortification," the boy suffered for a week. "A few minutes before he expired," John wrote, he "held up his arms embracing his mother in the most tender and affectionate manner that is possible to conceive and desired her not to cry, and then slept in Jesus."

John's son James, two years older than Benjamin, attended school at Harvard through the middle years of the Revolution. The family ken for business escaped him, but John, perhaps longing for a confidant, wrote him letters filled with business news as well as family affairs and friendly counsel. The correspondence reveals John as humble and even meek, attributes that might surprise many of his contemporaries. Addressing James in 1779, John complained of the loss of several privateers captured at sea, but was quick to recall his good fortune. "O how thankful we ought to be to him who rules and governs all events, that we have full possession of our health, and . . . a sufficiency of wealth to make us comfortable. . . . I repine not, but to the contrary I believe there is but few who can bear misfortune with more composure of mind than myself, which philosophical temper I freely and fully acknowledge to have come from and be continued in me by my creator and preserver."

John wrote in the same tone to his daughter Sally, just eight years old, in 1781. "Permit me to caution you, nay, warn you against pride. Consider from dust we came and to dust we must return. Treat all with decency and good manners, despise no person from their poverty, but be sure to respect all virtuous persons. Our family is all well for which and other blessings we enjoy we are not sufficiently thankful."

John's three daughters, Abigail, Sally, and Alice, seemed to embrace his guidance—they would rebel later, in their choice of husbands—but James seemed more resistant. That didn't stop John; he chided James constantly for not writing more often, and weighed in on any matters that caught his attention. "Your marr and sister from what they have heard, are considerable uneasy for fear you have fixed your affections on a Lady considerably older than yourself," John wrote in 1782. "For my own self I cannot consider you so imprudent . . . a lady 4 or 5 years older than yourself will probably be worn out and bowed down & round-backed as a monkey by the time you are middle-aged." As it turned out, John didn't have to worry on that score. James never did marry.

It was true that John had much to be thankful for. As the war progressed, many fortunes were lost in Providence and throughout America, but John only prospered. At the outset of the war he owned or shared interest in more than seventy-five ships, and while many were lost to the enemy—ten were seized in 1777 alone—John more than covered his losses with prize ships and returns from trade. Combined with earnings from the Hope Furnace and from his contracts with Congress, John managed to turn the war into a personal bonanza.

His phenomenal gains are evidenced by his investments. During the course of the war, John and his brother Nicholas banked heavily on securities issued by the states and by the Continental Congress. The prices of these bonds fluctuated wildly, but long experience trading in a variety of foreign currencies had honed their skills in arbitrage, and together the brothers amassed the largest single stake in government debt in Rhode Island. Around the same time, beginning in 1780, John went on a real-estate buying spree, purchasing a large waterfront tract on Aquidneck Island outside Newport and an eight-hundred-acre farm on Prudence Island. On the east shore of Narragansett Bay he obtained a lovely, grassy estate on a promontory near Bristol known by the Indian name Poppasquash, which he renamed Point Pleasant; on the west shore, he bought from the Greene clan five hundred well-watered acres at Namquit Point south of Patuxet, overlooking the spit of land that had grounded the *Gaspee* a decade before. This he dubbed Spring Green Farm, and it alternated with Point Pleasant as a summer retreat for his family.

Most of the properties John obtained were bargains. Some of the estates were confiscated from Tory sympathizers—the farm on Prudence Island formerly belonged to Joseph Wanton—and were resold at a discount by the wartime government. And farmland valuations were especially low. But John had had ample cash reserves to skim the cream off the depressed market. There is little question that, by the end of the Revolution, John had emerged as the richest man in Rhode Island.

John Brown's closest look at the war itself came in 1778, soon after the French decided to enter the conflict. That August, Vice Adm. Comte d'Estaing steered a fleet of twelve ships of the line, four frigates, and transports carrying four thousand troops across the Atlantic. Judging the approaches to New York too confining, d'Estaing headed north, to challenge the fortified British position at Newport. It would be the first joint operation between American forces and their new allies.

Washington dispatched several of his top commanders, including James Mitchell Varnum and Nathanael Greene of Rhode Island, to join Gen. John Sullivan in Providence and help direct the expedition. Col. John Laurens and the Marquis de Lafayette marched from New York at the head of a force of two thousand Continental soldiers; their arrival at Providence brought Sullivan's force to eleven thousand. These movements took time, however, and for two weeks, d'Estaing was forced to stall, his ships anchored off Dyer's Island, five miles north of Newport in Narragansett Bay.

John Brown was in the thick of all this activity, playing a role somewhere between river guide and Chamber of Commerce booster. He made one of his ships available to Nathanael Greene, and ferried him on several visits to d'Estaing; in conference with the French commander, John shared his smuggler's knowledge of the waters off Aquidneck to help position French warships and cut off British communications.

The invasion of Aquidneck commenced on August 10, but was interrupted, just as the French regiments were landing, by the arrival of a British fleet under command of Lord Richard Howe. Despite the pleadings of General Sullivan, d'Estaing promptly called back his troops and sailed off to meet the threat. For the next forty-eight hours the two European fleets maneuvered for the crucial advantage of windward position in what would have been the first full naval engagement of the Revolution, but now weather intervened—a gale, which escalated into a full-blown hurricane, wrecking both fleets and lashing Sullivan's army in camp on Aquidneck. When the weather finally broke, on the fifteenth, d'Estaing returned in his dismasted and nearly disabled flagship, only to inform Sullivan that he would set out immediately to Boston for repairs.

This was terrible news. D'Estaing's departure would upset the balance of force on Aquidneck and scuttle the first enterprise of the Franco-American alliance. Sullivan sent Lafayette and Greene to implore d'Estaing to change his mind; he sent along as well, as his personal representative, John Langdon, the New Hampshire shipmaster then in Rhode Island in command of a troop of militia. The delegation sailed out from Aquidneck on one of John Brown's ships, and John went along as their escort.

The conference went on all day aboard d'Estaing's battered ship. Lafayette, Greene, d'Estaing and his captains carried on the debate in the admiral's quarters, while John Brown and John Langdon paced uncomfortably across the deck. By nightfall, the verdict was in: D'Estaing was willing, but his captains were unanimous in opposition. Now it was the Americans' turn to decide: should they continue the assault alone, or retreat from the island?

Sailing back to Aquidneck that gloomy evening, the ship gliding quietly over the dark water, John talked strategy with Greene. They made an odd couple—John wheedling and garrulous in his silk stockings and velvet coat; Greene more reserved, cloaked in army blue. Greene was just thirty-six years old—four years younger than John—but he'd been seasoned in some of the bloodiest fighting of the war, and by the winter at Valley Forge. As John pressed Greene to make a landing on Aquidneck's southern shore—they would take the redcoats by surprise!—Greene reviewed in his mind the horrors that befell even the best-trained troops seeking to dislodge entrenched defenders; at Bunker Hill or, worse, at Red Bank, on the Delaware, where six hundred Hessians died in an assault on Fort Mercer, and the Americans lost just fifty men. John goaded him, insinuating that the commanders of the expedition would have to answer for failure to take Newport. But Greene had already decided: lacking the French guns and troops, any attack would be foolhardy.

Sullivan made his retreat on August 29, pursued by five thousand British regulars and Hessian mercenaries. The fighting lasted throughout the day, with Nathanael Greene leading a daring and crucial counterattack. Lafayette called the orderly withdrawal "the best-fought action of the war," but it was a retreat nonetheless, and Newport remained in British hands. In Providence, John Brown made his disappointment public, denouncing the campaign as "ill-planned and worse-conducted," and disparaging by name both Sullivan and Greene.

This was more than Greene was willing to swallow. Stopping at his home in Coventry before heading south to rejoin Washington, Greene paused to compose a lengthy reprimand that he sent to John. After a detailed defense of his and Sullivan's conduct, Greene addressed John directly: "I cannot help but feel mortified that those that have been at home making their fortunes, in the lap of luxury and enjoying all the pleasures of domestic life, should be the first to sport with the feelings of officers who have stood as a barrier between themselves and ruin."

John was abashed by this reproach, but there was little he could say in his defense. He did what he could in a letter of apology to John Sullivan, who continued in his station at Providence. "Disappointed persons will always, especially at the moment of misfortune, say harder things than they would do at another hour," John advised the general. "Perhaps at this moment I might have called it an inglorious campaign & perhaps worse in its consequences . . . but even this I do not remember saying." Five months later, John was still making amends, joining Jabez Bowen and Theodore Foster on an assembly committee appointed to commend Sullivan for his "abilities, and good conduct, as an officer."

The British finally departed Newport of their own accord in October 1779. As the fighting moved south, to the Carolinas and finally to Yorktown, John continued to support the war effort from his seat in the assembly and at home in Providence. When the British laid siege to Charleston, South Carolina, in 1780, John bet one of his ship captains a beaver hat that the Americans would prevail (as it happened, when the bet was laid, the town was already in British hands). When George Washington visited Providence that same year, John was a member of the welcoming committee that hosted an "elegant entertainment" at the statehouse. And when the French army under Jean-Baptiste de Rochambeau tramped through Providence, in 1781 and again the following year, John opened his home to the officer corps. "Our house, wharf, stable and lot is jock full of French men, horses and waggins," John wrote cheerfully to his son in November 1782. "Every gentleman in town takes [an] officer."

Clearly, John's experience of the war for independence was something quite different from the grim struggle endured by the Continental troops, or the gloomy privation that settled over everyday life. For John it was a time of exhilaration, of windfall gains and easy pickings, of balls for the generals and huzzahs for the troops. Freed at last from the constraints of the British laws of trade, John delighted in his newfound liberty. But if he was exuberant in saluting the allied forces and the patriotic ideals they fought for, John was less fervent when the bill for the fighting came due.

Liberty, 1782

FROM THE OUTSET OF THE REVOLUTION, the Continental Congress financed the war by printing paper money. This currency—distinct from the interest-bearing bonds that John and Nicholas invested in so heavily—quickly lost value, depreciating in some cases on a scale of four or five hundred to one. Congress tried to back its operations by issuing requisitions on the states, but collections lagged at a fraction of the total debt. Public revulsion at the miserable state of finances was widespread; in one colorful twist on Revolutionary practice, citizens in Philadelphia tarred a dog and feathered it with worthless Continental scrip, and then paraded behind the unfortunate cur outside the hall where Congress was meeting. More ominous was the mutiny, in January 1781, of two Pennsylvania regiments stationed in New Jersey, which had served three full years without pay or new uniforms. The rebellion was crushed at a cost of eight men dead, but the message was clear. Describing the events in a letter to his home government, Connecticut congressman Jesse Root said plainly, "The time for paying the army is arrived."

The solution was simple enough—raise revenue—but it exposed a fundamental problem that the colonies had managed to avoid through the first years of the conflict with England: would the new United States comprise a single nation, or stand as a league of independent states? The colonies had spoken with a single voice when they declared independence in 1776, but they remained skeptical of one another, and of investing power in a central government. These doubts were embodied in the Articles of Confederation, which established a "firm league of friendship . . . for their common defense," but asserted the "sovereignty, freedom and independence" of each state. Crucially, Congress was empowered to incur "all charges of war," but the powers of taxation were reserved to the states.

The deepening financial crises forced a reckoning with this mixed mandate, which Congress answered by appointing Robert Morris to the new post of superintendent of finance. Morris proved energetic, creative, and selfless, establishing a national bank, slashing expenditures—he fired 146 revenue officers in a single day—leveraging foreign loans, and, for a time, meeting the army payroll by issuing notes of credit against his own fortune. These measures were crucial but ultimately stopgap; what the government needed was a steady stream of funds.

Morris offered a plan in February 1781. The states were jealous of their power to tax land or other property, but they might accept the notion of a general duty on foreign trade. Morris proposed an impost of 5 percent; it would not yield enough revenue to retire the debt, but could at least fund the interest due on the loans from France, and the cost would be spread among consumers of imported goods throughout the states. There was a catch, however. The Articles of Confederation would have to be amended to allow direct taxes by the federal government. Any amendment would require the unanimous approval of the states. This would be the first test of whether the union forged by war would survive the peace.

The Impost, as Morris called his plan, was hailed in Congress, and by the summer of 1782, eleven states had ratified the amendment. With Georgia still occupied by British forces, assent from Rhode Island would put the plan into action. There, however, it was received with silence, and then growing antagonism. Rhode Island was first among the colonies to declare independence from England, and it would be last of the thirteen states to swear a new allegiance.

The leaders of the opposition, almost alone at first, were John and Nicholas Brown. The logic was simple: they had fought the British for freedom from duties and limits on trade, and they were damned if they were going to see the same infringements levied by any other authority. This line of thinking was, of course, entirely self-serving, subverting the groaning needs of the army and the new central government to the profit interests of a small class of shipping merchants. Clearly, it had to be dressed in more appropriate, more high-minded language, and represented to the public by a man with less obvious stakes in the outcome.

David Howell met both requirements. A linguist trained in the law, Howell was eloquent enough to formulate the argument and ambitious enough to carry it before the public. A native of New Jersey, Howell came to Rhode Island at the invitation of James Manning, whom he joined in 1766 as the first tutor at Rhode Island College. Howell soon forged strong ties with the family that had dominated the struggle over founding the college, marrying, in 1770, Mary Brown, first cousin to the Brown brothers. Voluble and eager to please,

Howell was one of the few figures in Providence to maintain a lasting connection to both John and Moses Brown. Howell prospered under Manning's direction, but the wartime closure of the college left him underemployed and near penniless. He twice ran for Congress, in 1778 and 1781, but was handily defeated both times. Thus Howell was primed to step in for John and Nicholas and speak against Congress's urgent appeal for a new, federal tax.

The case in favor of the Impost was presented in Rhode Island by James Varnum, who had been a student of Howell's before joining the army, and was elected to Congress by Rhode Island in 1780. Upon returning home from Philadelphia, Varnum wrote a series of articles for the *Providence Gazette* depicting the financial straits facing the Congress and the important role that a reliable revenue stream would play. But Varnum went further, reproving the strictures in the Articles of Confederation and extolling the rise of the federal government as the crowning achievement of the Revolution.

Howell launched his rebuttal to Varnum in March 1782, writing in the *Gazette* under the pseudonym "A Farmer." He delivered a jarring, biting critique. A vote for the impost, Howell wrote, would parallel "that fatal day when the Stamp Act was hatched by an infernal junto of British Ministers." He had the same low opinion of the power grab by Congress implicit in the request for authority to tax. The patriots of Rhode Island should be vigilant in rejecting the aims of "a tyrant, though shrouded under the name of parent, friend, or brother."

It was a daring challenge, for Howell to assume the mantle of patriot and paint Varnum, a veteran of fierce fighting on the Delaware and the frozen winter at Valley Forge, as a stalking horse for a new, "foreign" ministry. But it was effective, setting states' rights against the specter of an unrestrained federal power that would endure, "like Adam's fall, unalterable." And it was subtle: the feigned identity of the Farmer papered over the growing division between the farmers in the rural countryside and the mercantile seaports, and veiled Howell's ties to the shipping interests of Providence.

Most important, the Farmer letters tapped into Rhode Island's deep, spiritual tradition of independence, sparking such a surge of submissions to the *Gazette* that publisher John Carter felt compelled to print an apology, explaining that he did not have the space to print all the letters and articles. Most of them were critical of the Impost; it would "destroy all the liberties of the several states," while "tending to the establishment of an aristocratical or monarchial government." All of this ire accrued to Howell, who in the spring of 1782 ran once more for a seat in Congress. This time, in a campaign backed by the Browns and the other leading merchants of Providence, he prevailed, replacing James Varnum and earning a seat in the same government body he had so excoriated in print.

With Howell in Philadelphia, John Brown continued to foment opposition to the Impost from his seat as a deputy to the General Assembly. Echoing Howell, John couched his position in chauvinist terms, stressing the threat to the "sovereignty and independence" of Rhode Island.

The Congress, and Robert Morris, watched these proceedings with growing dismay. They had expected opposition—the matter of states' rights led to close votes in Massachusetts and New York—but they had won the question in every other colony, and now all their energy focused on little Rhode Island. Morris wrote a series of letters to Gov. William Greene (Nicholas Cooke had died in office), as did George Washington, but Greene demurred, and the General Assembly several times postponed a final decision. By July 1782, with the question still hanging, Congress dispatched two of its members, Jesse Root of Connecticut and Joseph Montgomery of Pennsylvania, to present their case before the Rhode Island legislature. They were politely received, and politely turned away.

The fate of the Impost was finally decided, on John Brown's motion, on November 1, 1782. John had spent the entire week lobbying his colleagues and leaning on the laggards, and he was confident of the outcome, but even he was impressed with the result. During a full day of hearings, the delegates sat through lengthy readings of letters from Robert Morris and from David Howell. Toward sunset, with the statehouse "the most crowded with respectable spectators I ever knew," as John recorded, the question was called, and the Impost defeated by unanimous vote. "Thus ended the long and much talked-about 5 percent duty and I wish never to have it introduced into this free state til time shall be no more," John wrote to his son.

John had reason to be proud. The vote against the Impost was a show of force, a measure of his ability to shape perceptions and steer the lawmakers of his home state. His achievement was all the more impressive in light of the observations of Ezekiel Cornell, a former delegate to Congress who passed through the rural districts of the state in the days after the assembly vote. "I am more and more surprised every day when I reflect that the Impost was voted out by a unanimous voice," Cornell wrote to a friend in the army, "for I can assure you upon my honor that there has not been one out of twenty among the inhabitants of the country that is opposed to the measure. They are much in favor of it. . . . It grows more and more popular every day in the country but it is held by the Providence people to be worse than treason to speak in favor of duties."

The unanimous vote of the General Assembly spelled the end of the Impost, but not the controversy over Rhode Island's opposition. News of the decision shook the new nation, emboldening provincial legislators and undermining confidence in the future of the still-tentative union between the states. The failure to achieve sanction for federal taxes prompted first Virginia, and then several other states, to repeal their own ratifications, and to introduce plans to renounce their Continental obligations and pay off federal debt and local army regiments piecemeal.

The division over the Impost was quickly shaping up as the first confrontation between nationalists, like Washington and Alexander Hamilton, and the antifederalists, who would mount a steadfast challenge to the rise of a national government. With the defeat of Cornwallis at Yorktown in 1781, the imminent threat of invasion had been banished, and regional leaders like George Clinton of New York were ready to return to the colonial era of separate, sometimes competing states. In the weeks after the vote against the Impost, David Howell gave voice to the emerging antifederalist position, publishing new attacks on the federal system in the Philadelphia press.

The nationalists, and particularly Robert Morris, believed the champions of regional autonomy were dangerously shortsighted. England remained formidable, with regiments still on the continent and warships enforcing an embargo on the high seas. And there was the debt, to the army and to the several foreign allies that had fronted vast sums to finance the Revolution. Defaulting on those obligations would bankrupt the union, cripple American commerce, and dishonor the sacrifice of thousands of patriot lives.

To the nationalists, the Impost remained the only viable alternative, and Rhode Island remained the obstacle. In December, the Congress voted to send a second delegation to lobby the lawmakers at Providence and impress upon them the "absolute necessity," as Hamilton termed it, of the funding program. David Howell was on hand to cast the sole vote against the plan.

Robert Morris reached the same conclusion as Congress, but relied on his own resources in attempting to break the impasse at Rhode Island. He wrote Gov. William Greene directly, asserting that Congress "cannot obtain loans without credit, and they cannot have credit without funds." At the same time, he sent Thomas Paine, the renowned tribune of the Revolution, to make the case in person.

At the time of his publication, in 1776, of *Common Sense*, Tom Paine became the crystallizing voice of the era, whose formulations on freedom, individual rights, and continental destiny helped define Americans' ideas about themselves and their Revolution. An activist as well as a polemicist, Paine had joined the Continental Army and became fast friends with George Washington and Nathanael Greene. And he was a welcome presence in Congress, serving for a time in the Committee on Foreign Affairs. But Paine was always impecunious—he had devoted his royalties from *Common Sense* to funding the American cause—and in 1782 Washington, Robert Morris, and Foreign Secretary Robert Livingston secretly agreed to pay Paine a small salary to produce nationalist tracts.

When Howell's arguments against the Impost began appearing in the Philadelphia press, Paine immediately set about composing a reply. By early December he had published two rejoinders in the *Pennsylvania Packet* and other papers there, but he realized he was addressing the wrong audience. On December 7 he stopped by Morris's office to propose traveling to Rhode Island and continuing the series there. He knew Varnum, the soldier and former congressman, and felt he might be able to make a difference. Two days later, Morris agreed.

Paine set out the next day on a rented horse, wending his way through the now-silent battlefields he had tramped with the army in New Jersey and New York. He was to be followed by the delegation from Congress, but the day they left Philadelphia, on December 22, they learned that Virginia had repealed its ratification of the Impost. Believing the cause to be lost, they turned back. Paine heard the same news, but he continued on, driven by his conviction that the Congress was facing an urgent crisis, and by hubris: he really believed his argument could swing the balance in favor of the Impost.

In Providence, John Carter had already published two of the famous writer's submissions; the series continued in weekly installments after Paine arrived. Few details survive of Paine's sojourn at the head of Narragansett Bay, but he remained more than a month, and it appears from the columns he published that his visit was becoming increasingly acrimonious.

His first columns, published in December and early January, did little more than reprise—in more trenchant terms—the arguments Morris presented in his letters to Governor Greene. By the time of his fifth installment, however, Paine had been on the scene long enough to learn something of the nature of the local opposition to the Impost, and his columns shifted from extolling the virtues of vigorous government to challenging the motives of its critics. He did not mention John and Nicholas Brown by name, but Paine was getting personal.

"The objectors to the measure, not choosing to begin the question where it ought to be begun, have formed into an ambuscade to attack it in disguise,"

Paine wrote January 18. "And this ambuscade consists originally of about ten or a dozen merchants, who have self-interest in the matter, and who, with a very profitable trade pay very little taxes in proportion . . . and who likewise, by their present opposition, are drawing themselves away from the common burdens of the country, and throwing them upon the shoulders of others. And this, forsooth, they call patriotism."

Paine scolded them sternly. "Be ashamed, gentlemen, to put off the payment of your just debts, the payment of your suffering army, and the support of your national honor, upon such illiberal and unbelieved pretenses." Indignant as he was at the Providence merchants, Paine reserved special venom for David Howell. "There is one gentleman who has raised all his present fame upon his opposition to the measure, and he has trudged laboriously in service of those who encouraged him; but I will apply to him a simile I once applied to another person . . . that as he rose like a rocket, he would fall like the stick."

Paine was, of course, correct—opposition to the Impost lay principally with a small clique headed by the Browns. But as his columns drifted into invective, the town of Providence and the pages of the *Gazette* rallied to the defense of their most prosperous and prominent citizens. Half a dozen writers, all pseudonymous, attacked Paine directly, exploiting their knowledge of his personal proclivities. He was "a mercenary writer" and "a bankrupt urging the necessity of a punctual discharge of our debts," they wrote. One wag twisted Paine's attack on Howell to dig at Paine's well-known penchant for liquor: "Men of modesty choose to fall, if they must fall, 'like a stick'; but we observe in him a striving to keep up a blaze even in his descent. This, however, may be wholly owing to a continual supply of *inflammable spirits*."

In his final column, Paine answered with disdain. "I have heard a great deal of the angry dislike of a few men, whose niggardly souls, governed only by the hope of the high price which their next or present cargoes may bring." Obviously chagrined, he closed by citing letters of commendation he'd received from Revolutionary heroes Nathanael Greene and Henry Laurens. But it was clear that Paine had failed in his mission; almost single-handedly, at a critical juncture in the life of the new nation, John Brown had derailed the momentum for establishing a central government and thrown the faltering federal leadership into disarray. During the month Paine stayed in Rhode Island, Robert Morris tendered his resignation in Philadelphia. The Congress persuaded him to stay on, but by 1784 Morris was gone, and it would be another three years of crisis and discord before the nation returned to the idea of a strong federal union.

The fact is, Tom Paine was never going to hector the merchants of Providence into compliance. It was true, what Paine had written about John Brown and his cronies, about their methods and their motives. But Paine was too much of an idealist to grasp the visceral nature of what he was dealing with. He was convinced that political freedom would bring with it a new, more holistic consciousness, a sense of shared obligation. What he didn't count on was the corollary, that the war of national liberation would unleash passion as well as conscience, impulse along with justice.

In fact, a strict analysis of his own self-interest would have led John Brown to adopt quite a different course. His stake in Continental securities—John held at least fifty thousand dollars worth, more than anyone else in Rhode Island—would dictate a firm allegiance to the requirements of the federal treasury. But John was driven by something deeper, the same fiery individualism that had led a bickering band of iconoclasts to follow Roger Williams to Providence in the first place. It wasn't cold calculation that prompted John to torch the *Gaspee*, it was sheer indignation, a surge of ire and blind will. John turned the same temper against the Impost: he never stood easy under the dictates of monarchical ministers, and he would regard the new tribunes of democracy with the same jaundiced eye.

10

Equal Rights

DURING A SULTRY AFTERNOON in late August 1783, Moses Brown made his way to John Carter's print shop to pick up copies of a new pamphlet arguing against the slave trade. He set a bundle of the freshly minted pamphlets on the bench of his one-horse surrey and set off to make a round of deliveries.

The streets of Providence were crowded that season, as the town stirred itself to throw off the torpor of the war years. Newport had been all but demolished during the British occupation, and Providence was quick to assume its place as the commercial center of the region. New buildings were being raised, including the Golden Ball, a huge, four-story inn on Benefit Street fronted by a double-decker balcony, that soon became the venue of choice for balls and state dinners. The town was expanding west as well, onto the marshy flats across the Great Salt River, where two new aqueducts brought springwater to supply new homes and businesses. From Prospect Hill to the cow pastures south and west of Weybosset, the air rang with the sounds of hammer and adze, and elegant carriages jostled with heavy wagons hauling lumber and brick along the cobblestones.

Moses was already familiar to the town's longtime residents; now he was becoming known as something of an eccentric. He had replaced the fine clothes of a successful merchant with the drab garb of the Quakers, wearing his broad-brimmed hat even in warm weather. And where most carriages of the day featured roofs of gray or black cloth, Moses had his upholstered in white, to keep it cool in the summer. When he steered his way through the bustle of carts and crowds along Towne Street, people knew just who was coming.

One of his last stops, at the south end of town, was at the merchant house of Clarke & Nightingale. Like John Brown, John Innes Clarke and Joseph Nightingale had profited handsomely off the war, running privateers and doing business through the committee building frigates for the navy. Now the firm was preparing to resume its maritime trade; one of its first ventures was an expedition to Africa.

John Clarke knew Moses well—he was a longtime member of the Baptist church, married to Jabez Bowen's sister—and Clarke met Moses cordially. They were indeed fitting out a ship for Africa, Clarke assured him, with a cargo of rum from their in-house still, but only to trade in ivory, beeswax, and gold dust—the so-called legitimate trade. Moses returned to Elmgrove that evening confident at least that he had been heard.

He learned soon after that Clarke had misled him; that the ship fitting for Africa was in fact a slaver. Moses promptly sat down and wrote a lengthy plea to Clarke and Nightengale, asking that they "give orders to the captain not to suffer any Negroes to be brought on board." Where his other tracts against slavery, addressed to legislators and to the public, stressed the iniquities of the trade and the ordeal of the slaves, in this letter Moses was more personal, asking his merchant friends to consider their own consciences, to save their own souls. Moses said his own decision, years before, to engage in the trade despite "averse convictions," had led to "the most uneasiness, and has left the greatest impression and stain upon my mind of any if not all my other conduct in life." His remorse was especially acute, Moses wrote, when he paused to think how his conduct might appear in judgment before God. Moses felt moved, then, by "some engagement for your preservation from so great an evil as I have found the trade to be." He implored them to reconsider, "that you may avoid the unhappy reflections which I have had."

If that was not prodding enough, Moses added an audacious dig to jar the merchants' sensibilities close to home. One of their own bondsmen had approached him some time ago, Moses confided, seeking release from "the burden of slavery." Moses said he counseled the slave to be patient, but he asked the merchants to consider, if a slave sought relief from their own kind treatment, how much worse must be the anguish of those slaves sold to a life of toil in the tropics.

Moses' appeal had no effect; the Clarke & Nightingale sloop *Providence* set sail soon afterward for Africa and proceeded thence to the Caribbean with a cargo of slaves. The voyage marked a turning point in the course of the American slave trade: during the years of fighting with England, the trade had entirely ceased, but with the signing of the Treaty of Paris, the sea lanes were open again to commerce, and the merchants of New England lost no time in returning to the most risky but most profitable trade of the era. In late 1784, when Moses had his encounter with John Clarke, merchants in Boston, Salem, and Newport were also laying plans to send out slaving vessels. By the summer of 1785, when the *Providence* made her return, a correspondent in Africa reported seeing six American ships anchored off the Slave Coast, "and more daily expected."

The sailing of the *Providence* marked a turning point for Moses as well. Since the beginning of the Revolution, Moses had been content to restrict his political efforts and his drive for social reform to the confines of the Quaker church. Similarly, he had answered his concern over the fate of Africans in America through personal acts of philanthropy and intervention, as in the case of John Clarke. But it was fast becoming clear that the question of slavery was too large and too important to be left to individual judgment or ecclesiastical argument. England was no longer sovereign, meaning that America would be charting her own course, with Americans at the helm. For Moses that meant returning to the public forum and pressing his antislavery agenda.

In this Moses was not alone. Quakers throughout the former colonies, and especially Moses' friend and correspondent Anthony Benezet, recognized that cessation of hostilities with Britain presented a unique opportunity to bring the new language of human rights to bear on the reality of slavery. Benezet swung into action, reviving his publishing campaign and pressing the Pennsylvania–New Jersey Yearly Meeting in 1783 to lodge a formal petition with the Continental Congress calling for a ban on the slave trade. That October, a Quaker delegation including Benezet, James Pemberton, and Warner Mifflin traveled to Princeton, New Jersey, where the Congress was sitting, to present their petition.

The Quakers made their impassioned arguments, but they got short shrift from the Congress. The president of the body, Elias Boudinot of New Jersey, was an opponent of slavery, and met personally with Benezet, but the best he could do was win referral to a committee, in December, led by David Howell. Howell was also sympathetic to the abolitionist cause, but he was already deeply engaged in the battle over the Impost, and approved a compromise measure referring the petition to the individual states. The committee's timorous report set the tone for all the government's future dealings with the question; the word "slavery" was not even mentioned, but invoked by reference to "the object of the second article in the association entered into . . . [in] October 1774"—the ban on slave trading installed at the outset of the Revolution. At any rate, in January, the report itself was rejected.

It may simply have been too soon: the Congress was at that time beset by the funding crisis and hamstrung by flagging interest in the very idea of a central federal government. After the move to Princeton, taken in part to escape the ravages of yellow fever in Philadelphia, many delegates weren't even both-

ering to show up. At the same time, as the lawmakers made explicit in conference with the Quakers, their actual powers of legislation were strictly limited
by the Articles of Confederation. The abolitionists would have to wait for a
more competent forum to take shape.

Moses Brown undertook his new campaign against slavery in earnest that September 1783. He submitted a fresh round of articles against slavery to John
Carter, including draft legislation patterned closely after the emancipation
bill Moses had touted in 1775. A month later, he sat down with the Quaker
committee that had lobbied against the slave trade back in 1774, including
Tom Hazard and David Buffum, and together they drew up a new petition for
the General Assembly. The plan was ambitious, calling for more comprehensive antislavery legislation than anything that had come before, including
gradual emancipation and a strict ban on any residents of the state taking part
in the slave trade.

The petition made explicit reference to the Revolution and the new circumstances arising from independence; the institution of slavery "is not an
evil which has taken place in the present day," but now that America was
awakened to the "blessings of liberty," slavery represented "a national evil,
with accumulated guilt." America having prevailed in the war with England,
the Quakers pleaded "that the general joy may not be any longer interrupted
by the sighs of those who yet labor under bondage."

Enthusiastic as they were, Moses and his Quaker allies were also deliberate. Moses drew up a list of all sixty-six delegates to the General Assembly and
broke it down by their prospective votes; he could anticipate outright opposition from twenty-five, and firm support from just sixteen. Moses' brother John,
a delegate from Providence, was counted as undecided. The committee decided to wait until after the October elections in hopes the new assembly
might prove more amenable. The petition was submitted in December, and
promptly referred to committee; a bill was produced a week later for consideration at the February session.

Moses had been down this road before; his lonely crusade in 1775 had produced only frustration. This time he was more systematic, and more expansive. He and his Quaker allies presented their petition to town councils across
the state, seeking instructions compelling their delegates to support the bill.
Separately, Moses reached across the usual denominational divides, writing a
passionate appeal seeking the support of several key religious leaders. This was
an unusual breach of practice, because Quakers, like the other Protestant

sects of that era, were jealous of their doctrine and convinced that rival congregations were wrong, if not damnably misguided.

Yet Moses knew that the proposed ban on slave trading had already aroused
strong opposition, and he believed a voice from the pulpit would be essential
to a winning strategy. Writing to James Manning of the Baptists, and to the
Congregationalist ministers Enos Hitchcock of Providence and Samuel Hopkins of Newport, Moses proposed that it was "honorable for men of virtue,
however they may differ in modes or forms, to be united in using their influence," especially in a cause so urgent as bringing an end to slavery. Moses
reiterated the account he gave Clarke and Nightengale of his own guilty involvement in the slave trade, and made the blunt demand, "The conduct of
Christians must be changed."

The success of Moses' appeal was evident when the bill was discussed at the
Providence town meeting of January 31, 1784. James Manning arrived "with a
number of sober and respectable members" of his flock, as Moses termed
them. And while Joseph Snow, a Congregationalist from the west side of town,
was too ill to attend, he called members of his church to his home and showed
them Moses' letter before sending them off with orders to vote their consciences. There is no record of the debate at the meeting, but John Brown apparently stood silent as the vote was taken: 108 in favor of the abolition bill and
58 against. During the next few weeks, freemen at four other town meetings
directed their delegates to support the bill.

The matter finally came before the General Assembly on February 25, and
the hearing lasted for most of two days. The bill itself, as issued from the committee of the lower house, was dressed in full Jeffersonian regalia. "Whereas,
all men are entitled to life, liberty, and the pursuit of happiness," the preamble
read, "and the holding of mankind in a state of slavery, as private property . . . is
repugnant to this principle, and subversive of the happiness of mankind. . . ."
The text went on to propose that for all children born after the first day of
March, the institution of lifelong servitude would be "taken away, extinguished, and forever abolished." Further—and this was the more controversial
section—the bill prohibited any resident of the state from engaging in the slave
trade, and required that owners of vessels fitting out for Africa post a bond of
one thousand pounds to ensure that slaves were not included in the cargo.

The debate was joined after the bill was read. Moses anticipated a vigorous
contest, and he may have looked forward to the opportunity finally to confront
his foes in a public forum, and with meaningful legislation at stake. What he
did not anticipate, and what caused him deep dismay, was to find his brother
taking the floor as the leader of the opposition.

John Brown never intimated, in conversation or at the town meeting, his deep antipathy for the bill. He had no direct interest at stake—like the other slave traders in Rhode Island, he had quit the business upon the order of the Continental Association—and it was John who had requested direction of the freemen at the town meeting. But John had already demonstrated, in the campaign to stop the Impost, that he would challenge any effort to place limits on maritime commerce. And like Moses, John understood that decisions made in the wake of the war would set precedent for years to come. His instinct told him that now was the time to fight for the prerogatives of the merchants.

There may have been, as well, an element of family rivalry in John's adamant opposition to Moses' initiative. The brothers had been partners for years—in business, as Sons of Liberty, in winning the college for Providence—and while they usually stood as allies, John may have tired of sharing laurels with his more pious brother. Similarly, while John was grateful to Moses for winning his release from British custody, there had to be an attendant aspect of humiliation, one only underscored when John reneged on the agreement Moses had made with the military authorities in Boston. Within the family, as in the town at large, John wielded great influence, but Moses seemed to enjoy greater respect. Nicholas, for example, was John's business partner during the war, but when his second son was born, in February 1775, Nicholas chose to name him Moses.

Besides, John was defiant by nature, especially so in the face of conventional wisdom. When Zephania Andrews, master builder for the Brown family projects, wrote to chastise John for ignoring the direction of the town meeting, John answered that he would be "politically dead" and "useless to my family and friends" if he did not trust and follow his own counsel. As to the vote of the freemen, John had decided that "the majority of the town was misled," though he did not elaborate how.

In any event, after Moses had marshaled a coalition of clergy to swing the vote at the town meeting, John turned the tables at the General Assembly. Animated, agitated, his raspy voice echoing across the statehouse chamber, John spoke early and often, pausing to introduce witnesses and then resuming his own discourse. He had help, from the Newport delegation and from Joseph Nightengale, another Providence delegate who ignored the directions of the town meeting. The debate ranged across the full range of issues posed by the question of slavery, from practical to ideological, from political to scriptural.

John opened his case by challenging the comfortable orthodoxy of the abolitionists, arguing that the slave trade was "a piece of humanity," as slaves who remained in Africa were often simply destroyed. To support his point, he called on a veteran of the African trade named Benson to share his experience from the coast. Benson described tribal kings who slaughtered their enemies, and monuments made of skulls. One African woman, passed over for purchase at a slave mart, had begged him to buy her, Benson said, as she would be slain if left behind.

Considered at the remove of two centuries, at a time when slavery has been outlawed by every country on Earth, this argument appears almost absurd. But it was a genuine question at the time, and still provokes debate among academic investigators today. Slavery was a scourge, certainly, but slavery was widespread in Africa long before the rise of the European trade, and even at the height of the plantation system, more Africans were slaves in Africa than in all the plantations of the Americas. While it is hard to credit the European slavers with any pretense to "humanity," it was at least plausible to suggest that transport to the Americas might be preferable to bondage at home.

John was not alone in asserting this moral defense of slavery. The rise of abolitionism as a genuine political force was attended, in the decade preceding the General Assembly debate, by the publication of several tracts articulating the proslavery position. One of the most accomplished was produced by Richard Nisbet, a Caribbean slaveholder educated at Oxford who made occasional visits to the abolitionist stronghold of Philadelphia. In 1773, Nesbit answered the reformers with *Slavery Not Forbidden by Scripture*, proposing that black slaves working the British plantations had "fewer cares, and less reason to be anxious about tomorrow, than any other individual of our species." And while Nisbet's depiction is contradicted by many contemporaneous sources, the fact remains that African-Americans in bondage came to know longer life expectancy than those left behind. The point is not that John was right, but that he had an argument to make, and in calling Benson as a witness, he made it with some authority.

John then turned the floor over to Esek Hopkins, elected as a delegate from North Providence after his dismissal from Continental service. Esek had apparently patched things up with John after their bitter struggle over naval affairs—possibly because John had secured him a position on the board at Rhode Island College—and now he was ready to read lines from John's script. Esek questioned the ethics of Quakers who opposed slavery but readily partook of the rum, sugars, and indigo produced on the plantations of the West Indies. Taking the question further, Esek called on Jonathan Arnold, a Quaker merchant and a delegate to Congress, demanding to know if Arnold hadn't recently sent a trading vessel to the Caribbean.

Next to stand was Nathan Miller, a deputy from Warren and a member of the committee that drafted the bill. Slavery was endorsed in the Bible, Miller said, reprising the debate between Samuel Sewall and James Saffin eighty years before.

John Brown returned to the rostrum to take up the more practical elements of the question. The resolve of Congress against the slave trade, passed in 1774, had expired, John said, and the recent petition of the Quakers was still pending. Leave the matter for Congress to decide, John said. In the meantime, consider the economic consequences to Newport if the slave trade were abandoned. Here John produced chalk and a blackboard, and proceeded to tally up the costs of crippled trade and idle distilleries, guiding the assembly through his calculations like a professor at a seminar.

The success of John's argument was secured when William Bradford, the speaker of the lower house, a lean patrician from Bristol, rose to sum up the debate. Rhode Island had gone far enough by passing a law to bar the import of slaves, Bradford said. Any additional effort by "this little state" would be futile, "like the smallest spot in the face of the sun, and would no more stop the trade if we passed the new act than ye spot would the light." This was especially disappointing to Moses, as Bradford had been an ardent champion of liberty on the colony's committee of correspondence. In opposing the slave-trade bill, Bradford demonstrated once again the limits of the Revolutionary appeals to natural rights.

When the vote was called, the ban on slave trading was defeated by a margin of two to one. It was a devastating reversal, the triumph, in Moses' estimation, of "interest and influence" over "the justice of the subject." It didn't help, Moses noted, that the bill had been sponsored by Quakers, who were widely reviled for their pacifist opposition to the recent war. "We were much flung at by several," Moses recorded dolefully.

It wasn't a total loss. The assembly did approve the manumission bill, setting the stage for the gradual abolition of slavery throughout New England. And in a separate vote, it repealed the earlier amendment to the ban on imports that allowed traders to bring surplus slaves into the state for as long as a year pending sale in the West Indies. Thus Moses prevailed on key elements of the legislation he had sponsored eight years before, and Rhode Island joined Pennsylvania and Connecticut in the post-Revolutionary movement of the northern states to end the institution of slavery. While Massachusetts and New Hampshire followed haltingly—the status of slaves there remained in limbo for decades—the close of the Revolution brought into sharp relief the divide within the new union between the southern and northern states over the question of slavery.

But while Moses achieved a partial victory at the legislature, he also learned that his most persistent and resourceful adversary would be his own brother. Moses' campaign against slavery would no longer pit him against a remote and morally fathomless opposition; from here forward, the struggle would lead to intimate and sometimes painful confrontations, forcing him to question his basic assumptions about family, community, and the nature of the human spirit.

Moses' postwar campaign to end Rhode Island's involvement in the slave trade also brought him into an important new alliance with Samuel Hopkins, pastor of the First Congregational Church at Newport. A disciple of Jonathan Edwards, one of the leading proponents of the Great Awakening, which brought a new emphasis on sin and the renewal of faith, Hopkins had spent twenty-five years preaching to a small parish in rural Massachusetts before being called to Newport in 1770. Soon after his arrival there Hopkins published a new treatise, *True Holiness,* an extension of Edwards's doctrine that unselfish love and benevolence represented the one true path to salvation. As refined by Hopkins, the doctrine of benevolence required the virtuous individual to abandon all ambition for worldly success in favor of unceasing, altruistic endeavor on behalf of the poor and the oppressed. This was a radical new formulation that rejected the customary routines of the church in favor of concrete engagement in the affairs of men. It soon led Hopkins to an ambitious attack on slavery.

Hopkins's theology had little to say about slavery at first—Edwards had several slaves, and Hopkins owned one himself—but after he moved to the seat of the American slave trade, Hopkins could no longer ignore it. By 1776, when Congress was weighing the dangers of independence, Hopkins issued his book-length *Dialogue Concerning the Slavery of the Africans.* Addressed and dedicated to "the Honorable Continental Congress," the *Dialogue* was framed as a carefully reasoned argument between a slaveholder and a freeman who espoused the principles of liberty. Hopkins targeted "the gross, barefaced inconsistence" of patriots who held slaves in bondage, and specifically called upon Congress to establish "universal liberty to white and black." Others had decried the hypocrisy of Americans holding men and women in bondage, but Hopkins went further than any of his contemporaries, demanding immediate emancipation, and suggesting that the war itself was evidence of God's anger at the prevalence of slavery. "We have no reason to expect deliverance," Hopkins wrote, "till we put away the evil of our doings."

Coming during a lull in the early abolition movement, when matters of liberty took a backseat to the affairs of war, the pamphlet failed to make much of an impression on Congress, but it served to broaden the early abolitionist movement beyond the exclusive domain of the Quakers. Hopkins's challenge to slavery was further muted by the British occupation of Newport at the end of 1776, forcing him to spend the next four years preaching at pulpits scattered around southern New England. But by 1784, when Moses called on the clergy to rally against the slave trade, Hopkins became a close and influential ally. Their correspondence serves as a window on the early movement against slavery, its accomplishments, and its setbacks.

Writing to Hopkins after the debacle at the General Assembly, Moses reported that "the influence of the mercantile interest" had carried the day, but he remained convinced that, "notwithstanding the vote of the Assembly there is a considerable majority of the state against the trade, and what is wanting is to call those feelings into action in the cause of reason, humanity and religion."

Hopkins responded two months later, after the spring elections, and commended Moses for his perseverance, confiding, "I am apt to sink under discouragements which you seem easily to surmount." To explain his doubts, Hopkins described his own tenuous situation. "I have dared publicly to declare that this town is the most guilty, respecting the trade, of any on the continent, as it has been, in a great measure, built up by the blood of the poor Africans. . . . This has greatly displeased a number, and I fear the most are far from a disposition to repent, especially they who have the greatest share of the guilt. . . . This gives me a gloomy prospect of our future circumstances!"

As much as Moses and Samuel Hopkins had in common, they also had grounds to differ. Hopkins was an early advocate for repatriating freed slaves back to Africa. "Colonization," as the plan was known, would avoid the problem of integrating free blacks into a hostile society, and offer the added benefit of spreading the gospel in heathen Africa. The scheme had broad appeal, winning support from racists who believed blacks and whites could not coexist, as well as from abolitionists—indeed, the two camps sometimes overlapped. When Hopkins proposed the idea, Moses gently demurred. His time was best spent in the campaign against the trade, Moses said, but he would share the colonization plan with other Quakers and report back on how it was received. In later years Moses flatly denounced the idea, but in 1784 it was still novel. Besides, in his effort to end slavery, Moses needed all the friends he could get.

In the same month that Rhode Island struck its grudging compromise with Moses and the abolitionist Quakers, Congress was wrestling with a new demand that it square the republican ideals of the Revolution with the institution of slavery. This challenge came from within the government, and could not be brushed off as another extremist initiative.

The question arose as the new Confederacy wrestled with the prospect of opening up the western frontier to settlement. The Revolution had stalled the progress of westward expansion, but even before the fighting was over pioneer families were streaming over the Appalachian Mountains to the well-watered valleys beyond. This raised important questions of how the new territories should be governed, both for the white settlers and for the Indians who already lived there. At the same time, sale of the western lands was viewed as a potential windfall for the nation, especially by David Howell, who touted proceeds from land sales as an alternative to the Impost for paying down the federal debt.

The first plan for governing the West was posed by the army—it was the army, after all, that had the strongest claim against the Treasury. Soldiers would accept land in lieu of cash in settlement of back pay and other obligations. The plan was designed by Timothy Pickering, the quartermaster general of the army under Washington. Pickering was that odd bird for his time, a second-generation abolitionist—his father was a Presbyterian deacon and gadfly in Salem, Massachusetts—and his draft of a governing ordinance called for "the total exclusion of slavery."

That first initiative was soon incorporated into a more vague but more expansive plan endorsed by Alexander Hamilton, again devised to help pay off the army. It then went to a committee comprising Thomas Jefferson, David Howell, and Jeremiah Chase of Maryland. With Jefferson absent for much of the discussion, it fell to Howell to craft the final ordinance.

Howell was an admirer of Moses as well as John Brown, and he counted himself an abolitionist, so Moses had hopes that the new ordinance for the western territories would serve as a bulwark against slavery. As with the campaign against the African trade, a measure to hem the expansion of the institution would represent an important step toward its final elimination.

But Howell's interests were not limited to slavery, and in his committee work, he paid far more attention to the size and autonomy of the prospective states—he agitated for immediate self-rule, as opposed to interim government by Congress—than to civil rights. Consequently, Howell signed off on new language submitted by Jefferson, a watered-down version of Pickering's hard line against slavery that delayed abolition in the new territories until the year 1800.

When the bill was reported to Congress, Pickering immediately challenged the new wording. "To introduce [slaves] into countries where none now exist," Pickering argued, "countries which have been talked of, have been boasted of, as asylums to the oppressed of the earth—can never be forgiven." But when the debate was joined, the representatives of the southern tier challenged even the revised version, and demanded a vote. Howell, who was shepherding the bill on the floor, was quickly outmaneuvered, allowing the question to be posed in the negative: "Shall the words moved to be struck out stand?" The vote was six in favor and three opposed, with one state divided and two absent, but as the motion required a majority of seven, the measure failed, and the prohibition on human bondage was dropped. Another crucial opportunity to limit the advance of slavery had been lost.

For Moses Brown, the decision at Congress had to be especially dispiriting. He had learned around the same time of the death of Anthony Benezet, and of the rebuff by Parliament of a new Quaker petition against the slave trade. And at home, Moses' wife and daughter were both ill and showing little sign of recovery. But once again Moses displayed the determined optimism that so impressed Samuel Hopkins. In a letter to Howell a month after the vote on the western lands, Moses managed to be complimentary and forward-looking. "I was glad to find you were so thoughtful of liberty as to [seek to] prevent slavery in the new states sixteen years hence," he wrote. "I wish the old ones might be engaged no longer to abridge its black inhabitants of those rights which they have been so long contending for, I mean Liberty."

Moses went on to encourage Howell to revive before Congress the proposal to ban trade with Africa, and speculated hopefully that Virginia might join Rhode Island and Connecticut by introducing gradual abolition. He then asked a startling and critical question: "Has General Washington freed his Negroes or has he not?"

Considering the well-known history of Washington's stony silence on the question of slavery, and that he finally manumitted his 123 slaves only upon his decease, Moses' query seems wildly off base. Yet recent scholarship examining Washington's attitudes and his personal struggle with the limits on manumission in Virginia suggest there may have been foundation for such speculation. Washington's experience with black soldiers during the war appears to have softened his feelings toward Africans in general, and the officers closest to the commander, particularly Alexander Hamilton and the Marquis de Lafayette, were adamantly opposed to the continued practice of slavery in the new republic.

As early as 1783, upon learning that a treaty of peace had been concluded,

Lafayette wrote to Washington a letter of congratulations, which he closed by proposing that they both join together and "try the experiment to free the Negroes." Well aware of Washington's stature as liberator, Lafayette made explicit that "such an example as yours might render it a general practice." Washington replied with evident enthusiasm, even acknowledging that such a precedent might "encourage the emancipation of the black people of this country," and promised to discuss the matter when he next saw Lafayette in person. That meeting took place in 1784, and while Washington finally demurred, a houseguest at Mount Vernon recalled that Washington said then he "wished to get rid of his Negroes." The following year, another visitor, a Methodist bishop, recorded in his diary that Washington had proclaimed his opinion against slavery. Rumor of such a dispensation may well have reached the ears of Howell in Congress, and thence been relayed to Moses.

Of course, it may just have been wishful thinking on Moses' part, to suppose that a landed Virginia aristocrat would relinquish so substantial a piece of his estate. But that goes to demonstrate the increasing desperation of Moses and the other abolitionists. The war had been waged and won in the name of liberty and equal rights, but it was fast becoming clear that the southern states were loath to apply those principles to the chained and branded Africans who tilled their plantations, and that Congress was unwilling to test the South's resolve. A grand gesture by Washington may well have been the last, best chance to mount a meaningful challenge to the institution of slavery in America. Certainly Moses perceived the irony that attended Washington's standing as a slaveholding freedom fighter. If the general were to keep his slaves, Moses observed to Howell, "this will indeed be a paradox to posterity."

John Brown does not appear to have dwelt at any great length on his decision to oppose Moses' slave-trade initiative. He denounced the plan as "a shallow policy," orchestrated the floor fight against it, and moved on. So far as John was concerned, there were far more pressing matters to attend to.

John was, at the close of the Revolution, at the height of his powers and at the height of his influence — "the Providence Colossus," as some in town referred to him. Moses had speculated, in a letter to Samuel Hopkins, that the freemen of Providence would oust John from the assembly for ignoring the instructions of the town meeting, but just the opposite occured: in May, John was elected to Congress. Whether he campaigned for the post is hard to say, but certainly his feelings about the federal government were ambivalent. He expressed continuing interest in Robert Morris's plan to establish a national currency, but he scoffed at the main project then occupying Congress—its doomed effort to resurrect the Impost. In any event, having won the job, John chose not to serve. The assembly then issued explicit instructions sending the state's delegates to Congress, but John ignored them.

Many other delegates made the same decision. By that time Congress was all but itinerant, meeting, successively, in Princeton, Annapolis, Philadelphia, and then Trenton, sneered upon by the public and by its own members—Virginia delegate John Francis Mercer called it "a vagabond, strolling, contemptible crew"—and powerless to address the intractable problems of the army and the debt. So disenchanted was John that, in 1785, he spurned his appointment, arranged by David Howell, as one of three commissioners named to supervise construction of a new seat of government at the District of Columbia. It is apparent that the antipathy was mutual. That same year, a petition filed by John and by James Manning seeking compensation for wartime damages to Rhode Island College was approved in committee, but rejected by the full Congress, in part to punish the state for opposing the Impost. The following year Manning, sent to Congress in John's place, wrote home that "the politics of Rhode Island are *damned* by all I hear speak of them."

Rather than attend Congress, John occupied himself with the affairs of his vast estate and his growing family. In the early 1780s, the Great Salt River was jammed with close to sixty wharves and John was seeking room to grow. The candle business had declined during the war, idling the Browns' eleven-acre manufactory at Tockwotten, a south-facing waterfront below the end of town. Consequently, John set about refurbishing the wharves and storehouses on the Tockwotten property to serve as headquarters for an expanded shipping operation. His mercantile fleet had been diminished by wartime captures, but the losses were far outweighed by profits from privateering gains that left him huge sums to invest. These he plunged into a renewed presence in the Caribbean—despite a new British embargo on trade with her colonies there—into European imports, and into a fleet of sixteen new fishing vessels, small schooners rated at just twenty-five tons apiece, with which he hoped to capture a substantial piece of the cod market so long dominated by Massachusetts. The fishing operation taxed John's imagination more than his purse; rather than name the new boats he assigned them letters of the alphabet, his account books recording the exploits of schooners A through P.

At the same time he moved his business operations, John decided to move his home as well. Enlisting the help of his brother Joseph, John laid plans for a grand new mansion to be situated on Benefit Street, above the commercial fray of the town's main street but still close enough for him to keep an eye on his many interests. The imposing brownstone-trimmed brick structure would be the largest private residence in town, three stories high, with views of the bay, the wharves along the river, and to the northwest, the gleaming steeple of the First Baptist Church. The mansion was built around a grand staircase with railings anchored in twisted newel posts; flanking rooms opened onto the central hall through double doors topped by elaborate carved pediments. The walls were papered in French cloth, the fireplaces clad in Philadelphia marble. For all the elegance, John gave prominent placement in the foyer to a carved squirrel, a homage to his personal ethic of busy industry.

The business of the home was attended in outbuildings. There was a freestanding kitchen, and a bathhouse, and the slaves' quarters. There was a carriage house as well, where John kept a variety of coaches, including the one he'd obtained from General Gage. They were a mark of distinction in a town that boasted but a handful of personal vehicles; John's favorite was a four-wheeled chaise his son had bought in Philadelphia. Called a chariot in the vernacular of the day, it was custom-finished with glass windows and pleated curtains, the exterior painted a soft robin's-egg blue and edged in gold. The interior was built to seat two on a padded, forward-facing bench, but John, with his prodigious girth, used it as a solo conveyance, riding in style as he made the rounds of his various enterprises and properties.

Even as he was laying out his new home, John was struggling to keep his household together. With all else in transition, five of his male slaves escaped, leaving their berths in John's home and workshops and making their way to Boston, where they settled in with the free black community. They found liberty there but they also found destitution, and three of them returned to Providence soon after, being received upon a promise to "behave better." John took this all in stride, attributing the desertion of his slaves to the meddling of the Quaker idealists, and their voluntary return to his benevolent tutelage. Still, it had to be unsettling, to John's business operations if not to his conception of his own benevolent nature.

John appears to have had only slightly better relations with his own children. His son James, having graduated from college, was frequently on the road, ostensibly to attend to business matters but usually more for pleasure. John wrote him constantly, offering advice, pleading with him to "turn your thoughts to business," and chiding him for spending lavishly and keeping loose company. John's eldest daughter, Abby, though still in her teens, was also getting restless. She fell in love with John Francis, the son of John's close Philadelphia associate Tench Francis, whom she met during a visit the young man made to Providence in 1783; two years later, John felt compelled to implore

John Francis, just twenty-two years old, not to entice his daughter to move away to Philadelphia. The mere thought of her departure, John wrote, "fills my eyes with rivers and my heart with pain." John's solution to the problem became apparent in February 1786, when he announced he was taking John Francis on as a partner. John Francis and Abby were married two years later.

Still, the life at home wasn't all tension. Writing to John's daughter Sally when she was out of town later that spring, a friend described the family dynamic: "Abby and your mama are next door with your aunt, your papa is in the front room with a numerous junto of politicians, and Jimmy is down at Point Pleasant. Thus stationed I suppose agreeably to their inclinations."

John also strove to maintain his familial connections with his brothers. He ended his partnership with Nicholas at the close of the war, but while they often competed in the same lines of business, they always remained cordial, sometimes helping to finance each other's ventures. Relations with Moses, of course, were more delicate. Neither of the two brothers broached any direct discussion of their confrontation at the General Assembly over the slave bill; the incident appears to have passed in silence, with both men too proud, or too uncomfortable, to acknowledge the gulf growing between them. Their continuing rivalry was evidenced in their philanthropy: in a grand gesture, in 1784, John offered to match any and all donations to the library at Rhode Island College, spurring a subscription that raised more than fifteen hundred pounds. Rather than join that effort, Moses made his own, much more modest contribution that same year, importing from England twenty pounds' worth of books—mostly religious titles—which he delivered to the library in person.

But John was careful to signal to Moses his continuing esteem. In April 1785 he wrote a short note, signed also by Nicholas Brown and John Jenckes, asking Moses to accept an appointment as a Providence deputy to the General Assembly. Joseph Nightengale had been elected but declined to serve, and the three asked Moses to step in "as no man can be thought of who will do the town that real service as you can." The request was probably made just for show—Moses had made it abundantly clear that he was no longer interested in public office—but it was a substantial peace offering.

John, Moses, and Nicholas were reminded again of the bonds of kinship that December, when Joseph Brown died of what appeared to be a stroke. Joseph had been stricken a year before, and while he recovered most of his faculties, he was enfeebled through the final days of his life. While never so prominent in business as his brothers, Joseph had served several turns in the General Assembly, and the monuments he designed—the college building, the market house, the new Baptist church, and his own handsome home on

Towne Street—ensured him a prominent place in the story of the town. His passing drew his brothers together for several days of sorrowful observance, together with their families and that of Jabez Bowen. As John described it in a letter to his children, "We are taught that it is better to go to the house of mourning than the house of feasting, especially when a breach is made among the four brothers which have so long survived."

John respected Moses and cultivated his friendship, but he was never going to allow that consideration to restrict his decisions in business or in politics. Driven, self-directed, skeptical of and perhaps incapable of compromise, John might try to seek accommodation, but always in the end he listened to his own counsel. In 1786, with his fishing venture foundering and commerce in general slipping into doldrums, John decided to return to the slave trade.

He sent his first ship to Africa early in the year. As with the *Sally*, that voyage met with disaster—his ship returned in September having lost half of a cargo of seventy slaves, along with the captain and the first mate. John suffered this debacle in silence, possibly out of chagrin for his role in still another episode of profound human suffering, but probably also because he didn't want to supply his critics with more ammunition. Moses certainly would have remarked on the incident had he learned of it, but he never did—the only account of this disastrous voyage that survives is a notation in a diary kept by John Francis, who learned of it from a sea captain and wrote his father-in-law to share the bad news.

The debacle certainly entailed a financial setback, but John was obstinate, and late that fall, he began fitting out a second ship for the Guinea Coast. Moses caught wind of this venture and quickly composed a letter of protest to John. It made the same moral arguments he'd made to Clarke and Nightengale, and added the more practical observation that, for all the pain they caused, slave voyages often failed even to return a profit. Moses included with his letter a recent pamphlet arguing against the trade, and dispatched the package the afternoon of November 27. It was delivered by Moses' son Obadiah, just as John was sitting down to a meal.

John decided to come clean with his brother, responding with a letter that was at once conciliatory and defiant. Yes, it was true; his ship had been four months in preparation and had just begun taking on ballast. But there was no turning back. "I have no doubt of your sincerity in your exertions to discourage the slave trade," John wrote, "and did I consider it as you do I would by no means be concerned in it." But despite the recent desertion of his own chattel,

John was convinced "the slaves are positively better off that is brought from the coast than those that are left behind." Moreover, John had directed his captains to sell their cargo at Hispaniola, "where all accounts agree they are better treated than in any part of the English West Indies."

John emphasized again: "When I am convinced as you are that it is wrong in the sight of God, I will immediately desist, but while it's not only allowed by the Supreme Governor of all states, but by all the nations of Europe . . . I cannot think that this state ought to decline the trade."

These were the same arguments John had made before the General Assembly; whether he truly believed them, or was simply rationalizing, is hard to say, but John went on to detail his motivations explicitly. He confirmed that he'd sustained losses, "sometimes very graitly, in almost every voyage to Guinea," though he did not share the grim news of his most recent failure. But John remained convinced of the bonanza that a successful venture would yield. "All the estates that have been acquired" in Newport had been won through slaving, John wrote.

Clearly, John felt he had little choice. "I owe an enormous sum of money in Europe, and am striving in every trade which appears lawful and right to me, to pay as much of that debt as possible." John enumerated his ventures in shipping tobacco and in cod fishing, so far with no profits to show.

John closed with another elaborate bid to appease his brother. John had recently been elected to another term in the assembly, but he would gladly relinquish that seat to Moses, and would do nothing to oppose a new bill against the slave trade. "I am fully sensible that you can serve the town and state at large all better as a legislator than I can, and wish with all my heart you would once more consent to serve the public that way."

John was laying it on thick. "Tho I am not endowed with the divine light to see the Guinea trade with the same eyes as you do, I respect you as a brother and a friend." If that fraternal reference were not enough, John added, "I respect your children and sincerely wish they might be indulged to be more familiar with mine, I am sure my children has a particular regard for yours." At last, John signed off, "Your affectionate brother."

We can only imagine what Moses made of this extraordinary letter. Certainly he was disappointed, as John was clearly determined to ignore his brother's advice. But Moses could not have been surprised; John had already demonstrated that he would listen only to his own counsel. Besides, John's intransigence followed a pattern. The lawmakers of New England had written a spate of new laws against slavery, but in towns that had pledged blood and treasure in the cause of liberty, and in the rural countryside where the minutemen drilled in ragtag formations, blacks continued to be marginalized and despised, returned to bondage by former masters, or kidnapped and sold to the south.

The status of black mariners on the New England waterfront was especially tenuous, as shipowners and captains treated their black seamen as a sort of hybrid cargo and crew, hiring them with promises of manumission only to renege or, worse, sell them off at ports away from home. Such was the case with Cato, a slave who sailed out of Providence for John Clarke and Joseph Nightengale. Like Priamus during the war, Cato was promised his freedom, but when his ship reached New York in 1784, the owners had him jailed for an alleged debt. A Quaker abolitionist there wrote to ask Moses to intervene on Cato's behalf, but Moses answered that, based on his prior experience with the two merchants, "no application would be of use." Moses felt obliged to add a note on the character of the two Providence merchants. "By this time thou mayst think them men of bad principle," Moses wrote, "but I can assure thee they stand high in reputation as merchants here, and I may say, having dealt largely with them, I have ever found them as punctual in business as most, their conduct in the case of slavery notwithstanding." As for Cato, Moses could only advise that his friend post bail and keep him "out of their reach."

As the incidents multiplied, Moses relied on a small cadre of fellow activists to help pursue legal and other responses, but by 1786 he lamented that they were "but few and those mostly employed . . . their time alone would hardly admit of attending to all the cases." As bad as conditions were in Providence, Newport was worse. When Samuel Hopkins wrote another of his tracts against the slave trade, the publisher of the *Newport Herald* agreed at first to print it, but then recanted, fearing to offend his many readers and advertisers engaged in the trade. Pessimistic by nature, Hopkins despaired of any progress in the legislature and presumed that the deepening crisis of the federal government was divine retribution for America's "depravity, unrighteousness and cruelty."

And yet, for all the kidnappings, all the outrages, and all the disappointments, Moses sensed that public opinion was turning his way. In 1784, the Methodist Conference in Baltimore required its members to manumit their slaves; in 1785 the New York Manumission Society was formed and the Baptists of Virginia moved to condemn slavery. Writing to Hopkins that year to report a string of recent manumissions, Moses proposed that "the testimony gains ground for freedom." Later, describing for a British Friend the political situation in New England, Moses wrote that "the trade is carried on from these states yet the general voice of the people is against it." There were powerful mercenary interests supporting the trade, Moses acknowledged, but "if the tenderness of the people can be kept alive, time may work for the deliverance of the captives."

The intellectual tide was turning against slavery along with public opinion. Anthony Benezet had passed on, but his writings gained wide circulation in Europe as well as America. In London, Cambridge University created a sensation when it offered a prize for the best essay on slavery; the result was Thomas Clarkson's seminal *Commerce of the Human Species*. The book-length tract, which drew on Benezet and saluted the early work of the Quakers, was published on both sides of the Atlantic and spurred the formation, in 1787, of Britain's first nondenominational abolition society.

These were sober and deliberate compositions; it was left to Samuel Hopkins to inject an element of wrath into the discourse. Hopkins was a curiosity for the clergy of the time, a pedantic speaker whose sermons could barely hold his congregation, but he was influential for the sheer righteousness of his dogma. The *Dialogue* that he addressed to Congress was ignored at first, but came to be embraced as a fundamental text by the abolitionists; in 1787 he added a warning, titled simply "The Slave Trade and Slavery," and published in two parts in the *Providence Gazette* over the pseudonym Crito.

"The Slave Trade" dealt only briefly with cataloguing the horrors of the traffic; Hopkins's mission was to alert readers to the price of their complacency. Slavery, he declared, "is become a national sin, and a sin of the first magnitude—a sin which righteous Heaven has never suffered to pass unpunished in this world." It was not just the slave traders who would have to pay the price, Hopkins warned, but "all those who have had any hand in this iniquitous business," even those who failed to oppose it, "are guilty of the blood of millions who have lost their lives by this traffic in the human species." This was the language of Benjamin Lay, but Hopkins made his jeremiad more pointed. Having fought and won a war in the name of liberty, Americans had only increased their culpability. "We are guilty of a ridiculous, wicked contradiction and inconsistence, and practically authorize any nation or people, who have power to do it, to make us their slaves." For Hopkins, as for Moses Brown and a broad constituency who took their principles seriously, slavery remained the one burning question yet to be answered by the American Revolution.

This growing consensus of elite and general opinion crested at a critical juncture for the new nation. The financial crisis John Brown had done so much to aggravate had by now spread to the states; heavy taxes on land, levied to help

defray war debts, sparked resentment and, in Massachusetts, the bloody uprising known as Shays's Rebellion. Rhode Island and several other states issued
large drafts of paper currency, which quickly depreciated, engendering angry
recriminations between debtors and creditors. Strapped for funds, states
began taxing one another with tariffs and trade duties. And with the disputes
turning inward, Congress, empowered to act only by consensus, was neutralized.

The prospect of a solution arose out of a call from Virginia for a conference
of the states to devise a uniform system of commerce. Rather than revise the
Articles of Confederation, the delegates, meeting at Annapolis in 1786, decided on the more ambitious project of drafting a new federal constitution. At
last, the leaders of the new nation would confront the question of just what
they had wrought.

The Constitutional Convention met in Philadelphia for a period of four
months, beginning May 28, 1787. Sequestered in a room forty feet square,
their deliberations kept secret to encourage candor and compromise, the delegates spent long hours hammering out ingenious and enduring answers to
the questions of proportional representation and securing the rights of large
and small states. Congress was granted crucial powers to raise taxes and to reg-
ulate commerce. These were matters where rational men might agree to disagree; the issue that sparked divisive debate and threatened to wreck the entire
national project was the practice of slavery.

The first contest between North and South arose over the question of representation, and resulted in the three-fifths clause that allowed southern states to
count slaves, at that ratio, for the purposes of representation in Congress. That
measure provoked some dissent from northern interests fearful of ceding influence to the South, but for weeks the delegates avoided direct reference to
the moral implications of keeping Africans in bondage. On August 7 Gouverneur Morris of Pennsylvania, the aristocratic protégé of (though not related
to) Robert Morris, broke the ice by declaring he would "never . . . concur in
upholding domestic slavery," which brought "the curse of heaven on the states
where it prevailed."

Crippled by the loss of one leg in his youth, accomplished in business and
celebrated for his wit, Morris dispensed with any pretense of respect for the
slaveholders' position. The plan to count slaves in southern representation
"when fairly explained comes to this: that the inhabitant of Georgia and
South Carolina who goes to the Coast of Africa, and in defiance of the most sacred laws of humanity tears away his fellow creatures from their dearest connections and condemns them to the most cruel bondages, shall have more

votes in a government instituted for protection of the rights of mankind, than the citizen of Pennsylvania or New Jersey who views with a laudable horror, so nefarious a practice."

The southern delegates received this tirade in silence; they knew they had the votes, and Morris's motion to delete the three-fifths clause lost by a wide margin. Two weeks later, the convention took up the more explosive question of allowing import duties, potentially prohibitive, on slave cargoes. This was the only challenge raised at the convention toward limiting the institution of slavery in any regard; emancipation and even gradual abolition were simply too radical to contemplate, but the trade was the most heinous element of the business, and would represent a first step toward reform. In addition, the southern faction was divided on the question; Virginia, Maryland, and Delaware already had a surfeit of slaves, and their delegates were willing to acknowledge the "infernal" nature of the trade. These defections left the Deep South, principally Georgia and South Carolina, isolated and intransigent.

It was left to the New England delegates, especially those of Connecticut, to counsel in favor of compromise. Oliver Ellsworth would not consider the "morality or wisdom of slavery," but advised instead that "what enriches a part enriches the whole." The next day, Ellsworth's associate, Roger Sherman, offered a more pragmatic argument. He personally disapproved of the slave trade, Sherman confided, but the survival of the union was his primary mission.

Sherman was strangely suited to his role as the convention's apostle of expediency and moral capitulation. He was, as one colleague recorded, "the oddest shaped character I ever remember to have met with. . . . The vulgarisms that accompany his public speaking . . . make everything that is connected with him grotesque and laughable." Yet Sherman was also "extremely artful in accomplishing any particular object," and his goal in Philadelphia was to cement the union, not to settle the question of slavery. To those who raised moral qualms, Sherman counseled patience. "The abolition of slavery seemed to be going on in the United States," Sherman averred, "and the good sense of the several states would probably by degrees complete it." Thus did the early abolitionists fall victim to their own limited success.

Other voices were raised in opposition, but by then the outcome was clear: the New England states would allow slavery to persist in return for southern acquiescence to federal regulation of trade. This "dirty compromise," as historian Paul Finkelman has aptly termed it, was codified in the final document. The word "slavery" was never mentioned, but the Constitution provided for legal recovery of fugitive slaves, pledged to raise the militias against slave insurrections, and included three-fifths representation—though of course no vote—for people in bondage. The one slim concession to the abolitionists was to allow Congress to abolish the slave trade, but not for another twenty years. By then, as James Madison observed, the trade "will produce all the mischief that can be apprehended from the liberty to import slaves."

Moses Brown and the other American abolitionists got news of the disappointing results from Philadelphia only gradually—the debates were conducted in secret, and Rhode Island boycotted the entire affair, for fear the new government would erase the state's paper currency. But word began to circulate soon after the new Constitution was forwarded to the states for ratification. "I am hurt by the doings of the convention respecting the slave trade," Samuel Hopkins wrote Moses on October 22. "I fear this is an action which will bring a curse." But Hopkins was ambivalent on what course to advocate, as rejecting the Constitution would lead only to anarchy. It was a dilemma that would dominate public discourse for the next several months.

One solace Moses could take from the decision at Philadelphia was that his old mentor Stephen Hopkins had nothing to do with it. Hopkins, the early apostle of American liberty and signer of the Declaration of Independence, did not live to see the formation of the new government. Hopkins died in July 1785, at his home on Towne Street. His later days were painful ones, attended as they were by the advance of his "shaking palsy"—probably Parkinson's disease—and by the death of his second wife Anne, whom he lamented with the epitaph, carved on her gravestone, "O my companion, thou hast left me to finish my journey alone." But Hopkins was not truly solitary. In his final days, he was attended by his stepdaughter Ruth, and entertained regular visits from Theodore Foster, who was helping Hopkins record a history of Providence, and from Moses. How Hopkins would have contributed to the constitutional debates is hard to say, but he settled his accounts with his slaves upon his decease, declaring in his will, "I wish to give all my negroes their freedom."

By early November William Rotch, a merchant from Nantucket and a leading Quaker activist, was taking a hard line against the new constitution. Writing to Moses in impassioned tones, Rotch said, "My heart has been often pained since the publication of the doings of the convention. I had entertained some hope that so many wise men would have formed some system of government founded on equity and justice, . . . and that we [Quakers] might lend our aid in establishing it as far as it tended to peace and morality. But we may say in truth that the wisdom of men can or shall not work the righteousness of God, and whatever high encomiums are given to the Constitution, it is evident to me it is founded on *Slavery*, and that is on *Blood*."

Moses himself chose less incendiary terms, but he shared the disappoint-ment of Rotch and Hopkins. "Alas," he wrote to a Philadelphia friend in No-vember, "instead of extending humanity and good will to [the Africans], the convention has I think very unhappily wounded the cause of liberty and the rights of man." Another opportunity to realize and codify the ideals of the Rev-olution had been allowed to pass by.

Bad as the news was from Philadelphia, it was tempered by news from New York. There, operating in the shadow of the Constitutional Convention, the Continental Congress was still attempting to conduct business. And in July, even as some key delegates were shuttling back and forth to attend both coun-cils, the Congress approved a new ordinance for government of the western frontier. This version of the bill was more limited than the Ordinance of 1784, covering only the lands lying north of the Ohio River. But this time, the ordi-nance prohibited slavery throughout the Northwest Territory.

The legislative history of the bill does little to redeem the character and foresight of the Congress. The provision barring slavery was tacked on as an af-terthought, at the request of Manasseh Cutler, a developer who paid a million dollars for rights to develop a large section of the fertile Ohio Valley. Cutler was no abolitionist, but he asked for the slavery amendment in deference to Timothy Pickering, whose soldiers Cutler viewed as his prime customers. Nathan Dane, the Massachusetts representative charged with writing the new ordinance, decided to drop the antislavery clause, as he expected the southern states to veto it. A week later, however, after the southern section was ex-empted from the jurisdiction of the ordinance, Dane found that opposition to the clause had evaporated, possibly because the slave interests feared new competition if plantation labor were allowed north of the Ohio. Conse-quently, in Dane's words, "after we had completed the other parts, I moved the article [barring slavery], which was agreed to without opposition."

It was apparent, then, that despite the "dirty compromise" made in Philadelphia, the future of slavery remained in flux. And in Rhode Island, while he was tracking the progress of the momentous debates to the south-ward, Moses Brown was doing his best to keep his own campaign for aboli-tion alive. At the New England Yearly Meeting in June, Moses sponsored still another legislative petition against the trade. The appeal, approved by the Quaker meeting and presented to the General Assembly June 13, con-sisted of a general prayer for any law that might "prevent that cruel and unjust trade, and finally to abolish that barbarous custom of holding mankind as slaves." The legislature agreed to take up the matter at its October session.

Just why Moses decided to resurrect his campaign against the slave trade that summer remains something of a mystery. The composition of the legislature had not changed appreciably since the defeat three years before, and the state's economy continued to worsen, rendering the lure of an African venture all the more powerful. But Moses had enough experience in politics to know that persistence and focus could steer events in surprising ways; hadn't the British Parliament been forced to repeal the Molasses Act? And Moses still believed that the people of the state were behind him.

In August Moses learned that his brother, at least, would stand aside for this round of debate. John had not undergone any sort of moral conversion; rather, he'd revised his business strategy. Three years before, the Philadelphia financier Robert Morris had staged a successful trade mission to China. Now John was planning to follow suit, sending his three-hundred-ton ship *General Washington* to the Orient.

With preparations under way to assemble a cargo and outfit the ship, John invited Moses to invest in the venture. That was unlikely, as Moses continued to foreswear business engagements, but it showed just how far John's feelings for his brother had swung. Perhaps to sweeten the offer, John assured Moses that, with this new business before him, "I shall not be any more concerned in the Guiney Trade." Moreover, though John continued to represent Providence in the General Assembly, he promised Moses that "you can do what you think is right respecting the proposed prohibition to the Guinea Trade." John even offered to step down if Moses would take his seat.

Moses was unimpressed with John's dramatic change of heart—"I don't expect his leaving the trade is so much from principle as interest," he wrote later—but it augured well for the slave bill, removing its most vocal and most influential opponent. Still, Joseph Nightengale remained a delegate from Providence, and like the Newport faction, he gave no indication of following John's lead. To the contrary, the Newport slavers were growing more militant.

Samuel Hopkins complained to Moses in August that the slave-trade lobby continued to intimidate the publisher at the *Newport Herald*. "That wicked set of men have got the printer in their hands and have silenced the press," Hopkins fumed. As to the General Assembly, Hopkins advised, "If they do not wholly dismiss the petition, I shall be glad. I have pretty good evidence that some of them speak fair words to you and your friends; who yet are determined against doing anything against the slave trade." Of course, Moses had stronger contacts in the legislature than Hopkins, and may have harbored a different sense of their inclinations.

Moses pressed ahead. Two weeks before the October session, he got the Crito essay published in Providence. Hopkins, however, remained dour. He had tried to rally support for the Quaker petition among the Newport clergy, but few signed on. The gospel ministers considered the assembly leadership to be "destitute of all principles of justice," and an appeal to their mercy would only invite their contempt. The Quakers would have to proceed on their own.

When the day of decision came, at the white-clapboard courthouse in South Kingstown on October 31, 1787, Moses and four fellow Quakers won permission to present the bill to the General Assembly, and to defend against any objections that might be raised. The debate was surprisingly brief—there was no John Brown to contend with, no sea captains to share tales of the trade—and the vote stunningly one-sided: forty-four votes in favor, and just four against, each of them from members involved in the slave trade directly, or through ownership of distilleries.

With the lower house in hand, the Quaker committee hurried across the hall to find Gov. John Collins and his ten "assistants"—the legislature's upper house. Collins was a lifelong Newport resident, but he was no aristocrat. A former blacksmith who ran away to sea, Collins was a committed patriot whose politics derived largely from an instinctive mistrust of the state's merchant class; in his view, "their religion is trade and their God is gain." Aware, presumably, of the Newport merchants' long attachment to the slave trade, Collins embraced the Quaker bill and it passed the upper house by unanimous vote. That afternoon, the prohibition on slave trading became law.

As with the earlier, limited ban on slave imports, this bill opened with a soaring preamble invoking "justice, and the principles of humanity, as well as the laws of nature." But this was no symbolic victory. Where most colonial measures limiting the slave trade dealt with embargos on imports, the Rhode Island bill made it illegal for any citizen of the state to "directly or indirectly import or transport, buy or sell, or receive on board their vessel . . . any of the natives or inhabitants of any state or kingdom in that part of the world called Africa, as slaves or without their voluntary consent." And the act carried penalties: one hundred pounds for each slave transported, and one thousand pounds for each ship, with the fees to be divided equally between the state and the person who filed the complaint.

After so many disappointments, this was an unmitigated triumph for Moses, the strongest blow against the slave trade yet to be levied by the abolitionist movement. But Moses was too modest, too sober, to celebrate outwardly; writing to relate the good news in his careful Quaker diction, Moses called the decision "agreeable." It was left to Samuel Hopkins, the relieved pessimist, to exult in their unexpected victory. "Is it not extraordinary," Hopkins wrote a fellow minister in November, "that this state, which has exceeded the rest of the states in carrying on this trade, should be the first legislature on this globe which has prohibited that trade? Let them have the praise of this."

11

The Society

IN THE LATE SUMMER OF 1788, an aspiring Providence merchant named Cyprian Sterry paced back and forth atop a pier that jutted into the broad wash of the Thames estuary at the foot of downtown New London, Connecticut. Sterry's vessel wallowed heavily in the brackish water, her hold crammed with a full cargo of rum and tobacco, her captain and crew on board.

Sterry was a clever and resourceful man—during the war, he'd escaped from a British prison and lived incognito in London for several months before returning to Providence. Now, at thirty-six years of age, despite the new law in his home state, Sterry was risking everything for a stake in the slave trade. But if Sterry was worldly and ambitious, he was also pious, and he delayed his venture long enough to seek the customary blessing of the ship before setting out to sea.

At last he saw his messenger returning down the steep cobblestones of State Street—alone. After learning that the ship was bound for Africa, the Congregational minister to whom Sterry had applied for benediction had declined to perform the service.

The incident at New London highlighted two key developments in Moses Brown's campaign to stop the slave trade. The first was the extent to which ecclesiastic opinion—not just Quaker opinion—had turned against the trade. The second was the limits of the triumph Moses had scored at the General Assembly in Rhode Island. Sterry was a Providence resident, a close friend of Joseph and John Brown. Determined to stake his claim in the revived trade to Africa, Sterry had simply sailed with his ship to Connecticut—an easy day trip on the placid waters of Long Island Sound—and obtained her clearance papers at the customshouse there. The Rhode Island law was a hindrance, but a minor one.

Like Samuel Hopkins, Moses saw passage of the first legislative prohibition against slave trading as a milestone in the larger crusade against slavery. But they both recognized as well that, once the federal government renounced jurisdiction over the slave trade, the abolitionists would have to fight their battles state by state. In the fall of 1787, at the same time he was lining up votes in the General Assembly, Moses traveled to Boston to present the New England Yearly Meeting's memorial to the legislature there. The Massachusetts courts had all but abolished slavery, based on the declaration, adopted as part of the new state constitution in 1780, that "all men are born free and equal." Yet in other respects the situation for blacks remained as dire as in Rhode Island—slave ships were departing from Boston and Salem, and free Africans were being kidnapped and transported north to be sold as slaves in Canada.

The Massachusetts legislature reacted coolly to the Quaker petition, raising doubts about the limits of state jurisdiction, and holding out the prospect of congressional action. The state Senate declined at first even to consider a ban on slave trading. But Moses and the Quakers were persistent as ever; Moses traveled again to Boston in the spring of 1788, and kept up a close correspondence with Friends in the Bay State. Their efforts got a boost when a notorious kidnapping mobilized the Boston Association of Ministers, and within weeks, Massachusetts became the second state to make the slave trade illegal, though its fines were less than half those of Rhode Island.

Connecticut was a more difficult case. Not only were slavers moving to the state's ports, but since passage of its gradual abolition law, slaveholders had taken to shipping their underage charges south for sale. Moses traveled there as well, not long after his trip to Boston, to meet with a legislative committee in New Haven. The lower house embraced the petition against the African trade and a second clause banning the export of slaves, but as in Massachusetts, the upper house scuttled the bill. Moses returned the following year, working with the Connecticut clergy to revive the legislation. Samuel Hopkins paved the way, writing letters of introduction to Levi Hart, an influential minister in the town of Preston, and to Jonathan Edwards, a minister in New Haven and the son of Hopkins's famous mentor. Hopkins was effusive in praising Moses as "an honest, sensible man . . . brother to the famous John Brown, the rich merchant in Providence." Hopkins explained that Moses had once been involved in the slave trade, but now saw it his duty to stop the traffic and to end slavery. "We have no men of any other denomination in these states, who appear to be conscientious, discerning, faithful, and zealous, in this matter, as these Quakers do," Hopkins wrote. It was rare for a Congregationalist to offer such acknowledgment to a rival sect, but certainly warranted.

Moses spent several days with Edwards in New Haven, treating with the governor and the committee drafting a new bill. The meetings went well; Moses was especially pleased to authenticate the rumors that Cyprian Sterry was evading the law of Rhode Island by shipping through Connecticut. Again, Moses left town confident of a good result, but again, his hopes were disappointed. The ban on slave trading passed intact, but the prohibition on slave exports was dropped by the upper house. Writing to describe the late developments, Edwards proclaimed himself "mortified"—without the ban on slave exports, "I expect that now the poor creatures will be carried out in shiploads"—and lamented that Moses and the Quakers had not tarried in New Haven a few days longer to ensure passage of the complete bill. Moses, however, was more attuned to the two-steps-forward, one-step-back pace of legislative change, and pronounced the new bill a credit to the state.

This was a good season for Moses, and not just in the legislatures of New England. He had retreated during the war years into the closed society of the Quakers, repelled by the anger and violence—not to mention the hypocrisy—of the patriots. Now, as the conflict with England receded, Moses reconnected with the larger community. Though he had renounced "worldly" engagements and refused to take a seat in the state legislature, Moses did consent, in October 1783, to accept the post of surveyor of streets for Providence, reprising his work on Benefit Street before the war. Two years later, Moses agreed, with his old friend Jabez Bowen, to reroute Benefit Street and lay boundaries for a new town cemetery. Moses thoroughly enjoyed these tasks; they were duties of high trust that called for precision and meticulous attention to detail.

Moses was able to pursue these new public responsibilities in part because the palsy that had so disabled him toward the end of the war appears to have left him. His wife, Mary, and his growing children all seem to have enjoyed a respite from their various infirmities; by 1787, Moses was able to write to a friend, "My family and friends are in general well." Indeed, Sarah, now in her early twenties, was well enough to engage in courtship with William Almy, a Providence Quaker a year younger than she, who held the important post of clerk in the Smithfield Monthly Meeting. Almy joined Moses in his work against slavery, and traveled with him to lobby the legislature in Connecticut.

To judge from his correspondence, Moses' relations with his children were distant and formal, constrained within a narrow Quaker framework, as if Moses hoped to raise them as models of devotion to his adopted faith. Writing to his son when Obadiah was just twelve years old, Moses admonished him to "often set down when alone and endeavor to be still and give room or place for the *Spirit of Truth* to appear to thee whether it has to reprove thee for anything thou mayst have been doing, or to fill thy mind with tenderness and love and in this state open to thy mind what thou shouldst do . . . by obedience thereto thou wilt grow more and more in favor with the Lord." So pleased was Moses with this letter that he promptly wrote out a copy and sent it to his daughter.

Yet, stilted as his manner might appear, it gave rise to warm and close bonds with both of his children. Obadiah was perfectly dutiful; while away at school in his early teens, he vowed to his father that he would "make use of this opportunity in giving attention to learning as youth is the best time for improvement." And Sarah was unfailingly affectionate. Despite the high standards he set, Moses never had to reprimand rebellious offspring the way John did.

With his family in health and his fortune intact, Moses found time during this period to pursue several reformist concerns apart from the ongoing campaign against slavery. One was the promotion of education. Quakers, like Baptists and several other Protestant denominations, were generally skeptical of formal schooling, but Moses considered that a backward and mistaken position, and led a movement at the Meeting for Sufferings to open a nondenominational primary school that would offer scholarships to the poor. His goals were twofold—to encourage learning and industry among Quaker children, and to spread Quaker teachings among the larger community. A small school, opened at Portsmouth in 1785, was closed soon after for lack of funds, but Moses never gave up his dream of a Quaker academy. In the meantime, in 1785, Moses joined his brother Nicholas and Jabez Bowen on a town schools committee, though it was not until 1800 that free schools were mandated by state law.

Moses' other great postwar engagement came as part of a national effort to jump-start American manufactures. Peace had brought a surge in British imports, idling thousands of workers and raising the prospect that England would regain through the marketplace the primacy she had lost on the battlefield. The most critical sector was textiles, where twenty years of industrial innovation had given Britain a daunting advantage in productivity and output. John Brown flaunted his competitive spirit by wearing a simple, homespun suit during an address to the General Assembly in January 1789, a symbolic act emulated by George Washington at his first inauguration, four months later. But where John always enjoyed a flamboyant gesture, Moses adopted a quieter and more effective approach.

This was a major departure for Moses, a return to business affairs after a hiatus of more than a decade. But it made sense in several important ways. Unemployment was a growing social problem, the sort of cause to which Moses was so often drawn. And investment in manufacturing helped open a new career path for William Almy, who joined Moses' family when he married Sarah in the spring of 1789. It helped, too, that most of the small-scale entrepreneurs working to develop mechanized textile production around Providence were Quakers.

Moses was not alone: business leaders in Philadelphia and Massachusetts had put up investment capital and bounties to lure European artisans who might bring the latest industrial expertise across the Atlantic. But the British guarded their industrial secrets closely, establishing fines and prison terms for the export of plans or machinery, and barring the emigration of skilled craftsmen.

Moses began seeking out information on the latest methods of textile production as early as the fall of 1787, when he spent several days on the road visiting experimental mills funded by the legislature to promote manufactures in Massachusetts. By November 1788, he had obtained several rudimentary spinning and carding machines, fabricated by a small clique of Quaker wood and metal workers from drawings of the Massachusetts models. These first machines Moses housed in a room at the market house, and after a winter of trial and error, he decided to enter the business in earnest. In April 1789 he entered a formal partnership with his cousin Smith Brown, son of Uncle Elisha, and William Almy. Moses contributed two-thirds of the capital, Smith Brown one-third, and Almy the day-to-day management. By the summer of 1789 the firm had obtained all the major textile processing equipment in Rhode Island, and had rented a water mill on the Blackstone River in Pawtucket, north of Providence, to drive its spinning apparatus. The machines required constant modification and repair; Moses found the entire enterprise "more arduous than I expected," but hired a small team of craftsmen and pursued the project doggedly.

Throughout this period of renewal, Moses enjoyed something of a thaw in his relations with his brother John. Having renounced his position in the slave trade, John stayed mum as Moses scored legislative victories across southern New England. John may have been holding his tongue in hopes that Moses would help underwrite John's ambitious new venture in the nascent China trade. Just as likely, John was simply preoccupied.

The most pressing matter on John's busy agenda in the fall and winter of 1787 was the impending marriage of his young business partner, John Francis, to his daughter Abby. John tried at first to quash their courtship—he appears to have had no particular objection to John Francis, just to the idea of losing his daughter—but when the two lovers persisted, John brought the young man into his shipping firm. Then John struck upon a transparent ruse: he would send John Francis to the Orient as supercargo on the *General Washington*, delaying the wedding by at least eighteen months. But John Francis would have none of it. He would separate from the firm rather than ship out to sea, and the wedding would go forward.

Thwarted, John hastily changed course. Yes, there would be a wedding, and it would take place in Providence, in the extravagant style that John brought to all his endeavors. The date was set for New Year's Day 1788, and preparations were made all in a rush, complicated by the fact that the *General Washington* was set to sail that same week. December 27 found John at Newport, attending the final loading and packing of his cargo for China—anchors, cannon, and raw steel; rum, wine, and a dozen other varieties of spirits; ginseng, cordage, codfish, beef, and five tons of ham. At nine o'clock that night, John finally departed the quarterdeck. He hailed his captain and crew, they answered with a three-gun salute, and the *General Washington* was under way, her white sheets ghostly against the evening sky.

Returning to Providence the next day, John threw himself into the preparations for the wedding. The reception was planned for John's new house on Benefit Street, but there was a hitch—the house wasn't nearly complete. For two days John did what he could to get the upper floors finished and painted, while his wife, Sarah, attended to the bride. Come January 1, Abby, at least, was ready, trussed in white satin and strings of pearls. Three bridesmaids attended, also dressed in white, and each sporting tall white feathered plumes atop elaborate cane headdresses. The ceremony was followed by a dinner for forty-four, with just ten guests from outside the immediate family. No guest list survives, so we can't be sure if Moses was on hand, but it seems likely, as John was still hoping his brothers would invest in his China ventures.

The party was over soon after midnight, but that was just the beginning. John was famous for his entertainments, and he wouldn't let the marriage of his eldest daughter pass without a full salute. For the reception, held four days later, John printed up a set of his trademark calling cards—a fanciful rendering of a king of hearts on the front, with the invitation and address inscribed on the reverse—and invited more than one hundred friends, including most of the business and political elite of Providence. This revel was held in the new house on the hill, on the second floor, at the head of a grand staircase. The place was still unfurnished, but a collection of chairs sufficed, along with benches covered in green felt. Dinner was served in one room and cards dealt in another; the balance of the floor, two spacious rooms, was devoted to dancing. "We behaved with decorum until about 11," one guest wrote later. Then, somebody called for a jig, and the party got started in earnest.

John Brown caught the spirit, draping himself in "the drollest mixture of male and female dress," and led the men of the party in a riotous round of cutting in on the paired dancers. "Never were such shouts, such bursts, such exclamations as when the older gentlemen stepped in," recorded Anna Bowen, Jabez's sister. "When the novelty of the jigs were over, we played Blind Man's Bluff, and Col. [Joseph] Nightengale made a great deal of fun by throwing himself in the way of the blind man, who happened to be Mr. Brown." The party continued until about three in the morning, Bowen recalled approvingly; "a merrier crew I never laughed with." The festivities continued for days; the newlyweds sojourned at Boston, accompanied by James and Sarah Brown, then returned for another family gathering on the sixteenth, and finally another dance, at Spring Green Farm, toward the end of February.

The excitement of the wedding and the opening of the China trade provided John with a distraction—and probably a welcome one—from the state's deepening political wars. Not since the battles between Stephen Hopkins and Samuel Ward had Rhode Island been so sharply divided over questions of leadership and policy. In a very real sense, John Brown had initiated the dispute by raising the hackles of the farmers and landowners against the taxing authority of the Continental Congress. Now, as trade dwindled and most of the former colonies sank into economic depression, John and the other merchant leaders of the state performed a political about-face, rallying behind the new federal government, calling for endorsement of the Constitution and, remarkably, for institution of a federal impost. To their dismay, most of the landed interests in the state declined to follow.

The most glaring fissure at the state level was over the question of a new emission of paper money. The idea was proposed as a means to finance the crushing burden of state and Continental debt, and a way to revive trade stymied by the lack of hard currency. The merchants of Providence and Newport immediately denounced the plan, fearing that the new currency would rapidly depreciate, allowing debtors to pay off loans in worthless state notes. The General Assembly managed to stave off the paper-money faction until May 1786, when the new Country Party, representing the desperately impoverished rural farmers, swept into power. That same election saw John Brown returned to the General Assembly to represent Providence and lead the merchant faction, now in the unaccustomed role of minority bloc.

When the new legislature convened in June it lost no time in approving the issue of one hundred thousand pounds in paper bills. The scrip would be loaned to landowners against mortgaged equity, to be repaid over a period of fourteen years; in the meantime, the new currency was deemed legal tender for all contracts past and present. Refusal to accept the new money extinguished the debt outright, and subjected such creditors to escalating fines.

John Brown and the Providence delegates entered a series of formal protests to the acts authorizing the new currency, but they were brushed aside by a confident majority led by John Collins and a fiery orator named Jonathan Hazard, dubbed by his enemies the "Machiavel of Charleston." John made an easy target for the Country Party ideologues: they blamed the merchants in general for the state's fiscal woes; in addition, John's large holdings of state and federal bonds, including soldiers' pay certificates bought at steep discounts, left his motives open to suspicion. John felt the sting of public resentment one afternoon as he clattered down the street in his lustrous hand-finished chariot; passing by a cooper's shop, a workman growled out from the gloomy workshop, "Soldier's blood makes good varnish." Long aligned along geographic lines, the electorate was now dividing over matters of class, and for the first time, John's opulence was a liability, the source of resentment and mistrust.

The rift over paper money quickly spread to the question of joining the new union: the Country Party, with John Collins a notable exception, opposed the Constitution as a threat to the paper-money solution, while the merchants saw the federal government as their best chance to put down the rural insurgency. Thus, by 1787, John Brown, the former champion of state's rights in the battle against the Impost, found himself the leader of the Rhode Island Federalists. That year, when the assembly voted to boycott the Constitutional Convention, John formed a committee of merchants to denounce that decision. They outlined their objections in a letter to the convention, pronouncing their allegiance to the union and their belief that "the full power for the regulation of the Commerce of the United States . . . ought to be vested in the National Council."

Little had changed by the fall, when the Constitution was presented to the General Assembly for ratification. Rather than convene a ratifying convention, as the delegates to the federal convention had advised, Country Party leaders proposed a referendum conducted at town meetings across the state. Recognizing they could never sway sentiment in such disparate forums, John Brown and the federalists boycotted the entire process. The referendum went forward, however, and in March 1788 the Constitution was defeated by a margin of ten to one, with Providence and Newport isolated as lone Federalist strongholds.

The depth of the political crisis gripping Rhode Island became apparent in July 1788, when the Federalists in Providence announced a public Independence Day feast to celebrate New Hampshire's vote to become the ninth ratifying state. The night of July 3, with an ox already roasting on a spit, more than a thousand armed men gathered in the woods nearby, determined to prevent any public displays of fealty to the union. At a peace parley hastily arranged the next morning, the Country Party militia agreed to stand down provided the celebration was limited strictly to independence, with no reference to the Constitution or to New Hampshire.

The Federalists were chagrined, but not cowed. Later that month, news reached Providence that Virginia had ratified, leaving only Rhode Island and North Carolina in dissent. The Federalists answered with a cannonade and a parade, and erected a symbolic protest on Weybosset Bridge. On the south side of the bridge they raised eleven large American flags, each bearing the name of a state and the date it adopted the Constitution. On the north rail two poles were lashed to the rail; one with a flag for North Carolina, leaning at a thirty-degree angle with the motto "It will rise," and a second, bare, at an angle of forty-five degrees, over a sign that read, "Rhode Island in hopes."

The controversies over paper money and the Constitution represented new territory for John. In the battles against the British customs authorities and the successful effort to capture Rhode Island College, his wealth and brash audacity had made John the darling of his peers, his harsh elocution the voice of his community. After the raid on the *Gaspee*, John had enjoyed the silent protection of the entire community—stevedores and tavern drunks as well as politicians and lawyers—who all ignored the handsome reward posted by the king. Now John's prominence was working against him: the very bombast he had deployed against the Impost was fueling the Country Party movement. It seems fair to suppose that by February 1789, John was feeling frustrated, confused, perhaps a bit fearful of the future. At least that would help explain John's visceral reaction to Moses' latest initiative in his campaign against slavery.

～～～

Even as Moses was traveling to Connecticut to endorse its law against the slave trade, he was aware that new legislation could provide only part of the answer to slavery and the continued maltreatment of free blacks. Cyprian Sterry, for example, was criminally liable in Rhode Island for the venture he launched from New London, but without an active lobby to press for enforcement, he could ignore the law with impunity. The model for such a lobby was the Pennsylvania Society for the Relief of Negroes Unlawfully Held in Bondage, organized by Anthony Benezet in 1775 and revived by James Pemberton in 1784 as the Pennsylvania Abolition Society. Dominated by Quakers but open to all comers, the abolition society wrote legislation, and more important, it took on specific cases, hiring lawyers and demanding prosecutions.

As the abolition movement gained momentum, attachment to such societies became a mark of distinction in certain patriotic circles. In 1785, John Jay, the jurist and former president of the Continental Congress, was named head of the New York Manumission Society; in Philadelphia, Benjamin Rush joined the abolition society, and in 1787, Benjamin Franklin became its president. Even where there were no laws against slavery, as in New York, the abolition society found plenty to do, sponsoring abolitionist lectures, printing essays, and registering free blacks to prevent their being forced back into slavery. When Moses Brown made his second trip to lobby the Connecticut legislators at New Haven, the New York society sent a delegation as well.

By November 1788 Moses was convinced of the need to form a society in Rhode Island, but he was stymied for a time by the search for "a suitable person to put at the head of it." Several Friends had proposed Moses for the post, but he believed a non-Quaker should fill the office, making it harder to dismiss the society as a secretarian project. Moses finally settled on David Howell, the former congressman, then employed as the state attorney general. Howell was close to John Brown, but he was first and foremost a politician, and was happy to accept such an honorable and prominent position.

That winter saw the departure of half a dozen slave ships from Rhode Island. Moses did what he could to intervene: accompanied by Samuel Emlin, a Quaker preacher visiting from Philadelphia, he went to the home of Cyprian Sterry, then fitting a ship out at Newport. In the course of a lengthy conference, the pair warned Sterry that they would seek prosecution of any merchant found violating the law. Sterry offered what was becoming the stock answer for slavers confronted by abolitionists—that his latest African venture was concerned with ivory and gold, not slaves.

During the same sojourn in Providence, Emlin received a more candid appraisal of the new law against slave trading from none other than John Brown. Emlin knew John's wife, who continued to worship at the Quaker meetinghouse. Encountering John during a stroll up Towne Street, Emlin pointed out a ship on the waterfront loading a cargo of rum and asked whether John knew if it were bound for Africa. John offered the jaunty reply that he couldn't say

260

for sure, "But in my opinion there is no more crime in bringing off a cargo of slaves than in bringing off a cargo of jackasses."

Such casual defiance of state law spurred a final round of organizing meetings at the clapboard Quaker meetinghouse in Providence. On the wet, blustery Friday afternoon of February 20, the Providence Society for the Abolition of the Slave Trade adopted bylaws and named a slate of officers: Howell as president, Moses Brown as treasurer, and Thomas Arnold as secretary. It was an auspicious beginning for the antislavery faction. Howell was suitably famous to stand at the top of the masthead, and along with Arnold, who had been trained in the law, he could be relied on for free legal advice. And there would be little problem getting the word out: while not a member of the group, John Carter, publisher of the *Providence Gazette*, manumitted his two slaves the same week that the society was formed, and readily made space in his paper for abolitionist tracts from as far away as Philadelphia and London.

Yet Carter was a printer, not an activist, and even before he published notices that the group had been formed, he gave prominent play to an anonymous attack on the new society. The author, who dubbed himself "A Citizen," excoriated the abolitionists for questioning the character of the slave traders, and for seeking to deprive them of their legal livelihoods. He cited in particular the encounter between the Quakers and Cyprian Sterry, whom the Citizen alleged had been subjected to an intimidating intrusion and threatened with "utter ruin" if he continued in the slave trade.

The whole debate was misplaced, the Citizen asserted. American ships carried just a fraction of the total traffic from Africa; a local prohibition would be pointless so long as the great nations of Europe continued the trade. As to slavery itself, the Citizen held that it reflected God's will; that as some are born with superior intellect or vigor, so are others born to indolence, servitude, and in some cases, bondage. In all, it was a jarring piece, alerting the members of the still-inchoate society that they would not assume the moral high ground without a contest.

Thomas Arnold took the bait, responding February 19—a day before the official launch of the society—with a sharply worded rejoinder printed in the *United States Chronicle*, a competitor to the *Gazette* that had begun publishing five years before. Writing under the pseudonym "A Foe to Oppression," the Quaker convert derided the form and the content of the Citizen's essay, questioning his version of the visit to Sterry and calling him to step out from behind "the Figlean screen of a fictitious signature." He closed by denouncing the Citizen's fatalistic defense of slavery. According to the Citizen's logic, Arnold wrote, "The thief in the night, the robber on the highway, and the murderer . . . may equally with the slave trader, plead in his justification that he was but fulfilling the designs of Providence."

The Citizen answered in the next edition of the *Chronicle* with a quick, biting piece. The society was a "combination"—a damning epithet for the time—"who assemble together to devise methods to deprive their fellow-citizens of their lawful property . . . and will be considered as dangerous to the community, and in strictness of justice and law will be held accountable for the loss of all slaves which may be induced away from their owners." This was not just a challenge, but a threat.

Two days later, the Citizen returned with a lengthy harangue in the *Gazette* addressed directly to the Foe to Oppression. Slavery was "right, just, and lawful, and consequently practiced every day," and thus enjoyed the protection of the Constitution. To make his case, the Citizen cited extracts from recent histories of Africa showing tribal slavery and warfare to be ancient traditions. It was the abolitionists who were the lawbreakers; the slaveholders of Rhode Island comprised "the very best men in Newport and other parts of the state," as demonstrated by their uniform opposition to the "wicked plan" of the paper-money party. Far from being oppressors, the slaveholders were victims of abolitionist schemes to spirit away their servants with no compensation for their lost investment. "Now, Sir," asked the Citizen, "who appears to be the thief?"

By now the shadow debate in the pages of the *Gazette* and the *Chronicle* had become something of a sensation, the subject of excited speculation over the names of the anonymous authors, and a source of consternation within the new abolition society. The most distressed was Moses Brown, who feared, as was widely rumored, that the Citizen was actually his brother John. Hoping to short-circuit a debate that was robbing the society of stature and momentum—and that threatened to breach the circle of his family—Moses went to the print shop under the sign of Shakespeare's Head and pleaded with John Carter to reveal the name of the Citizen. Carter was cagey: his hands were tied, he said, but he would deliver a letter to his anonymous correspondent. Two days later came the reply: the identity of the Citizen would remain secret. Carter shrugged; he wished people would write "less pointedly," but he could not refuse printing such a topical debate.

Now, reluctantly, Moses jumped in. Writing as "A Friend, Though a Monitor, to the Citizen," Moses offered a detailed rebuttal to the Citizen's defense of the slave trade, and then proposed that both sides "bury the hatchet." This column prompted a round of confession. His curiosity piqued, John wrote Moses a quick, private note confirming that he was indeed the Citizen; now

John wanted to know, was Moses the Monitor? With John's messenger standing in the hallway awaiting the reply, Moses answered immediately. Yes, he was the Monitor, and he wanted this unseemly public exchange to stop. He sought to placate John, assuring him that no threats were made during his meeting with Cyprian Sterry, but John had his own version of the encounter, and he stuck to it.

Where the brothers found common ground was in their suspicion of the printer Carter. John averred in his note that Carter had advised him not to identify himself, prompting Moses to complain that Carter "wished to see a quarrel going on in his paper." If that was the case, Carter played his hand adroitly: instead of dying out, the controversy only accelerated. John's answer to the Foe to Oppression had been picked up by the *Newport Herald* and emblazoned across the front page. For most of his life, John had yearned for the stature of Newport's merchant elite; now he was the toast of that circle, their champion in the public lists. Far from backing down, John continued to publish, raising the debate over slavery to a new pitch of intensity and exposing for all to see the Brown family's own painful experience in slaveholding.

❧

David Howell took a brief turn as the object of the Citizen's wrath; mistakenly assuming Howell was the Foe to Oppression, John had ridiculed him in the *Gazette* as "a gentleman known to be over-fond of popularity." But Howell quickly retired from the field, submitting a signed piece for the March 7 *Gazette* that disavowed any hand in the published challenges to the Citizen, and lamented John's harsh handling of his "best friends."

Despite Howell's reticence, and despite the private exchange with Moses, John responded with the journalistic equivalent of a blunderbuss. Having no choice but to answer the "torrents of abuse" heaped upon the slave traders, John dismissed Howell as a dupe to Thomas Arnold, then slammed Arnold as "a sinner covered in hypocrisy." Turning next to the Friend Though a Monitor, John agreed to "close our controversy" by sharing publicly "the effects of the exertions of these good people in poisoning the minds of the slaves." With that, John told the tale of his runaway slaves.

In John's telling, the story became one of his own toleration, of the wrongful meddling of the abolitionists, and of the inherent inability of blacks to handle a life of freedom. The five black men "left my service," John said, and ran away to Boston, but soon found themselves ostracized. "They were all well clothed before they ran off," but John encountered two of them several years later, and found them "miserable and naked"; when he bought them new clothes at a marine supply shop, they agreed to return to his employ. "Another of them, having more ability, kept himself tolerably well-clothed, and returned home of his own accord," John wrote, and the fourth, "having his wife in Boston," was allowed to remain there.

The fifth runaway "was more daring than the rest," and "much better acquainted at the house of your Treasurer"—an overt reference to Moses—"from whose Negroes' advice and counsel he was determined to be free." Naturally, his destiny would be more dire. "I am sorry to tell his fate," John wrote, though tell it he did; "he went to Virginia, and there was hanged for house-breaking." Apocryphal or not, the story served its purpose, fixing responsibility for a tragic death on the abolitionists, and Moses in particular.

Not satisfied with this searing indictment of the leadership of the new society, John addressed a separate, lengthy column to the Friend Though a Monitor—to his brother Moses. This time, John promised, he would "endeavor as much as possible to keep my pen within the bounds of decency and moderation," but that did not bar sarcasm or contempt from the passage that followed.

Knowing now that Moses was his Monitor, John delved deeply into their spiritual divide. "I feel myself perfectly willing to be judged by the tribunal of the public, whether my meek and worthy brother has shown more of that moderation and Christian spirit, which he is so well known to possess, than the Citizen, who does not pretend to make any extraordinary profession of religion; though my wish and endeavor is to venerate the real Christian professor, of whatever denomination." John acknowledged, in mock humility, "It is true that I frequent a different meeting from my friend, because I was brought up that way, as were my worthy parents before me."

John spent several paragraphs quibbling with the Monitor's idea of altruism, but then he changed gears. Leaving aside the moral question of slavery, John opened the political question then facing the nation. "Permit me remind you," John wrote, "that it cannot be long before this state becomes a member of the Union; and I beseech you, in the most friendly manner, not to become the means of dividing the general government against itself, by influencing the northern part, through your mistaken zeal for the abolition of slavery, to create a war between the two extremities of the Confederacy." Thus, even before the Constitution had been adopted, John held out the prospect of a civil war over the question. "Many bloody wars have ensued from less beginnings," John warned. "A little fuel has sometimes kindled a great fire." To emphasize his attachment to the incipient union, John now signed himself "A Citizen and True Federalist."

That was enough for Moses. The next week he dispensed with his pseudonym and, over his own name, published an appeal "that all personal publications cease." To be blamed for the destruction of John's executed slave "is unkind as it is unjust," but Moses would let the matter rest in order to restore "peace and cordiality."

Thomas Arnold, on the other hand, was far from finished. The same day of John's private exchange with Moses, Arnold appeared again in the pages of the *Chronicle*, under the new pseudonym "Monitor the Younger." He started with a rebuttal, demanding that John prove or retract his charges that the Quakers had threatened Sterry, and that Quaker farmers, taking advantage of the paper-money policy, were paying hired laborers in depreciated currency. Then he turned more personal, accusing John of engaging in illegal trade to Jamaica and, now treading into the sacrosanct domain of familial relations, denouncing John for "daily prosecuting, with personal abuse, a brother." This charge Arnold compounded by pointing out the brother in question had "sometime past hazarded his life and fortune to rescue him from captivity in some respects like that he is now attempting to rescue his fellow-men from." The reference to Moses' trip to Boston to gain John's release from a British brig—by then a famous episode from the early days of the war—made clear to all who didn't already know that this war of words was dividing the most prominent family in Providence.

Of all the charges Arnold had levied, the accusation that John was abusing his brother in print—true on its face, of course—drew the sharpest rejoinder yet. "Abominable!" roared the Citizen. "I shudder at the thought of its being possible for any man to be so depraved. . . . You must know, to the contrary of your assertion, that there is the strictest harmony and brotherly love between me and the brother you refer to. We differ in opinion, it is true, with respect to liberty of conscience . . . but [I] will just inform you, that I feel much gratitude to my worthy brother, and I dare say the same feelings are reciprocal, notwithstanding your wicked endeavors to prevent them, and for which I pity you from my heart."

~

We can only imagine Moses' dismay watching his brother and his close friend and in-law attack each other in an unprecedented display of public rancor— with Moses himself as the subject. Yet Moses must also have felt some inner satisfaction to see John avow in public his abiding brotherly love. Remarkably, Moses never stepped forward to contradict John or defend Thomas Arnold, in print at least, or in any of his surviving correspondence. Instead, with Arnold and David Howell, Moses huddled twice a week at John Carter's print shop, scanning the new edition of the *Gazette* to find the latest chapter in the spiraling acrimony. To that point, neither Arnold nor John was willing to let the feud lie.

Like captains of a pair of battling frigates, John and Thomas Arnold had spent days tacking and yawing for position, seeking the best angle for attack; now they drew up parallel, trading simultaneous broadsides in the *Gazette* and the *Chronicle*, devastating barrages that filled entire pages of newsprint. According to John, Arnold himself had engaged in the illegal Jamaica trade. Arnold had joined the Society of Friends only in order to "obtain a fortune with a pretty girl"—a reference to John's cousin Mary Brown. And Arnold might wield an "embellished pen . . . and I a very blunt one," but that was only because Arnold had the advantage of attending the very college that John had played such a prominent role in founding.

Arnold volleyed back. "I now undertake to remove a pile of rubbish"—a "huge" one at that—"from the path through which I hope many will be conducted from Egypt to Canaan, from slavery to freedom." The invective flowed from there. John had concealed his illegal trade to Jamaica from public scrutiny by destroying public records. He was a mere "*tool* of the slave traders." Lastly, Arnold provided a final installment to the story of John's slaves, "whose industry and faithfulness . . . contributed no small share to that *affluence* in which you are *floating*." This anecdote involved Yarrow, one of the slaves owned jointly by the four Brown brothers, who spent his days in labor at the candle works. In his document of manumission, Moses had relinquished his quarter share in Yarrow's bondage, but John held him fast to his dying day. On his death-bed, Yarrow had delivered an "indignant message: 'Tell him,' said Yarrow, 'to come and take his quarter, or I shall soon be free.'"

This, of course, only incensed John. His next piece, in the *Chronicle*, was addressed "To Tommy the Quaker." Here was a new round of accusation, and a healthy dollop of breast-beating. The three leaders of the abolition society—Arnold, Howell, and Moses—had been harassing the editors of the Providence newspapers, scheming to "prejudice the minds of the public against the good name of the Citizen." But "my name will still appear in the eyes of all unprejudiced men, *as gold tried in the fire*." John was veering between pride and self-pity. What about charity? John asked. "Is not the benevolent man entitled to some esteem?"

The nature of the game had shifted, John complained. "You seem to have quitted the field on which the controversy began, vis the abolition of slavery, and turned your whole strength . . . into personal slander and abuse." It was true—by this point, the debate was revealing more about the character of the combatants than the merits of human bondage. John showed the pugnacity he had shown all his life, the brazenness, the unquestioning self-assurance, the total engagement that he brought to every endeavor. But here we see as well the depth of his fury, unleashed on his friends and closest relations, his willingness to take public any damning material he could get hold of, his blind commitment to victory. We see too Thomas Arnold, usurping his station in the clan to confront his powerful brother-in-law, enduring withering attacks on his public reputation to deliver the same to John. And we see Moses, or at least, we see his reticence. He was appalled at the public bloodletting—it violated every principle of decorum and reserve that so attracted him to the Quaker ethic. But Moses wasn't willing to relinquish the press, the single source of news and opinion of that era, an instrument so crucial to his mission. He joined the contest but in a more muted, more deliberate manner than the other contributors. Working in the manner of Anthony Benezet, Moses published two long pieces during the debate, correcting the Citizen's representation of the nature of the slave trade, illuminating the dolorous conditions in Africa and on the Middle Passage. He cited the same texts as John, but followed the passages further to show the painful human costs of institutional slavery. With emotions cresting all around him, Moses was steadfast, never losing sight of his distant goal.

John also recognized that slavery remained at the root of their dispute. For all the charges and gossip, the excursions into the Jamaica trade and the Country Party's paper-money policy, slavery remained the source of their most damning accusations against him. He could not let the story of Yarrow lie unanswered.

John had never heard of Yarrow's dying declaration, the Citizen wrote, nor had anyone in his family. That accusation aside, Yarrow had died in comfort and in the care of his lifelong household. Manumission was simply inappropriate: John could not have freed Yarrow without freeing his fellow slaves who had worked so faithfully in John's own home. Those he would attend to posthumously, in the fashion of his uncle Obadiah, that "worthy gentleman" whose estate had devolved, by bequest and by marriage, to Moses and then to Arnold. Now John rounded to his point: if Moses and Thomas Arnold were to relinquish just a fraction of the estate they had inherited, they could purchase the freedom of every slave in Providence. "Why is not the sin as bad in you and his holding such property, as it is for a man to profit by the labor of such slaves? You as the receiver are as bad as the thief, and the receiver as bad as the kidnapper." In a society laced with slavery, the bright lines of guilt and innocence were hard to draw. Again, it was John who was aggrieved. "I do not condemn your holding property which was got from the labor of slaves, but I condemn your partiality, that you are so unwilling that others should acquire property in the same way yours was got."

By now the public clash had raged for more than a month, and the primary combatants had exhausted their arsenals of invective and intimate gossip. Several other correspondents had joined in the fray, writing from both sides of the dispute under names like "Reason," "Rejoinder," "Conviction," and "Thorn, jun.," the printers of Providence and Newport always willing to find space for such provocative prose. But for all the bluster, the landscape remained largely the same. The abolitionists had the law and now the society, but the slavers continued putting out for Africa. Writing from his vantage at Newport, Samuel Hopkins assayed the situation for Moses. "I am pleased to find you are able to maintain such a degree of calmness and fortitude under the abuse you and your friends have received from one who, unprovoked, is casting firebrands, arrows and death, and fighting creatures of his own imagination," Hopkins wrote. "I have the pleasure, however, of believing the mad opposition the Citizen is making to the Abolition Society . . . will be the means of strengthening it, and promoting the design for which it was formed." Newport, however, would continue to be hostile territory. "The combination and influence in this town is strongly exerted against [the society]. And many who reprobate slavery and the slave trade in their own minds do not choose to appear openly against it, because they feel themselves in some way dependent on those whom they should thereby offend."

It comes as little surprise, then, that the first action undertaken by the abolition society arose out of Newport but was pled from New Bedford, Massachusetts. The brigantine *Hope*, owned in part by Caleb Gardner, a prominent Newport captain and merchant, and helmed by John Stanton, also of Newport, had sailed for Africa in 1787 and made two trips around the triangle, each time delivering more than one hundred slaves to the West Indies. While she lay at Boston fitting out for yet another venture, Caleb Gardner made the mistake of applying at New Bedford to change the name and the owners of the vessel. This subterfuge came to the attention of William Rotch, a Quaker merchant and abolitionist who occasionally did business with the Brown brothers.

Rotch moved quickly to alert the sheriff, who arrested Gardner, his partner, and Captain Sheldon for violation of the new Massachusetts law. Rotch then wrote to Moses Brown requesting that the abolition society take over the case and fund the prosecution. It would become the first case ever tried in the United States for violation of a law against participating in the international market for slaves.

Moses and the other leaders of the society were glad for the chance to forget their war of words and take action against an actual slave trader. They assumed the cost of the case and helped assemble depositions from the crew of the *Hope*. The slavers of Newport did what they could to bribe and threaten the witnesses against them, but by the time the case came to trial, in March 1791, the facts of the case were beyond dispute. David Howell made the opening argument and after a week of trial the Newport slavers were found guilty. Crucially, the Massachusetts judge ruled that the state statute, which governed the conduct of American seamen abroad, presented no conflict to the provisions in the new U.S. Constitution protecting the slave trade in America.

The toughest question facing the plaintiffs was how hard they should strike. The Massachusetts law called for fines of two hundred pounds for the ship and fifty pounds for every slave transported; the tally at hand could reach as high as six thousand pounds. But Caleb Gardner was a hugely popular figure, a hero of the Revolution—like John Brown, Gardner had provided important assistance to the French admiral Comte d'Estaing—and a member of the upper house in the General Assembly. And as the plaintiffs would receive half the fines levied in the case, Moses Brown and other Quakers feared such a large award would carry the taint of profiteering. As early as May 1789 Moses warned Rotch against seeking the full judgment; stopping the trade, not money, was the object of the case.

Rotch agreed, but reluctantly. Though Rotch was a Quaker, he was not so retiring as many of his sect. Rotch displayed his fiery nature when, early in the Revolution, he accepted a consignment of guns and bayonets in payment for a debt. Rather than participate in the fighting by arming the combatants, he sold the muskets off for fowling pieces and dumped the bayonets into the sea.

In the Massachusetts case, having snared Gardner and his partners, Rotch wanted to make an impression: the suit should be "carried to a length that will clearly convince those traders they are fully within our power." Others were more reticent. As one Quaker elder put it to Moses, "Be careful not to tamper with or by any means partake of the disposition which thirsteth or seeketh to get the upper hand, that thirsteth for power and outward grandeur." Beset on both sides, Moses opted to steer a middle course.

In the case of the brig *Hope*, Moses' counsel held sway: the plaintiffs sought damages only against the ship, and the owners were fined just two hundred pounds. It was a victory for the new society, reflected in the steady growth of its membership roster. Renamed the Providence Abolition Society in 1790, it counted 170 members. They included, in addition to some of leading politi-

cal figures in Providence, Samuel Hopkins and Thomas Robinson of Newport, a Massachusetts chapter led by William Rotch and the Boston clergyman Jeremy Belknap, and a Connecticut chapter that included Levi Hart and
Jonathan Edwards.

But the verdict against Caleb Gardner was not the decisive blow Rotch was
looking for: the *Hope* returned to Africa four times in the next four years.
Other compromises brought similarly disappointing results; in one case, the
society voted to forgo prosecution in favor of a written pledge to desist from the
trade, but eight months later, the merchant in question dispatched his vessel
to Africa. The society's cautious approach left some abolitionists fuming. "The
past neglect to prosecute, and the known hesitation respecting it, has had a
great and apparent effect already," Samuel Hopkins wrote Moses in November 1789. "The slave traders are more bold and resolute to go on in the trade,
and entertain a low and contemptuous thought of the Society . . . anything
that looks like irresolution, neglect and dilatoriness, will fix a slur on the Society which cannot easily be wiped off."

Much as Moses sought to avoid public confrontation in seeking to enforce the
state laws against slavery, once the society was established, the cases crowded
in from all over the state. At Newport, Caleb Gardner continued putting slave
ships out to sea. In Bristol, the aptly named slaver James D'Wolf was charged
with murder for strangling an African woman aboard ship—he absconded before a trial could be held. And in Providence, Moses and the society found
themselves locked, once again, in a battle of wills with John Brown.

The showdown began with a plea to the society from a black seaman
named James Tom. Toward the end of the Revolution Tom had been sailing
under a British flag when his ship was captured by one of John Brown's privateers. Ever since, he and several other blacks had been pressed into service,
first on privateers, and then in John's merchant vessels. Now, during a brief
layover in port, Tom was asserting his freedom under Rhode Island's 1774 law
against slave imports.

The society agreed to take the case, and asked Moses to seek a settlement.
John answered in typical fashion, sending some dock hands to grab James
Tom forcibly off the street and hold him aboard one of his ships. Not to be ignored, the society that same day obtained a writ ordering Tom to be delivered
to the local court. But when the local sheriff went to John's Towne Street
wharf to serve the writ, John ordered his crew to let no man board his ship.
Moses stepped in again, offering to submit the question to impartial judges

from a neighboring state, but John only sputtered, denouncing the society and announcing to his brother, "You have as much right to the coat on my back as you do to my Negro."

The case was finally submitted to Superior Court in Providence, which rendered judgment against John and ordered James Tom to be set free. There is no record of a plea involving John's other black seamen; less resourceful than James Tom, it appears, they continued in bondage, sailing as slaves alongside the free crewmen of John's fleet.

Fearing that the derision and resistance of slaveholders like John was eroding the popular mandate for abolition, Moses returned once again to the General Assembly, seeking an explanatory act in 1791 that would formally acknowledge the society's standing in court and inject new vigor into the slave-trade statute. Moses and his allies put on a show of force, marshaling support from across the political spectrum, including Theodore Foster, the Providence politico and a leading Federalist; Arthur Fenner, venerable father of the new governor; and Job Comstock, a leader of the virulently antifederalist Country Party. The move nearly backfired, as the slave traders "exerted themselves to the utmost." The bill was approved by a vote of thirty-seven to twenty-two, but the slave traders quickly moved a watered-down replacement bill that carried the lower house as well. This maneuver was finally headed off in the upper house only by intervention of Gov. Arthur Fenner Jr., a Country Party moderate who had little patience with John Brown and his fellow merchants. The substitute bill was defeated by the margin of a single vote.

Moses had prevailed again, capping a period of remarkable gains in his campaign against slavery. In the space of just over three years, he had written legislation that struck at the heart of the American trade, blanketing the primary slave ports of North America with a prohibition that had already been tested in court under the provisions of the new federal Constitution. He had founded the sole abolition society in New England, and had himself been named the regional correspondent to the society in Philadelphia. Rather than wait for the councils of Europe, as the Citizen advised, he had forged ahead, serving as an inspiration to the Quakers in London then struggling—so far unsuccessfully—to wrest a ban on slave trading from Parliament.

And yet Moses could not escape the sensation of running on dry sand. For all he had accomplished—the laws, the votes, the society—the slave ships were still departing for Africa, still bringing their woeful cargoes to the Caribbean and the ports of the southern states. Quaker petitions were denounced and rebuffed in Congress, and slave traders continued to patrol the byways of the north, trolling for unsuspecting black quarry.

More painfully, Moses knew now—if he had any doubts before—that his nemesis was his brother. John embraced the role of ever-ready alter ego, dogging Moses, even ridiculing him in his quest for spiritual atonement. In his exasperation, Moses occasionally ventured explanations: to one British correspondent, Moses ruminated that John "has an overgrown fortune, and thinks himself I suppose pretty independent." Yet Moses never broke with John, never even rebuked him for his public attacks on his character. It was as if John had become the first object in Moses' mission of spiritual atonement: if he could not bring his own brother to share his sense of moral obligation, how could he expect to reform an entire nation?

12

The New Republic

THE PUBLIC FRACAS OVER SLAVERY and the new abolition society exposed for all to see the broad gulf that divided John and Moses Brown. In their diction, in their sense of propriety, in the basic values that led them to opposing poles on the moral question posed by slavery, the brothers could not have been more different. And yet, at the same time their controversy raged in the pages of the local press, another debate was unfolding that would push the brothers back onto common ground, and provide a foundation for ongoing collaboration, and even a sense of amity. The question was whether Rhode Island should ratify the Constitution and join the federal union.

The uncertain status of Rhode Island took on added urgency as the rest of the states fell in line. When New Hampshire became the ninth state to ratify, in 1788, Congress set about forming the new government, and the following April, George Washington was inaugurated as the first president. The Congress then turned its attention to the Bill of Rights, compiling a roster of fundamental protections to address the most glaring omissions in the Constitution. That document was presented to the states in September 1789, setting off another round of ratification and prompting a groundswell of national pride. Rhode Island, however, remained aloof. Skeptical of any central authority and jealous of its paper-money program, the Country Party and its agrarian base drew on the state's long tradition of fierce independence to resist every effort at the General Assembly to call for a ratifying convention.

The state had been down this path before, of course, in rejecting the federal Impost, but much had changed since then. No longer was the Congress governed by the Articles of Confederation, which required unanimous consent of the states for any change of policy. Rather than hang on the whims of any single state, then, the national government could simply forge ahead without it. And where before some other states had second thoughts, and followed Rhode Island's lead by rescinding their votes for the Impost, now they grew impatient. If Rhode Island continued to stand outside the union, the other states of the new union threatened to impose duties on Rhode Island exports. If that failed, the United States could institute an outright embargo on all trade from Narragansett Bay or, as was urged in the newspapers of Massachusetts and Connecticut, could simply invade, dividing the little state up among her neighbors.

John Brown found all of this enormously exasperating. An early champion of states' rights, he saw now that commerce with the other states, as well as with the other nations of the world, would be sorely hampered if Rhode Island had to negotiate separate treaties and alliances. Moreover, while John loved the brave posture of defiant independence, he grew increasingly uncomfortable with his state's pariah status. In June 1789 John was proud to show off his new mansion to Abigail Adams, who was traveling to join her husband, the new vice president, in New York. John put on one of his trademark dinner parties, and Adams was impressed, describing John's house as "one of the grandest I have ever seen in this country." (Adams also provided us with the sole surviving commentary on John's wife, Sarah: "The simplicity of her manners & dress with openness of her countenance & the friendliness of her behavior charmed me beyond all the studied politeness of European manners.") Yet when George Washington toured New England later that year, he pointedly avoided stopping in the holdout state, depriving John of an audience with a man he admired with unabashed fervor.

Most galling to John was the idea that he felt powerless to influence the state's entrenched majority. He wrote letters to Congress denouncing the Antifederalists, and crafted strategy with the Federalists of Newport, but the Country Party remained in power, its champions winning each election by comfortable margins. When John Adams wrote to John in February 1790 that "I am really much affected by the obstinate infatuation of so great a part of the people of Rhode Island," John could only commiserate.

For Moses, the question posed by the Constitution was not so much a test of pride as one of conscience. At the outset, like so many other Quakers, Moses rejected the new plan for government out of hand as a shameful compromise with the slave faction. But as the months went by, some of the Quakers he respected most began to moderate their position. In 1788, George Churchman wrote from England to suggest that on the question of slavery, the members of the Constitutional Convention "went about as far as they could go, without breaking to pieces and doing nothing." Churchman reminded Moses that "there is still a power that reigns over all . . . so if Faithful Friends in each part of the continent keep their places in singleness of heart, no doubt but that the way will gradually open."

By 1789, even William Rotch had begun to retreat from the passion of his initial reaction. "I was much disgusted when I first saw the Constitution," Rotch wrote to Moses, particularly with the section guaranteeing the freedom to import slaves. But after a conversation with Nathaniel Gorham, a delegate to the convention from Massachusetts, "I was fully reconciled to it, finding unless they suffered that clause, the whole matter must be broke up, which I think would have ended in great confusion and perhaps much bloodshed," Rotch wrote. "I now feel willing to contribute my might, so far as propriety will admit, to the settling of the government."

These ruminations had to have some influence — Moses was fond of Rotch, and relied on his counsel in business and church affairs — but Moses withheld his endorsement for the federal compact, especially when John touted the Constitution in his performances as the Citizen. This was, in fact, one source of John's fury. In their opposition to the Constitution, the Quakers had become fellow travelers with the Country Party and the other Antifederalists. Together, they were impervious to all the entreaties of the state's mercantile class, and were leading Rhode Island into a self-satisfied isolation that could only end in disaster.

Two developments brought this slow-moving crisis to a head. The first was the ratification of the Constitution by North Carolina. Legislators there had refused to join the union until a Bill of Rights was included to delimit the authority of the central government. When they finally agreed to come on board, in November 1789, Rhode Island was suddenly, perfectly, alone, an independent state surrounded by a hostile union. Second was the movement by Providence and Newport to secede from the state and seek their own compact with the federal government. The idea was floated by Jabez Bowen in a letter to George Washington, and gained wide attention in the regional press. Rhode Island had now reached the limits of her independence: she would either join the union or be dismembered herself.

With his beloved homeland threatened with dissolution from without and within, Moses finally broke his silence. In January 1790 he took a tour of the state, riding as far as East Greenwich on the western shore of Narragansett Bay to meet with Quaker leaders and advise that "the time is come when our acceptance of the new government will be better for us than to any longer stand out being alone." Moses explained his thinking in a candid letter to some of the other leading Quakers. Making no reference to slavery, he alluded only that he still wanted to see changes in the Constitution, but reasoned that "it is now only to be first adopted before we can attempt any amendments." In the meantime, the addition of the Bill of Rights promised that the new government "will be the best and the most peaceably founded, perhaps in all the world." Ratification, Moses concluded, would be "to the best interest of this poor, divided, lonely state."

After all the acrimony, this dramatic step by Moses came as a break in a family stalemate. His nephew Nicholas Brown Jr. voiced the sense of reconciliation when he wrote his uncle, "I am pleased to see you come out the friend of order and good government."

While Moses was entreating his fellow Quakers to support ratification, John was pursuing the same ends at the legislature, but after his own fashion. With the General Assembly meeting at Providence in January 1790, the Federalists once again called for a ratifying convention. The state's rural voters remained largely opposed to the union, but within the more sober forum of the statehouse, and faced with a packed gallery of Providence Federalists, their representatives began to waver. Indeed, some of them, even their leader, Jonathan Hazard, were already actively seeking jobs in the new federal government.

The debate took all of Friday, January 14. By the end, well after sundown, the House of Deputies agreed for the first time, by a five-vote majority, to call for a ratifying convention. But the upper house remained a Country Party bastion, and there, on Saturday, the resolution failed by a five-to-four vote. Encouraged by the close margin, and by their first victory in the lower house, the Federalist deputies promptly offered a substitute motion, this differing only by the date set for the convention, in hopes that momentum would swing their way. The motion prevailed again in the lower house, and again the upper house balked. But rather than reject it outright, the assistants agreed to extend the legislative session to Sunday, January 16.

John Brown was not a member of the assembly at the time, but he monitored the proceedings closely, and when the session was extended, he recognized an opportunity. As reported in the next edition of the *Gazette*, one of the Antifederalists was a minister, and as the meeting was continued to a Sunday, the preacher was "obliged to attend to the cure of Souls," and so missed the final vote. Another version suggests that in fact, the good reverend was induced by a bribe to forgo the crucial session. The story is recounted in the memoir of Welcome Arnold, the eldest brother of Thomas Arnold and a close associate of John Brown: "The Elder was doubtless greatly grieved, and distressed, that the wicked political men should take advantage of his pious call to preach that day," the memoir read. "And Mr. John Brown was so much grat-

ified by the pious Elder's attention to the spiritual concerns of his flock that
he, soon after, sent him a clear Deed of a very considerable farm in the vicin-
ity, as a reward for his religious zeal." With the reverend absent, the upper
house deadlocked four-to-four, allowing Gov. John Collins to cast the deciding vote in favor of the convention. Congress, informed that the logjam at
Rhode Island might be broken, agreed to put off for three months the punitive
duties planned for the renegade state.

The convention was set for March 1, at South Kingstown. Neither John nor
Moses was there, but the clan was represented by Uncle Elisha, then seventy-
four years old. Cantankerous as ever, Elisha was an Antifederalist holdout to
the end. After a week of debate, the convention adjourned without a decision,
agreeing only to meet again in Newport in May. There, after another weeklong session, the convention finally voted to adopt the Constitution by a majority of two, the slimmest ratifying margin of any of the thirteen states.

Surprisingly, as there were no prominent Quakers among the delegates,
the most extended debate turned on the question of slavery. As at Philadelphia, the critics of the Constitution cited their allegiance to liberty and their
revulsion at the idea that the new nation would countenance the slave trade.
And as at Philadelphia, the Federalists answered with pragmatism. Jonathan
Hazard, the Country Party leader turned Federalist, agreed that the critics of
the trade "acted on right principle," but warned that any move against slavery
would "stab at the vitals of the Southern States." Likewise, William Bradford,
the Bristol lawyer who had opposed Moses so effectively in the past, vowed, "I
abhor the slave trade," but warned against antagonizing the South. In the end,
the convention agreed to include, among a roster of proposed amendments,
one denouncing the slave trade as "disgraceful to the cause of liberty and humanity." It was no more than a principled gesture, but it was the only antislavery amendment proposed by any of the thirteen states.

Ratification of the Constitution, contentious as it was, closed the Revolutionary era in Rhode Island with a flourish. With her long tradition of independence, she had been the first of the thirteen colonies to make a formal
break with England. For eighteen years, since the torching of the *Gaspee*, the
state had been the scene of armed uprising, hostile invasion, and widespread
privation. Of all the original colonies, Rhode Island was the only one to actually lose population in the course of the war. Now, reluctantly, she had relinquished her sovereignty and become the last former colony to join the new
nation.

Mindful of the high price Rhode Island had paid, President Washington
celebrated her return to the fold by scheduling a state visit to the two primary

ports on Narragansett Bay. Washington sailed to Newport from New York on August 15, accompanied by Thomas Jefferson, his secretary of state; George Clinton, governor of New York; Theodore Foster, now a senator; and half a dozen other federal dignitaries. By the time they reached Providence, preparations had been under way for a week. The approach of the ship was marked by a volley of cannon, and a huge crowd gathered at the docks to see Governor Fenner greet the president. After spending the night at the Golden Ball, on Benefit Street, Washington on Thursday toured the town, making his way up Prospect Hill to see the college. That afternoon, John Brown had his moment. Washington agreed to join John in his coach—probably not the chariot, as that would have been too cramped for the long-legged president and his corpulent host—to visit the shipyard at India Point, where carpenters and caulkers were laboring over the skeletal frame of John's largest ship yet, a 950-ton behemoth called *President Washington*, the second of three ships John named after his hero. Stately and gracious, Washington must have gotten an earful from John, on the state of trade, the struggle with the Antifederalists, and the duties of the new government. Never bashful, John would make the most of a private audience with the nation's first chief executive.

Upon their return, Washington consented to stop at John's mansion for a round of punch served on china recently imported from Canton on the *General Washington*. Finally, John released him, and the president concluded his tour with stops at the homes of Governor Fenner and Jabez Bowen. Washington sailed later that evening, after a public dinner at the statehouse with two hundred invited guests. John partook lustily in the toasts that evening; after all the travail and all the politics, he had finally seen consummated his vision of Rhode Island standing as an equal among the states of a new nation, independent of Britain, master of her own fate.

Even before Washington's visit to Providence, John was working to ensure that the functionaries of the new government would conform to his principles and cater to his needs. On June 11, less than a month after Rhode Island endorsed the Constitution, John wrote Washington to remind him of the "Grait Exertions" made by the Federalists to achieve ratification, and warned him against appointing any of the "Anties" to federal office. Rather, John offered his own recommendations for "a core of Honest Faithfull and Vigilent Custom House Officers." Paramount on his list was Jeremiah Olney, a Baptist stalwart and veteran of the Revolution, and a candidate for the job of customs collector for the port of Providence.

Olney won the appointment, promising "upright, impartial, and faithful discharge" of his duties. It was a crucial post: like William Morris before him, Alexander Hamilton, Washington's choice as secretary of the Treasury, made revenues from trade duties central to his funding plan, and compliance in Providence, with its history of resistance to British tax collectors and the continental Impost, would pose a critical test of federal authority.

Olney soon learned that John Brown, despite his public support for the government and for Olney's appointment, would treat him with the same measure of contempt he had reserved for Lieutenant Dudingston. John set the tone in November 1790, when Olney announced that the customs office would be closed Saturday afternoons. John led several merchants in a sharp response to this initiative, warning Olney, "We are exceedingly sorry, *for your own sake*," that the collector would not reconsider his decision. "To what end doeth mankind live in society if it is not for the accommodations of each other?" John asked plaintively. More firmly, John added, "Every merchant will consider it as a grievance, if he cannot be indulged."

This dustup was just a preview of the problems Olney would encounter in his dealings with John Brown. More telling was Olney's effort to secure export manifests for the 280-ton ship *Warren*, which John was sending to Calcutta. Olney learned on Thanksgiving Day that the *Warren* was departing Providence for Newport, where she would load with wine and other trading goods. Encountering her captain, John Smith, on the street outside church, Olney asked Smith to alert John Brown to his obligation to file papers certifying the *Warren*'s cargo. To his dismay, John "thought proper to slight the friendly message, and in apparent contempt of the laws, dispatched the ship about eleven o'clock in the forenoon, without any application to me for a register or other papers!" Writing to Secretary Hamilton for direction, Olney proposed that "every breach of the revenue laws should be prosecuted, and if *wilful*, punished with rigour, however powerful the offenders might be." Hamilton fully concurred.

Olney heard from John directly soon after writing that letter, and John assured him the *Warren* would return to Providence, and file formal clearances, before setting out to sea. Thus Olney was especially disturbed to learn in December that, "contrary to what Mr. Brown informed me was his intention, the ship *Warren* did not return from Newport . . . but having completed her lading there, she sails." John finally filed papers on the *Warren*, but four days after she departed, leaving Olney no way to authenticate the cargo report. The incident caught the attention of Secretary Hamilton, who advised Olney, "It is fit that you pay more than ordinary attention to the vessels of Messr. Brown &

Francis . . . since a disposition to disregard the revenue laws has manifested it-self in them on this occasion."

It was foolhardy, of course, for John so quickly to antagonize the new fed-eral inspector at Providence, not to mention the new Treasury secretary. John's growing position in international trade—he was sending ships to Europe, the Baltic, and South America, as well as the Orient, and his return cargoes racked up duty charges of as much as one hundred thousand dollars—required constant contact with customs officials, and their favor could be essential to the business of juggling scarce capital.

Fortunately for John and his friends in Providence, Alexander Hamilton was inclined to cultivate the merchant community, believing as he did that fostering business enterprise was the key to survival for a new republic strug-gling to emerge from a postwar recession in a world still dominated by the im-perial ambitions of Europe. Moreover, as Hamilton well understood, the Treasury would have to rely on cooperation more than coercion to enforce the revenue laws. He had only ten revenue cutters to patrol the entire eastern seaboard, and he could ill afford a state of open enmity between merchants—many of them inveterate smugglers—and the officials of the new government. Hamilton expressed his sense of balance in enforcement of the trade laws in a private letter to Olney prompted by the continued carping of the Providence shipping interests. "I am aware that in a scene where [the merchants] have been accustomed to much relaxation, a spirit of exactness is particularly nec-essary. . . . But on the other hand I have considered it as possible that your ideas of precise conformity to the laws, may have kept you from venturing upon relaxations in cases in which, from very special circumstances, they may have been proper."

Hamilton now made clear his position. "The good will of the merchants is very important in many senses, and if it can be secured without any improper sacrifice or introducing a looseness of practice, it is desirable to do it." The customs inspectors, Hamilton made clear, should seek accommodation.

John would test Olney's patience and sense of propriety repeatedly over the next several years. But he would draw on Hamilton's amity more directly in pursuing one of his grandest and most abiding ambitions—the launching of a bank. This enterprise would require all of John's resources—his capital, his political connections, and his mercantile network. In addition, John felt he needed a partner in the project, one whose integrity was publicly acknowl-edged and above reproach, whose loyalty he could rely on implicitly, and whose judgment he regarded as equal to his own. For that sensitive, central role, John reached back to his roots—he turned to his brother Moses.

John Brown had begun agitating for a bank as early as 1784, the year the country's first regional banks were chartered in Boston and New York. Spurred by the success of the Bank of North America in Philadelphia, the nation's first bank, chartered by Robert Morris in part to finance the war, John joined with Jabez Bowen and John Jenckes to convene several organizing meetings and raise funds through subscription. But there was little capital available, and the funding stalled well short of the announced goal of one hundred fifty thousand dollars.

Launching a bank was, at that time, an act of daring and imagination. Prior to the Revolution, loans and credit were strictly private affairs, and the bank closest to the colonies was located in London. With independence came the opportunity to establish local banks, but in circumstances of enormous risk, with wildly fluctuating currencies, no organizational standards, and depositors accustomed to keeping their savings close at hand.

The first banks were situated, naturally, at the leading centers of commerce and population. As John was well aware, Providence was "insignificant, and I may add miserable in point of wealth, when compared to the four towns in the union who now have banks established." Still, John had advice and encouragement from his old friend Tench Francis, father of John's young partner. Tench Francis was a leader in Philadelphia's financial community and, beginning in 1787, the first cashier of the Bank of North America.

John believed that creation of a local bank would boost the local economy by answering pressing problems of credit and providing a stable medium for transactions after the chaos of the paper-money administration. And he feared that should Providence fail to answer the call, she would soon be eclipsed by those communities that did. "Without a spring to promote our young men in business here, they must and will continue to go to such places as will aid them with the means of business," John wrote to Moses. "In short all our wealth . . . must be transferred to those other states who by their banks promote all the valuable arts of mankind."

Of course, John had his own interests to serve as well. Easy access to credit was crucial in assembling the huge cargoes he was shipping to the Orient, and in settling his accounts with the new customs service. But he elaborated the public-benefit aspects of the project in seeking a state charter for the institution, and in newspaper ads calling for subscriptions. John was accustomed to claiming public interest while pursuing his own ends; in this case, as with the locating of the college in Providence, he may actually have had a point. Banks would play a vital role in early American economic development, and proliferated as the years went by.

More surprising than his support for the bank was John's determination to bring Moses into the project. Just a year before, John had savaged Moses in print, and neither Moses nor he had given any indication of reconciling their bitter division over the question of slavery. Moreover, Moses and John had differed over business affairs early on, leading to John's split from the family firm in 1771. Since then, Moses had roundly proclaimed his disaffection with commerce, and had formally retired from the world of business. He would seem an unlikely candidate for a pivotal role on the board of the new institution.

But John knew Moses better—he was not simply the retiring and self-effacing figure he presented to the Society of Friends and to the public at large—perhaps better than Moses knew himself. John knew, for example, that after Moses had announced his withdrawal from business, and from the family candle works and the Hope Furnace, Moses had dickered stubbornly over the value of his holdings, rejecting several overtures from John and dragging the talks out for more than six years. At one point, John complained, Moses was demanding "a grait deal more than you have any expectation of getting." John found these negotiations galling, but they confirmed his sense of Moses as a hardheaded businessman—the only one John had encountered who drove a bargain harder even than himself.

More recent experience showed John that, whatever principles he might espouse publicly, Moses was able to set aside his scruples when it came to the affairs of business. John had made the point, when writing as the Citizen, that the proprietors of the nascent textile works in Providence were using cotton raised by slaves in the West Indies. Yet in the year after those taunts were published, Moses received several consignments of Caribbean cotton from John. As usual, the two brothers dickered over the price, but no mention was made of the propriety of using slave produce—an omission that could not have escaped John's notice.

There was another, more tangible development that forced John to entreat Moses' support for the bank. In May 1791 Nicholas Brown, eldest of the four brothers, died after a long illness. John quickly learned of the event and rushed to his brother's house, where he found Nicholas sprawled across a bed, and "his widow and two children . . . on the floor in the greatest agony of grief, stricken on the scene." John attended to the body, but it was Moses who was named the executor of the estate, along with Nicholas Junior, in charge of distributing his effects and managing a portfolio of more than two hundred thousand dollars in public securities. That August, John put the proposition to Moses: "How can a considerable part of our worthy deceased brother's securities be put to better use than in a bank of our own?"

Lastly, John believed that Moses' high stature in the community would assure potential depositors of the bank's integrity. The fledgling textile works aside, he had no business interests, thus insulating himself from conflicts of interest in making loans.

But if John had a variety of reasons for approaching Moses, what of Moses? Committing his reputation and energies to founding a bank would require him to set aside his continuing feud with his brother, and to contradict his religious compunctions against becoming entangled in business affairs. The latter concern weighed heavily on Moses, but in the fall of 1791 he took up the work in earnest, meeting with John and Welcome Arnold, brother of Thomas, to review other bank charters, to plan reserve accounts and loan criteria, and to choose the board of directors.

Moses described his reluctant decision to join the enterprise in a searching "apology" he wrote to James Pemberton, the Quaker leader in Philadelphia. The depressed state of business affairs in Rhode Island had given rise to "overreaching and other moral deficiencies," he wrote; the bank might prove "a remedy to this evil." Still, when he was first approached and offered the post of bank president, he declined outright. When he was named a director at one of the early meetings, he declined again. But the other directors persisted, and in the end, "finding my name was wanted to give some credit to the institution which I really thought would or might if it were well managed prove useful even in a moral sense," Moses agreed to sign on.

Another factor Moses didn't mention to Pemberton—this was an apology, after all—was the great pleasure he took in organizing and directing the establishment of community institutions. He had demonstrated in the past his bottomless appetite for the meetings and minutia involved in launching schools, paving roads, and raising buildings. The founding of the bank would be a return to form.

Instead, in writing Pemberton, he dwelt on his sense of guilt. "I still have the same mind," Moses confided, "that Friends in our station"—presumably elders of the Quaker society—"have enough to attend to without being called to the place of the money-changers." Clearly, Moses remained conflicted in his decision. "If any friend mentions my name in the matter I hope I have said enough to manifest to them that I am not pleased with it. . . . I hope some good may come out of it yet I would not have others go into it any more because I am involved so far in it."

Moses had less to say about his brother John, but he must have felt ambivalent there as well. Even when they were not locking horns over the question of slavery, John's extensive and often contentious business affairs were a constant distraction to his brother. During this period Moses received several appeals from debtors pressed by John for payment; one, Christopher Whipple, wrote Moses in anguish to plead for "a convenient shed" for his wife and children while he languished in debtors' prison. Months later, Whipple was more indignant. "I am not to be cast into prison like a dog"; but jailed he was, his estate forfeit.

John was equally hard on his creditors, and they also turned to Moses for help. Champion & Dickason, the Browns' London agent, wrote to Moses in 1789 to complain that while John was engaged in launching ever-larger ships in the China trade, he was making no effort to settle a looming debt to them. "Your brother John treats us in the most unfeeling manner while he is carrying on considerable business and surely it may be said with our capital." Such conduct by a member of his family "must be painful to a man of your character and high sense of honor," the agents offered; for his influence on their behalf "we should be most thankfully grateful." Moses apparently did intercede, as the same firm reported six months later, "We are very much of opinion that your conversation with your brother has had some effect on him, as we have had by far a more agreeable letter from him lately than in sometime past." Moses may have been the younger of the two siblings, but he always felt responsible for his more venturesome brother.

John understood this, and knew whatever offense might drive them apart — be it renouncing his deal with the British at the outset of the war or his continuing interest in the slave trade — Moses was always open to restoring his familial connection. With death of their brother Nicholas, the bond grew stronger. Moses acknowledged John's influence in his letter to Pemberton: "My brother John was anxious for me to engage, manifesting more cordiality than for many months past and desiring to conciliate his affection in every way . . . being only two of us left, had weight with me."

Having made his decision, Moses entered into the bank project with all his usual energy. He consulted the charters of several other banks and relied on these to draw up the charter for Providence. Moreover, Moses helped raise capital, calling in personal loans and prevailing on his friend William Rotch to invest seven thousand dollars in the first months of operation.

With Moses on board, the citizens of Providence again witnessed the phenomenon of the Brown family joining together to shape the institutional life of the town. Advertisements appeared in the *Gazette* calling meetings to raise subscriptions, at the same time emphasizing the public spirit of the enterprise:

"Taught by the experience of Europe and America, that well-regulated Banks are highly useful to society, by promoting punctuality in the performance of contracts, increasing the medium of trade," and so on. As the project gathered speed, the tone of the notices shifted, warning, "Any persons who may neglect attending at the Court-House at the hour appointed . . . will do well to re-member, that they can blame none for themselves for their inattention to the business." By October, with bank funded with capital commitments for more than $180,000, the membership of the board was announced: John Brown, president, followed by Welcome Arnold, Moses Brown, Nicholas Brown Jr., John Innes Clarke, Jabez Bowen, and three others.

Once the charter for the bank was approved by the General Assembly, on October 3, 1791, John immediately began lobbying to have the bank desig-nated as a depository for federal funds, and to have banknotes deemed accept-able in payment of customs bonds. This was a brilliant stroke, expanding the scope of the bank and making the customshouse a virtual subsidiary of the merchant interests. Customs duties were required in specie, always a scarce resource for traders who relied on credit; the ability to pay in banknotes would allow far more flexibility in dealing with the government. And deposits of the customshouse receipts would mean the merchants' bonds were essentially being recycled, providing new funds for loan to the entrepreneurs of Provi-dence.

Already in his tenure at Treasury, Alexander Hamilton had made it clear he supported the formation of banks, and had ordered that customs receipts in Boston, Philadelphia, and New York be deposited at the banks there. Provi-dence was an exception—it was, as John had acknowledged, "miserable in point of wealth" by comparison, and would never rival the great ports for vol-ume of trade. But John was persistent, pushing his scheme with Benjamin Bourne, one of Rhode Island's delegates to Congress, and after several weeks of deliberation, Hamilton signed off, notifying Jeremiah Olney of his decision November 10.

Thus by the winter of 1791, John had succeeded in erecting an entirely new fiscal structure to manage shipping affairs and obligations to the govern-ment, with himself in the pivotal role of president of the new bank. And yet by the spring of 1792, John was already leaning on Olney for special dispensation in handling his accounts. That May, John applied to Olney for a seven-hundred-dollar advance against future duties; a month later, he paid duties with a banknote dated three days after the bond became due. Each time Olney reminded John of the "strict regard I have for punctuality," but each time, the collector acquiesced. He was a stickler for procedure, it was true, but he was also well aware of John's stature and influence.

It was not long, however, before John overplayed his hand, drawing the scrutiny of Alexander Hamilton himself, and demonstrating his sagacity in pressing his brother Moses into service. In October 1792, word reached Hamilton "through a channel so respectable as to claim notice," as he termed it, that the affairs of the bank were in "considerable disorder." This was of particular concern to the Treasury, as government deposits at the bank amounted to more than twenty-five thousand dollars.

Hamilton was worried, but he wanted to move cautiously. Concerned as ever with the broader ramifications of his every step, Hamilton explained his thinking in a letter to Olney: "Aware that a sudden order to withhold public deposits and withdraw public money might contribute to any partial derangement, which may exist, a total one, to the great prejudice of all concerned, I forbear to take such a step." Instead, Hamilton selected a delegation "who will combine a regard to the public interest with a disposition friendly to the Bank and to the Trade" to investigate and report back to him.

John Brown learned of the inquiry in a weekday morning visit from Jeremiah Olney, who stopped by John's countinghouse on Main Street and asked to speak with him privately. After they had stepped into a rear warehouse, Olney related that Hamilton had ordered an inspection "to know what state the bank was in, and whether the public deposits were safe." Alarmed, John asked if Olney would be satisfied with a look at the vault, but the inspector suggested that a conference with the board was in order.

The meeting, at seven o'clock that evening, degenerated into something of a power play. Olney arrived in company with John Dexter, the Treasury's collector of revenue for Rhode Island, and William Channing, the U.S. district attorney, both Newport men. Channing opened the session by reading a section from Hamilton's letter describing "the deranged state of the bank." The bank directors present—Moses was not—answered by suggesting the whole imbroglio was due to malicious rumors floated from jealous merchants at Newport. They would not open their books to Channing—only to Hamilton—and Channing would not share a copy of Hamilton's letter.

Another meeting was scheduled for the following night, and in the interim, John dispatched an urgent letter to Moses. He described the threat to the bank and exhorted him to step in, explaining that "I wish you to come down and see the letter in their hands, which they decline giving us a copy of but may show it to you." Clearly, Moses' reputation, and his more pacific demeanor, would be necessary to defuse the crisis. Just what transpired at the second session was not recorded, but the inspectors elected to leave the federal deposits untouched, and Moses composed a conciliatory letter to Hamilton.

As it turned out, he need not have bothered; even before the meeting took place, Hamilton wrote to notify his subordinates that "the information [regarding the bank] was a misapprehension." Yet the potential was there, in the showdown with federal authorities, for an ugly intervention that could well have shaken public confidence in the young institution. Realizing that his brusque style could cost him dearly, John once again had called on Moses to bail him out, and once again, Moses had come through.

This was a season of conciliation for the two surviving Brown brothers. It was as if, with the question of slavery in abeyance—the society remained active, but John suffered its efforts in silence—the brothers were seeking to affirm through public works the affinity that had so long eluded them.

The Browns put on an impressive display of amity through the winter of 1791 and the spring of 1792 as they wrestled over the question of where to site a bridge over the Seekonk River. Here, as usual, the brothers were rivals, each working to rally public support behind a competing plan. But this campaign they carried off with decorum, neither stooping to disparage the other.

There was, to be sure, a genuine basis for the dispute over the bridges. The Seekonk, a broader, stronger river than the Great Salt, flowed past the far side of Prospect Hill, separating Providence from the towns of Warren and Barrington, and from the rolling pastures of southeast Massachusetts. For generations, a pair of ferries sufficed to carry a light flow of travelers and farm wagons across the Seekonk, but by now the growth of Providence warranted erecting at least one bridge. John appears to have struck upon the idea first, proposing a span extending, naturally, from his wharf and warehouses at India Point, across the mouth of the Seekonk. Moses responded soon after, proposing a bridge several miles upriver at the landing for the "upper ferry," which would be served by a road leading through his farm. Both bridges would be financed by lottery, and paid off through tolls.

Both bridge schemes quickly became the subject of political controversy. Residents of the mill town of Pawtucket, twenty miles upstream, including such longtime friends of the Brown family as Oziel Wilkinson and several members of the Jenckes clan, were "very much alarmed" for fear that permanent structures, even with a draw in the middle, would impede the navigation of rafts, barges, and other vessels bringing lumber and farm produce to market. But Providence dominated the state assembly, and the idea of a bridge quickly gained momentum. John and Moses each set about gathering signatures in support of his respective bridge, each keeping his references to the other project discreet.

When the petitions were filed, John's encouraged approval of both projects, but "if one bridge only should at present be deemed necessary . . . it would be more beneficial to the public at or near the lower ferry than in any other place." John was so modest he didn't even affix his own signature, allowing his friends to carry his cause. Moses was equally civil; his petition simply emphasized the need for both bridges to be built. The signatures attached offer a glimpse of the allegiances each brother might summon: Clarke & Nightengale signed both petitions (in each case signing as a firm), as did James Arnold, Nicholas Power, and Stephen Dexter; Nicholas Brown Jr. and Jeremiah Arnold, the customs inspector, signed only for Moses.

Both petitions were approved, and both bridge companies incorporated. For years thereafter, travelers traversing the Seekonk chose between John's bridge and Moses' bridge. But if the brothers were amicable, they were still adversaries: in June, with the decision still in play, Moses wrote to friends in Newport to report that a new road might easily be laid to the site of his proposed bridge, "much better than the South Road to the Lower Ferry now is," and that this news should afford the Newport delegates "full satisfaction to appear in favor of the upper bridge." Eight years later, Moses was still playing the same game, buying up land to block a new highway leading from India Point—and John's bridge—straight through Barrington to Warren. Even when the brothers achieved public peace, they never resolved between themselves the question of which was the leader and which would acquiesce.

In December 1789, at a time when Moses was occupied in prosecuting slavers through the abolition society and wrestling with the dilemmas presented by the new U.S. Constitution, he received a letter from New York that would dramatically alter the prospects of his infant cotton manufactory. The author was Samuel Slater, an ambitious young mill worker from England who was seeking a management position in the cotton-spinning business.

For more than a year, Moses had been recruiting and vetting spinners and mechanics who might be able to advance the rudimentary state of the spinning jennies, looms, and carding machines that were the basis for industrial textile production. It had been a frustrating experience—the artisans, most of them recently arrived from Europe, commanded high wages and rarely stuck around long enough to see a project through. Moreover, none had direct experience working with Richard Arkwright, whose spinning jenny had revolutionized cotton production in England. Without Arkwright's innovation,

American textile production could never rival England for volume, price, or quality.

Samuel Slater represented a breakthrough. Raised next door to Arkwright's partner, Samuel Strutt, in Derbyshire, England, Slater was apprenticed at age fourteen in Strutt's mill, and spent the next seven years learning the intricacies of Arkwright's secret machinery. At age twenty-one, having assumed the post of superintendent under Strutt, Slater read of the bounties offered in the United States for industrial expertise. He knew of the strict laws against disseminating protected technologies but he was too impatient for the slow, steady climb up the management ladder. He decided to emigrate, setting in motion one of the earliest and most influential cases of industrial espionage on record.

That summer, Slater told his mother he was visiting London for the weekend, packed a single bag, and boarded a ship bound for New York. He arrived after a passage of more than two months and promptly found employment. But Slater was dismayed at the poor state of the equipment on hand, and soon began casting about for a more promising station. Moses was among the first mill operators contacted by Slater, and he immediately recognized the implications of Slater's expertise in Arkwright's secret technology.

Moses responded promptly, but was careful not to overplay his hand. "Thy being already engaged in a factory with many able proprietors, we can hardly suppose we can give the encouragement adequate to leaving thy present employ." Yet Moses demonstrated a fair grasp of the technology involved, and offered Slater all the profits from the enterprise after interest and maintenance costs. Then Moses played his trump card, assuring Slater of "the *credit* as well as the advantage of perfecting the first water-mill in America." This was just the sort of partnership Slater had in mind when he left Derbyshire. He booked passage on the next packet bound for Providence, and by early January he was in Pawtucket, touring the rented mill there with Moses, his son Obadiah, William Almy, and Smith Brown.

The timing could not have been better for Moses. He'd incorporated the partnership of Almy & Brown just months before, and his various mechanics had pretty well exhausted their expertise. Moses later described Slater's reaction to the assembled equipment as "disappointment . . . they are good for nothing," but that was probably unfair; for in just two months' time, working with Oziel Wilkinson and other local craftsmen, Slater had two water-powered spinning frames up and running. By April, a new partnership had been formed between Smith Brown, Almy, and Slater, with Moses providing the financing.

The move to Pawtucket was propitious for Slater as well. Assuming proprietorship of a factory had been his goal from the outset. And during the nights he spent boarding at Oziel Wilkinson's workshop he struck up a relationship with Wilkinson's daughter Hannah. The pair were wed in October 1791, which ensured that Slater, unlike so many of his fellow expatriates, would stay put.

The arrival of Samuel Slater and the success of the spinning operation won for Moses sudden prominence on a stage far removed from the familiar arena of politics and religion. In July 1791, Moses received from John Dexter, the Treasury official at Newport, a copy of Alexander Hamilton's circular letter soliciting information on the state of industry in each of the thirteen states. Dexter had turned to Moses, he explained, "from a full conviction, that as no one in the state has more at heart the encouragement of our infant manufactures—has been more indefatigable and liberal in the establishment, improvement and use of them than yourself, so no one can possibly possess a more competent knowledge of their commencement, progress, and present state, than yourself."

Moses took the charge seriously, and spent two months composing a detailed and comprehensive response for the Treasury. He spoke directly from his own experience. Prewar manufactures were in decline, he explained; the candle business was sinking as a result of the demise of the whaling business, which in turn was devastated by the war and by overfishing. Likewise, rum and sugar were in decline since the British had embargoed commerce with the West Indies.

Moses then turned his attention to textiles. He described the early experiments in water-powered spinning, the arrival of Samuel Slater, and the progress made since then. With the spinning technology finally perfected, a host of ancillary operations were now being pursued—picking and cleaning, soaping, drying, weaving, cutting, bleaching, and finishing—each process taking place in separate workshops, and each requiring time to develop skill and expertise. Their success was measured in yards of fabric—"velveteens, velverets, corduroys, thicksets, a variety of fancy cut goods, jeans, denims, velours, stockenets, pillows or fustians, etc."—all produced by hand at shops in Providence and East Greenwich from cotton spun at the Pawtucket mill.

Moses took as a given the public benefits of employment and capital formation that such enterprises would yield, elaborating only on the aspect of child labor. "As the manufactory of the mill yarn is done by children from 8 to 14 years old it is a near total saving of labor to the country," he stated. The dismal implications of youngsters spending their early years working twelve- to sixteen-hour shifts in the gloom of the textile mills, as became prevalent throughout the Northeast for much of the next century, apparently escaped Moses, as they did Hamilton himself. Both men were too focused on their goal to see pitfalls already close at hand.

Not content simply to relate the status of current production, Moses addressed several policy questions where the federal government could make a difference. The chief impediment to the future of American textiles, he wrote, was the dumping of surplus fabric by British traders who offered low price and long terms of credit. This was not just a market decision, Moses asserted, but a "policy of the English manufacturers, formed into Societies for the purpose . . . in order to break up the business." It had been deployed with success in Ireland a decade before; now it was being turned against the United States.

Such practices, Moses proposed, called for a response by the government, either in the form of bounties for domestic production, or tariffs on imports, or both. More particular, Moses explained that cotton from the West Indies was more carefully picked, and arrived cleaner, than from the southern states in America, a critical factor in mechanized production. Consequently manufacturers generally purchased foreign cotton despite import duties, "a circumstance truly mortifying" to U.S. producers. This should also be addressed through a combination of tariffs and bounties to encourage domestic production. Here again, Moses appeared to be losing sight of the larger consequences of his single-minded pursuit; he knew full well, from his brother's imprecations as well as his own experience, that southern cotton was a product of slave labor, yet he was advising Hamilton on how to promote it. Moses never addressed this surprising contradiction. The singular focus he brought to his endeavors was one of his great strengths, but sometimes led him astray.

Moses also appears to have overlooked the critical role his personal initiative played in the progress of his new enterprise. Several times in his essay for Hamilton, Moses applauded the efforts of government and business societies to foster the acquisition and development of industrial technology. Yet his own experience, as he pointed out in the same document, was quite different. In his pioneering efforts to raise a textile mill, Moses wrote, "No encouragement has been given by any laws of this state nor by any donation of any society or individuals but wholly began carried on and thus far perfected at private expense." He made the same observation two years before, pointing out to a correspondent that, at his new mill, "we mean to be managers ourselves[;] this is private, theirs are Societies of men that don't wish to labor and therefore employ others."

The wisdom of Moses' hands-on approach was only confirmed in the years that followed. Convinced that technology was the best means to economic advance, Hamilton himself presided over the first stock offering of the Society for Establishing Useful Manufactures (SEUM), a project that won enthusiastic backing from financiers in New York and New Jersey. The idea was to raise a new town on the Passaic River in New Jersey that would be devoted wholly to manufactures—of textiles, paper, shoes, hats, and beer—and would utilize new industrial techniques spirited from Britain in the same fashion Samuel Slater had done. Toward the end of 1791, the society purchased seven hundred acres, dubbed the new settlement Paterson, after the state's governor, hired a slew of factory supervisors, and commenced construction. But the stock of the consortium collapsed in a financial panic in 1792, tens of thousands of dollars were squandered or stolen, and four years later, its spinning, weaving, and printing operations were shuttered.

During the period of the SEUM's rise and fall, Moses pressed ahead with his mill works at Pawtucket. Progress was sporadic, and always arduous. In 1792, the partnership commenced work on a new factory building and a dam to service it. At more than six feet high and two hundred feet long, the dam was America's largest to date, and presaged the coming transformation of the rural landscape, along with the political disputes that would attend it. The night of August 31, the proprietors of a metal shop and a grain mill downstream crossed Moses' property, waded into the stream, and destroyed all the work done so far. Moses and his partners sued, but the vandals prevailed in the claim that the new dam would interrupt—albeit temporarily—the flow to their waterwheels. But while the suit was being contested, construction went ahead, and the dam still stands today. A second suit was brought by farmers concerned about the threat posed by the dam to spawning fish. In this case, Moses appealed to the General Assembly, and won an exemption to the state's Fish Act. As at the Hope Furnace, Moses' political clout proved critical in helping to assert the prerogatives of industry.

Other problems arose within the firm itself. In 1791 Smith Brown retired and his place was taken by Moses' son Obadiah. Under both formations, friction arose between Almy and Brown, who operated out of Providence, and Samuel Slater, who worked in Pawtucket, fashioning equipment with the aid of Oziel Wilkinson and his sons. Though still young, Slater was flinty and sometimes imperious; his partners in Providence regarded his constant demands for funds and supplies skeptically. Slater's frustration is apparent in the memos he sent his partners; in one he complained, "The mill is now destitute of the following articles: cotton to pick, corn, rye, coffee, tea, molasses and flour." Another was more firm: "Please send some fleece cotton . . . and a little money if not I must unavoidably shut down the mill next week."

Success came in spurts, and brought its own complications. Almy, Brown & Slater's debt to Moses grew from ten thousand dollars to more than double that figure. Some weeks, production outstripped demand, and yarn piled up at the warehouse in Providence; in others, Slater and his mill hands could not meet all the orders. Following in the path of his father's early career, Obadiah cruised north and south along the coast and traveled far inland to recruit new customers. At the mill, Slater's mechanical improvements progressed steadily, but managing America's first factory workforce proved a constant trial. Whole families were employed—children were essential, as they were the only ones small enough to climb inside the spinning frames when threads tangled or broke—and young Slater had to answer to the parents for his methods. Arnold Benchley protested vigorously when Slater insisted his children work by candlelight; Caleb Greene kept his children home when their pay was late. One summer day, Slater's entire workforce—parents and children together—left the factory on a mission to pick whortleberries.

Slater could be a tough taskmaster; he ran shifts of twelve hours in the winter, sixteen in the summer. But in some instances, Slater took the parents' side in his appeals to Almy & Brown. In 1794, Slater fumed, "You call for yarn but think little about the means by which it is to be made such as the children." Some appeals were downright plaintive: "Children are quivering this morning at seeing it snowy and cold and no stoves [in the factory]." On his own initiative, Slater introduced a Sunday school to provide his young charges a modicum of education, a practice he borrowed from the mills back in England.

Despite the growing pains, and technical setbacks, the mill made the transition from business experiment to going concern. By 1795, revenues reached more than twelve thousand dollars. In 1797, Slater opened a second mill, this one with Oziel Wilkinson as his partner; in 1799, William Almy and Obadiah Brown opened a second mill of their own. Within a decade, a dozen new mills had opened, and the industrial era in New England had begun in earnest.

One place it did not catch on was in Newport. When Moses composed his report on manufactures for Hamilton, he sent a draft to William Ellery, the customs inspector at the port and an old political ally, suggesting that the slave traders there could better devote their capital to textiles. Ellery was not encouraging. The men of property in Newport did not have the "spirit of enterprise" required of such an endeavor. Besides, Ellery noted dourly, "An Ethiopian could as soon change his skin as a Newport merchant could be induced to change as lucrative a trade as that in slaves for the slow profits of any manufactory."

As the textile business grew, Moses' role diminished. The business never became a source of income for him; while he recouped his initial loans, Moses said later, "not one penny of profit has ever come to my hand." But that was never the point. He'd provided the vision, the capital, and the entrepreneurial will; he was content to let the younger generation sort out the details of managing their growing concern.

13

Moses Goes to Congress

RETURNING TO BUSINESS was never part of the life plan that Moses Brown laid out when he joined the Society of Friends. But in the aftermath of the Revolution he felt called upon, as did so many of his generation, to step forward and lend his weight and influence in helping chart the course of the new nation. His skills and his life experience dictated that a primary contribution would be in the world of commerce—that was his training from an early age, and at the bank and at the mills in Pawtucket, his judgment and his foresight proved invaluable.

At the same time, Moses was determined to honor his other obligation, to his conscience and his faith, which from the moment of his conversion had manifested in the campaign against slavery. Here as well Moses brought a wealth of experience, as a Quaker elder and as a lawmaker. Undaunted by the setback at the Constitutional Convention, Moses set his sights upon the new national government.

He had little choice. Since the string of legislative victories in New England, and despite the prosecution of Caleb Gardner, slavers were flouting the ban on slave trading. In 1793, at least seventeen slave ships set sail for Africa from Providence, Newport, and Bristol—more Rhode Island slavers than in any year since the first shots were fired at Lexington. Energy for prosecutions waned even at the Providence Abolition Society, where monthly membership sessions gave way to quarterly meetings of a standing committee. If the state was unable or unwilling to enforce the law, perhaps the federal government, with its customs officers and its broader authority, would succeed.

Moses had little cause for optimism. From a high point in the early years of the Revolution, public attachment to the philosophy of natural rights had eroded steadily—especially when such beliefs required the loss of such valuable property as slaves. The shift was made conspicuous during the second session of the first Congress convened under the new Constitution, when a memorial was presented by Quakers from the mid-Atlantic states seeking a "remedy against the gross national iniquity of trafficking in the persons of fellow-men." In the ensuing debate, the southern representatives attacked the Quakers and the memorial in language James Madison described as "shamefully indecent," while the northern members looked on in silence. Madison finally closed the debate by offering language "that Congress have no authority to interfere in the emancipation of slaves, or in the treatment of them." There was a caveat, however, inserted perhaps as a sop to the abolitionists. While it took no action at the time, Congress retained the authority to restrain its citizens from engaging in the slave trade, and to prohibit foreigners from fitting out slave vessels in American ports. These provisions were not binding in the manner of the Constitution, but they signaled the sense of the body, and pointed the way to future action.

Congress spoke again on the question of slavery in 1793, and again, it affirmed the rights of the slaveholders. At issue was an effort by Pennsylvania to prosecute two Virginia men charged with kidnapping an escaped slave. The interstate dispute was referred to Congress, and the result was the Fugitive Slave Act, which entitled slave owners to claim runaways anywhere in the union, and set criminal penalties for obstructing the capture or assisting the fugitive slaves.

Across the sea in England, a burgeoning abolition movement also appeared to be foundering. The Parliament had conducted extensive hearings on the nature of the slave trade, prompted by the abolitionist attorney Granville Sharp and hundreds of Quaker petitions, but in 1791, after ferocious debate, a bill to ban the trade was defeated. The following year saw the chaos of the French Revolution, and economic depression spread across Europe. King George declared war on France, Edmund Burke led a conservative reaction in Parliament, and the moment for reform was lost. Clearly, if a blow was to be struck against the slave trade, it would have to come from the new republic that called itself the land of liberty.

Moses watched these developments through correspondence with other Quaker activists in London, Pennsylvania, and New York, and in the pages of the local press. "I would rejoice to see the members of Congress . . . take up the cause of the oppressed Africans as becomes the representatives of a free people, but there appears evidently a cloud over that body," he wrote to James Pemberton in 1793. "They need something to stir them up."

That instrument was close at hand. In the years since Rhode Island had barred her citizens from participating in the slave trade, every state in the union had installed some sort of embargo on the importation of slaves. This policy consensus was the product of several factors: the success of abolitionist propaganda in the North; the surfeit of slaves in the middle states, particularly

Virginia; and in the South, the fear of insurrection, spurred in part by the bloody slave rebellion in Haiti that began in 1791 and continued for more than a decade. With American ports closed to the slave trade, an extension of the Rhode Island statute against participating in the foreign trade seemed reasonable—and expressly within the powers of the Congress.

Not everyone agreed with this approach, even within the ranks of the abolitionists. As early as 1790, Jeremy Belknap, the Massachusetts minister included on the first roster of the Providence Abolition Society, objected vigorously to plans to petition Congress, for fear that "stirring up controversy on this subject may endanger the Union" of the states. Even the Pennsylvania Abolition Society, after its drubbing in the halls of Congress, counseled against efforts to secure an outright ban on slave trading. But Moses had seen his strategy work in Rhode Island, and he was ready for a national test.

He began his campaign in June 1793, convincing the New England Yearly Meeting that the time had come for another memorial to Congress. The Meeting named Moses and David Buffum, Moses' old colleague from the wartime aid project, along with William Rotch and Samuel Rodman, both of Nantucket, as a delegation to present the memorial to Congress in Philadelphia.

Similar plans were being laid in Philadelphia itself, where James Pemberton was working to organize all of the leading abolition societies in the nation under a new umbrella organization, the American Convention for Promoting the Abolition of Slavery. Moses was named the delegate for the Providence society, but when the convention held its first session, in January 1794, he was not present. It may be that Moses was delayed from his journey south by illness at home—his wife had been down with influenza, and his daughter Sarah was bedridden with a fever—or it may be that Moses preferred to present his case to Congress on his own.

In any event, Moses departed in early January, traveling overland by stage. It was a grueling trek even in good weather, all the more so in the dead of winter. But Moses was buoyed by his sense of mission, and by the warm endorsements he received from his family and friends. His son Obadiah, his son-in-law William Almy, his nephew Nicholas Brown Jr., and Nicholas's partner George Benson—together the leading lights of the new generation in Providence—were all enthusiastic supporters of the effort against slavery. Moses' expedition might be quixotic, but it was never lonely.

Moses reached Philadelphia to find that Rotch and Rodman, sailing from Nantucket, had arrived before him, and they greeted him with dramatic news:

they had obtained an audience with George Washington himself, and the president had agreed to introduce the petition of the New England Quakers before the Senate. This was an extraordinary and unexpected gesture, coming from a slaveholding president, and especially one so painfully circumspect on questions of public policy. In years past, in his private correspondence, Washington had been dismissive of just such Quaker appeals — after the debates in Congress in 1790, he wrote to a family member, "The introductions of the Memorial respecting slavery, was to be sure, not only an illjudged piece of business, but occasioned a great waste of time." But his flippant tone may simply have reflected "his need to prevaricate when speaking to his relatives," as one recent writer surmised. At any rate, the president's thinking appears to have evolved over the course of his first term in office. In 1794, writing to another relative, he bared his contempt for the institution of human bondage. "Were it not then, that I am principled against selling Negroes, as you would cattle in the market, I would not, in twelve months from this date, be possessed of one as a slave."

Washington never voiced his doubts about slavery publicly. But in their memorial on the slave trade, the New England Quakers had finally struck the seam between the president's private beliefs and his public stance. On the morning of January 21, addressing the Senate a month into his second term in office, Washington made brief remarks on the diplomatic mission to France, and then presented "the memorial of the people called Quakers, from the yearly meeting held at Rhode Island." To be sure, Washington didn't speak in favor of the memorial, but he didn't have to; his decision to introduce it personally, and to commend its sponsors as "a respectable committee of the Friends of New England," had a dramatic result. Whereas a raft of similar petitions had previously been shunted aside, this one was ruled subject to debate.

Sen. James Jackson of Georgia, following the pattern already established for attacking such petitions, immediately rose to challenge Washington's gambit. "Is it regular," he asked, "that petitions . . . should be introduced by members of the executive branch?" But Washington was far too august a figure to be undermined on questions of procedure. Theodore Foster, the senator from Rhode Island, rose promptly to call for a reading, and the debate was under way.

Jackson launched what had become the standard attack on Quaker petitions. "It is quite improper that the subject be given any consideration by Congress. We had some matters on this subject to consider three or four years back . . . they threw the whole body into great confusion and the bad temper which was raised in this room got into every measure which we had to consider for the whole year. Congress should have nothing to do with this subject." Jackson's recollection was apt, but with Washington's tacit support, the mood of the Senate had shifted. Henry Cabot of Massachusetts assured his colleagues that the New England petition would not affect "the character of the servitude of any description of persons now employed in the United States." The South, Cabot averred, had nothing to fear. "This measure affects the citizens of our northern states, not those of the south. All the northern states have passed laws which are intended to discourage those citizens involved in the West Indies slave traffic. . . . In order to give force to those state laws, it is desired that a federal regulation be obtained which will help back up the state enforcement machinery." This was not quite accurate—the Rhode Island law, for example, barred any engagement in slave trading—but it sufficed to calm the Senate. The memorial was laid upon the table, pending a decision from the House of Representatives.

Moses arrived at Philadelphia sometime after the Senate hearing—possibly a week later. After locating Rotch and Rodman—Buffum appears not to have made the trip—Moses submitted the petition of the abolition society, which was added to the Quaker memorial. A third petition, from the American convention of abolition societies, was submitted as well, and committees in the House and the Senate considered all three.

Over the course of the next week, Moses and his delegation made the rounds of Philadelphia to lobby against the slave trade. They found the Congress "somewhat divided on the question," Moses wrote in a letter home, but at least they were listening. In canvassing the members, Moses found, "They most generally if not universally reprobate the trade," though "some of them apprehend or pretend to fear the consequences" of any challenge to slavery.

One critical early encounter was a meeting with James Madison, then attending Congress as a representative. His central role in writing the Constitution made him an expert in the powers of the government, and his intellect and judgment earned him influence with delegates from the South and the Northeast. Madison had great reservations about slavery, but had set them aside at the Constitutional Convention. Like so many of the delegates then, his paramount concern was the survival of the union.

Receiving the New England Quakers at his apartment, Madison weighed the implications of the slave-trade memorial. The Constitution expressly forbade any limits on slave imports, but what of imposing penalties on American slavers? Considering the matter closely—which meant a political as well as an ethical assessment—Madison reached the same conclusion as Washington, his friend and fellow Virginian. "Congress has the power to suppress all immoralities," he said carefully. The foundation stone was in place.

With Madison's tacit endorsement, Moses and the Quakers sought interviews with as many congressmen as they could locate. To their pleasant surprise, they met with "as favorable a reception among the Southern members as we had reason to expect." In fact, the southerners warned that the greatest threat to the measure lay with the New England members, who were inclined to sidestep the controversy. On that score, Moses was glad to see the Philadelphia papers publishing tracts against the slave trade at the time, "making the object more conspicuous and less likely to be left to sleep."

The optimistic tone of Moses' correspondence was borne out when the slave-trade memorials were considered by the full House on February 17. With Moses looking on from the gallery, the House agreed after a brief discussion to appoint a committee to write a law barring American citizens from participating in the foreign slave trade. The bill took direct aim at the triangle trade, and with the ports of America closed to slaves, amounted to an outright prohibition on slaving. Remarkably, the tally was unanimous—so dramatically had the tables turned, Moses noted later, that the bill's critics found reasons to be absent rather than see their votes recorded in opposition.

Moses and his fellow Quakers were so confident of final passage that they planned to depart Philadelphia even before the committee returned the bill, but they tarried long enough to enjoy a celebratory meeting with Washington. Moses was glad to find that the president "appeared clear and decided for suppressing the trade," and he came to share with his brother—for entirely different reasons—an abiding veneration for the stately Virginian.

Sure enough, on March 22, following the lead of the House, the Senate approved "an Act to prohibit the carrying on the slave trade from the United States to any foreign place or country." The bill set two stages of penalties: First, any ship or vessel found in violation "shall be forfeited to the United States, and shall be liable to be seized, prosecuted, and condemned" in the federal court for the district where it was seized. Second, individuals who violated the act would be personally liable: "all and every person" engaged in fitting out a slave ship was to be fined $2,000, while captains and crews who took slaves on board ship for purposes of sale would be fined two hundred dollars per slave. President Washington signed the bill the same day.

While this was not the first such law in existence—that distinction belonged to Rhode Island—the federal act was tougher and carried heavier penalties than any of the measures passed in New England or the Atlantic states. Moreover, the bill represented the first breach in the stranglehold that the slave faction seemed to wield in Congress.

Yet despite its obvious import, the legislation failed to elicit anything like the sort of celebration that greeted the Rhode Island bill in 1787. This was not for lack of attention—the new law was trumpeted by the American convention of abolition societies, and notices of the bill were published in all the major ports. But the abolitionists, and the slave traders, had seen all this before. After their experience with the state laws, both sides were waiting to see how firmly this new measure would be enforced.

14

Prosecutions

THERE IS NO INDICATION, in his letters or by his circumstances, that John Brown paid any attention to his brother's mission to Philadelphia, or to the new federal legislation that resulted. By the middle of the 1790s, John was occupied in the things he liked to do—expanding his business operations, harassing government officials, and, beginning as early as 1794, when he was fifty-eight years old, talking about retirement.

The griping against Jeremiah Olney at the customshouse, which began almost as soon as Olney took the job, became a regular occupation for John. Early in 1793, after Olney had tangled in court with John's friend Welcome Arnold, John led a petition drive seeking Olney's removal from office. "We trust that the commerce of this district will never be made subservient to the caprice of the collector of its revenue," the petition demanded, "or that the citizens thereof be subjected to the mortification of submitting to *incivilities*." The signatures included what might be termed the usual suspects—John Brown, Welcome Arnold, Joseph Nightengale. Curiously, though the petition was addressed to President Washington, it was never sent; the idea, apparently, was simply to unnerve the customs office.

Not finding much cooperation from Olney, John turned to Congressman Benjamin Bourne, hoping to pry a discounted rate or a waiver of the duties claimed by the Treasury Department. Better yet, John suggested that his firm might "be indulged with a large discount [loan] in the National Bank." Of course, John had his own bank where he might seek funds, but there he was already overextended.

The constant cries and appeals might appear to be the thrashings of a desperate man, but in this case, they were simply expressions of character. In fact, John continued to be, as he had been in the past, wildly successful. His plant at India Point was thriving, with the addition of a gin distillery, which he established in the conviction—correct, as it turned out—that the taste for rum in

New England was waning. His ships to the Orient returned with ever-larger cargoes, save for one. That vessel, the nine-hundred-fifty-ton *President Washington*, which John had proudly pointed out to its namesake while under construction, had sailed for Calcutta in 1791 with Thomas Willing Francis, brother of John's partner and son-in-law, as supercargo. When he arrived, Francis found the place deep in drought, and subject to a blanket embargo on exports. Rather than sail home in ballast, Francis made the command decision to sell the vessel and make his own way back. When news reached John that he had lost his prized ship, according to one of his clerks, "Mr. Brown read the letter and sat for some time with tears streaming down his cheeks." It was five years before Brown could forgive Tom Francis.

But for that lone setback, at this point in his life, John was enjoying himself immensely. He had, of course, a lavish mansion and a devoted wife, but his domain was larger than that. He was a regular at the new Exchange Coffee House, on Market Square—which had a long, elegant bar on the first floor, dining rooms on the second, and a billiard table and card games on the fourth—and at John Howland's barbershop, a place rich in rumor and gossip on the town's west side. Also on the west side of the river, on the corner of a lot he owned, John saw the erection of Providence's first playhouse, in which he was the largest stockholder. It had to afford some sense of vindication when John attended the first performance in 1795, some thirty years after he tried, and failed, to force another band of thespians on a skeptical citizenry.

John began talking about retirement in letters to his son, perhaps only as a ruse to lure him into business. "I have thought of retiring from the counting house," he wrote in February 1794. "How shall it be done? Edward Dickens is active. Shall he be initiated with you or with you & Francis or with the latter only?" But James must have recognized the ploy; anyone who knew John recognized that business affairs were his greatest source of pleasure. That was his public face, imprinted indelibly on the people of the town, and captured in a reminiscence delivered years later by a man who grew up when John dominated the life of Providence:

John Brown . . . when I knew him was fleshy and rather unwieldy in movement and might be observed riding daily in all the business portions of the town in a one-horse sulky, driving bargains and personally superintending all the branches of his affairs at the counting house, at his stores, at the shipyard, on the wharves, at the bank, and wherever his business operations called. He had a peculiar voice, the tones of which I can well recollect, and in his employment was a black man who could imitate his voice so well that he would often deceive the clerks of the establishment who, expecting from the well known tones in the entryway that Mr. Brown was about to appear, would be surprised, when the door opened, to see no one but darky.

Against the backdrop of John's deep-rooted irreverence, his continuing attachment to the slave trade was as much an expression of character as a statement of ideology. Slaving was never a major part of his business, but it was always an option, and he wasn't going to let someone else, least of all his brother, take it away. Had it been coined at the time, John would have loved the phrase "politically incorrect," and his engagement in the slave business was an extension of that.

In some instances, it appears that John didn't even realize how strongly the people around him felt about the controversy over slavery. In 1794, when his nephew needed a business loan, John referred him to Charles D'Wolf, the eldest brother of a merchant clan in the little Narragansett port of Bristol. The D'Wolfs got into the slave business later than the Browns, but in similar fashion, when Mark Antony D'Wolf sailed for Africa in 1769. By the time of the Revolution, Mark Antony and Charles, his eldest son, had made seven trips in the triangle trade. Unlike the Browns, at the close of the war the family resumed the trade in earnest. Mark Antony had seven sons, and beginning in 1784, five of them became deeply involved in slaving. The exceptions were Samuel, who perished on his first voyage to Africa, and Levi, who, like Moses, renounced the business and turned to religion. James, notorious for his indictment in the murder of a slave aboard ship, sailed as captain of a slaving voyage for John in 1785. John counted the D'Wolfs as friends and political allies, and the family dominated Bristol as much as the Browns did Providence. "They was handsome, dashing and reckless," the legend goes, "but for morals something fierce."

On John's recommendation, his nephew Nicholas and George Benson composed a polite letter requesting a loan of five thousand to ten thousand dollars, "if it is convenient for you to do it." They proposed to pay interest of 6 percent, and asked that, should D'Wolf be unable to supply the funds, he might refer them to "any of your friends."

Charles D'Wolf replied from Bristol the next day. He had no funds handy, and what he did he could put to better advantage than 6 percent interest. "Besides, I should be fearful it would hurt the feelings for your Mr. Benson, as a person of his nice sensibility must conclude it smelt rank of inhumanity for it would be money arising from the sale of Negro slaves in the West Indies." In this instance, the pretense of collegial mercantile civility was cast aside.

D'Wolf closed the door in a postscript: "I do not know of any of my friends having any money to loan." And that may have been the case, as the D'Wolfs were ramping up their slaving activities, enough to make Bristol, for a time, the leading slave port in Rhode Island.

They were not without competition. Despite passage of the federal law—to say nothing of the state prohibition—the middle 1790s saw a surge of vessels putting out for Africa from every port and inlet on Narragansett Bay. The leader in Providence was Cyprian Sterry, who sponsored a staggering fifteen voyages in 1795 alone. Sterry was another friend of John's, a late entrant to the maritime fraternity who saw opportunity in the slave trade and pursued it almost exclusively. He soon found success, buying a home in town and maintaining seven black servants in his household, four of them slaves. John was impressed enough by Sterry's initiative that he secured for him a seat on the board at Rhode Island College, and Sterry became an occasional visitor at John's house on Benefit Street.

John Brown eyed the exploits of his slave-trading cronies with the avid fascination of a cat watching a fishbowl. In 1786, he had promised his brother that he would quit the trade, but that was some time ago. Hadn't they, since then, had their open, albeit venomous, exchange of views in the public prints? John had borne the public opprobrium of his support for the trade; wasn't he entitled to some of the benefits?

Besides, John had never taken his vow all that seriously. True, he'd refrained from commissioning new voyages to Africa. But he fudged the question in 1791, when he wrote to Tom Francis, then in New York and preparing to sail as supercargo on the *President Washington*, to offer advice on the contents of his return cargo. The ship would return by way of West Africa; it was not a prime slave district, but there was likely to be a market there. Two drafts of the letter survive. One was tentative: "If you go through the Mozambique channel you may stop and satisfy yourself whether you would be permitted to trade and take a cargo of slaves, hides, ivory, or not. Elephant teeth is very plenty there, I believe hides is also." The second was more definitive. "Sell your cargo at Bombay. . . . Load 400 or 500 hogsheads of water with which proceed to the Mozambique and purchase one thousand prime slaves and proceed with them to St Estatia for our further orders. Could we get admittance for them into the Savannah or Suriname they would fetch seventy thousand pounds lawful money at least but you have our liberty to do as you may think best for our interest." There's no telling if John actually issued orders to load his prized new ship with a cargo of slaves, and in the event, to John's dismay, no slaves were purchased, as the ship was sold in India. But it appears that John was willing to disregard the promise he'd made to Moses.

At any rate, in 1795, with slavers putting out all around him, John did exactly that. In August, he commissioned Peleg Wood, a Newport slaving captain, to lead a venture in the triangle trade. Toward the end of November, he fitted out an aging square-rigged ship named *Hope,* on the Providence waterfront, with the distinctive hallmarks of the African trade—chains, handcuffs, and plenty of rum. Soon thereafter, Wood sailed to the Slave Coast of West Africa, secured a cargo of captives, proceeded to Havana, and sold the slaves there, all in explicit violation of the new federal law. Nor was it a secret; John's venture was the talk of the wharves in Newport and Providence. After the *Hope* returned to Rhode Island from Havana, toward the end of 1796, Peleg Wood's son was overheard bragging that the voyage was commissioned as an "experiment . . . to try the strength of the law." The slavers of Newport were watching closely, young Wood said, to see what action might result.

The directors of the Providence Abolition Society moved slowly in answer to these provocations, waiting, perhaps, for federal authorities to take the lead. In August 1794, William Ellery, Jeremiah Olney's counterpart at the customshouse in Newport, wrote to his supervisor in Philadelphia requesting details of the bonding procedure for ships clearing for Africa, but while he was a strong critic of the slave trade, he initiated no suits against the Newport merchants.

In the meantime, the abolition societies in New York and Philadelphia were beginning to move ahead, collecting information on illicit slave ventures and forwarding their material to federal officials at those ports. The pattern was becoming clear: if the abolitionists wanted to see the law enforced, they would have to do the spadework themselves.

The Providence society finally acted in March 1797, petitioning U.S. District Attorney Ray Greene to bring separate actions against Cyprian Sterry and John Brown. They backed their petitions with depositions obtained from crew members who were interviewed after their return to Rhode Island. The society had numerous targets to choose from, but these two stood out: Sterry was the most egregious offender, and John the most obnoxious.

John reacted with the same venom he'd brought to his appearances as the Citizen. In a rambling letter to Moses he denounced the abolitionists for hypocrisy and vowed to rally political and popular support in a bid to repeal the federal law. The abolitionists were playing with fire, promoting "popular commotions" that could threaten the still-tenuous union of the states. The prosecution, he warned, would only backfire, steeling his will against the abolitionists and leaving him no recourse but to plunge ever more deeply into the slave trade. As to the federal law, the abolitionists were subverting the law themselves by making illegal threats to obtain evidence against him. And Thomas Arnold in particular was waging a vendetta, John surmised, rooted in Arnold's belief that John had opposed his efforts to obtain a loan from the bank.

The society's move against John, and John's angry reaction, left Moses in a quandary. Moses understood that without prosecutions the new federal law would be, like the state law before it, a dead letter. And yet the prospect of actually taking John to court was deeply disturbing. It would be an ugly fight— of that much Moses could be sure—which would tarnish the family name and destroy the modicum of friendship that he and John had cultivated so carefully. Still, he couldn't stop the suit on his own. The decision rested with the board of the society, and while Moses was certainly its most influential director, on this question he was compromised, and the other directors had their own feelings about his brother John.

Caught between friends and family, Moses reached out to both. He sent copies of John's letter to Thomas Arnold, to William Rotch, and to Thomas Hazard, soliciting their input but also, whether consciously or not, seeking friendly support to help him withstand the onslaught of his brother's indignation.

At the same time, Moses sat down to compose a letter to John. This was not one of the concise, pointed statements that he so often turned out on questions of business or politics, but more in the searching, almost stream-of-consciousness mode that he adopted in his religious epistles to fellow Friends. For once, Moses had John in a corner, and he could address him in tones that John normally would not tolerate. "I am very sorry that thou in thy declining years should give occasion for any to complain of a breach of a law of the United States, which from thy example, being as is said the first, diverse others have also done," Moses began, "and for the avowed purpose of trying the strength of the law, which if true is an additional cause of sorrow to me, that thou should be made a tool of to effect such a purpose."

Moses dwelt closely on the nature of John's offense—it wasn't just the act of engaging in the slave trade that so disturbed him, as the capacity of such a violation "to injure the moral sense of the inhabitants," leading to an "increase of hardness of heart toward the gentle reproof of the instruction in their own mind." This was a crucial point for Moses, that if John and the other slave traders each would only listen to his own conscience—"the tender operations of the truth in their own minds"—they would recognize the evil nature of their business. It was through "the love of self, or of money, or the setting up a strong will to be rich, [they] are led into habits [which] they in their simplicity and rectitude of mind would shudder at or despise."

This appeal went to the core of Moses' Quaker beliefs. The truth was there, instilled by God for anyone to see, if only they would listen. Moses wanted desperately to believe that John had been led astray—albeit by his own baser instincts—and that this prosecution would not so much force his submission as open his eyes to his own conscience. In a sense, Moses had as much at stake here as John did. If he could not bring his own brother to acknowledge the truth when it was laid out plain before him, it would undermine the whole Quaker construct—the power of the "inner light," man's innate propensity to see God's will and to follow it.

Were it up to Moses, he would not even bring a case against John. "I shall not be easy to see thee marked out alone, as I am clear in my mind that would not be wise or just," he wrote. Moses would rather rely on friendly persuasion, but the question was out of his hands. "Matters are so far advanced I see no way to prevent the prosecution."

That being the case, Moses suggested, if John could not be persuaded to renounce the trade of his own volition, perhaps he could be brought to see his own self-interest. John had best "make thy defense with all that moderation and temperance which thy cause will admit, and let no blood rise." This could have two good results. First, John was being sued under Section One of the new law, and stood only to forfeit his ship. "Thy vessel is old and perhaps if thou art quiet it may not be sold high." Second, it might preclude "larger prosecutions"—the prosecution was seeking forfeit of John's ship, but not the fines prescribed in the law. John should understand there was no plot against him, nobody scheming for his ruin. "The object of the prosecution is to stop the trade, not to get the traders' profits of it or their other money. But if those whose wills or inclinations for carrying on or supporting the trade are so strong as to refuse a compliance with the law they must expect to abide its penalties."

This was for his own good, Moses insisted. "Our Lord is said came with a sword against evil, but that sword was sheathed with so much love and meekness for those who transgressed his holy laws that he wounded only to heal them."

These plaintive tones had little effect on John. He dashed off another letter to Moses, one that echoed in tenor and argument the defense he mounted for his previous slave voyage, in 1786: he was faced with massive debts to the customshouse, and so had no choice. Quakers were lawbreakers, just like him; and besides, the slave trade was good for the Africans.

Moses answered, more sharply this time. "Will any slave trader put his hand to his heart and say I send for these poor wretches to save their lives and not for the love of gain?" Moses demanded. "Surely thou nor none other will be so lost to the truth as to thus pretend." And no, Quakers who refused military service were not lawbreakers in the same vein as slave traders. But Moses was no longer trying to convince John—just to let him know that the society would not be deterred. Moses had proposed to the other directors that prosecution be dropped if John would publicly disavow the slave trade, but they had refused. To their minds, John was the "first offender" of the law, and must be taken to task. At that point, Moses recused himself from the entire matter. John was on his own.

Letters from two key directors at the society convinced Moses to step aside. Thomas Arnold wrote mainly to defend himself—he never believed John was opposing his loan applications at the bank, but he would press ahead with the prosecution from "a sense of duty" rooted in twenty years' opposition to the slave trade.

It was left to William Rotch to express the outrage that prevailed on the board of the abolition society. Rotch was a committed Quaker like Moses, but he was less naïve when it came to questions of character, and he had known John for more than thirty years. "Far be it from me to feel any pleasure in contributing to the calamities of the merchants," Rotch wrote, "but I have ever considered John in a different point of light from most others, having been convinced that his object was less that of gain, or a preference to that mode of trade, than a determined resolution in the strength of his own power to defeat the law against it." This was a test of wills, and Rotch, for one, would not back down.

He knew of no transgressions in collecting evidence for the petitions, but had no qualms if such technical violations were established. It would be "much more tolerable to stretch the law in convicting criminals than it would be in that criminal to violate the rights of his fellow creatures so far as to force them from their native country into perpetual slavery."

John's continued defense of the trade left Rotch sputtering. "I am at a loss to conjecture what character John will expect us to form of him from the outlines he has given thee of his professions of humanity and care and compassion in transporting those unhappy people when we know in what manner they are treated, during their imprisonment in chains and handcuffs when they are on shipboard. And the arguments he uses in justification of the trade are too stale and have been too often refuted to suffer my patience to dwell upon them."

Rotch understood the painful position confronting Moses. "I feel much sympathy toward thee on this trying occasion, as I know the situation of thy brother's mind on this subject must be affecting to thee." Rotch even avowed his affection for John: "I owe him no evil, but most sincerely wish his present and eternal felicity." But until this matter was settled, Rotch wanted nothing more to do with John Brown. "I shall take it as a favor thou would sell my five bank shares, . . . as I shall not be willing to hold any property under the influence of such a man."

Moses was not ready to take such a drastic step. For several months after the flurry of communications in March, the question lay quiet, and Moses and John conferred routinely on shipping affairs and business at the bank. John was overextended, as usual, and reached out to Moses for help negotiating with creditors and the other bank directors. He also found opportunities to share with Moses his sense of humanity: "I often contemplate an expression of the worthy Governor Hopkins," John wrote in July, "that a man of business and usefulness to the society around him never departs this life better nor so much regretted as in his prime or middle age, when he is most useful to the community. On this principle I know my time is passed already but I do believe the sooner I am taken hence the more the impression will be on those I leave behind to contemplate what I have done for the place of my nativity."

It was an old pattern, John reaching outside the framework of their principled disputes to reveal himself to Moses as a person of feeling. It might be transparent, but it had worked before, and John was doing everything he could to win his brother's allegiance.

And Moses was receptive. In June, he went so far as to provide John with an updated membership roster for the society, which John requested in order to press his lobbying campaign. Moses again reminded John that he had done everything in his power to head off the prosecution, but his effort was "rejected by those who thought thou was the first that broke the law and ought to be the first prosecuted." He emphasized to John "how disagreeable it was, to nearly all thy friends, but to none more than to thy only brother."

It became apparent over the course of the summer that John was in fact being singled out after all. The case against Cyprian Sterry, who was much more deeply engaged in the trade, was dropped after Sterry provided a signed statement that he would send no more vessels to Africa. But Sterry did not have the same history of belligerent defiance that John did. And Sterry did not appear to have the means to violate his oath the way John had; the slave trade was his principal line of business, and with his operations stalled, he was forced to declare bankruptcy.

There would be no such abeyance in the proceeding against John, in large part because, apart from his dealings with his brother, John continued to protest that the prosecution was unfair. To Caleb Greene, a New Bedford Quaker with a merchant house in Newport, John asserted, "I have done with the trade and now assure you that I am never to be concerned in the trade again. I hope therefore you'll discontinue the action as it is very inconvenient to me to attend any law suits . . . and as we are told in the Good Book that unless we can forgive, how can we be forgiven?" Veering wildly, John then asserted that no evidence could be had against him, as the crew of his ship would never cooperate.

John addressed Thomas Arnold as well, but indirectly, through his brother Welcome. "Both you and he knows that I am not in the Guinea trade nor have been concerned but in one voyage," John wrote to Welcome Arnold. "Now sir is it good policy for the citizens of this place to be prosecuting their neighbors who are not in the trade while others of Warren, Bristol, Newport and etc. who are driving the trade are suffered to be unmolested? I think a few lines from you to your brother must open his eyes."

His pleadings were ignored, and the case was set for federal district court in Newport on August 5, 1797. To the end, John could not see the reason for his being singled out. He made a last appeal to Moses: "I call on you my brother as an officer to the society which is so cruelly and vindictively prosecuting me for *one* offense though I have so frequently declared I would not again be concerned in the trade. . . . You'll have none to prevent an accommodation unless it's your brother Thomas Arnold who I do not think may be as well employed otherwise as in his endeavor to destroy your brother."

Having made his arguments to the society, John did not bother presenting them in court. When the case was called against the ship *Hope*, no one spoke for the defense, and the district attorney presented sufficient testimony to show the ship had indeed sailed for Africa, and transported slaves from there to Havana. Judge Benjamin Bourne, the former congressman and a political ally of John's, found for the prosecution, held the ship forfeit, and ordered it auctioned at John's shipyard at India Point. It was a victory for the society, but a hollow one for Moses—what had he achieved, if the first man convicted under the federal law he wrote against slave trading was his own brother?

That was not the end of John's bout with the abolition society. Not satisfied with the forfeit of John's ship, the more adamant members of the board, likely led by William Rotch, filed a second suit seeking the fines prescribed under the federal act. This was the "larger prosecution" Moses had warned of.

The new filing set off another round of appeals from John, to Moses and to David Howell, offering to pay court costs and promising to abide by any settlement that the society might propose. At least that was how John presented himself in his letters; Moses saw John as continuing his intransigence. In a note he amended to one of John's letters, Moses held that John had rejected the "moderate" terms for a truce offered by the society, swayed by the "flattering of his friends at Newport." It was probably true, as well, that Rotch and Thomas Arnold were still inflamed by the lengthy tirades John published as the Citizen; at any rate, they were less impressed by John's occasional displays of humanity than was his brother Moses.

The suit for fines was a more substantial matter than the action against the ship, however, and would entail a trial by jury, not just a hearing before a judge. In this, John's enemies made a serious miscalculation—after all, the case was to be heard at Newport, where the slave trade continued to enjoy popular support.

When the trial was held in June 1798, John was exonerated and the society ordered to pay all costs. No official record of the trial survives, but when Moses summarized the decision two years later, he implied that John had finally been able to bring his high profile and powerful influence to bear on the proceedings. John won his verdict "by the *peculiar turn* of the jurors," Moses wrote. He added cryptically, "His complaints induced many to believe he would never more be concerned [in the slave trade] and others were induced into compassion considering his age, but there was something more which I forebear to describe that occasioned the difficulty to obtain a verdict of jury, though the most explicit charge of the court was given in favor of finding him guilty. . . . Perhaps no other man among us would have had so much favor shown him."

Whatever the means by which John prevailed, he was exultant in his triumph. Writing home to share the news with his family, he dropped any shadow of the humble tone he had adopted in his missives to Moses. He had won his verdict, John wrote, and though the lawyers for the society were considering an appeal, "I have no fears of their obtaining, as the further they proceed the more the people in general are against this wicked and abominable combination. I mean the Abolition Society." On the advice of John Clarke, who attended the trial with him, John was staying at Newport long enough to obtain a final ruling. In a postscript, John took one last dig at his tormentors. "The committee for the Society are very busy running around in the rain to git their Council together. . . . I tell them they had better be contented to stop where they are, as the further they go the worse they will fare."

The failure of the suit against John had a devastating effect on the abolition society. Regular meetings ceased, and it sponsored no more prosecutions. In the meantime, and despite the absence of Cyprian Sterry, departures for Africa from Rhode Island surged. Just twelve departures were recorded in 1798, the year John went to trial. The next year saw thirty-eight clearances—more than in any preceding year. Those ships bore away from Africa an estimated thirty-seven hundred slaves to lives of hard labor on plantations in the Caribbean.

It was, in many regards, a cruel year for Moses. In May, just before the trial at Newport, Moses' wife, Mary, died. Like Anna, she had been in fragile health for much of her adult life. But she had been a steady source of support for Moses, had traveled with him to view textile mills and to attend Quaker meetings throughout New England, and her demise stilled his once-busy household. His son Obadiah now had a family of his own, and his daughter Sarah had died late in 1795, at thirty years of age, leaving William Almy to raise their single child, a four-year-old daughter.

As a last service to Moses, Mary had introduced to him a friend of hers from the Quaker meeting, Phebe Lockwood, a widow, whom Moses married at a sober church ceremony in May 1799. Phebe idolized Moses; during her first marriage, she had named her son after him—Moses Brown Lockwood. But Moses was nineteen years her senior, and while Mary, and Anna before her, had been genuine partners in Moses' various endeavors, Phebe was more of an attendant. In his advancing years, Moses found himself increasingly isolated and alone.

15

John Goes to Congress

In the summer of 1798, flush with his victory over the Abolition Society, John Brown decided to run for office. He toyed with the idea of a bid for governor, but changed his mind, perhaps in the face of the continued popularity of incumbent Arthur Fenner, then serving the eighth of fifteen consecutive annual terms. Eventually he settled on Congress; he'd been elected twice before and had declined to serve, but that was in the days of the Confederation, and much had changed since then.

John ran as a Federalist, the party of President John Adams and, more important for John, the war party. After months of intrigue, the United States had recently chosen sides in the struggle for primacy in Europe, settling a pact with England. France now regarded America as her enemy and instituted a policy of open season on American shipping. No hostilities were declared, but by the spring of 1797, the French had seized more than three hundred American merchant vessels. The conflict came to be known as the Quasi-War with France.

John Brown, naturally, wanted to strike back. It was a "manly" stance, of course, but there was more to it than that. War meant military spending, and for John that meant profits. John acted promptly, offering to sell the eight-hundred-ton *George Washington* to the government for forty thousand dollars. John described her as well-built, copper-sheathed, and "one of the best sailers in America."

The navy balked, proposing that John instead lead the merchants of Providence to build or donate a ship at their own expense out of "public spirit." John ignored that suggestion, and waged a spirited lobbying campaign for the sale, writing to President Washington and Sen. Theodore Foster, and sending agents to call on Treasury Secretary Oliver Wolcott. By August 1798, needing ships for immediate service, the navy came around, albeit warily. In ordering the purchase, Navy Secretary Benjamin Stoddert, a merchant in civilian life, agreed to John's price, but warned his agent, "Mr. Brown, who seems to be a complete master of the art of bargain-making, will probably ask more. You must do the best you can with him, and let the public be screwed as little as possible." The warning was in vain; a succession of captains found the *George Washington* to be a miserable ship, "worse than useless," despite an overhaul that cost as much as the original sale price. Still, John got his money, as well as a spate of new contracts for the Hope Furnace.

John didn't hide his support for war when he asked Moses, in August, the same month he sold his ship, to back his run for Congress, but he didn't mention it, either. Instead, John made a plea for personal peace. "I wish to have all disputes on the abolition business cease and the hatchet buried," John wrote, echoing Moses' own appeal, in the *Providence Gazette*, nine years before. While he had no doubt of success, John wrote, he hoped to warrant the support of "the most respectable men of the state," among them Moses, Obadiah, and George Benson.

Remarkably, considering his pacifist beliefs and John's repeated betrayals, Moses signed on. John promised "that he would be friendly disposed to the poor blacks should anything come before Congress on their account," Moses recalled later, and that was good enough for him. That Moses would have believed his brother says something about his high threshold of credulity, but there has to be more to it than that. Some credit is due to John's powers of persuasion, the same charisma that induced the navy to buy a dull-sailing ship it could not afford. But in equal measure, Moses' acquiescence testifies to his stubborn refusal to give up on his brother. It was an act of faith, and faith was central to Moses' own identity. He clung to the idea that John could be reformed long after John had proved that conviction futile.

John won the election of 1799 handily, marking his first return to public office since he served in the General Assembly, a nine-year stretch that ended in 1787. The wonder is that it took so long. John loved the hobnob and the horse-trading of politics, and he loved having a stage from which to speak his mind. At home, his children had come to refer to him as Old Thunder, a phrase that captured his inclination as well as his demeanor.

But John had much to do before heading to Philadelphia to take his seat that December. After the untimely death of his partner and son-in-law, John Francis, in late 1796, John had begun in earnest to liquidate his assets and close down his business affairs. The following year he put "all his navigations and distillery" up for sale. Few buyers stepped forward with the means to acquire even a portion of his estate, however, and John had to content himself with winding down his shipbuilding and mercantile operations piecemeal.

These measures yielded John a huge amount of cash. His last cargo from the *George Washington*, which returned from Batavia before its sale to the government, netted more than three hundred thousand dollars. There were duties to pay, certainly, and outstanding debts, but John was no longer plowing his profits back into outgoing cargoes, and he was loath to let that kind of capital lie still. Some of it he devoted to ambitious new civic projects designed to secure Providence's commercial future, including several turnpike companies—at that time, interstate roads were private affairs—and a visionary plan to dig a canal to Worcester, Massachusetts, that would siphon trade from the western hinterlands south, away from Boston. But what captured John's imagination was America's westward migration. He bought thousands of acres in the Ohio territory, lands that he promptly transferred to his children. And he plunged deeply into a real estate venture in the Adirondack region of northern New York.

John came by this project through a series of accidents that began in 1795 when he sent John Francis to New York to sell a twenty-ton cargo of tea. It was purchased there by James Greenleaf, a thirty-year-old Boston native and land speculator whose partners included former Treasury secretary Robert Morris. As security to his promissory note, Greenleaf attached a second mortgage to the Adirondack land. A year later, Morris and Greenleaf went bankrupt when their land speculations failed. John had rashly canceled the Greenleaf securities, but with the prices falling, he sensed an opportunity, and in December 1798, he put down thirty-three thousand dollars to acquire title to two hundred ten thousand acres of rugged, rocky land.

Together with Greenleaf's default, the Adirondack tract cost him more than one hundred thousand dollars, but John never dwelt on the cost. On the contrary, the new property seemed to rejuvenate him, and he dove into the enterprise with an astonishing burst of energy and zeal. Before the purchase he had commissioned a survey and sent his son James to inspect the property, but now that it was his, John determined to see it for himself. In February, despite his age, the icy roads, and a rheumatic leg that rendered him close to lame, John set out from Providence, traveling to Albany and thence north, finally arriving at Herkimer County. What he found there can only be called forbidding—a frozen wilderness of weak soils and stony outcrops dominated by stands of beech, maple, spruce, and hemlock.

John saw something different. Upon his return to Providence he issued orders for a new survey that would divide the tract into eight townships and lace it with five hundred miles of new roads. Weeks later John headed back, this time staying on his sprawling north woods domain for more than six weeks. He lived in an unfinished log cabin, dined on potatoes and sour bread, and spent his days harassing a hardy crew of woodsmen assigned to clear land and cut roads. His sudden adaptation to this pioneer mode, after so many years of unbounded affluence, suggests just how strongly John was seized by his vision; one early Adirondack historian termed it "monomania."

It was more than just greed that was driving John—though he ruminated constantly about the potential growth in the value of his holdings. This was an exercise in pure ambition, turning loose his will and verve in the wastes of the Adirondacks. His forefathers, with just a handful of friends, had built a town from a rudimentary camp on the bank of the Great Salt River; just as improbably, his own generation had thrown off British rule and seen Providence surpass Newport as the commercial center of the entire region. The venture in upstate New York was slightly more preposterous—no towns ever rose there, and it remains wilderness to this day—but John was accustomed to plunging ahead when the outcome still lay far over the horizon.

He may have been obsessed, but John had not completely severed his moorings. He remained a man of means and obligations—and a congressman-elect—and in late June, he headed home to Providence. Upon his return John learned disturbing news: the abolition society might be in abeyance, but the collector of customs at Newport had taken it upon himself to enforce the federal law against slave trading.

William Ellery was a diminutive Harvard-educated lawyer who, on several occasions, found himself thrust by circumstance onto the stage of history. A Newport politico and Son of Liberty who helped instigate prewar riots against the Tories, Ellery was selected to replace Samuel Ward in the Continental Congress after Ward died in office. Arriving at Philadelphia in May 1776, Ellery missed most of the debate, but was on hand to sign the Declaration of Independence. He likewise had little to do with establishing the Continental Navy, but after the departure of Stephen Hopkins in September, Ellery served a thankless term on the Marine Committee, trying at a distance to police the machinations of the frigate committee in Providence.

The war years drained the small fortune Ellery inherited from his merchant father, and he came to depend on the stipend he earned as a government loan officer. When the customs post came open, Ellery plied his Federalist connections and won a sinecure that he would cling to for more than twenty years. Ellery was not so exacting as Jeremiah Olney, who supervised a separate district in Providence, but he was committed to upholding the law. And Ellery had mixed feelings on the slave trade—his own father had sent several ships to Africa—but after the failure of the second case against John Brown, the slavers of Newport and Bristol became even more brazen. In the middle of 1799, at Ellery's direction, the government finally began to move against them.

Ellery and U.S. Attorney David Barnes filed the first of half a dozen cases against Rhode Island slavers in April. They moved cautiously, chastened by the verdict in John's jury trial, and sought only the confiscation of the ships involved. But the slave traders quickly developed a counterstrategy, rigging the auctions so that they could repurchase their vessels for a nominal fee—in some cases as little as ten dollars. Ellery answered with a little subterfuge of his own—he would send his own agent to bid at the auction, ensuring a competitive price, and if his agent prevailed, adding a new ship to the Treasury's little naval force.

Ellery debuted this new wrinkle in a proceeding against the *Lucy*, a new two-masted schooner sailing under command of Captain Charles Collins and owned by Charles D'Wolf. The prosecution showed that Collins and the *Lucy* had recently returned from a slaving trip to Africa, and on July 8 Judge Bourne, sitting at Bristol, ruled the vessel forfeit. Ellery then ordered his surveyor at Bristol, Samuel Bosworth, to attend the auction and bid for the ship. Bosworth was a longtime resident of Bristol who knew the power and the temper of the D'Wolf clan, and asked Ellery to name someone else to attend to that "disagreeable business." When Ellery insisted, Bosworth consented "with considerable fear and trembling."

As the date of the auction approached, Bosworth tried to keep his assignment secret, but word leaked out. The night before the *Lucy* was set to go under the hammer, Bosworth answered a knock on his door to find John Brown standing on the stoop with Charles and James D'Wolf. John was a frequent visitor to Bristol—his Poppasquash estate lay nearby—but his appearance with the D'Wolfs rendered the encounter exceptional. Peering dumbfounded at the three men huddled before him in the gloom, Bosworth asked what brought them to his door. The answer was succinct: he should refuse the appointment to attend the sale of the *Lucy*. It did not fall in his line of duty, and his status as a volunteer would render him a turncoat in the eyes of his neighbors. By his own account, Bosworth firmly turned them away.

John Brown headed back to Providence that night, but at dawn the next day, the D'Wolfs called on Bosworth again. So agitated were the sailors on the

Bristol waterfront, Charles warned Bosworth, he could not guarantee the surveyor's safety if he showed up for the sale of the *Lucy*. Bosworth repeated that he would obey his orders. At ten o'clock, the hour appointed for the auction, Bosworth left his house and set off for Charles D'Wolf's wharf, a route that took him along the rim of Bristol's busy harbor. Sure enough, with D'Wolf's wharf already in sight, half a dozen jack tars laid hold of Bosworth and dragged him, struggling and yelling, onto a waiting sailboat. Several people witnessed the kidnap, according to Bosworth, including Charles Collins, a sea captain who sometimes sailed for the D'Wolfs, but Collins and the rest watched in silence as he was trundled off the dock.

Bosworth's assailants quickly made way, sailing out of Bristol's compact harbor and then east, finally dumping him on the wooded shore two miles from town. Making his way back to Bristol, Bosworth found that the auction took place as scheduled and the *Lucy* was sold to a Cuban captain who sailed for the D'Wolfs. Faced with this and a dozen other more trivial evasions, Ellery continued filing cases against the slave traders, but only sporadically. In the meantime, having already reneged on his latest promise to his brother, John Brown headed for Philadelphia to take his seat in Congress.

⁓

John set out in November 1799, traveling overland in a private carriage, staying at inns that he knew and keeping a practiced eye on the prices of land and commodities at the towns along the way, gauging potential investment opportunities. This was a familiar route; John traveled to Philadelphia at least once a year, often accompanied by a child or grandchild, and usually staying with Tench Francis, where he was embraced as a member of the family.

This time, on his first evening in town, John stopped by the Francis mansion north of the town center, but he didn't stay. John continued on to a boardinghouse three blocks from Congress Hall, his accommodations for the next several months. The next day, a Monday, he made the short stroll to Congress on foot. John immediately felt at home—the building, of brick with white trim, was similar to the statehouses back in Rhode Island, with the House chambers in a corner room on the second floor; and the politics were familiar, with an embattled core of avowed Federalists seeking to hold on to power even as they feuded among themselves. On the first day of the session John tarried in his apartment to write letters home, but he arrived in time for President Adams's speech welcoming the members of the Sixth Congress.

John attended the sessions regularly, but the more important work took place outside Congress Hall. John made the most of his off-hours, dining with

Navy Secretary Benjamin Stoddert, who welcomed him graciously despite early word of the deficiencies of the *General Washington*, and buttonholing Treasury Secretary Wolcott to secure extra deposits for the Providence bank. Another dinner partner and key contact was Harrison Gray Otis, the Boston Federalist and nephew of Revolutionary firebrand James Otis. A regular guest at John's home in Providence, Otis was then just thirty years old but already entering his second term in the House. John was new to the conventions of the capital, but he was acclimating quickly.

These quasi-public pursuits were interrupted by the staggering news that George Washington had died on December 14 at his estate at Mount Vernon. Word reached Philadelphia soon after, and on December 18, when early reports were confirmed, Congress immediately adjourned. For the next week church bells were muffled as they tolled the news, and the doors of Congress were draped in black. The official observance was held December 26, when the city turned out in mourning dress to observe a solemn procession from Congress Hall to the steps of the Lutheran church. A military parade was followed by Washington's riderless white horse, and then the members of Congress, who filed into the church to hear a eulogy delivered by Henry "Light-Horse Harry" Lee, the famous general then sitting as a representative from Virginia. His speech commemorated Washington as "first in war, first in peace, first in the hearts of his countrymen."

John reveled in the sentimental public salutes to the leader he liked to refer to as "the best man in the world." He won appointment to the joint House-Senate committee charged with commemorating the first president, and helped author the resolution to erect "a marble monument . . . in the City of Washington," a task not completed until sixty-five years later. On the committee, he formed a strong bond with General Lee, "who," John wrote home, "in a particular manner has congratulated me in the most complimentary terms on my sentiments in politics coinciding so exactly with his in every instance."

Two weeks later, John was still gushing with enthusiasm. He obtained a copy of Lee's speech and sent it home with the request that his young grandson commit the entire text to memory. "I contemplate the pleasure of hearing him repeat [the speech] extemporary," John wrote. "Nothing certainly can be more pleasing, more useful nor more entertaining than to hear repeated the good, great and brilliant career of our excellent Washington." This was more than just busywork; John was clearly devoted to John Brown Francis—"our dear boy," as he termed him—and he wanted to inculcate in his grandson graces that had never come easily to him.

Throughout this period, John wrote his family regularly to convey his orders and advice on business matters back home and relay the highlights of his stay in Philadelphia. He attended a dinner with President Adams and thirty members of Congress—Abigail Adams was the only woman present, and genially recalled her visit to the Brown home in Providence. And he had several more dinners with Stoddert, during which he proposed establishing a naval dry dock south of Providence. Stoddert was polite but, perhaps wary of another sales pitch from John, rebuffed the plan.

John also related his successful effort to win—by a single vote—the long-delayed federal funding grant to repair damages sustained during the Revolution to the buildings at Rhode Island College. But John discreetly omitted any mention of the debate that occupied two full days in the first week of January 1800. That debate concerned the slave trade, and John distinguished himself for having one of the sharpest tongues in the House.

The question first arose in December, when James Hillhouse, a Federalist delegate from Connecticut, proposed amendments to toughen the Act of 1794. Hillhouse may not have been aware that his colleague from Rhode Island already had been convicted of violating the law, but he knew that it was being flouted, and wanted criminal penalties added to the fines already in place. Hillhouse's motion was referred to committee without comment, but on January 2, Robert Waln of Pennsylvania opened the question again by offering the petition of Absalom Jones, a free black from Philadelphia, who sought a range of measures to limit the reach of the Fugitive Slave Act, for "amelioration" of the "hard situation" of those currently held in bondage, and for more effectively restricting the slave trade. Waln proposed referring the petition to the slave-trade committee.

This more expansive petition provoked a sharp if predictable reaction from John Rutledge Jr., whose father had led the southern defense of slavery at the Constitutional Convention. "Already had too much of this new-fangled French philosophy of liberty and equality found its way" into the plantations and the slave pens of the south, Rutledge warned. The very subject was "improper and unconstitutional," and the petition should be summarily rejected.

This opened the gates to the entire debate over slavery, the question that continued to hang like a lowering cloud over every session of Congress. The representatives assumed what by now were familiar positions: the southern delegates sounded dire alarms at the potential violence that could arise from openly discussing the question; most northern delegates lamented the institution of slavery but saluted the constitutional limits on their authority to banish it; and a few scattered voices asserted a moral obligation to uphold the petition. Slavery was "a cancer of immense magnitude," declared George

Thatcher of Massachusetts, one that had fostered "700,000 enemies in the very body of the United States."

To this mix of tried—not to say tired—rhetoric, John Brown brought a new element of candor and his own brand of no-nonsense pragmatism. This was just the sort of occasion Moses had in mind when he extracted his brother's promise to set aside his personal feelings about slavery. But whatever weight John may have attached to his vow to Moses, in the event, John simply couldn't resist. He rose to answer Thatcher, offering his first speech as a member of the House.

John first addressed the challenge to the Fugitive Slave Act. Every member from the northern states should have seen by now, he said, "the impropriety of encouraging slaves to come from the Southern States to reside among them as vagabonds and thieves."

John warmed to his subject, drawing on some of the favorite themes he introduced as the Citizen. "I do not hold a slave in the world," John asserted, "but I am as much for supporting the rights and property of those who do as though I owned them myself." Slaves were personal property, John said, as much as a farm or a ship. And challenging the right to such property could only foster division between North and South.

Addressing the petition itself, John, like several speakers before him, dismissed the free-black authors as a front for the organized abolitionists, "a combination of people who have troubled Congress for many years past, and who I fear will never cease." And he had no fear of the slave uprisings Thatcher had inferred; America's 5 million free citizens could subdue them at any time. Then, playing off the partisan spirit of the times, John asked Waln and Hillhouse to withdraw voluntarily their support for the petition. He was sorry, he said, to see such a divisive document sponsored by "two such worthy members of the House, both good Federalists." This drew a guffaw from the delegates, perhaps the only time that a congressional debate over slavery was punctuated by laughter.

After a theatrical pause, John turned to the question of the slave trade. This was the one point where the abolitionist critique had achieved consensus; after the deluge of horrific testimonials from the coast of Africa and from the captains and crew of slave ships, even the supporters of slavery had conceded that the trade was too cruel to countenance. To John, these humane sympathies were entirely misplaced. "We want money," John thundered. "We want a navy, we ought therefore to use the means to obtain it. We ought to go farther than has yet been proposed, and repeal the bills in question." Everyone in the House that day knew this was a reference to the law barring participation in the slave trade, but few if any knew it had been written by his own brother. "Why should we see Great Britain getting all the slave trade to themselves? Why may not our country be enriched by that lucrative traffic?" Questions of right and wrong had nothing to do with it: "There would not be a slave more sold" if American ships joined in competition with the British, "but we should derive the benefits by importing from Africa as well as that nation."

That was enough; John resumed his seat. It was not a particularly persuasive argument and had no impact on the strong majority supporting the slave-trade prohibition. It was more a performance piece for John—he had stood at the podium in countless town meetings and at each of the several state houses in Rhode Island; now, he'd entertained the United States Congress, rattling its delicate sensibilities with his dollars-and-cents pragmatism.

But John's statement was something of a landmark in the already voluminous annals of the slave debate in Congress, the first affirmative defense of the slave trade. Slavery's critics had suspected for years that New England's easy compliance with the demands of the southern states was rooted in the North's ties to the slave trade. As early as 1776, when his attack on King George for fostering the trade was struck from the first draft of the Declaration of Independence, Thomas Jefferson surmised the hand of self-interest in the North as well as the South: "Our Northern brethren also I believe felt a little tender . . . for tho their people have very few slaves themselves yet they have been pretty considerable carriers of them to others." The same influence was suspected in the "dirty compromise" that made room for slavery in the body of the Constitution; now, a New England delegate had made explicit and put on the record the North's ambivalence, and the source of it.

Word of John's perfidy reached Rhode Island before the month was out. Moses was dismayed, but he was not surprised. From the moment he learned that Congress would consider amendments to the slave-trade act, Moses said, "I feared the agitation of that subject would agitate my brother . . . he having a peculiar irritability when it ever has been mentioned." Moreover, Moses had heard that John's allies in Rhode Island—most likely including the D'Wolfs—had begun circulating petitions calling for repeal of the federal ban on slave trading.

Moses didn't bother confronting John on his statement in Congress. He may, at long last, have finally resigned himself to John's utter intransigence on the question; he certainly didn't need to hear another apology, or another defiant outburst. Instead, Moses wrote to Dwight Foster, a senator from Massachusetts who had introduced a companion bill to Hillhouse's slave-trade amendment. Moses wasn't going to challenge John directly, but he wanted to limit the damage he could do.

Moses was uncertain of the nature of Foster's bill, but he hoped "to encourage the friends of humanity to perseverance, however fierce and zealous my brother may be." John might argue, in his zeal, that popular sentiment favored a return to the slave trade, but this was illusory, "like a jaundiced man may see others like himself." As to John's appeal for revenue to fund a navy, Moses argued that the African trade "is a grave for seamen, more men being lost in it than nearly all other trade, and of course [it] strikes directly at the plan they espouse for a navy . . . indeed there is no light in which the trade can be viewed but it will appear repugnant to the best interest and feelings of our country."

Surprisingly, considering the initial performance of the law, Moses cautioned against efforts to expand its penalty provisions. "The law as it stands is competent if it was carried onto effect by officers of the government. . . . My object in writing this letter is to excite a caution against aiming at more than can be obtained in the House nor to increase the penalty so much as to prevent the execution of the law." It appears that, while Moses had failed in restraining his brother, he still preferred moderate persuasion over outright enforcement. But he had no illusions about the stakes involved. "It is said by the encouragement of having the law repealed there are more vessels contemplated to be sent into the trade than there ever has been." The cadre of prospective slavers included John himself: "He has now a ship he has been refitting which if he does not sell I fear he would again be tempted to send on a slave voyage if by his exertions he could procure a repeal."

On that score, at least, Moses need not have worried. Foster replied in February that the prohibition on the slave trade remained popular with Congress. But he could not agree with Moses on the question of penalties. "The evil has been increasing in the country and the law since enacted has been shamefully violated. . . . Some further penalties to prevent this traffic must and I think will be adopted."

The amendments to the slave-trade bill were reported out of committee to a joint session of Congress on Saturday, April 26. John was the first to speak. He reprised the arguments he made in January—the role of the Quakers, people who "do little to support the government"; the need for trade revenues—and then he went further. Penalizing the slave trade "was wrong, when considered in a moral point of view, since, by the operation of that trade, the very people themselves much bettered their condition."

John Rutledge followed with a lengthy endorsement of John's points on revenue, and asserted that the law was adequate as it stood, without new amendments. But the majority of the Congress was growing impatient with arguments that bordered on the absurd. Sen. Wilson Cary Nicholas, of Virginia, objected to John's attacks on the Quakers and asserted that already, "the people of the Southern states were wiping off the stain" of slavery. Not to be outdone, Robert Waln, the author of the House amendments, asserted that Pennsylvania was "unanimously in favor of the trade being put an end to most completely." And Waln had done his homework; "great evasions" of the law were then taking place, including rigged auctions of forfeited vessels.

After a final review in committee, the bill was reported back to the House on Saturday, May 3. It had been a tough week for John; his friend and adviser Tench Francis had died late Thursday, and John had been up most of the night consoling his grieving in-laws. But he was in Congress the following morning, and he was on hand Saturday to hear the final text. The act forbade any American citizens from having any interest in slaving ventures to foreign ports, set prison terms of two years in addition to any fines, and directed ships sailing for the federal government to seize any suspect vessels. John Brown and John Rutledge argued gamely, but to little effect. The vote was resounding, with sixty-seven in favor and just five votes against.

John headed back to Providence two weeks later. His first session in Congress had been pretty much a bust, considering the heavy majority that had rallied behind the bill he'd devoted most of his legislative skills to defeat. But John never expressed any regrets. He'd made his stand, he hadn't backed down, and besides, it didn't cost him financially—his last venture in the slave trade was already behind him.

That has always been the puzzling aspect of John's passionate defense of the slave trade. True, he'd underwritten an occasional voyage to Africa, but it was never a mainstay for him, and there were always other merchants more deeply engaged than he. But he willingly assumed the mantle of spokesman for the slaving interests, from the day back in 1784 when he defied the directives of the Providence town meeting. It's hard not to assume that it was rooted, at least in part, in reaction to his brother's equally vigorous crusade against slavery. But if that's an explanation, it doesn't change the fact: just as Moses made the abolition of slavery the defining struggle of his life, so John chose to make his defense of the slave trade the centerpiece of his public life and integral to his legacy. In taking the fight to the floor of Congress, John Brown ensured that his name would always register prominently in the annals of American slavery.

Moses Brown was on John's mind during his tenure in Philadelphia, but not as his nagging monitor. Twice in his letters to his children, John spoke fondly of his brother, observing once that "it is good both in the sight of God & man for relations to respect and esteem each other." And in the sole surviving letter that he addressed to Moses during his stay in Philadelphia, John wrote at length on the tedious conventions of the Congress, but made no mention of the slavery debates. Rather, he dwelt closely on the business of the Providence Bank—construction plans, the rate of the next quarterly dividend, how much capital to hold in reserve.

It was an interest that John and Moses shared. Despite his early misgivings, Moses proved to be an assiduous and effective director at the bank, attending to every aspect of its operation, even down to ensuring that bonds from the bank officers were signed, executed, and on file. During John's hiatus in Providence before his return to Congress, the brothers regularly attended the meetings of the bank board, leaving at the door their awkward conflict over slavery.

The serene relations with Moses contrasted with a sharp reversal in John's political fortunes. The Federalists had come to power as the party of a strong central government, ready to punish its enemies at home and abroad. But when relations with France deteriorated, President Adams had opted for diplomacy over confrontation, prompting an ugly rift with the arch-Federalist Alexander Hamilton that led to a debilitating—and ultimately fatal—identity crisis for the party. John was among the early casualties of this surprising political shift: in statewide balloting in August for the term beginning in 1801, John and the rest of the Rhode Island Federalists were swept from office. John fared especially poorly, collecting only 138 of 3,240 votes cast, perhaps in consequence of his unpopular support for the slave trade. John would return to the capital for the second session of the Sixth Congress, but he would attend as a lame duck.

John's domestic life was another source of discord during this period. Since the death of her husband, John Francis, Abby and her son had returned to her parents' household, and the boy was a constant source of delight to his grandparents. But Abby's sisters, Sarah and Alice, were each engaged in romances that would lead to marriage. In both cases, the primary impediment to their troth was their father.

Alice, the youngest sister, was the most impetuous of John's children. An occasional painter and something of a beauty, Alice had begun a liaison with James Mason, a businessman three years older than she. James Mason grew up near Providence and attended Rhode Island College, but carried something of an air of mystery. He spent several years in the South—long enough to marry and become widowed—before returning to Providence in 1798. He soon earned a reputation as a gambler, a fortune hunter, and something of a ladies' man, qualities that apparently only endeared him to Alice.

The budding romance caused much anxiety in the family, which only increased when Alice announced her engagement to Mason. John was away in Philadelphia for the climax of this domestic crisis, and by the time he got back, the outcome was already fixed: Alice, then twenty-three years old, was pregnant. Stephen Gano, the pastor of the First Baptist Church, was drafted to preside over a "private wedding," and Alice and John Mason were wed on July 18. Abby Mason, named after her beloved aunt, was born the next day. Whatever John made of this sudden denouement is hard to say, but familial cordiality soon prevailed; by June 1801, Alice's young family had moved into John's old house on Main Street. Soon after, John Mason was appointed a trustee at Rhode Island College.

Sally Brown's suitor at this time was Charles Frederick Herreshoff, the son of a Prussian aristocrat who emigrated to New York in 1787. Herreshoff entered the import trade and met Sally when he came to Providence in 1798 to talk business with her father. Herreshoff proposed marriage the next year; he was ten years older than Sally. John Brown approved of Herreshoff at first, but over time, as with each of his daughters, he deemed the polished Prussian insufficient material for a son-in-law. It didn't help matters when, in October 1799, Herreshoff lost most of his fortune speculating in European sugar stocks. This only confirmed John's skepticism, and he made his feelings clear.

Sally was more patient than her sisters in dealing with her father. She stayed in his orbit, lulling him with concertos on the pianoforte in the music room of the mansion on Benefit Street. Of all his children, Sally was the most accomplished, pursuing studies in mathematics and astronomy as well as music. But if Sally was dutiful, she also had a life to live, and by the time of John's return to Congress, late in 1800, she laid the line down plainly. "Dear Sir," she addressed her father. "To judge from your conduct toward me the summer past and the extreme prejudice you have all along entertained against Mr. Herreshoff, I have little reason to think you ever mean to give your consent to our marriage." She would still appreciate his approval, but with or without it, the pair would be wed in the spring.

John Brown departed Providence on December 1, 1800, setting sail from the town wharf just before winter ice closed the mouth of the Great Salt River. He was traveling by sea this time, and to a new destination; this session of Congress would convene in the new capital, Washington, D.C. John had much to consider during his passage southward, even apart from the turbulence at home. The political picture was clouded by a close electoral battle between John Adams, the Federalist incumbent; Thomas Jefferson, the incumbent vice president and Republican (or Antifederalist) champion; and Aaron Burr, the New York attorney and assemblyman running on Jefferson's ticket.

And John had urgent business to transact in the final stretch of his term. The tougher penalties in the new slave-trade act had had a decided impact— of nineteen clearances for Africa from Rhode Island for the year 1800, only one was entered after the new act took effect. Now, six months later, some of the more aggressive shipmasters of Bristol and Newport were fitting out ships to test the law once more, but even the most brazen were leery of William Ellery and his prosecutors. Together with his friends Charles and James D'Wolf, John had hit upon a creative solution: establish a new customs district at Bristol, one outside the jurisdiction of the enterprising Ellery. This would be a delicate matter as the two existing Rhode Island districts were already plainly sufficient, but John could expect cooperation from his Federalist Party connections. It was worth a try.

John was not the only political figure enlisted in this scheme. In a testament to the power and influence of the D'Wolf clan, his allies in pushing the new customs district included both Benjamin Bourne and Ray Greene, the judge and prosecutor in the slave case against John. Bourne remained on the bench, while Greene had recently been selected to replace William Bradford as the United States senator from Rhode Island. Bourne and Greene had each fulfilled his official obligations by enforcing the law against John, but it appears that for both men, the bonds of local political faction were stronger than the moral sway of the abolitionists.

John arrived at Baltimore after several days at sea, and made his way by stage to the new capital city. It was a daunting prospect, a handful of buildings surrounded by a broad swath of tree stumps and boggy hollows. The Capitol was a hulking brick structure without dome or marble, and the president's house was still not finished. The members of Congress stayed at half a dozen boardinghouses, their needs serviced by a tailor, a single washerwoman, and a lone oyster house. The settlement was drained by a fetid open sewer dubbed, unfortunately, the Washington Canal.

There was no social life in the rudimentary Federal City, no balls or taverns as in Philadelphia. It was more like an austere political club. The representatives found rooms according to allegiance, and John boarded with fifteen other Federalists. Like most of the members, John ate his meals at his boardinghouse; breakfast and dinner were served on slab tables for anyone on hand. "Not a drink of Cider to be had for love nor money, so you may judge whether

I had rather be at my own table or here," he wrote home after his first week in town.

John made his first appearance at the Capitol on December 8, three weeks into the session. He trudged the six hundred steps from his boardinghouse on foot—he counted them—as there were no carriages available for lease or sale. One leg was nearly lame from rheumatism, but John gamely managed the stairs at his living quarters, and those leading to the second-story chamber of the House of Representatives, without complaint.

The early days of the session were devoted largely to formalities—how best to memorialize Washington; where stenographers should sit in the new congressional hearing room—but the great preoccupation was the selection of the president. It was clear, by the first of January, that Adams had been defeated; the question now lay between Jefferson and Burr, and would be decided in the House. John leaned toward Burr, whom John had retained briefly in the legal tangle surrounding his New York tract, but Jefferson was more active in seeking the support of the Federalists. John met with Jefferson several times, the aristocratic Virginian once stopping by John's boardinghouse to confer with John and Ray Greene.

John related these affairs to his brother in a series of letters from Washington. Moses responded in kind, describing an injury he sustained while attempting to mount a horse, and advising John how to answer new calls on hard currency at the bank—a plan of which John "fully approved." It appears the two had reached a new stage of amity, both conscious that their days were growing short. But this was strictly personal: on the question that had so long divided the brothers, there would be no late reconciliation.

In late December, Treasury Secretary Oliver Wolcott moved to ratchet up the government's campaign against the slave trade, sending a New York sea captain named John Leonard to take over the prosecution of the New England slave merchants. Leonard met with Moses in Providence just after Christmas, soliciting contacts among the abolitionists there and in Boston. Aware of the volatile nature of his mission, Leonard asked that his activities be kept secret. But he moved quickly, filing his first case on December 31, naming the sloop *Fanny*, owned by James D'Wolf.

Captain Leonard made clear at once he would press harder than his predecessor Ray Greene, charging D'Wolf under four counts of the federal law and seeking damages of twenty thousand dollars. The case was scheduled for trial before a Newport jury with Judge Bourne presiding. Not to be intimidated, the

D'Wolfs hired a team of three lawyers led by Asher Robbins, a Yale-educated attorney and future U.S. senator.

The new prosecutor soon learned the price of challenging the D'Wolfs on their home turf. After several days of argument, the jury reported a quick verdict, finding that "the said James D'Wolf owes nothing." Not satisfied with their triumph at the bar, the D'Wolfs gathered outside the courthouse with some of their more unsavory friends and waited for Leonard to appear. When he did they confronted him; a shoving match ensued and one of the ruffians took a swing at the prosecutor and knocked him to the ground.

Word of the assault on the courthouse steps soon reached Washington, provoking outrage in the Congress and at the Treasury Department. The timing could not have been worse — just a week before, Ray Greene had quietly introduced the Bristol petition in the Senate, where it was referred to the Committee on Commerce and Manufacturers. It was expected to win easy approval there, but the House had yet to see the bill. Now, John Brown would have to do what he could to limit the damage.

"The violence used in Newport . . . will put it out of my power to get the law through this session," John lamented in a letter to Judge Bourne. Fortunately for John, however, the House was just then engaged in its deliberations over selection of the president, a political marathon that took six days and thirty-six ballots before finally settling on Jefferson. Partisan that he was, John voted each time for Burr.

The Bristol customs bill was reported from the Senate to the House on February 18, the day after that momentous decision was rendered, and promptly referred to committee. John did what he could to protect it, but the D'Wolfs' blunder at Newport had made a strong impression. John painted a dismal picture in a letter to Judge Bourne. "This outrageous conduct will add to the jealousy of all those, and you know they are not a few in Congress, who are prejudiced against the Bristol merchants on account of the African trade," John wrote. Though the Senate had approved the new district without opposition, the House committee "have made up their unanimous minds to report against the district."

John was frustrated, but he was as skilled in politics as he was in business, and there was still time. At the close of the session on Friday, Samuel Smith, chairman of the House Committee on Commerce and Manufactures, rose to report the committee's vote against the district. John intervened, imploring Smith to hold his report back through the weekend. It was a question of fairness, John argued; the committee was frustrating the enterprising spirit of the small ports in favor of the larger firms operating out of Philadelphia and New

York. That was absurd, Smith retorted. He couldn't care less about the customs district, and the other members of the committee were emphatically opposed. But Smith was a Federalist, and a wealthy merchant like John, and he was willing to give him a reprieve. He agreed to delay his report to the following Monday.

Over the weekend, John treated with each of the six members of the committee. John never described the substance of those conversations, but by noon Monday, he'd effected a complete reversal. "I now have the pleasure of informing my Bristol friends," John wrote Judge Bourne that afternoon, "the report of the said Committee on Commerce and Manufactures has now just been made and passed without a dissenting vote and is accordingly *enacted*." All that remained was to shepherd the selection of the collector for the new district, a choice that his colleagues would leave to the esteemed representatives of Rhode Island.

Passage of the Bristol district wasn't John's greatest political victory. It couldn't compare to the unanimous vote against the Impost, or the sweet taste that came after years of struggle with the razor-thin vote to bring Rhode Island into the union. But this was more finite, more of a score, and it carried a different sense of satisfaction. It had come in Congress, in the new capital, the nexus of wealth and power for a new nation that had, in his lifetime, been unthinkable. He'd pulled it off himself, by sheer force of character. There were no minions, no machine to work with, just Federalist glad-handing and a liberal dose of personality. His children called it thunder; John preferred the phrase "acrimony of spirit."

And it was loaded with personal meaning. Creation of the Bristol district did serious damage to the federal apparatus established to police the slave trade, handing a deepwater port to a clan of notorious slavers. John could have spent his energies battling excise taxes on liquor—the issue was then before the Congress, and John's gin distillery was operating at capacity. His focus on the slave trade appears almost pathological. Moses thought so; a "peculiar irritability," as he termed it, which he attributed to an outsized love of money. John certainly had that, but Moses didn't account for his own place in the picture. It was sibling rivalry on a grand scale. John was never going to cede to Moses the question of what was right and what was wrong.

With the Bristol district settled, John's political work was over. His party and its leader had been swept from office, and most of the critical appointments had been made—in February, John had seen Judge Bourne elevated to the Circuit Court of Appeals, and Ray Greene named to replace Bourne on the federal bench in Rhode Island. He attended each day as the session wound down, staying well into the evening as the House closed out its business March 3. John liked the pageantry, and he savored the clubby relations with his colleagues. For the Federalists, the inaugural was all anticlimax— Adams departed the night before, scuttling plans for a send-off. But John didn't seem particularly distressed. He'd had his heyday. "After this," he wrote, "the Feds may part, never to meet in this transitory world again."

16

Legacies

JOHN BROWN RETURNED FROM WASHINGTON to find his affairs in various stages of disarray, and he set about shoring them up with his usual energy and ingenuity. His son James had been busy in his absence, doing what he could to maintain the family enterprise and keeping in close touch with his sisters, but the critical moves had been left to the aging patriarch.

John quickly sought peace with his daughter Alice, who was by then nursing her second child. Recognizing her new family as an accomplished fact, John reverted to form, inviting James Mason to join him as a business partner. Mason consented, and in June 1801, Alice, James, and their children had moved into John's old house on Main Street. Soon after, James Mason was appointed a trustee at Rhode Island College.

John stuck to his pattern, as well, in his dealings with Sally—he spurned every entreaty from Sally and from Charles Herreshoff, pushing his daughter and her fiancé to make their plans without him. Since his near bankruptcy in 1799, Herreshoff had recovered sufficiently to lease a farm in Westchester, outside New York, and to buy a country estate on Shelter Island, off Sag Harbor, at the eastern end of Long Island. Independent but not impetuous, Sally arranged for Herreshoff to present his finances for review by Thomas Poynton Ives, a business partner of her cousin Nicholas. On July 2, 1801, with Ives's approval but without her father's, Sally and Charles were married in Providence. No descriptions of the wedding survive, but the newlyweds spent an evening with the Masons at their new home on Main Street, and another with the Iveses, before sailing back to Westchester. Once again John was forced to make amends, proposing local business ventures to Herreshoff in a belated bid to effect Sally's return to Rhode Island.

John had no better success enforcing his will in the wilds of upstate New York. In the first years that he owned the Adirondack tract, John spent twenty-five thousand dollars on roads, bridges, and causeways to open the land to settlers. But he recognized from the outset that grain and other crops would have to be established before the homesteads and towns he envisioned might be realized. In correspondence with the caretaker he employed to supervise the property, John emphasized the need for "sowing and planting as much ground as you think bids fair," but no harvests materialized. It was all the caretaker could do to repair the roads each spring from the damage sustained the previous winter.

At the same time, John had to struggle to clear his title to the property. He learned, soon after his purchase, that a wealthy London merchant had asserted claim to the land through the legal offices of Aaron Burr in New York. John retained Alexander Hamilton to defend his title, but the dispute became entangled in the much larger intrigues between Burr and Hamilton. The question was finally resolved in John's favor by an act of the New York legislature in 1804.

At sea, at least, John's old manner still prevailed. His once-great fleet had dwindled to just two trading vessels, the *Hope* and the massive *General Washington*, but his captains continued to venture far and wide—the *Hope* to Europe and the *General Washington* into the Pacific. In a report of her exploits that John received via Philadelphia, he learned the *General Washington* had slipped a trade embargo to put in at a small port in Peru, where "she succeeded in smuggling all her cargo." She was last seen sailing west, out to sea and headed for Canton, easily outpacing two Peruvian cruisers sent in futile pursuit.

With his more risky investments lying far beyond his reach, John focused his energies on his estate in Providence. Along with supervising the operations of his thriving gin distillery, John spent the summer of 1801 directing teams of laborers in building and paving roads running by his several properties and cultivating farm acreage near town. "All these attentions together with a new wharf at India Point has kept me in my sulky from the break of day til nite excepting only an hour at breakfast and an hour at dinner," John wrote in September.

It was a remarkable pace for a man of his age and his physique, and it couldn't last. In March 1802, John's sulky veered into a ditch and overturned, causing severe injury to his leg. For two weeks he was confined to his bedroom, and afterward he rarely walked more than a few paces, but he resumed making his rounds in his chariot. At home John was comforted by the constant attention of his wife and his daughter Abby, who lived with her parents in her widowhood. In the evenings his grandson John Brown Francis made a custom of massaging his grandfather's aching legs.

In July 1803, John took an afternoon ride in his chariot from Providence east and then south to Spring Green Farm, across the fragrant green country-side, the air heavy with humidity and pungent with the smell of sea grass and tidal marsh wafting up from the Great Salt River. From a rise in the road just below Patuxet, John could look out from his cushioned seat and see the scrubby profile of Namquit Point, the sandy spit where he and his audacious crew had boarded and torched the *Gaspee* under a midnight sky thirty years before.

That evening, John's lungs became congested, an edematous condition that persisted through the steamy Rhode Island summer. He slept only fitfully, and his indomitable spirit seemed at last to yield to depression at the prospect of his mortality. On September 20 his family was pleased to find John in a bet-ter mood than he'd exhibited in weeks—James was on hand at the brick house on the hill, and Abby and her son, John Brown Francis, as well as Sally and Charles Herreshoff. John conversed and laughed well into the evening, re-tiring to his bedroom around nine, accompanied by his grandson. After receiving his customary rubdown, John gazed at John Brown Francis and murmured, "Good night my dear boy. Good night my dear dear dear boy." Those were his last words; ten minutes later, John expired.

His death, perhaps inevitably, took his wife and children by surprise—they simply couldn't anticipate the demise of someone who had so dominated, for so long, the life of his family and of his community. But John himself had pre-pared thoroughly for the event, toiling for weeks more than a year before the event over what might be considered his crowning masterpiece—the final summary of his estate.

Comprising eleven folio pages, copied out in fine hand by one of his clerks, the roster of his holdings is impressive for its sheer volume, and all the more so in its precision and detail. The first section, covering his land holdings, enu-merates forty-seven properties, some small but most quite substantial. His "homestead house" in Providence leads the list, valued at $18,000, followed by "a beautiful meadow," a half mile up the hill. John helpfully advised that the lot might be divided into house lots worth $4,000 apiece, but he modestly appraised the current value at half that figure.

The listing continues, outlining the fruits of a lifetime of relentless enter-prise: the various lots, wharves, and structures at India Point, including the re-mains of the old candle works; his one-sixth share of the Hope Furnace property; various town lots on both the east and west sides of Providence; three farms on Prudence Island featuring "kind and easy plow land" and totaling more than sixteen hundred acres; the family retreats at Bristol and Spring

Green; the India Point bridge and the surrounding properties; two thousand acres along the banks of the Connecticut River; nearly nine thousand acres of farmland in southern Massachusetts; land rights in Ohio valued at nineteen thousand dollars; and of course, the Adirondack tract. Most of his holdings John valued conservatively, but New York lands he priced according to his aspiration, at a dollar an acre, a figure that would not be realized for generations. Still, leaving the New York land aside, his real estate holdings were worth a quarter of a million dollars—an astounding figure for his time, and a lasting legacy for his children.

The summary under the heading "Trading Stock and Personal Estate" told its own story: shares in the Providence Bank, in two new insurance companies, and in two turnpike associations; the equipage at India Point, including his shipyard and two remaining ships, the gin distillery, and sixty cannon (worth four thousand dollars "at the beginning of a war" but valued at twelve hundred dollars in peacetime); and John's plate and furniture, which he valued at four thousand dollars but which is now held in various museums and brings millions of dollars at auction. His personal effects—apparel and a watch—John did not trifle with, throwing them in with his coaches, carriages, and horses. John also included here more than twenty outstanding personal loans, some as small as twenty pounds, calculated with interest, and a number of them forgiven, due to his debtors' "embarrassed circumstances."

He closed his tally with few debts of his own, which are noteworthy anomalies in light of his vast holdings. He owed the Providence Bank—*his* bank—one hundred thirty-five thousand dollars, nearly double the value of the bank stock in his portfolio. He owed twenty-six thousand dollars to Simeon Potter, a notorious Bristol trader and mentor to the D'Wolf family. And he owed twenty-three hundred dollars to Charles Herreshoff and five hundred dollars more to James Mason—apparently loans to John were part of the price of entry to his family circle.

Taken together, his accounting of his accumulated assets highlights some of the attributes that set John Brown apart from even the most successful of his fellow merchants. He was a businessman, to be sure, but one possessed of a vision acutely tuned to his times and the direction that America was headed. The sheer range of his enterprises, from farming and manufacturing to shipping and finance, was extraordinary. And while he was a man of property, he was never obsessed with his possessions—other wills of the time enumerated personal property in painstaking detail, but John didn't bother. For John, the pleasure was not in the spoils but in the hunt, and in the stature that came with material wealth. As John once explained in a letter to his son, "before I was seven years old I knew what property was and consequently what a despicable figure I myself and my children after me would cut without a share thereof."

It may presume too much to say that John's death spelled the end of Moses Brown's campaign against slavery, but it's hard not to see a connection. Moses remained invested in the cause of Africans in America, and continued his personal engagement in attending to their welfare. But after 1803, he did not author another piece of legislation relating to slavery or the slave trade, nor did he take any steps to orchestrate lobbying efforts by the abolition society.

It may be that Moses was simply exhausted by twenty-five years of politics, advocacy, and agitation. It's possible that, according to some unspoken calculus, Moses decided he had paid off the debt he incurred by his role in the voyage of the *Sally*. And it is true that the abolition movement as a whole lost momentum around the turn of the century, having achieved much of its agenda in the North and seeing little prospect of success in the South. But in Moses' case, it appears there was something else at work. It was not like him to leave off a pursuit he cared about so deeply as slavery simply because the political winds had shifted. And though he was growing old, he remained active in several fields, realizing some of his greatest successes late in his long life. His abrupt retreat on the question of slavery suggests that in this most personal and most heartfelt quest, the looming presence of his brother was a more powerful factor than Moses ever acknowledged, even to himself.

Moses first exhibited reservations over punishing transgressors in the battle against slavery and the slave trade when the Providence Abolition Society first initiated legal proceedings against Caleb Gardner. He persuaded William Rotch then not to seek full enforcement of the penalties under state law; later, when John Brown was the defendant, Moses voiced qualms about the entire prosecution. It appears that while Moses was enthusiastic about the idea of legislation, he had no taste for the ugly business of holding his peers—and ultimately his brother—to account. It appears as well that, with John gone, Moses had lost his personal stake in the contest.

Whatever the source of his ambivalence, Moses' withdrawal from the field was evidenced by a deepening silence. As early as 1801, the American convention of abolition societies, to which Moses was a corresponding member, sounded a general alarm for enforcement of the federal law Moses helped draft: "Notwithstanding the prohibitions of most of the states on this subject, and the strict instructions of those of the general government, upwards of two hundred vessels, belonging to our own citizens, are employed in the purchase and transportation of slaves from Africa to the West Indies, and the southern parts of this country.

"This rage for the traffic is so far extended by avarice that many persons have risked their all in its pursuit . . . that we are induced to earnestly call on our brethren in those parts, to aid in its suppression." In Rhode Island, home to the first law against the slave trade, this appeal was quietly ignored. So brazen were the slavers of Bristol that an abolitionist who sponsored the prosecution of a ship there was assaulted in his sleep and had one of his ears cut off.

Another appeal to action was addressed to Moses in 1805, but Moses handed the matter off to David Howell, in his capacity as president of the abolition society. Howell's review of the situation can only be called disheartening. Several slavers had been successfully prosecuted, Howell wrote, "but the failure in others has occasioned discouragement to so general a pursuit and prosecution as otherwise might have been the case; the violence used in some cases, on those who have been complainants, has also tended to lessen that pursuit. . . . Most of those concerned in the oppressive commerce, having been successful in the mammon of unrighteousness, and thereby acquired a *forcible* influence, which the peaceful and legal measures of the society, are not able to counteract." This was the sort of language that, a few years earlier, Moses or Rotch or Thomas Arnold would have used to incite their cohorts to action; now it was the language of capitulation.

Howell did not mention, but Moses was certainly aware, that the biggest factor contributing to the success of the illegal slave trade in Rhode Island was the coup John scored in his final trip to Congress by establishing a separate customs district at Bristol. The significance was not apparent at the outset, as the first collector appointed to the new post, Jonathan Russell, proved as active in upholding the law as William Ellery and the other Treasury officials. But the D'Wolf clan promptly focused their energies on Russell's removal. James D'Wolf, by then a member of the state General Assembly, sponsored a petition drive among the assembly deputies to have Russell replaced by Charles Collins, who helmed slavers for D'Wolf and was related to James by marriage. Crucially, D'Wolf was a Republican, and when Thomas Jefferson moved into the White House, D'Wolf's petition received a full hearing.

President Jefferson resisted at first, finding little fault in Russell's performance. But the Republican faction in Rhode Island, led by William Ellery's nephew Christopher, named to replace Ray Greene in the Senate, made the customs post a top priority in their communications with Washington. In February 1804 the president gave way, firing Russell and naming Collins to replace him. When Russell learned of the decision, in March, he lodged a stern protest with Treasury Secretary Albert Gallatin. He did not object to his removal, Russell emphasized, but rather to the selection of Collins. "He has been bred and brought up from his youth in the slave trade," Russell wrote, and had engaged in "numerous and notorious" violations of the law. On the same day he received his appointment, Collins had celebrated the arrival in the West Indies of his own brigantine sailing from Africa with a cargo of slaves. Worse, Russell wrote, Collins had been party to the kidnap of Samuel Bosworth, the federal official charged with bidding on D'Wolf's ship *Lucy*.

But the damage was done. As Senator Ellery wrote to James D'Wolf, "There is now, dear sir, nothing more to be done for Bristol—everything which she asked is granted." From that day forward, slave prosecutions in the Bristol district ceased, and clearances of ships sailing for Africa soared. With the floodgates open, William Ellery stood aside as well, and the traffic from Newport reached its highest volume ever. In 1805, for the first time, more than fifty slave ships departed Rhode Island for Africa. It was as if the abolitionist campaign against the slave trade had never taken place.

The pattern set at Bristol, of legislation followed by halting enforcement and then wholesale violations, anticipated the course of the larger struggle. The greatest legislative triumphs of the early movement against slavery came in 1807, the year the constitutional protections for the slave trade were set to expire. On the earliest possible date, March 2, President Thomas Jefferson signed into law the "Act to prohibit the importation of slaves into any port or place within the jurisdiction of the United States." Three weeks later, on the other side of the Atlantic, the English Parliament followed suit, enacting a universal ban on British participation in the slave trade. Before long, all the great powers of Europe joined the prohibition. The first great goal of the abolition movement, once so distant it was hard even to envision, had at last been realized.

Yet the institution of slavery continued to prosper, in Cuba, in Brazil, and especially in the southern United States, where it was extended to the new lands incorporated through the Louisiana Purchase. The slave trade grew commensurately, and the statutes against it were openly flouted. By December 1810, President James Madison warned Congress that "American citizens are instrumental in carrying on a traffic in enslaved Africans, equally in violation of the laws of humanity, and in defiance of those of their own country." Twelve years later, a House committee reported that "the African slave trade now prevails to a great extent." More recent studies have found that, despite the legislation and naval patrols, "the actual volume of forced African slave migrations to the Americas tended to follow the pattern of growth and decline in American labor demand." Simply put, the legislation against the slave trade had no effect whatsoever.

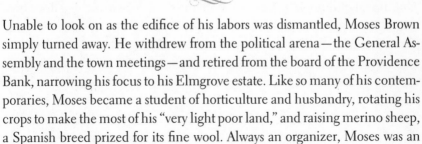

Unable to look on as the edifice of his labors was dismantled, Moses Brown simply turned away. He withdrew from the political arena—the General Assembly and the town meetings—and retired from the board of the Providence Bank, narrowing his focus to his Elmgrove estate. Like so many of his contemporaries, Moses became a student of horticulture and husbandry, rotating his crops to make the most of his "very light poor land," and raising merino sheep, a Spanish breed prized for its fine wool. Always an organizer, Moses was an early member of the Rhode Island Agricultural Society.

While he stayed busy supervising teams of farmworkers during plantings and harvests, his family circle grew steadily smaller. In June 1808, Phebe Lockwood was taken ill with a full-body fever. She never recovered, and in October, Moses buried his third wife. Widowed once again, he never remarried, but he derived some comfort from the presence at Elmgrove of Phebe's sister Avis, her niece Avis Harris, and several long-term boarders.

Moses was, of course, concerned with his own mortality. He'd had long periods of recurring illness, beginning as far back as the early 1770s, when he'd elected to withdraw from the family business. But Moses proved resilient, far outlasting his brothers and, to his great disappointment, his son Obadiah, who died in 1822, at age fifty-two, leaving no heirs. In his bereavement, Moses could only wonder, "What am I continued so long here for?"

As if in answer, in the later years of his life, Moses renewed his longstanding interest in education, finally achieving goals that had eluded him for decades. In 1814, he revived the idea of a boarding school that would inculcate Quaker and other children in the ways and values of the church. The first attempt, at Portsmouth on the northern end of Aquidneck Island, had failed in 1786, in part for lack of funds and in part because few Quakers wanted to send their children to such a distant location. Moses decided to try again, this time on land he owned adjacent to Rhode Island College, on the hill above Providence. As he did at Portsmouth, Moses insisted that the school take on poor children without charge, and that it be open to students of all religious affiliations. He petitioned the Meeting for Sufferings to take up a new subscription to fund the project, and he donated more than forty acres of land for the campus. Construction began in the spring of 1816, with the work hired out to Almy & Brown, the firm headed by Moses' son and son-in-law.

As before, the progress of the school was hampered by a lack of funds, but that was resolved with the death of Obadiah. Moses' son had prospered in the textile business, and in his will he bequeathed to the Friends School the sum of one hundred thousand dollars, the largest single gift made to that date to an educational institution in America. With the struggle of launching the school behind him, Moses took an office in the new building, served as treasurer of the endowment, and spent many of his days visiting with teachers and students. By 1824, he was able to report to a friend that "our school has become too large." Parents living near campus were asked to take their children home due to overcrowding in the dormitory.

Moses had retired from politics, but did not entirely withdraw from the affairs of the larger world. He became engaged in a succession of reform movements as they swept the evolving consciousness of the nation; he helped found the Rhode Island and Providence Plantations Bible Society in 1816, and mentored Thomas Arnold and George Benson when they founded the Rhode Island Peace Society in 1818.

Nor did Moses forsake his original and most heartfelt social cause, the plight of black Americans. He maintained, as he had for years, his correspondence with and occasional assistance to his former slaves, their families, and their children. Some of them had settled in town and worked for Moses, while some traveled farther afield. Peggy Harrison moved to Boston after Moses set her free, and corresponded with him intermittently, always addressing Moses as "Dear Master." In 1804, she asked him for "a little money" to help found an independent black Baptist church, and Moses gladly pitched in. Four years later, not long after the church began holding services, Harrison finally addressed Moses as "Dear Friend."

This was more than an exercise of noblesse oblige on Moses' part, but an effort to demonstrate that, given the opportunity, blacks could assimilate into white society. Unlike many fellow abolitionists, Moses saw blacks not just as pitiable objects for philanthropy but as equal to whites in every human capacity. This was a radical notion at a time when blacks were uniformly uneducated and, if free, only recently released from servile bondage, and Moses was constantly looking for proof of his conviction. He found a form of physiological evidence in the case of Henry Moss, a free black born in Virginia who, as he reached middle age, found his skin turning from sable to white. Today this would be recognized as vitiligo, a fairly common syndrome that results in depigmentation of the skin, but at the time it posed a conundrum to the paradigm of Caucasian superiority.

Henry Moss first noticed his changing color around 1792, and quickly recognized the larger implications of his blanching complexion. Moss presented himself for inspection in Philadelphia in 1796, drawing the fascinated interest of such prominent men as George Washington, Thomas Jefferson, and Benjamin Rush—Rush, a physician, went so far as to blister Moss's skin with chemicals to see if it reverted to black. It did not.

Moses Brown got his chance to meet with Henry Moss during a trip Moss made to Providence in 1803. Moses arranged for a close physical examination, which satisfied him that "his back below his shoulders is mostly as white as white people his age, as are parts of his breast and even his nipples." Other parts of Moss's body remained black. "He appears now to be neither wholly black or white." To Moses, this obviated any distinctions based on the color of skin. "Me thinks it is an evidence of the sameness of human nature and corresponding with the declaration of the Apostle, that, 'God hath made of one blood all nations of men.' For we see in him one and the same blood sustains a man that appears to our sense, both black and white."

Moses demonstrated his abiding conviction in racial equality in more challenging circumstances in the years to come. After the Revolution, and especially after the turn of the century, the Old World decorum of Providence began to break down as strangers and unemployed drifters began to swell the population and throng the streets and taverns. In the old and poorer sections of town, particularly on the east side north of Market Square, prostitution and bawdy houses became a glaring new public vice. The district was also home to most of the free blacks in Providence, a community of close to a thousand people sharing small homes and crowded tenements with sailors, laborers, and other working-class whites. Vice and race soon became commingled in the minds of the town's civic reformers, and a rash of petitions complained of racial mixing and the harmful influence of "colored" people.

Not surprising, Moses Brown was a leader in the local reform movement, but he explicitly avoided letting the blacks suffer the blame alone. In 1817, Moses headed a drive that collected sixty-seven signatures protesting "divers houses of bad fame not only among the colored people but even among the whites who come here from neighboring states and collect women of prostituted character." The town council responded by ordering noncitizens of dubious character to be removed from the city limits, an ineffectual throwback to earlier, simpler times. The complaints continued, as did resentment against poor blacks, giving rise to an ugly race riot in 1824, and an antiabolition backlash that reached from Boston to Cincinnati.

Ostracized by white society and hungry to establish social standards and a sense of dignity from within their own community, northern blacks began to form their own independent associations. As early as 1787, blacks in Newport formed the Free African Unity Society, seeking to forge new identity out of the "calamitous state" of their impecunious freedom. A similar society was founded around the same time in Providence, but its activities and its profile in the community were limited. A generation later, around 1812, a school was founded for the education of black children, and the drive for a separate black establishment gained new momentum. In 1819, backers of the school joined with the officers of the African Union to propose erection of a combined school and meetinghouse, which would provide a permanent seat for black worship, education, and community work. This project would afford Moses Brown the venue for his last great contribution to the welfare and prospects of blacks in Providence.

Led by a black preacher named Nathaniel Paul, the African Union raised funds in cities from Boston and Salem to New York and Baltimore, as well as five hundred dollars from black families in Providence itself. It was enough to begin construction of a building; all that was needed was the land. The organizers turned to Moses, who agreed to buy a lot for them at any site they chose on the east side of Providence. Once the land was selected, Moses made the purchase, assigning the land to the town council "to be applied to and for the use of the people of color forever." The conveyance bore all the hallmarks of Moses' deliberate, perspicacious brand of philanthropy. He specified that the school adopt a Lancasterian plan of instruction, which emphasized the use of advanced students in teaching the younger children, and that the hall of worship be open to all denominations. As was his custom, Moses attached a preamble, asserting his conviction "that Almighty GOD our Heavenly Father 'hath made of one blood all nations of men,' and that a time will come when by suitable opportunities being offered them for learning, civilization and Christian instruction, they will more generally be brought to the knowledge of the blessed truth." The school opened in 1820, accompanied by stories in the *Providence Gazette* extolling the efforts of the African Union and profiling the intellectual accomplishments of several free blacks in America, anecdotes selected to refute "the stale imputation of inferiority in [black] mental faculties."

The land grants to the African Union and to the Friends School were the landmarks of this final phase of Moses Brown's long life of striving. He wasn't fighting anymore. Removed from the constant ebb and flow of political reform, his concerns were at once more modest and more durable. Moses was making sure his legacy would be meaningful, tangible, and lasting.

Moses Brown died at Elmgrove on September 6, 1836, three weeks short of his ninety-eighth birthday. An epitaph authored by William Goddard, son of Moses' old friend the publisher of the first newspaper in Providence, captured the pathos of Moses' last days. "Successive bereavements took away from the aged pilgrim his staff and the companions of his journey, but they taught him to lean with more confidence upon an Almighty arm and to look forward with a more sustaining hope to a communion with the society of Heaven." In its language and its piety, it was a memorial of which Moses would have approved, one he might have written himself. He was a seeker and a striver who had let his conscience guide his life, always following the direction of his own inner light.

Yet it's hard to look at Moses Brown's long course of struggle and achievement without concluding that his life was a tragic one. He lived to fulfill his destiny as a lawmaker and a moral leader. By dint of determination and perseverance, he'd won many battles in his greatest moral struggle, writing the first laws against slavery and the slave trade, and bringing the malefactors to the bar of justice. He had awakened the social consciousness of his community and engaged the apparatus of the government to secure the demise of the institution of human bondage. But it was all to no avail.

John Brown, Moses' brother and in many ways his alter ego, had no such cause for remorse. His was a life of conquest and triumph, a buccaneer's dream of ambition rewarded. John gambled and won and gambled again, indulged every passion and every appetite. He reaped huge profits and dispensed huge donations. Fiercely independent, he acknowledged no sovereign but his own will. He was always the largest man in the house and the loudest voice on the floor, "Old Thunder," a force unto himself.

Each of the brothers left legacies that long survived him. Moses had no heirs but was memorialized by the children of his brother Nicholas—his daughter Hope, who married Thomas Poynton Ives, named her first son Moses Brown Ives. And *her* daughter Charlotte, who married William Goddard, named her son Moses Brown Ives Goddard. John's name also echoed through the generations: Sally Brown's grandson, the second John Brown Herreshoff, became world famous as a designer of yachts that dominated the America's Cup competitions toward the end of the nineteenth century. And the grandson John doted over, John Brown Francis, won distinction as a U.S. senator and the eleventh governor of the state of Rhode Island.

John's most ambitious project, the settlement of the Adirondacks, proved a great burden to those he left behind. Both his sons-in-law, first James Mason and then Charles Frederick Herreshoff, spent years on and off the tract, seeking to establish roads and industry and to induce settlers, but to no effect. Herreshoff finally set up residency on a lonely hillside, to the dismay of Sally and their six children, who remained on the family estate in Bristol. Herreshoff was on the tract at the end of the cold month of December in 1819 when an iron quarry, one of the enterprises he'd worked so hard to develop, was flooded. Apparently distraught at one more failure on the unyielding land, Herreshoff picked up a pistol and ended his life.

Responsibility for the tract, now tainted with suicide, passed to John Brown Francis. It was a "moon shine inheritance," Francis wrote in 1830, "giving me the appearance of wealth but in reality fastening poverty upon me." At last, in 1850, the tract was sold off in pieces, the largest share, about one hundred sixty thousand acres, bringing the paltry sum of twelve thousand five hundred dollars. But if the land speculation in upstate New York was an act of folly, it does little to tarnish the memory of John's foresight and sagacity. While many of his most accomplished contemporaries fell prey to such grand blunders—Robert Morris's speculations landed him in debtor's prison—John built much more than he squandered.

John's most illustrious bequest was the one he built with his brother Moses. Rhode Island College was John's constant preoccupation—he served as its treasurer for twenty-one years, retiring from that post in 1796, and four years later secured from Congress federal compensation for damages sustained during the Revolution. It was only after his death, however, that John's efforts were commemorated. In 1804, acknowledging a grant of five thousand dollars from Nicholas Brown Jr., the trustees changed the name of the institution to Brown University. The family remained intimately involved in the affairs of the school; from 1841 to 1854, John Brown Francis served in the office of chancellor.

Moses Brown, of course, had the satisfaction of seeing the school adopt his family's name, but he too received his utmost personal encomium posthumously. It was not until 1904 that the New England Yearly Meeting moved to venerate Moses' "generous charity and far vision . . . his sterling character and great soul" by designating the boarding school he had founded as the Moses Brown School.

Yet for all their works and all their deeds, the most ephemeral legacy left by John and Moses Brown was the most profound—the story of their great fraternal battle over the moral question of slavery. This was no theoretical exercise, no friendly disputation over manners or etiquette, but an elemental struggle over the meaning of rights and the extent of individual liberty. It was a human story, certainly, but it was also quintessentially American.

Roger Williams, the intrepid founder of Rhode Island, is rightly renowned for his foresight in drawing an emphatic line between the affairs of religion and the affairs of state. Less well remembered, but just as important, was that the charter Williams obtained from the British Parliament in 1644 established the tiny colony of Rhode Island as the first practicing democratic state since the fall of Athens. John and Moses Brown thus were steeped in the traditions of political and religious liberty, their attitudes distilled through four generations of individual self-rule. They both exercised their heritage of autonomy and freedom in trade and in religion, in the Revolution against England and in the creation of a new national government. There was much that they shared, but they divided over the same moral question that divided the nation.

John and Moses weren't the only members of America's founding generation to engage in the debate over slavery. Moses was part of a movement, and followed the lead of Quakers like Anthony Benezet and the Pemberton brothers. And the proslavery interest was strong enough to write its will into the Constitution, though few northern voices were so unabashed as John's. What set the Brown brothers apart was the depth of their mutual engagement, their personal stake in the outcome. No other abolitionist had to face the reality of the slave trade so close to the center of his identity; no other slave trader had to fend off so persistent and so intimate a challenge to his prerogative.

By the currents of history, by confluence of circumstance, and by force of their own will, John and Moses each adopted the great moral question of the day as the focal point of his identity. They emerged as American archetypes, the robber baron and the social reformer, thunder and light, a dichotomy in the national character that echoes to this day. John may have regarded his ultimate triumph over Moses as purely personal—he always had a taste for revenge—but it suggests something much larger, a tragic dimension at the core of the American experiment.

Notes on Sources

In order to make the text of this book as accessible as possible, I have modernized the spelling and punctuation of the letters written by the Brown brothers and their correspondents. Much of the spelling of the time was phonetic, and the results ranged from charming to comical, but the unique spellings could be distracting, and make certain passages confusing and hard to decipher.

Most of the letters and documents cited in this book can be located in the Moses Brown Collection at the Rhode Island Historical Society, a venerable private repository that Moses helped found, and to which he bequeathed his extensive personal papers. Some of John Brown's papers and letters also turn up in that collection, but the great majority of materials pertaining to John were lost during a hurricane in 1815, when surging floodwaters swept John's old warehouse off India Point.

Several generations of writers have consulted the Moses Brown Collection, and their footnotes usually rely on the folder-and-document-number reference system originally used to catalogue the collection. More recent, however, almost all the Moses Brown papers were photographed and reproduced as a microfilm series under the title "Papers of the American Slave Trade," available on loan from the Library of Congress. This excellent resource is arranged chronologically, and consequently, the reference notes for this book consist simply of the date and the abbreviated title of the repository, "RIHS."

There are a few crucial John Brown letters that turn up in other collections at the historical society. When those papers are cited, they are referenced by date, the name of the collection, and RIHS.

The John Carter Brown Library at Brown University contains another extensive collection of Brown family materials, but rooted more in the family businesses and less in the personal correspondence of individual family members. These materials formed the basis for James B. Hedges's 1952 work, *The Browns of Providence Plantations*, a seminal study in early American enterprise. Papers from that collection are referenced herein by date and the abbreviation "JCBL."

A third source of primary material used for this book is the extraordinary personal collection maintained by Henry A. L. Brown, an author and amateur historian who is related to the Browns of this book by marriage and who lives to this day on John Brown's Spring Green Farm. Henry Brown did honor to his avocation by sharing his extensive collection of original documents, family journals, and letters. Some of those materials are also on file with the Rhode Island Historical Society, but those I obtained directly from Henry are referenced here with his initials, "HALB."

Another important source with numerous references in the notes is *Rhode Island History*, the journal published with varying frequency for more than sixty years by the Rhode Island Historical Society. Some articles consist of a single document recently donated to the society, while others delve deeply into the society's archives to illuminate a particular period or aspect of the state's rich history. Also invaluable were the Gaspee Virtual Archives, a remarkable online resource that makes available a vast trove of primary and secondary materials relating to that landmark event.

ABBREVIATIONS

RIHS   Rhode Island Historical Society

JCBL   John Carter Brown Library

HALB   Private collection of Henry A. L. Brown

RICR   John Russell Bartlett, ed., *Rhode Island Colonial Records* (Providence, 1865), 10 vols.

1. JAMES BROWN PUTS OUT TO SEA

Page

5 shipwright John Barnes: Gertrude Selwyn Kimball, *Providence in Colonial Times* (Boston, 1912), 232.

5 James was able . . . to watch: The physical topography of early Providence is described in Richard Mather Bayles, *History of Providence County, Rhode Island* (New York, 1891), 134.

6 first shipyard in Providence: William B. Weeden, *Early Rhode Island: A Social History of the People* (New York, 1910), 114.

8 the sale of home lots was restricted: Alice Collins Gleeson, *Colonial Rhode Island* (Pawtucket, 1926), 151.

8 "no more than necessity": Weeden, op. cit., 96.

9 "heaps of stones and rubbish": Ibid., 323.

9 "You have struck me as with roses": For the story of Obadian Holmes, including his will, see http://homepages.rootsweb.com/~sam/obadiah.html.

10 The colonel was the leading Providence merchant: Col. Nicholas Power is profiled in Kimball, op. cit., 229–30.

10 "refuse Eror and Chuse Truth": James Browne's sermon can be found in *James Browne: His Writings in Prose and Verse* (Boston, 1917), 4.

11 Africans had proven the best: One contemporary argument for the "urgent need for Negro slaves" is made by Alonso de Zuazo, the Spanish judge of Hispaniola. His statement, dated 1518, is published online by the Gilder Lehrman Institute of American History, at www.gilderlehrman.org/collection/document.php?id=196.

11 more than 6 million Africans: A census of the international slave trade is provided by Paul E. Lovejoy, *Transformations in Slavery: A History of Slavery in Africa* (Cambridge, 1983), 19.

12 "no trade to be made without rum": Jay Coughtry provides an indispensable survey of the Rhode Island slave trade in *The Notorious Triangle: Rhode Island and the African Slave Trade 1700–1807* (Philadelphia, 1981). The 1725 quote on rum is from factors at Cape Coast Castle, quoted in Coughtry, 108.

12 craftsmen there had learned: Sarah Deutsch, "The Elusive Guineamen: Newport Slavers, 1735–1774," *New England Quarterly* 60, no. 2 (June 1982): 241. See also Coughtry, op. cit., 85.

12 "West India rum never will sell": Richard Miles to Ross and Mill, 8/10/75, quoted in Coughtry, 114

12 "Negroes at Jamaica": Joseph Manesty to John Bannister, 4/3/47, quoted in Elizabeth Donnan,

Documents Illustrative of the History of the Slave Trade to America (Washington, D.C., 1930), III:141 n. 2.

13 sitting on his wharf . . . six months: For molasses see James Brown to Sir, 3/15/36, quoted in John Carter Brown Woods, ed., *The Letter Book of James Browne of Providence: Merchant 1735–1738* (Providence, 1929), 23.

13 now he was determined: For James Brown's Africa venture see James B. Hedges, *The Browns of Providence Plantations: Colonial Years* (Cambridge, 1951), 71.

13 "I should be very glad": James Brown to Sir, 1/28/36, quoted in Woods, op. cit., 19.

13 "I want my money": James Brown to Mr. Turtolow, 1/27/36, quoted ibid., 18.

13 "if you have any money": James Brown to Captain Remington, 6/14/36, quoted ibid., 34.

14 A ledger: Entries cited in Kimball, op. cit., 246.

14 "loden with staves": James Brown to Sir, 3/15/36, quoted in Woods, op. cit., 23.

16 some slave ships tarried: There is a wide range of sources detailing the conditions of the slave trade on the African coast. One of the best in Robert Harms, *The Diligent: A Voyage Through the Worlds of the Slave Trade* (New York, 2002). Jay Coughtry's *Notorious Triangle* is also valuable.

16 "more honor and honesty": Esek Hopkins to Nicholas Brown & Co., 10/29/66, in Hedges, op. cit., 39.

16 "Hamond hath bin heair": John Cahoone Jr. to Stephen Ayrault, 10/27/36, quoted in Donnan, III:130.

17 "make dispatch": James Brown to Obadiah Brown, March 1737, quoted in Kimball, op. cit., 246.

17 "the Arivol of my Ginemon": James Brown, quoted ibid., 248.

17 "Othniel Herndon": Mary Brown's will is detailed in Abby Isabel Brown Bulkley, *The Chad Browne Memorial: Consisting of Genealogical Memoirs of a Portion of the Descendants of Chad and Elizabeth Browne 1638–1888* (Brooklyn, 1888), 23.

17 "my body may be opened": James Brown to neighbors, May 1738, quoted in Kimball, op. cit., 232.

18 "ye heavy nuse": Obadiah Brown to Hope Brown, 7/16/39, quoted in Hedges, op. cit., 8.

18 "little molasses-faced Moses": I. B. Richman, *Rhode Island: A Study in Separatism* (Boston, 1905), 162.

18 George Taylor: Mack Thompson, *Moses Brown: Reluctant Reformer* (Chapel Hill, 1962), 10. See also Kimball, op. cit., 217.

18 Entering Market Square: The walking tour of old Providence is based on Henry Richmond Chace, *Owners and Occupants of the Lots, Houses and Shops in the Town of Providence in 1798, Located on Maps of the Highways of that Date; Also Owners or Occupants of Houses in the Compact Part of Providence in 1759* (Providence, 1914).

19 a giant of a man: Bulkley, op. cit., 13.

19 "John Brown the Cleverest": John's cipher book and lessons are described in Kimball, op. cit., 215–17.

20 "Broke the Meeting Hous windows": Bowen to Moses Brown, quoted ibid., 236.

20 The business grew steadily: Hedges, 8–9.

20 an arcane process: Patty Jo Rice, "Beginning with Candle Making: A History of the Whaling Museum," *Historic Nantucket* (summer 1998), available online at www.nha.org/history/hn/HNWhalingmus.htm.

21 Vanderlight's role: Vanderlight is discussed in Hedges, 89, and Bulkley, 16.

21 John and Moses joined in: The brothers' respective roles are outlined in Hedges, 12–16.

21 more than sixty vessels: Moses Brown's tabulation of the family shipping interests is reproduced in Weeden, 228.

21 Obadiah listed ten black slaves: For the New Orleans slaving venture see Hedges, 54.

21 She never returned: The *Wheel of Fortune* is referenced in Hedges, 72, and Kimball, 276.

22 "Such Gales of Wind": James Brown to Nicholas Brown, February 1749, quoted in Kimball, 254.

22 He died at York: Ibid., 255.

23 "penetrating astutious Genius": Ezra Stiles, quoted in Richman, op. cit., 178. n. 1.

23 these were not the grandees: Reminiscence of Samuel Thurber, quoted in Samuel G. Arnold, *History of Rhode Island and Providence Plantations* (New York, 1859), II:603.

24 "a large water engine": Weeden, 227.

24 a lending library in Providence: Hedges, 199.

25 John was outraged: John's theater protest is recounted in Kimball, 305–9.

26 "the best tavern in Tauton": Hedges, 96.

26 John distinguished himself: Kimball, 269.

26 raising silkworms: Thompson, 43.

26 public health: Ibid., 15.

26 When John was wed: Ibid., 25.

27 a new home: Wendy A. Cooper, *Furnishing the John Brown House* (Rhode Island Historical Society Publications, 1962), 68.

27 Moses was married: Thompson, 72.

27 John stayed behind: Ibid., 19.

27 "a handsome fortune": Ibid., 26.

28 the largest shipping concern: Hedges, 15.

2. BROWN BROTHERS INC.

Page

29 eighty-five vessels: From records made by Moses Brown, cited in William E. Foster, *Stephen Hopkins: A Rhode Island Statesman* (Providence, 1884), I:94.

30 "ticklish times here": Hedges, *Browns of Providence*, 5.

30 five days in the brig: Ibid., 7.

30 "trade against raid": James, *Colonial Rhode Island—A History*, 270.

31 "a desolate little hole": Richard Pares, *War and Trade in the West Indies, 1739–1763* (Oxford, 1936), 457–59.

31 "Flags of Truce": One admiralty court ruling pegged the profits at an astronomical 5,000 percent. Ibid., 408.

32 Obadiah was empowered: *RICR*, VI:6.

32 the appointment of Uncle Elisha: Hedges, 52; *RICR*, VI:6.

32 "he became more undisguised": Gov. James Hamilton to William Pitt, 11/1/60, in Gertrude Selwyn Kimball, ed., *Correspondence of Pitt* (Cambridge, 1903), II:351.

32 "inhabited by the buccaneers": Bernard to Pitt, 5/9/61, quoted in George Louis Beer, *British Colonial Policy 1754–1765* (New York, 1907), 93.

32 For the *Speedwell*: Ibid., 57–63.

33 "every master": Ibid., V:445.

33 Hopkins issued at least thirty: Stephen Hopkins to Pitt, 12/20/60, in Kimball, ed., *Correspondence of Pitt*, 373.

33 the pretext of flags: Maj. Robert Rogers, *A Concise Account of North America* (1765; reprint, New York, 1966), 56.

33 "the enemy may avail themselves": Charles Hardy to Pitt, 3/11/57, in Kimball, ed., *Correspondence of Pitt*, 23.

34 free trade had established: Hopkins to Pitt, 12/20/60, ibid., 373.

34 "some of our leading men": Joseph Sherwood to Stephen Hopkins, 5/30/60, ibid., 320.

35 he won the office: Edward Field, ed., *The State of Rhode Island and Providence Plantations at the End of the Century: A History* (Boston, 1902), I:202.

35 social and hospitable: Foster, *Stephen Hopkins*, I:49.

35 "when he wrote at all": Ibid., 65.

37 "a long large rope": John Brown to Edward Dexter, c. 1796, RIHS.

37 "his personal organ": Frederick Bernays Weiner, "The Rhode Island Merchants and the Sugar Act," *New England Quarterly* III (1930): 464–500.

38 "party virulence": *RICR*, VI:549.

38 "a madman's life": Field, *The State of Rhode Island*, 203.

38 "he that distributes": Rogers, *Concise Account*, 58.

39 "procuring the free votes": David S. Lovejoy, *Rhode Island Politics and the American Revolution* (Providence, 1958), 25.

39 "a hard battle": Kimball, *Providence in Colonial Times*, 284.

39 "farmers get their estates": Lovejoy, op. cit., 21n.

39 "the violence of our enemies": Jos. Wanton to Nic. Brown & Co., 4/7/65, JCBL.

39 "Mr. Ward and Uncle Brown": John Brown to Jos. Winsor, 4/8/65, JCBL.

40 "that damned little Moses": Zebediah Hopkins to Moses Brown, 5/24/64, RIHS.

40 The table was ready: Mabel Munson Swan, "A Blockfront Secretary," *Rhode Island History* VII, no. 4 (October 1948): 120.

40 a family coat of arms: Robert P. Emlen, "Wedding Silver for the Browns," *American Art Journal* (spring 1984), 39.

41 "You will excuse me": John Brown to Palmer & Co., 1/7/64, JCBL.

41 "we had cleared it out properly": Joseph Rotch to Jacob Rivera et al., 7/31/64, RIHS.

42 "all the merchants . . . should meet": Ibid., 471.

43 "clandestine trade": Richman, *Separatism*, 200.

43 "grand committee": Weiner, *Rhode Island Merchants and the Sugar Act*, 475.

43 a great blizzard: Ward L. Miner, *William Goddard, Newspaperman* (Durham, NC, 1962).

44 "the iniquitous schemes": Lovejoy, *Rhode Island Politics*, 32.

44 "Essay on the Trade": Carl Bridenbaugh, *Silas Downer, Forgotten Patriot* (1974), 14, 45. Moses Brown retained drafts for "State of the Trade" in his personal papers.

44 "a Dictatorial Manner": *Providence Gazette*, 1/21/64.

44 "the utmost Insolence": *RICR*, VI:378.

46 "miserable condition": Ibid., VI:416.

47 gunners at the harbor fort: Ibid., VI:427.

47 "the general combination of the people": Ibid., VI:458.

47 a mob ruled the town: Lovejoy, 103.

48 "the whole town of Boston": Nicholas Brown & Co. to Capt. George Hopkins at Surinam, 9/8/65, quoted in Hedges, 202.

48 to adopt a set of resolves: Bridenbaugh, *Forgotten Patriot*, 22; William Staples, *Annals of the Town of Providence* (Providence, 1843), 210.

49 "No other colony": C. A. Weslager, *The Stamp Act Congress* (Newark, 1976), 90.

49 Foster penned an affidavit: John Foster declaration, 12/12/65, with note by Moses, RIHS. See also Thompson, 37; Robert Morton Hazelton, *Let Freedom Ring* (New York, 1957), 10.

50 Providence joined the other cities: *Providence Gazette*, 8/8/66, 8/23/66.

50 "business seems to wear a gloom": Hedges, 163.

51 "business being so poor": Ibid., 111.

51 "The merchants sustained very great losses": *RICR*, VI:473.

3. THE *SALLY*

Page

53 John and Moses Brown sailed: Nicholas Brown to John, Joseph, and Moses, 9/12/64, in Donnan, *Documents Illustrative of the Slave Trade*, III:206.

53 Within the harbor itself: Carl Bridenbaugh, *Cities in Revolt*, 38.

54 The very streets of the town: *RICR*, IV:190.

54 at least a third of that product: John J. McCusker, "The Rum Trade and the Balance of Payments of the Thirteen Colonies, 1650–1755," *Journal of Economic History* 30 (March 1970): 244.

54 "My appetite failed": John Woolman quoted in Amelia Gummere, ed., *The Journal and Essays of John Woolman* (Philadelphia, 1922)

54 "drew his brothers": Moses Brown to Dwight Foster, 1/30/00, RIHS.

55 the number of slavers setting out from Newport: Jay Coughtry, *The Notorious Triangle: Rhode Island and the African Slave Trade, 1700–1807* (Philadelphia, 1984), 27 and passim. Coughtry's estimates are conservative.

56 Samuel Sewall in Boston: Lawrence Towner, "The Sewall-Saffin Dialogue on Slavery," *William and Mary Quarterly* XXI, no. 1 (January 1964): 40.

57 "One Negrow feller": John Brown Ratable Estate, 11/10/67, JCBL.

57 the sale of "one Negro girl": Bill of sale, 11/19/1763, RIHS

57 "Grandfather Brown was born in Africa": William J. Brown, *The Life of William J. Brown of Providence* (Providence, 1883), 5.

57 slaves made up more than 15 percent: Alexander Boyd Hawes, *Off Soundings: Aspects of the Maritime History of Rhode Island* (Chevy Chase, 1999), 116.

57 ten to twenty slaves: Robert K. Fitts, *Inventing New England's Slave Paradise: Master-Slave Relations in 18th Century Narragansett, Rhode Island* (New York, 1998), 85.

57 Slave auctions were held: Johnston, *Slavery in Rhode Island*, p. 135.

57 One 1763 letter: Quoted in William D. Johnston, *Slavery in Rhode Island, 1755–1776* (RIHS Publications, 1894), 137.

58 "to prevent all persons": Ibid., 116.

58 "jolly darkies": Ibid., 137, 138.

58 "We shall largely be concerned": Hedges, 74.

59 other merchants had stepped into: Donnan, III:206n.

59 Their first choice was William Earl: Darold D. Wax, "The Browns of Providence and the Slaving Voyage of the Brig Sally, 1764–1765," *American Neptune* XXXII, no. 3 (July 1972): 171.

59 His conquests in command of privateers: Edward Field, *Esek Hopkins, Commander-in-Chief of the Continental Navy During the American Revolution, 1775 to 1778* (Providence, 1898), 12.

59 a remarkable oil painting: Robert W. Kenny, "Sea Captains Carousing in Surinam," *Rhode Island History* 36, no. 4 (November 1977): 107.

60 "If Esek is willing to quit": Wax, "The Browns of Providence," 175.

61 The shore was divided: Walter Rodney, *A History of the Upper Guinea Coast* (Oxford, 1970), 3.

62 "trade . . . has been miserable": Donnan, *Documents*, II:528.

62 "17 sail . . . of Europeans": Wax, op. cit., 175.

62 slaves . . . were more rebellious: David Richardson, "Shipboard Revolts, African Authority, and the Atlantic Slave Trade," *William and Mary Quarterly* VXIII, no. 1 (January 2001).

62 the region between the Gambia and Sierra Leone: Rodney, *History of the Upper Guinea Coast*, 103–6.

62 travelers routinely carried firearms: Ibid., 259.

62 the custom of the trade: Alexander Falconbridge, *Account of the Slave Trade on the Coast of Africa*, excerpted in George Frances Dow, ed., *Slave Ships and Sailing* (Salem, 1927), 133.

63 "the malady of the land": Robert Harms, *The Diligent: A Voyage Through the Worlds of the Slave Trade* (New York, 2002), 273.

63 mortality rate among slave crews: Herbert S. Klein, *The Atlantic Slave Trade* (Cambridge, 1999), 152.

63 "went ashore to meet the king": All references to Hopkins's transactions on the coast of Africa derive from the "Trade Book of the Brig *Sally*," JCBL.

63 Africans overwhelmed the British slave ship *Dove*: Harms, *The Diligent*, 122.

63 most of the trade: Rodney, *History of the Upper Guinea Coast*, 200–222.

66 "the sea, and a slave ship": Equiano quoted in Philip Curtin, ed., *Africa Remembered: Narratives by West Africans from the Era of the Slave Trade* (Madison, WI, 1968), 96.

66 "dew as you shall think best": Nicholas Brown & Co. to Esek Hopkins, 12/30/64, JCBL.

67 "We have not received a line from you": Nicholas Brown & Co. to Esek Hopkins, 7/15/65, JCBL.

67 The *Sally* was "up the River Gamby": Benjamin Gardner to Nicholas Brown & Co., 5/15/65, JCBL.

67 Hopkins had lost all his hands: Gertrude Selwyn Kimball, *Providence in Colonial Times* (Boston, 1912), 273.

68 "Such a favorable account": Moses Brown to Nicholas Brown & Co; Moses Brown to Esek Hopkins, 7/17/65, JCBL.

69 one slave in ten perished: Klein, *The Atlantic Slave Trade*, 140.

69 uprisings were far more frequent: Richardson, "Shipboard Revolts."

69 "Soon after he left the coast": *Newport Mercury*, 11/18/65, in Donnan, *Documents*, III: 213.

69 he was pleased with his innovation: Hopkins quoted in Moses Brown, letter undated, probably 1796, RIHS.

70 An average crossing: Harms, *The Diligent*, 302.

71 "I cannot carry them again to sea": Moses Brown, letter undated, probably 1796, RIHS.

71 "presented a revolting picture": Harms, *The Diligent*, 347.

73 "lost 88 slaves": Hopkins quoted in Wax, "The Browns of Providence," 178.

73 "We knowing your capacity submit": Nicholas Brown & Co. to Esek Hopkins, 11/16/65, JCBL.

4. SUCCESS

Page

75　Schlesinger wrote of colonial children: Arthur M. Schlesinger, *The Birth of the Nation: A Portrait of the American People on the Eve of Independence* (New York, 1969), 23.

76　Hopkins was again at sea: Esek Hopkins to Nicholas Brown & Co., 11/16/66, JCBL.

77　Moses began absenting himself: Moses Brown to Gentlemen, 7/6/68, RIHS.

77　Moses found himself beset: Thompson, *Moses Brown*, 40.

77　new fields of business: Hedges, *Browns of Providence*, 177.

77　"regular course of living": Moses Brown to Gentlemen, 7/6/68, RIHS.

77　another Guinea expedition: Coughtry, *Notorious Triangle*, 73, 98.

78　"Our Jno. Brown": Nicholas Brown & Co. to Benjamin Mason, 12/12/69, in Donnan, *Documents*, III:244.

79　"Fortune is a round stone": Letter quoted in Hedges, *Browns of Providence*, 15.

79　"I am much obliged to you": John Brown to Moses, 1/20/72, RIHS.

80　The plan was controversial: Thompson, *Moses Brown*, 51.

80　"It would be a very easy matter": Hedges, *Browns of Providence*, 193.

81　Moses was named with Jabez: Staples, *Annals of Providence*, 496.

82　the General Assembly authorized a charter: RICR VII:6.

83　"Great expectation": Hedges, *Browns of Providence*, 191.

83　Mud was slung: Lovejoy, *Rhode Island Politics*, 129.

83　"no peace could be expected": *RICR*, VI:549.

84　Moses served as the party whip: Lovejoy, *Rhode Island Politics*, 141. My analysis of the final years of the Hopkins-Ward dispute is derived primarily from Lovejoy's excellent account.

85　"seminary of polite literature": Reuben Aldridge Guild, *History of Brown University, with Illustrative Documents* (Providence, 1867), 7.

85　they dispatched James Manning: Ibid., 10.

85　they turned to Ezra Stiles: Walter C. Bronson, *The History of Brown University* (Providence, 1914), 15.

86　the first official holiday: Guild, *History of Brown*, 12.

86　from across New England and as far as Georgia: Bronson, *History of Brown*, 40.

86　the colony's "metropolis": Joseph Wanton to the Earl of Hillsborough, 6/16/72, produced in *RICR*, VII:90.

86　"institutions of this kind": Guild, *History of Brown*, 185.

87　wrote to the neighboring towns: Ibid., 191.

87　John and Moses repurchased: Moses Brown to Frances Wayland, 5/25/1833, quoted ibid., 207.

87　Manning refused to call the meeting: James Manning to Hezekiah Smith, 2/70, quoted ibid., 196.

88　"Newport hath raised a larger sum": *Newport Mercury*, 1/15/70, quoted ibid., 193.

88　"great noise and high tumulto": Theodore Foster to Jedediah Foster, 4/7/70, cited in Thompson, *Moses Brown*, 67.

88　"moved by their unreasonable enmity": Quoted in Guild, *History of Brown*, 201.

88　"sometimes undue warmth": Quoted ibid., 196.

90　trustees and ministers gathered around: Ibid., 234.

90　Ledgers of expenses: Building accounts, Nicholas Brown & Co., reproduced ibid., 237.

91 "The governor's wig": Quote from John Howland, in Arthur E. Wilson, *Weybosset Bridge in Providence Plantations: 1700–1790* (Boston, 1947), 192.

91 becoming an accomplished architect: J. Walter Wilson, "Joseph Brown, Scientist and Architect," *Rhode Island History* IV no. 3 (July 1945): 67.

92 he refused: Guild, *History of Brown*, 203.

92 "the title of scholar": Quoted by Moses Brown in a letter to Frances Wayland, 5/25/33, reproduced ibid., 207.

92 "a serious division": Ibid.

93 "singing in public worship": *Outline of the History of the First Baptist Church* (Providence, 1889), 3.

93 British colonies produced 15 percent: Edwin J. Perkins, *The Economy of Colonial America* (New York, 1980), 23.

94 agreed on their business plan: Terms of incorporation for the Hope Furnace and details of its formation are from Hedges, *Browns of Providence*, 123–54.

95 an exemption to the Fish Act: Frederic P. Fitts, "Water Rights in Rhode Island, 1790–1840: The Commodification of the Landscape," *Rhode Island History* LXI, no. 2 (summer 2003): 28.

95 a similar petition was granted: Gary Kulik, "Dams, Fish, Farmers: Defense of Public Rights in Eighteenth Century Rhode Island," in Steven Hahn and Jonathan Prude, eds., *The Countryside in an Age of Capitalist Transformation* (Chapel Hill, 1985), 25.

96 "Use your best judgment": Nicholas Brown & Co. to Rufus Hopkins, 8/3/67, JCBL.

96 "long and tedious": John Brown to Nicholas Brown & Co., 6/27/67, JCBL.

96 "got to blows": Rufus Hopkins to Nicholas Brown & Co., 12/20/67, JCBL.

98 Newport followed suit: Hedges, *The Browns of Providence*, 203.

98 Boston and New York threatened their own boycott: Ibid., 204.

98 committees of inspection: Staples, *Annals of Providence* (Providence, 1843), 226.

99 Saville was jumped by a gang: Gaspee Virtual Archives, "Revolutionary Fire: The *Gaspee* Incident" (Rhode Island Committee for the Humanities,1984), www.gaspee.org.

99 "unmercifully to the point of death": Lovejoy, *Rhode Island Politics*, 156.

99 "more Tenderness and Lenity": Quoted ibid.

100 "a voluntary act": *RICR*, VI:588.

100 the colony never paid reparations: Lovejoy, *Rhode Island Politics*, 111.

100 "the resolution of the colonies": Moses Brown to Joseph Sherwood, 7/3/70, reproduced in Gertrude Selwyn Kimball, *Correspondence of the Colonial Governors of Rhode Island* (Boston, 1902), II:420.

101 "material prosperity and political calm": Arthur M. Schlesinger, *The Colonial Merchants and the American Revolution, 1763–1776* (New York, 1918), 240.

5. THE GASPEE

Page

102 "the original coast guard cutters": Neil R. Stout, *The Royal Navy in America 1760–1775: A Study of Enforcement of British Colonial Policy in the Era of the American Revolution* (Annapolis, 1973), 59.

102 Dudingston's first command: www.gaspee.org.

102 Wanton was also a seafarer: Hawes, *Off Soundings*, 162.

103 Dudingston made a careful reconstruction: Lieutenant Dudingston to Admiral Montagu, 5/22/72, in *RICR*, VII:65.

103 Dudingston contracted a local pilot: *RICR*, VII:76.

104 Dundas drew his sword: Deposition of Rufus Greene, ibid., VII:145.

104 the lieutenant could not go ashore: Richard Showman, ed., *The Papers of General Nathanael Greene* (Chapel Hill, 1976), I:30 n. 3.

104 "every invention of infamous lies": Ibid.

105 "No commander of any vessel": *RICR*, VII:60.

106 "I will send the sheriff of this colony": Governor Wanton to Admiral Montagu, 5/8/72, ibid., VII:64.

107 one of her seamen said later: Deposition of Peter May, 1/19/73, in ibid., VII:151.

107 one version posits that John was a passenger: James Otis Kaler, *When We Destroyed the Gaspee* (Boston, 1901), text at www.gaspee.org. Kaler said his fictional rendering was based on letters by Justin Jacobs, but those letters have never surfaced.

107 He himself had been stranded: Moses Brown, "Journal of a Voyage to Philadelphia, 1760," RIHS; cited at www.gaspee.org.

108 John "immediately resolved": Statement of Ephraim Bowen, 8/29/1839, in *RICR*, VII:68.

108 a pirate raid: This account is a composite drawn from the statements of Ephraim Bowen and John Mawney, both raiders of the *Gaspee*, from Lieutenant Dudingston, from several members of his crew, and from the *Providence Gazette* of 6/13/72. There are some important discrepancies— none of the navy men mentioned chasing the *Hannah*—but I consider this to be the most reliable version. All these statements, except for the newspaper article, are presented in *RICR*, VII.

108 as many as five hundred: *Saturday Evening Post*, 8/22/29.

109 "They used us very ill": Deposition of Midshipman William Dickinson, 1/6/73, *RICR*, VII:67.

109 the single firsthand description of John: Ibid.

110 "let me dispatch the piratical dog": Deposition of Midshipman William Dickinson, 6/11/72, *RICR*, VII:84.

110 As his grandson recounted: R. A. Guild, *The Life, Times and Correspondence of James Manning, and the Early History of Brown University* (Boston, 1864), 171.

110 Justin Jacobs . . . was seen cavorting: The story is attributed to John Howland, the first director of the Rhode Island Historical Society, and can be found at www.gaspee.org.

111 the details of the story were known firsthand: Solomon Drowne Jr. to his brother, 6/23/72, in Edward Field, ed., *State of Rhode Island and Providence Plantations: A History* (Boston, 1902), II:465.

111 "dangerous circumstances": Deposition of Darius Sessions, 1/9/73, in *RICR*, VII:129.

112 "he desired it all might die with him": Darius Sessions to Joseph Wanton, 6/11/72, in ibid., VII:77.

113 "Dudingston told me": William Checkley to Commissioners of Customs, 6/12/72, in ibid., VII:87.

113 a jury found against him: Samuel W. Bryant, "Rhode Island Justice—1772 Vintage," in *Rhode Island History* XXVI, no. 3 (July 1967): 65.

113 "the prevailing opinion of the gentlemen": Darius Sessions to Joseph Wanton, 6/11/72.

114 "they beat a drum around Providence": Admiral Montagu to Governor Wanton, 6/11/72, in *RICR*, VII:82.

115 "five times the magnitude": Quoted in Neil L. York, "The Uses of Law and the *Gaspee* Affair," in *Rhode Island History* L, no. 1 (February 1992): 3.

115 "he was accustomed to sleep away from home": Guild, *The Life, Times and Correspondence of James Manning*, 172.

116 rough handling by the British: Aaron Briggs himself described his confinement and threatened whipping; *RICR*, VII:139. A seaman later confessed the decision to extort his testimony; *RICR*, VII:187. Brigg's personal background is provided by the diarist Ezra Stiles, in *The Literary Diary of Ezra Stiles* (New York, 1901), I:348.

117 Montagu dispatched five men-of-war: Neil R. Stout, "The *Gaspee* Affair," in Raymond Friday Locke, ed., *Great Military Battles: Selected Readings from Mankind Magazine* (Los Angeles, 1971), 16.

118 "The King's proclamation was posted": Field, ed., *Rhode Island and Providence Plantations*, II:465.

118 "a court of inquisition": Americanus, attributed to Stephen Hopkins, in York, "The Uses of Law."

118 Hopkins himself vowed not to cooperate: Stiles, *Diary*, I:349.

118 "awaken the American colonies": Samuel Adams to Darius Sessions, 12/28/72, at www.gaspe.org, citing S. A. Wells, *Samuel Adams and the American Revolution*.

119 "the time of terror": York, "The Uses of Law," 9.

119 the commander of the Goat Island gun crew: *RICR*, VII:148.

119 "burn the town of Providence to ashes": Ibid., VII:113.

120 a more moderate course: Stiles, *Diary*, I:331.

120 "the Tory bellowing": Ibid., I:346.

122 "Stand alarmed!": In *Political Sermons of the American Founding Era: 1730–1805*, at Liberty fund.org.

123 "so unreasonable, and so unconstitutional": Lee quoted in Eugene Wulsin, "The Political Consequences of the Burning of the *Gaspee*," *Rhode Island History* III, nos. 1 and 2 (January and April 1944): 10.

123 "A court of inquiry": Jefferson quoted ibid., part I.

124 "Virginia has led the way": Cooper and Franklin quoted ibid., II, p. 58.

124 a committee of correspondence: *RICR*, VII:228.

125 "laughed at by Rhode Islanders": Quoted in John C. Miller, *Origins of the American Revolution* (Boston, 1943), 329.

125 "an end to collecting a revenue": Ibid., 328.

125 "a downright democracy": Horsmanden to Dartmouth, in *RICR*, VII:130.

125 "the actors must be known": Smythe to Dartmouth, in York, "The Uses of Law," 15.

125 "something severe would have been done": Stiles in Wulsin, II:62.

125 "The whole continent was alarmed": Douglass Adair and John Schutz eds., *Peter Oliver's Origin and Progress of the American Rebellion: A Tory View* (Palo Alto, 1961), 99.

125 frequently at Newport: John Brown to brothers, 11/26/72, JCBL.

126 "a confederacy of smugglers": Richard Oswald to Lord Dartmouth, 2/9/75, in Schlesinger, *The Colonial Merchants*, 59.

6. ANNA

Page

127 "She collapsed": Thompson, *Moses Brown*, 73.

127 "several fitts": James Angell to Moses Brown, 9/16/65, RIHS.

127 forced to curtail his travels: Moses Brown to "Dear Sir," 10/20/67, RIHS.

127 Obadiah was all but lame: Thompson, op. cit., 88.

127 Joseph Brown . . . married his first cousin: *Chad Brown Memorial*, 33.

128 "an English gentleman of fortune": Ibid., 37.

128 an easy course of polite manners: Augustine Jones describes the "rules" of the household in "Moses Brown: His Life and Services," an address delivered to the Rhode Island Historical Society in October 1892. Jones was an orthodox Quaker and sometime historian who became headmaster at the Moses Brown School in Providence.

129 "Nature must be dissolved": Moses Brown to brothers, September 1772, quoted in Thompson, op. cit., 74.

129 Moses began attending: Thompson, op. cit., 74.

129 "There is time and space": From *Life and Recollections of John Howland*, quoted in Guild, *Brown University*, 248.

129 "my brothers, mother and only sister": Moses to William Wilson, 8/18/73, RIHS.

130 "I have need of every aid": Moses Brown to James Emlen, 8/3/73, RIHS.

130 "I saw my slaves with my spiritual eyes": This quote is attributed to Moses Brown and has been widely reproduced, but without a specific source. It turns up prominently in Augustine Jones, *Moses Brown*.

131 Pero was hit in the back of the head: Jabez Bowen to Moses Brown, 9/21/70, RIHS.

131 "My father during his youth": op. cit. Brown, *The Life of William J. Brown*.

132 "After the most deliberate consideration": Moses to "Dear Brothers," 8/27/73, RIHS.

132 "Dear brothers": Thompson, *Moses Brown*, 79.

133 Moses "has removed": Hedges, *Browns of Providence*, 18.

133 "I am sensible": Mary Brown deed of manumission, 11/4/73 (recorded 11/16/73), Providence City Hall.

133 "Whereas I am clearly convinced": Scene described in Thompson, *Moses Brown*, 82. Manumission recorded 11/12/73, in probate records, Providence City Hall.

134 "We cannot go the length of those Protestants": Robert Barclay, *Barclay's Apology in Plain English* (Albertis, PA, 1967), 46.

135 *The Selling of Joseph*: Samuel Sewall, *The Selling of Joseph: A Memorial* (Boston, 1700). On Sewall owning slaves, see Lawrence W. Towner, "The Sewall-Saffin Dialogue on Slavery," *William and Mary Quarterly* XXI, no. 1 (January 1964): 40.

136 "Cowardly and cruel": Towner, "The Sewall-Saffin Dialogue."

136 "frowns and hard words": Arthur Zilversmit, *The First Emancipation: The Abolition of Slavery in the North* (Chicago, 1967), 60.

136 efforts to limit or ban the slave trade: W. E. B. Du Bois, *The Suppression of the African Slave-Trade to the United States of America, 1638–1870* (New York, 1970 [1896]), 27–39.

136 "let them go free": Thomas E. Drake, *Quakers and Slavery in America* (New Haven, 1950), 6.

137 "perpetual slavery is an aggravation": Ibid., 13.

137 Quaker merchants in Philadelphia: William J. Frost, "The Origins of the Quaker Crusade Against Slavery: A Review of Recent Literature," *Quaker History* LXII, no. 1 (spring 1978): 42.

137 Quakers there were fearful of offending: Sydney V. James, *A People Among Peoples: Quaker Benevolence in Eighteenth-Century America* (Cambridge, 1963), 119.

137 Lay was publicly disowned: Drake, *Quakers and Slavery*, 45.

138 the New England Yearly Meeting was confronted: Ibid., 31.

138 that admonition was expanded: Ibid., 50.

138 "I saw in these southern provinces": Ibid., 53.

139 The response was electric: Ibid., 62.

139 "We fervently warn": Gummere, *The Journal and Essays of John Woolman*, 66.

139 "deep exercises": Caroline Hazard, *Thomas Hazard Son of Robt Call'd College Tom: A Study of Life in Narragansett in the XVIIIth Century* (Cambridge, 1893), 168.

139 a spate of manumissions: Kenneth L. Carroll, "Religious Influences on the Manumission of Slaves in Caroline, Dorchester and Talbot Counties," *Maryland Historical Magazine* LVI (June 1961): 176.

140 scattered reports of Quaker manumissions: Herbert Aptheker, "The Quakers and Negro Slavery," *Journal of Negro History* XXV (January 1940): 331.

140 The manumissions induced by Woolman: Frost, "Origins of the Quaker Crusade," 45n.

140 Tom Hazard . . . refused to accept possession: Hazard, *College Tom*, 51.

140 the Yearly Meeting directed: Zilversmit, *The First Emancipation*, 78.

140 virtually unprecedented in Rhode Island: A comprehensive survey of deeds recorded in eighteenth-century Rhode Island found Moses Brown's to be the first instance of multiple manumissions. The survey was made by Austin Meredith; his results are posted at www.kouroo.info/general/Manumission.pdf.

140 the Quakers had turned inward: Margaret H. Bacon, *The Quiet Rebels* (New York, 1969), 4.

141 Montesquieu in France and the Scot jurist George Wallace: David Brion Davis, "New Sidelights on Early Antislavery Radicalism," in Paul Finkelman, ed., *Articles on American Slavery* (New York, 1989), XIV:105.

141 "We have in common": David Brion Davis, *The Problem of Slavery in the Age of Revolution, 1770–1823* (Oxford, 1999), 276.

141 slavery was often more intimate: John Wood Sweet, *Bodies Politic: Negotiating Race in the American North, 1730–1830* (Baltimore, 2003), 62.

141 "my Negro man Jeffrey": Arthur E. Wilson, *Weybosset Bridge in Providence Plantations, 1700–1790* (Boston, 1947), 228.

142 "the Testimony of Stephen Hopkins' denial": Minutes, Monthly Men's Meeting, New England Society of Friends, in RIHS.

142 he continued to worship: Drake, *Quakers and Slavery*, 79.

143 a town meeting, called by warrant: *RICR* VII:272.

143 the metaphor had become ubiquitous: See F. Nwabueze Okoye, "Chattel Slavery as the Nightmare of the American Revolutionaries," *William and Mary Quarterly* XXXVII, no. 1 (January 1980): 3.

144 "the present disposition of people": Nicholas Brown to Keen Osborn, 11/30/74, quoted in Sweet, *Bodies Politic*, 244.

144 Moses sat down with Stephen Hopkins: William D. Johnston, "Slavery in Rhode Island, 1755–1776," *Rhode Island History* (RIHS, 1894), 132.

144 "Whereas the inhabitants of America": *RICR*, VII:251.

145 It was a time of anticipation: Moses Brown to William Wilson, 3/22/74, RIHS.

145 "repugnant to the first impressions": Patrick Henry to Anthony Benezet, copy in Moses Brown papers, RIHS.

145 he had left too soon: Moses Brown to William Wilson, 3/22/74.

146 Thus the colony united: Lovejoy, *Politics,* 169. See also Patrick C. Conley, *First in War, Last in Peace: Rhode Island and the Constitution, 1786–1790* (Providence, 1987), 8.

146 "remove as far as may be the evil practice": Caleb Greene Deed of Manumission (Moses Brown and Job Scott, witnesses), sworn 12/15/74; recorded 5/13/78, Providence City Hall.

146 "there is no getting possession of them": Nicholas Brown to Keen Osborn, 11/30/74, JCBI. (I am indebted to John Wood Sweet for alerting me to this document and providing me a transcript.)

147 to promote his cause in print: Thompson, *Moses Brown,* 99; Sweet, *Bodies Politic,* 245.

147 "all the lawyers of principal note": Nicholas Brown to Keen Osborn, 11/30/74.

147 "a Negro boy": Hedges, *Browns of Providence,* 186.

147 "Orin Briggs" was John's code word: Leonard Stewart Smith Jr., ed., *The Gaspee Affair: Prelude to a Tea Party* (Narragansett, 1972).

148 "I am not without hope": Thomas Arnold to Moses Brown, 9/8/74, RIHS.

148 "lobbying by Anthony Benezet": Zilversmit, *The First Emancipation,* 97.

148 "We will neither import nor purchase": *Journals of the Continental Congress,* 77.

149 "poor Africans": Thompson, *Moses Brown,* 80; see also Moses Brown, letter to unknown, 11/24/74; John Pemberton to Moses Brown, 12/24/74; John Pemberton to Moses Brown, 12/26/74, in RIHS.

7. CAPTURE AND RELEASE

This chapter is based in the main on the series of articles "The Patrol of Narragansett Bay (1774–76) by HMS *Rose,* Captain James Wallace," which consist primarily of letters by John and Moses Brown, and by Captain Wallace and other British authorities, compiled and transcribed by William G. Roelker. The articles were written and annotated by Clarkson Collins III, and published in *Rhode Island History* in six parts, beginning in volume VII no. 1 (January 1948), and continuing through volume IX no. 2 (April 1950). A final installment, under the title "John Brown's Attempt at Conciliation with the British," consisting of a last exchange of letters between John and Moses, and of John's speech to the General Assembly, was published in vol. X no. 2 (April 1951).

Page

150 General Assembly met: Lovejoy, *Rhode Island Politics,* 181; *RICR,* VII:310.

151 "Such a measure": Ibid., VII:311.

151 seventy-five cadets: Elkanah Watson, *Men and Times of the Revolution, or, Memoirs of Elkanah Watson* (New York, 1856) 19.

152 Wallace took note: Hope S. Rider, *Valour Fore & Aft: Being the Adventures of America's First Naval Vessel* (Annapolis, 1978), 9.

153 Captain Wallace knew: Ibid.

154 "I was from four o'clock": Quoted ibid, 13.

154 "impossible for our forces": James Angell to the Massachusetts Congress, 4/28/75, in Peter Force, ed., *American Archives,* 4th ed., II:431.

156 Elkanah Watson: Watson, *Men and Times,* 21.

LIBERTY, 1775

Page

169 Moses pursued this remedial legislation: The campaign is described in Thompson, *Moses Brown*, 102; the treatise "Observations and Historical Remarks upon the Slave Trade," n.d., is on file at the RIHS.

171 a separate position paper: Moses Brown, "Notes on Manumission," n.d., RIHS.

171 "that no instructions be given": Town Meeting Records, Providence City Hall.

171 another slap at the abolitionists: Johnston, "Slavery in Rhode Island," 133.

172 John Adams considered it too "divisive": Zilversmit, *The First Emancipation*, 111.

172 Quakers in New Jersey: Ibid., 91.

172 "Rights of British America": Reproduced in Merrill Peterson, ed., *The Portable Thomas Jefferson* (New York, 1985), 14.

172 Duties on slaves: Darold Wax, "Negro Import Duties in Colonial Virginia," in Paul Finkelman, ed., *Articles on American Slavery*, vol. III, *Colonial Southern Slavery* (New York, 1977), 435.

172 Jefferson ignored the rhetoric of liberty: John Chester Miller, *The Wolf by the Ears: Thomas Jefferson and Slavery* (New York, 1977), 12–21.

173 a diabolical scheme for emancipation: Ari Helo and Peter Onuf, "Jefferson, Morality, and the Problem of Slavery," *William and Mary Quarterly* LX, no. 3 (July 2003): 585.

173 fifty thousand slaves deserted their masters: John Hope Franklin, "The North, the South, and the American Revolution, in Paul Finkelman, ed., *Articles on American Slavery*, vol. IV, *Slavery, Revolutionary America, and the New Nation* (New York, 1989), 20.

173 he wrote Hopkins an impassioned letter: Foster, *Stephen Hopkins*, II:247

173 "The gun and bayonet alone" Edwin M. Stone. *Life and Recollections of John Howland* (Providence, 1857) p. 199

8. MOSES AT WAR

Page

174 Moses Brown rode north: The following account is derived from two sources, both by the hand of Moses Brown. One is his diary of the expedition to distribute aid in Boston, reproduced in Mack Thompson, "Moses Brown's 'Journey,' " "Moses Brown's 'Journey to Distribute Donations 12th Month 1775,' " in *Rhode Island History* XV, no. 4 (October 1956), 97. The other is a letter, Moses Brown to William Wilson, 1/2/76, published in "An Unwritten Chapter in the History of the Siege of Boston," *Pennsylvania History*.

176 "Whatever bustlings or troubles": Quotations from Rufus M. Jones, *Quakers in the American Colonies* (New York, 1962), 563.

176 "vain imaginations": Moses Brown to Dorcas Earl, 6/27/75, RIHS.

177 It was not a novel idea: *RICR*, VII:249, 284.

177 Second Continental Congress explicitly recommended: Arthur J. Mekeel, "New England Quakers and Military Service in the American Revolution," in Howard Brinton, ed., *Children of Light: In Honor of Rufus M. Jones* (New York, 1938), 245.

177 leaders . . . were persistent: Quotations from Mack Thompson.

177 Quakers at Philadelphia had begun to come around: Israel Pemberton to Moses Brown, 6/7/75, RIHS.

179 three thousand troops quartered in Providence: Nancy Fisher Chudacoff, "The Revolution and the Town: Providence 1775–1783," *Rhode Island History* XXXV no. 3 (August 1976): 71.

179 "Strange to tell": Quotations from Manning and Sullivan, ibid.

180 "you have often been the means": Mary Westrand to Moses Brown, c. 1770, RIHS.

180 "Whilst thou are, I hope, usefully employed": Ezekiel Burr to Moses Brown, 1/21/77, RIHS.

180 The crisis was finally relieved: Chudacoff, op. cit.

180 residents of Aquidneck abandoned the island: Bridenbaugh, *Cities in Revolt*, 324.

180 "The great distress of the poor in this town": Philip Wanton to Moses Brown 1/24/76; Marie Callender to Moses Brown, 1/24/76, RIHS.

181 "generous offer": Marie Callender to Moses Brown, 2/7/76, RIHS.

181 "I am at times jealous over myself": Moses Brown to William Wilson, 6/21/76, RIHS.

182 "Debt is the pretended occasion": Joseph Alpin to Moses Brown, 7/19/75, RIHS.

182 The John Smith involved: Charles William Farnum, "John Smith, the Miller, of Providence, Rhode Island, Some of his Descendants," *Rhode Island History* XXI, no. 3 (July 1962): 95; see also John Fitzhugh Millar, *Building Early American Warships: The Journal of the Rhode Island Committee for Constructing the Continental Frigates Providence & Warren 1775–1777* (Williamsburg, VA, 1988), p. 156.

182 "Smith's still holding him is illegal": Thomas Robinson to Moses Brown, 5/23/76, RIHS.

182 The new law: Sweet, *Bodies Politic*, 248.

182 the case of Priamus: John Pemberton to Moses Brown, 8/11/81; Thomas Hazard to Moses, 9/8/81; Thomas Robinson to Moses, 9/8/81, all in RIHS. Also see Hazard, *College Tom*, 183; Sweet, *Bodies Politic*, 246.

183 Moses described their case: Moses Brown to Theodore Foster, 9/3/78, RIHS.

183 "your noble and distinguished character": John Quamine to Moses Brown, 6/5/76, quoted in Thompson, *Moses Brown*, 105.

183 traveling as far as New Hampshire: The New Hampshire manumissions are cited in Drake, *Quakers and Slavery*, 80 n. 32.

184 one of the great experiments with emancipation: Lorenzo J. Greene, "Some Observations on the Black Regiment of Rhode Island in the American Revolution," *Journal of Negro History* XXXVII, no. 2 (1952), 142.

184 Joseph Brown and Nicholas Power wanted Prince: Sidney S. Rider, "An Historical Inquiry into the Attempt to Raise a Regiment of Slaves," *Rhode Island Historical Tracts* no. 10 (Providence, 1880), 58.

185 Prime Brown . . . had befriended Cesar Lyndon: The story of Little Cesar and Prime Brown is recounted in Sweet, 159–60.

185 Mary stayed at his home: Moses to Unknown, 11/24/74, RIHS.

185 Arnold was courting Mary Brown: Hazelton, *Let Freedom Ring*, p. 40.

186 Arnold's decision caused a lasting breach: Franklin S. Coyle, *Welcome Arnold, Providence Merchant* (Master's thesis, Brown University, 1972), p. 9.

186 they were married: Thompson, *Moses Brown*, 168.

186 a young boarder named Job Scott: Job Scott, *Journal of the Life, Travel and Gospel Labors of That Faithful Servant and Minister of Christ, Job Scott* (New York, 1797), 27–29.

186 "I find his company very agreeable": Moses to William Wilson, 5/21/74, RIHS.

187 Jemima Wilkinson: Herbert A. Wisbey Jr., *Pioneer Prophetess* (Ithaca, NY, 1964); see also J. Bruce Whyte, "The Public and Universal Friend," *Rhode Island History* XXVI, no. 4 (October 1967): 103.

187 Elisha Brown, who attended several of her meetings: Elisha Brown to Moses Brown, 1/4/79, RIHS.

188 they refused to comply with official requisitions: Refusals enumerated in Mekeel, "New England Quakers and Military Service," 245; Quaker protest quoted in Chudacoff, "The Revolution and the Town."

188 On the first of May 1776: Glenn LaFantasie, "Act for All Reasons: Revolutionary Politics and May 4, 1776," *Rhode Island History* XXV, no. 2 (May 1976): 39.

189 establish a noncombatant status: Margaret E. Hirst, *The Quakers in Peace and War: An Account of Their Peace Principles and Practice* (New York, 1923), 331.

189 "I call upon you Moses": Jabez Bowen to Moses Brown, 6/13/78, RIHS.

189 "the Quakers remained intransigent: Mekeel, "New England Quakers and Military Service."

190 "the honors of applause": Moses Brown to John Hancock, 10/3/78, RIHS.

190 "Render unto Caesar": Anonymous to Moses Brown, 7/16/75, RIHS.

191 "I fear a desire": Timothy Davis to Moses Brown, 4/22/76, RIHS.

191 Davis had threatened Quaker unity: The contacts between Moses Brown and Timothy Davis are treated in Mekeel, "Free Quaker Movement in New England During the American Revolution," Friends' Historical Association *Bulletin* XXVII, no. 27 (1938): 72; and Thompson, *Moses Brown*, 136.

192 "palsy and apoplexy": Moses Brown to John Pemberton, 12/22/80, RIHS.

192 "atonia, or relaxation of the nerves": Abraham Choock to Moses Brown, 1/14/81, RIHS.

193 "almost constant infirmities of writing": Moses Brown to William Wilson, 4/20/83, RIHS.

193 *nomen est omen:* For consideration of nominative determinism, see Sam Roberts, "Ms. Rose, by Any Other Name, Might Still Be a Florist," *New York Times*, 3/27/05, D-7.

193 Pemberton finally demurred: James Pemberton to Moses Brown, 5/21/84, RIHS.

193 he helped steer the Meeting for Sufferings: Sydney V. James, *A People Among Peoples: Quaker Benevolence in Eighteenth-Century America* (Cambridge, 1963), 250.

9. JOHN AT WAR

Page

195 "scourge the rebels": Vice Adm. Samuel Graves to Capt. James Wallace, in William Bell Clark, ed., *Naval Documents of the American Revolution* (Washington, 1964–94), II:881.

195 his troops burned homes and shot the occupants: Nicholas Brown to John Brown, 12/11/75, ibid., III:54.

195 an hourlong cannonade: *New York Gazette*, 10/23/75, ibid., II:420.

196 John Brown invited the entire regiment: Nathanael Greene to James Mitchell Varnum, 6/2/75, in Richard K. Showman, ed., *The Papers of Nathanael Greene* (Chapel Hill, NC, 1976), I:83.

196 John was appointed: Appointments of John Brown, Zephaniah Andrews, in Force, ed., *American Archives*, 4th ed., II:607.

196 Hopkins was named to command: Edward Field, *Esek Hopkins: Commander in Chief of the Continental Navy During the American Revolution 1775 to 1778* (Providence, 1898), 40, 60.

196 "Our want of powder": Washington quoted in Hedges, *Browns of Providence*, 219.

196 50 percent higher: Washington contracted for powder at four shillings per pound in October. George Washington to John Fisk, 10/24/75, in Force, ed., *American Archives*, 4th, ed. III:1167.

196 "most exorbitant": Stephen Moylan to John Brown, 11/27/75, Ibid., III:1688.

196 the faithful Elkanah Watson: Watson, *Men and Times of the Revolution*, 20.

196 John capitalized: Exception to the Continental Association described in John Brown to Rhode Island General Assembly, 11/29/75, Rhode Island State Archives.

197 the mainstay of John's business had been shut down: Nicholas Brown to Captain Sylvanus Jenckes, 9/25/75, in Clark, ed., *Naval Documents*, II:202.

198 creation of a Continental Navy: The birth of the American navy is described in William Fowler Jr., *Rebels Under Sail: The American Navy During the American Revolution* (New York, 1976) 39–71.

198 "the most wild, visionary, mad project": John Adams quoted in Clark, ed., *Naval Documents*, II:308.

198 "Governor Hopkins . . . kept us all alive": Lyman Butterfield, ed., *Diary and Autobiography of John Adams* (Cambridge, MA, 1961), III:349.

198 "an antiquated figure": Nathan Miller, *Sea of Glory: A Naval History of the American Revolution* (Annapolis, 1992), 56.

199 John had joined the team: Contract in Clark, ed., *Naval Documents*, III:879.

200 "A lucky affair": Hedges, *Browns of Providence*, 222.

200 It was a convivial group: Biographical notes on committee members can be found in Millar, *Early American Worships*, p. 152–158. See also Journal of the Committee Appointed to Build Two Continental Frigates in Rhode Island, in Clark, ed., *Naval Documents*, III:677.

201 working "constantly": Clark, ed., *Naval Documents*, III:766.

201 the deal they struck with the assembly: *RICR*, VII:417.

201 a second contract: Clark, ed., *Naval Documents*, III:879, 1153.

201 the first of three trading vessels: Hedges, *Browns of Providence*, 232.

201 "most profitable business": Clark, ed., *Naval Documents*, III:54.

202 The Naval Board was unmoved: Ibid., III:1099, 1132.

202 "letters of marque": *RICR*, VII:481.

202 Nicholas and John Brown had carted: Hedges, *Browns of Providence*, 274.

202 "no time ought to be lost": Clark, ed., *Naval Documents*, V:1026.

202 Providence celebrated: Force, *American Archives*, 5th ed., II:582.

203 bounty enough to enrich: *Providence Gazette*, 8/17/76, in Clark, ed., *Naval Documents*, VI:214.

203 "Come all you young fellows": Ibid., VI:116.

203 the Browns heeded their private interest: Richman, *Rhode Island*, 200.

204 she keeled over: Journal of the Committee Appointed to Build Two Continental Frigates, RIHS.

204 "rotten rigging supplied by John Brown": Millar, *Building Early American Warships*, p. 18.

204 Langdon was a proud and forceful character: John Langdon is profiled at SeacoastNH.com.

204 "We can launch at any time": John Langdon to William Whipple, 5/12/76, in Clark, ed., *Naval Documents*, V:62.

205 Langdon . . . visited Providence: Fowler, *Rebels Under Sail*, 242.

205 Langdon knew better: John Langdon to Josiah Bartlett, 9/14/76, in Clark, ed., *Naval Documents*, VI:815.

205 "disgust" among officers: James Warren to John Adams, 8/11/76, ibid., VI:143.

206 The deal had changed again: John Langdon to Josiah Bartlett, 9/14/76.

206 stern letters to the committee at Providence: Naval Committee to Providence Committee, Stephen Hopkins, 10/9/76, in Force, ed., *American Archives*, 5th, ser. II:954.

207 the entire group resigned: Staples, *Annals of the Town of Providence*, 268; Richman, *Rhode Island*, 220; Field, *Esek Hopkins*, 148. See also Miller, *Sea of Glory*, 127.

208 "I am at a loss": Field, *Esek Hopkins*, 167.

208 Cooke agreed to Hopkins's plan: Richman, *Rhode Island*, 220; Esek Hopkins to Naval Committee, 12/10/76, in Clark, ed., *Naval Documents*, VII:435.

209 appearing personally before the sheriff: The Richard Marvin affair is detailed in Field, *Esek Hopkins*, 220.

209 "A few minutes before he expired": Passage from "Brown Bible," Norman Herreschoff collection, courtesy HALB.

210 "O how thankful we ought to be": John Brown to James Brown, 6/13/79, RIHS.

210 "Permit me to caution you": John Brown to Sally Brown, 9/30/81, RIHS.

210 "Your marr and sister": John Brown to James Brown, 2/18/82, RIHS.

211 John Brown was in the thick of all this activity: Otis G. Hammond, ed., *Letters and Papers of Major-General John Sullivan, Continental Army* (Concord, NH, 1931), II:183.

213 "I cannot help but feel mortified": Showman, ed., *Papers of Nathanael Greene*, II:513.

213 "Disappointed persons will always": Hammond, ed., *Major General John Sullivan*, II:329.

213 John was still making amends: Ibid., II:523.

213 John bet one of his ship captains: "John Brown Bets a Hat," *Rhode Island History* XII no. 2 (April 1953), 63.

213 John was a member of the welcoming committee: Staples, *Annals of Providence*, 261.

214 "Our house, wharf, stable and lot": John Brown to James Brown, 11/11/82, RIHS.

LIBERTY, 1782

Page

215 citizens in Philadelphia tarred a dog: Edmund Cody Burnett, ed., *Letters of the Continental Congress* (Washington, 1906), VI:79 n. 3.

215 "The time for paying the army": Jesse Root to Gov. John Trumbull, 1/8/81, ibid., V:520.

215 "firm league of friendship": Articles of Confederation reproduced by the Avalon Project at Yale Law School, www.yale.edu/lawweb/avalon/artconf.htm.

216 Morris proved energetic: Frederick Wagner, *Robert Morris: Audacious Patriot* (New York, 1976), 86.

216 eager to please: Henry Marchant, onetime Rhode Island attorney general, described Howell as "unsteady . . . too much led by motives of present applaudits." Marchant to Alexander Hamilton, 9/12/93, in Gaillard Hunt, "Office Seeking During Washington's Administration," *American Historical Review* I (January 1895), 270.

217 He delivered a jarring, biting critique: Howell's campaign against the Impost is detailed in Irwin H. Polishook, *Rhode Island and the Union: 1774–1795* (Evanston, IL, 1969), 53–80.

218 John Brown continued to foment: William R. Staples, *Rhode Island in the Continental Congress* (Providence, 1870), 379.

218 all their energy focused on little Rhode Island: Washington letter, Congressional delegation referenced in Joseph Brown to David Howell, 7/13/82, John Hay Library, Brown University.

218 "Thus ended the long and much-talked about 5 percent duty": John Brown to James Brown, 11/3/82, RIHS.

218 "I am more and more surprised": Ezekiel Cornell to Gen. Benjamin Lincoln, 11/19/82, in Burnett, *Letters of Congress*, VI:542 n. 2.

219 a second delegation: The debates in Congress on how to answer Rhode Island's vote against the Impost are detailed in the headnotes to a Robert Morris letter to Thomas Paine in John Catanzariti and E. James Ferguson, eds., *The Papers of Robert Morris*, vol. VII, November 1, 1782–May 4, 1783 (Pittsburgh, 1973), 83.

220 he had published two rejoinders: Dates of publication and text for Tom Paine's "Letters to Rhode Island" are in Philip S. Foner, *The Complete Writings of Thomas Paine* (New York, 1945), II:333–66.

222 more than anyone else in Rhode Island: Hedges, *Browns of Providence*, I:322.

10. EQUAL RIGHTS

Page

224 "give orders to the captain": Moses Brown to Clark & Nightingale, 8/26/83, RIHS.

224 Moses' appeal had no effect: *Providence* to Africa, in Donnan, *Documents*, III:334 n. 2.

225 "more daily expected": Report from the *Charleston Evening Gazette*, 10/25/85, cited in Elizabeth Donnan, "The New England Slave Trade After the Revolution," *New England Quarterly* III, no. 2 (April 1930): 260.

225 Boudinot . . . met personally with Benezet: Drake, *Quakers and Slavery*, 94.

225 a compromise measure: Paul Smith, ed., *Letters of the Delegates to Congress* (Washington, 1980), XXI:266, n. 3.

226 as the lawmakers made explicit: Du Bois, *The Suppression of the African Slave-Trade*, 51.

226 Moses drew up a list: Moses' legislative campaign is described in Thompson, *Moses Brown*, 175–87.

227 "The conduct of Christians": Moses Brown to James Manning, Enos Hitchcock, and Samuel Hopkins, 1/26/84, RIHS.

227 at the Providence town meeting: Moses Brown to Samuel Hopkins, 2/5/84, RIHS.

228 "politically dead": John Brown to Zephania Andrews, quoted in Thompson, *Moses Brown*, 184.

228 John turned the tables: The best authority on John's performance is Moses Brown, who took detailed notes on the General Assembly debate. Undated ms., RIHS.

229 slavery was widespread in Africa: For a summary of contemporary scholarship, see Paul E. Lovejoy, "The Impact of the Atlantic Slave Trade on Africa: A Review of the Literature," *Journal of African History* XXX (1989): 365.

229 *Slavery Not Forbidden*: Richard Nisbet quoted in Larry E. Tise, *Proslavery: A History of the Defense of Slavery in America 1701–1840* (Athens, GA, 1987), 28.

230 John produced chalk and a blackboard: Hazelton, *Let Freedom Ring*, 79.

230 remained in limbo for decades: Zilversmit, *The First Emancipation*, 116.

231 Hopkins went further than any of his contemporaries: The best studies of Samuel Hopkins are David S. Lovejoy, "Samuel Hopkins: Religion, Slavery, and the Revolution," *New England Quarterly* XL, no. 2 (June 1967): 227; and Joseph A. Conforti, "Samuel Hopkins and the New Divinity: Theology, Ethics and Social Reform in Eighteenth-Century New England," *William and Mary Quarterly* XXXIV (October 1977): 572.

232 "the influence of the mercantile interest": Moses Brown to Samuel Hopkins, 3/3/84; RIHS.

232 "I am apt to sink": Samuel Hopkins to Moses Brown, 4/29/84, in Donnan, *Documents*, III:335.

232 Moses gently demurred: Moses Brown to Samuel Hopkins, 5/14/84, RIHS.

233 designed by Timothy Pickering: For Pickering see Garry Wills, *"Negro President:" Jefferson and the Slave Power* (Boston, 2003), 19.

233 "the total exclusion of slavery": Jay A. Barrett, *Evolution of the Ordinance of 1787* (New York, 1891, 1971), 8.

233 it fell to Howell: For Howell's primary role see Robert J. Berkhofer Jr., "Jefferson, the Ordinance of 1784, and the Origins of the American Territorial System", *William and Mary Quarterly* XXIX, no. 2 (April 1972), 231.

234 "To introduce [slaves]": Pickering quoted in Wills, *"Negro President,"* 22.

234 the measure failed: Barrett, op. cit., 25.

234 "Has General Washington freed his Negroes": Moses Brown to David Howell, 5/3/84, RIHS.

235 Washington replied with evident enthusiasm: Henry Wiencek, *An Imperfect God: Washington, His Slaves, and the Creation of America* (New York, 2003), p. 260–63.

235 another visitor: Dorothy Twohig, " 'That Species of Property': Washington's Role in the Controversy over Slavery," http://gwpapers.virginia.edu/articles/slavery/index.html.

235 "a paradox to posterity": Moses Brown to David Howell, 5/3/84.

236 explicit instructions: *RICR*, X:42, 56.

236 "a vagabond, strolling, contemptible crew": John Francis Mercer to Jacob Read, 9/23/84, in Burnett, ed., *Letters of the Continental Congress*, VII:591.

236 John spurned his appointment: David Howell to Gov. Jabez Bowen, 6/24/85, ibid., VII:149 n. 5.

236 compensation for wartime damages: Massachusetts delegates to Gov. James Bowdoin, 9/28/85, ibid., VIII:223, n. 2.

236 "the politics of Rhode Island are *damned*": (emphasis in original) James Manning to Nicholas Brown, 7/15/86, in Smith, ed., *Letters of the Delegates*, XXIV:400.

237 They were a mark of distinction: By 1790 just five men in Providence owned carriages. Hope Kane and W. G. Roelker, "The Founding of Providence Bank," *Rhode Island Historical Society Collections* XXXIV:116 n. 8.

237 five of his male slaves escaped: *Providence Gazette*, 3/14/89.

237 "turn your thoughts to business": John Brown to James Brown, 11/26/82, HALB.

237 spending lavishly and keeping loose company: John Brown to James Brown, 10/5/82; 1/21/83; HALB.

238 "fills my eyes with rivers": John Brown to John Francis, 11/1/85, RIHS.

238 "Abby and your mama": Unknown to Sarah Brown, 4/16/86, HALB.

238 John offered to match: R. A. Guild, *Early History of Brown University*, 242.

238 "no man can be thought of": Nicholas Brown, John Jenckes, John Brown to Moses Brown, 4/19/85, RIHS.

239 "We are taught": John Brown to "Dear Children," 12/3/85, HALB.

239 that voyage met with disaster: Diary of John Francis, 10/9/86, HALB.

241 Cato was promised his freedom: Cato's predicament is discussed in Joseph DelaPlaine to Moses Brown, 9/9/84, and Moses Brown to Joseph DelaPlaine, 10/20/84, RIHS.

241 "but few and those mostly employed": Moses Brown to Joseph DelaPlaine, 5/29/86.

241 public opinion was turning his way: Methodists, Baptists in Davis, *Slavery in the Age of Revolution*, 26.

241 "the testimony gains ground for freedom": Moses Brown to Samuel Hopkins, 3/2/85, RIHS.

241 "the trade is carried on": Moses Brown to Thomas Wagstaffe, 12/29/85, RIHS.

242 "is become a national sin": Samuel Hopkins, "The Slave Trade and Slavery," in Hopkins, *Timely Articles on Slavery* (Boston, 1854), 613.

244 "the oddest shaped character": Sherman was described by William Pierce, delegate from Georgia. Pierce's character sketches of his fellow delegates are available at www.laughtergenealogy.com/bin/histprof/misc/pierce.html.

244 "The abolition of slavery": Quotes from the Constitutional Convention, including those from Finkelman, derive from notes made by James Madison. They can be found online at www.sagehistory.net.

245 "I am hurt by the doings of the convention": Stephen Hopkins to Moses Brown, 10/22/87.

245 Hopkins's final days: Dorothy G. McCarten, *Stephen Hopkins*, Typescript (RIHS, 1975) p. 41.

245 he settled accounts with his slaves: Foster, *Stephen Hopkins*, II:161.

245 "My heart has been often pained": William Rotch to Moses Brown, 11/8/87, RIHS.

246 "instead of extending humanity": Moses Brown to unknown, 11/13/87, RIHS.

246 The provision barring slavery was tacked on: Barrett, op. cit., 76.

246 opposition to the clause had evaporated: Staughton Lynd, "The Compromise of 1787," *Journal of Negro History* LXXXI, no. 2 (June 1966): 225.

246 "I moved the article": Barrett, op. cit., 77.

247 "I shall not be any more concerned": John Brown to Moses Brown, 8/16/87, RIHS.

247 "I don't expect his leaving": Moses Brown to Samuel Emlin, 11/6/87, RIHS.

247 "That wicked set of men": Samuel Hopkins to Moses Brown, 8/13/87, RIHS.

248 he was no aristocrat: Collins background in John P. Kaminski, "Political Sacrifice and Demise—John Collins and Jonathan J. Hazard 1786–1790," *Rhode Island History* XXXV, no. 3 (August 1976): 9.

248 Collins embraced the Quaker bill: Thompson, *Moses Brown*, 182. For details of the assembly hearing, see Moses Brown to Samuel Emlen, 11/6/87, RIHS.

248 no symbolic victory: See text, "An Act to Prevent the Slave Trade," *RICR*, X:262.

249 "Is it not extraordinary": Samuel Hopkins to Levi Hart, 11/27/87, in Donnan, *Documents*, III:344 n. 2.

11. THE SOCIETY

Page

250 Sterry was a clever and resourceful man: Background on Cyprian Sterry can be found at www.zipworld.com.au/~rsterry/gen/wbsmith/notes; note I0098.

250 Sterry had applied for benediction: Moses Brown to Samuel Hopkins, 10/24/88, RIHS.

251 The Massachusetts courts: William M. Wiecek, *The Sources of Antislavery Constitutionalism in America, 1760–1848* (Ithaca, 1973), p. 47.

251 slave ships were departing: Donnan, "New England Slave Trade," 260.

251 free Africans were being kidnapped: Peter Thatcher to Moses Brown, 9/21/87, RIHS.

251 The state Senate declined at first: William Rotch to Moses Brown, 12/1/87, RIHS.

251 Moses traveled again to Boston: Moses Brown to the Massachusetts Committee, 11/1/87, RIHS; also Moses Brown to Ed Prior, 4/12/88, RIHS.

251 a notorious kidnapping: Zilversmit, *The First Emancipation*, 157.

251 Massachusetts became the second: Du Bois, *Suppression of the African Slave-Trade*, 33.

251 "an honest, sensible man": Samuel Hopkins to Levi Hart, 11/27/87, in Donnan, *Documents*, III:335 n. 1.

252 "will be carried out in ship-loads": Jonathan Edwards to Moses Brown, 10/20/88, ibid., III:345.

252 pronounced the new bill a credit: Moses Brown to Jonathan Edwards, 12/16/88, RIHS. For more on Moses' travels to support abolitionist legislation, see James Francis Reilly, "Moses Brown and Rhode Island Antislavery," master's thesis (1954) on file at RIHS.

252 surveyor of streets: Thompson, *Moses Brown*, 80.

252 reroute Benefit Street and lay boundaries: William C. Pelkey, ed., *Early Records of the Town of Providence* (Providence, 1892), XVIII: 21.

252 Almy joined Moses: William Almy to New Haven in Moses Brown to William Wilson, 11/10/88, RIHS.

253 "often set down when alone": Moses Brown to Obadiah Brown, 6/20/83, RIHS.

253 "make use of this opportunity": Obadiah Brown to Moses, 6/22/85, RIHS.

253 A small school, opened at Portsmouth: Moses Brown to David Barclay, 3/19/87; see also Thompson, *Moses Brown*, 158–67.

253 Moses joined his brother Nicholas: Nicholas Brown to Moses Brown, 5/1/85, RIHS.

253 wearing a simple, homespun suit: Bulkley, *Chad Brown Memorial*, 36.

254 bounties to lure European artisans: George S. White, *Memoir of Samuel Slater, the Father of American Manufactures* (Philadelphia, 1836), 47–62.

254 British guarded their industrial secrets: Barbara M. Tucker, *Samuel Slater and the Origins of the American Textile Industry, 1790–1860* (Ithaca, 1984), 48.

254 he spent several days on the road: Hedges, *Browns of Providence*, II:161.

254 a winter of trial and error: James L. Conrad, *Entrepreneurial Objectives, Organizational Design, Technology, and the Cotton Manufactory of Almy and Brown, 1789–1797*, available online at www.h-net.org/~business/bhcweb/publications/BEHprint/v013/p0007-p0019.pdf.

254 had obtained all the . . . equipment: Paul E. Rivard, "Textile Experiments in Rhode Island 1788–1789," *Rhode Island History* XXXIII, no. 2 (May 1974): 35.

255 He hailed his captain: Hedges, *Browns of Providence*, II:18.

256 "Never were such shouts": Descriptions of the Abby Brown wedding from HAL. Brown and Richard A. Walton, *John Brown's Tract: Lost Adirondack Empire* (Canaan, NH, 1988), 37.

256 a new emission of paper money: Irwin H. Polishook examines the paper money and constitutional controversies in *Rhode Island and the Union 1774–1795* (Evanston, II, 1969), 103–29; see also Kaminski, "Political Sacrifice and Demise," 91–92.

257 the leader of the Rhode Island federalists: Hillman Metcalf Bishop remarked on the irony in "Why Rhode Island Opposed the Federal Constitution," *Rhode Island History* VIII, no. 2 (April 1949), 116. He wrote, "Since the most prominent Federalists had insisted only a few years earlier that freedom and power were opposites, they were now in a position of trying to undo the effects of their skillful propaganda against the Continental Impost."

257 a letter to the convention: Richman, *A Study in Separatism*, 250.

258 the political crisis gripping Rhode Island: The partisan protests are related in Staples, *Annals of Providence*, 328.

259 he was stymied for a time: Moses Brown to James Pemberton, 8/11/88, RIHS.

259 half a dozen slave ships: Moses Brown to Unknown, 1/27/89, RIHS.

260 "there is no more crime": John Brown writing in the *United States Chronicle*, 3/26/89.

260 John Carter . . . manumitted his two slaves: Sweet, *Bodies Politic*, 444 n. 24.

260 it was a jarring piece: *Providence Gazette*, 2/14/89.

260 "The thief in the night": *United States Chronicle*, 2/19/89.

261 The Citizen answered: *United States Chronicle*, 2/26/89.

261 Slavery was "right, just, and lawful": *Providence Gazette*, 2/28/89.

261 Moses went to the print shop: John Brown to Moses Brown, Moses Brown to John Brown, both 3/9/89, RIHS.

261 "A Friend, Though a Monitor": *Providence Gazette*, 3/7/89.

262 Howell . . . submitting a signed piece: Ibid.

262 the tale of his runaway slaves: *Providence Gazette*, 3/14/89.

263 John delved deeply into their spiritual divide: Ibid.

264 he dispensed with his pseudonym: *Providence Gazette*, 3/21/89.

264 "Monitor the Younger": *United States Chronicle*, 3/9/89.

264 "Abominable": *United States Chronicle*, 3/19/89.

265 The nature of the game had shifted: *United States Chronicle*, 3/26/89.

267 "I am pleased to find you are able to maintain": Samuel Hopkins to Moses Brown, 3/30/89, RIHS.

268 Moses warned Rotch: William Rotch to Moses Brown, 5/16/89, RIHS.

268 dumped the bayonets into the sea: Margaret H. Bacon, *The Quiet Rebels* (New York, 1969), 74.

268 Rotch wanted to make an impression: William Rotch to Moses Brown, 5/16/89, RIHS.

268 "Be careful not to tamper": Peleg Almy to Moses Brown and Oziel Wilkinson, 8/26/89, RIHS.

268 170 members: For the charter of the abolition society, as approved by the General Assembly, see *RICR*, X:382.

269 the *Hope* returned to Africa four times: Hawes, *Off Soundings*, 194. The prosecution of Gardner et al. is recounted in Hawes, 194, and in Coughtry, *Notorious Triangle*, 207–11. A contemporary account of the trial is reproduced in Donnan, *Documents*, III:352.

269 the society voted to forgo prosecution: Coughtry, *Notorious Triangle*, 211.

269 "The slave traders are more bold": Samuel Hopkins to Moses Brown, 11/18/89, RIHS.

269 D'Wolf was charged with murder: George Locke Howe, *Mount Hope: A New England Chronicle* (New York, 1959), 105.

269 a battle of wills with John Brown: The story of James Tom is told in Sweet, *Bodies Politic*, 225; see also Moses Brown to James Pemberton, 4/26/90, RIHS.

270 seeking an explanatory act: Moses Brown to James Pemberton, 7/19/91, RIHS. See also Thompson, *Moses Brown*, 201.

271 John "has an overgrown fortune": Moses Brown to William Vassal, 11/86, RIHS.

12. THE NEW REPUBLIC

Page

273 "The simplicity of her manners": Abigail Adams to Elizabeth Smith Shaw, 6/28/89, in "Mrs. Vice-President Adams Dines with Mr. John Brown and Lady," *Rhode Island History* I, no. 4 (October 1942), 97.

273 he pointedly avoided stopping: Polishook, *Rhode Island and the Union*, 208.

273 "I am really much affected": John Adams to Brown & Francis, 2/28/90, RIHS.

273 "there is still a power that reigns over all": George Churchman to Moses Brown, 7/10/88, RIHS.

274 "I was much disgusted": William Rotch to Moses Brown, 2/25/89, RIHS.

274 The idea was floated by Jabez Bowen: For the secession movement see Kaminski, "Political Sacrifice and Demise," also Polishook, *Rhode Island and the Union*, 210.

274 "the time is come": Moses Brown to Isaac Lawton, Jacob Mott, and others, 2/4/90, RIHS.

275 As reported in the next edition: Polishook, *Rhode Island and the Union*, 212.

275 "John Brown was so much gratified": Tristam Burgess, *Memoir of Welcome Arnold*, (Providence, 1873) 25; Polishook references this account.

276 The convention was set for March 1: Details of the debate over the Constitution are related in Robert C. Cotner, ed., *Theodore Foster's Minutes of the Convention* (Providence, 1929). See also Patrick T. Conley, *First in War, Last in Peace: Rhode Island and the Constitution, 1786–1790* (Providence, 1987).

276 the only one to actually lose population: Bureau of the Census, U.S. Department of Commerce.

276 Washington celebrated her return: John Williams Haley, *Washington and Rhode Island* (Providence, 1932), 36–39.

277 John offered his own recommendations: Gaillard Hunt, "Office-Seeking During Washington's Administration," *American Historical Review* I (January 1895): 280.

277 Paramount on his list was Jeremiah Olney: Hunt's edited version of John Brown's letter to Washington omits the specific reference to Olney, but John Brown's support for Olney is detailed in Fred Dalzell, "Prudence and the Golden Egg: Establishing the Federal Government in Providence," master's thesis, Brown University, December 1991.

278 "upright, impartial and faithful": Dalzell, "Prudence and the Golden Egg," 4.

278 "We are exceedingly sorry": Emphasis in the original. Quoted ibid., 7.

278 John "thought proper to slight the friendly message": Jeremiah Olney to Alexander Hamilton, 11/29/90, in Harold C. Cyrett, ed., *Papers of Alexander Hamilton* (New York, 1961), VII:168.

278 Hamilton fully concurred: Alexander Hamilton to Jeremiah Olney, 12/13/90, ibid., VII:210.

278 "contrary to what Mr. Brown informed me": Jeremiah Olney to Alexander Hamilton, 12/24/90, ibid., VII:381.

279 he could ill afford a state of open enmity: Dalzell, op. cit., 23–24.

279 "The good will of the merchants": Alexander Hamilton to Jeremiah Olney, 4/2/93, in Cyrett, ed., *Papers of Hamilton*, XIV:276.

280 Brown began agitating for a bank: Field, ed., *Rhode Island and Providence Plantations*, III:261.

280 "Without a spring to promote": John Brown to Moses Brown, 8/14/91, quoted in Hope F. Kane and W. G. Roelker, "The Founding of the Providence Bank," *Rhode Island Historical Society Collections* XXXIV: 114.

281 John knew Moses better: See John Brown to Moses Brown, 11/3/73; 9/10/74; 11/3/74; 12/4/74; 1/24/78; all in RIHS.

281 "a grait deal more": John Brown to Moses Brown, 11/3/74, RIHS.

281 Moses received several consignments: John Brown to Moses Brown, 8/18/89; Moses Brown to John Brown 1/20/90; John Brown to Moses Brown 1/25/90; RIHS.

281 John put the proposition to Moses: John Brown to Moses Brown, 8/14/91, in Kane and Roelker, "Founding of the Providence Bank."

282 a searching "apology": Moses Brown to James Pemberton, 11/2/91, RIHS.

283 "I am not to be cast into prison": Christopher Whipple to Moses Brown, 4/10/89; 4/30/89; 10/14/91; RIHS.

283 "Your brother John treats us": Champion & Dickason to Moses Brown, 11/6/89, RIHS.

283 "We are very much of opinion": Champion & Dickason to Moses Brown, 4/30/90, RIHS.

283 prevailing on his friend William Rotch: William Rotch Jr. to Moses Brown, 11/17/91, RIHS.

284 membership of the board: Kane and Roelker, "Founding of the Providence Bank."

284 Hamilton signed off: Alexander Hamilton to Jeremiah Olney, 11/10/91, in Cyrett, ed., *Papers of Hamilton*, IX:489.

284 John was already leaning on Olney: Dalzell, "Prudence and the Golden Egg," 28.

285 "Aware that a sudden order": Alexander Hamilton to Jeremiah Olney et al., 10/22/92, in Cyrett, ed., *Papers of Hamilton*, XII:605.

285 John learned of the inquiry: Olney's visit to John Brown and John's appeal to Moses are contained in John Brown to Moses Brown, 11/1/92, RIHS.

286 "the information was a misapprehension": Alexander Hamilton to Jeremiah Olney et al., 10/25/92, in Cyrett, ed., *Papers of Hamilton*, XII:619.

286 John once again had called on Moses: The episode of the bank inspection is treated in Hedges, II:192; in Thompson, 253–54; and in Hazelton, 111.

286 "very much alarmed": Petition of North Providence to the General Assembly, 3/1/92, Rhode Island State Archives.

287 The signatures attached: Petitions to the General Assembly, both in June 1792, Rhode Island State Archives.

287 Moses wrote to friends in Newport: Moses Brown to Unknown, 6/19/92, RIHS.

287 Eight years later: John Brown to James Brown, 12/29/99; 1/16/00; HALB.

288 "Thy being already engaged": Moses Brown to Samuel Slater, 12/10/89, in White, *Samuel Slater*, 73. Emphasis in the original. Mack Thompson also offers an overview of Moses Brown, Samuel Slater, and the cotton business in *Moses Brown*, 206–33.

288 by early January he was in Pawtucket: Smith Wilkinson to George White, 5/30/85, in White, *Samuel Slater*, 76.

288 that was probably unfair: Conrad, "Entrepreneurial Objectives," 10. See also Paul E. Rivard, "Textile Experiments in Rhode Island 1788–1789," *Rhode Island History* XXXIII, no. 2 (May 1974): 35.

289 The pair were wed: Field, op. cit., III:342; see also White, 102, and Thompson, 226.

289 The dismal implications . . . escaped Moses, as they did Hamilton: In his Report on Manufactures, 12/5/91, Hamilton was explicit: "Women and children are rendered more useful and the latter more early useful by manufacturing establishments." In Cyrett, ed., *Papers of Hamilton*, X:153.

290 "No encouragement has been given": Moses Brown to John Dexter, 10/15/91, ibid., IX:432–41.

290 "we mean to be managers": Moses Brown to J. Bradburn, 10/30/89, in Conrad, "Entrepreneurial Objectives," 9.

291 a new town on the Passaic River: Ron Chernow, *Alexander Hamilton* (New York, 2004), 370–88.

291 waded into the stream, and destroyed all the work: Gary Kulik, "Dams, Fish, and Farmers: Defense of Public Rights in Eighteenth Century Rhode Island," in Steven Hahn and Jonathan Prude, eds., *The Countryside in an Age of Capitalist Transformation* (Chapel Hill, 1985), 25.

291 "The mill is now destitute": Slater to Almy & Brown, 4/25/01; quoted in Tucker, *Samuel Slater*, 53.

292 "Please send some fleece": Slater to Almy & Brown, 2/19/96, quoted in James L. Conrad, "Evolution of Industrial Capitalism in Rhode Island 1790–1830," Ph. D. thesis, Brown University, 1973, 114.

292 debt to Moses: Tucker, op. cit., 55.

292 managing America's first factory workforce: Conrad, "Evolution of Industrial Capitalism," 106, 107.

292 One summer day: Ibid., 105.

292 Slater could be a tough taskmaster: Tucker, op. cit., 77, 79.

292 "You call for yarn": Slater to Almy & Brown, 11/14/91; quoted in Conrad, "Evolution of Industrial Capitalism," 107.

292 "revenues reached more than $12,000: Ibid., 142.

292 "An Ethiopian could as soon change": William Ellery to Moses Brown, 12/5/91, RIHS.

293 "not one penny of profit": Hazelton, *Let Freedom Ring*, 92.

13. MOSES GOES TO CONGRESS

Page

294 Energy for prosecutions waned: Coughtry, *Notorious Triangle*, 211–12.

295 Madison finally closed the debate: Gary B. Nash, *Race and Revolution* (Madison, WI 1990), 38–41.

295 they signaled a sense of the body: Du Bois, *The Suppression of the African Slave-Trade*, 78–80.

295 result was the Fugitive Slave Act: Wienek, *Antislavery Constitutionalism*, 98.

295 a burgeoning abolition movement also appeared to be foundering: Moses Brown's London correspondents included James Phillips, 6/21/91, 1/26/92, 2/23/93, and Thomas Wagstaffe, 6/5/92. See also Dale Porter, *The Abolition of the Slave Trade in England, 1784–1807* (New Haven, 1970), 40–89; David Brion Davis, *The Problem of Slavery in the Age of Revolution 1770–1823* (New York, 1999), 426–34.

296 Not everyone agreed: Richard S. Newman, *The Transformation of American Abolitionism: Fighting Slavery in the Early Republic* (Chapel Hill, 2002), 32 (for Belknap), 43 (for PAS).

296 The Meeting named Moses and David Buffum: Moses Brown to Job Scott, 6/9/93, RIHS.

296 Moses was named the delegate: Samuel Collins to Moses Brown, 12/29/93, RIHS.

296 he was not present: James Pemberton to Moses Brown, 1/7/94, RIHS.

296 illness at home: Obadiah Brown to Moses Brown, 1/26/94, RIHS.

297 "The introductions of the Memorial": Washington quoted in Wiencek, *An Imperfect God*, 276.

297 "his need to prevaricate": Ibid.

297 "I am principled against selling Negroes": Quoted in Twohig, " 'That Species of Property,' " 12.

297 his decision to introduce it personally: None of the writers who have explored the subject of Washington's views on slavery have mentioned this important break from past practice by the first president. That is likely due to the fact that Washington's introduction was expressly omitted from the *Annals of Congress* (Washington, D.C., 1834), IV:36. The entry is telling, however; the introduction of the Quaker memorial is inserted, without reference to the president, between two other presentations that *are* credited to Washington. That the president did personally introduce the memorial is attested to in a letter to Moses Brown from Theodore Foster, the senator from Rhode Island, who was present at Congress and penned his account the same day (1/21/94, RIHS). Foster gave an unusually close report of the proceedings, from which all the quotes of the debate are drawn.

299 "Congress has the power": Moses Brown to John Quincy Adams, 12/1/1833, RIHS.

299 "making the object more conspicuous": Moses Brown to Obadiah Brown, 2/8/94, RIHS.

299 the president "appeared clear": Moses Brown to Dwight Foster, 1/30/00, RIHS.

299 "all and every person": Text of the bill, *Annals of Congress*, IV:1425.

14. PROSECUTIONS

Page

301 John led a petition drive: Dalzell, "Prudence and the Golden Egg," 17–21.

301 John turned to Congressman Benjamin Bourne: Ibid., 41–43.

302 "Mr. Brown read the letter": Quoted in Brown and Walton, *John Brown's Tract,* 49.

302 "John Brown . . . when I knew him": Clarkson A. Collins, ed, "Pictures of Providence in the Past, 1790–1820: The Reminiscences of Walter R. Danforth," *Rhode Island History* X, no. 1 (January 1951): 11.

303 The D'Wolfs got into the slave business: Coughtry, *Notorious Triangle,* 47–49.

303 "They was handsome": White, *Mount Hope,* 98.

304 a surge of vessels: Professor Coughtry breaks down the traffic in close detail in *Notorious Triangle,* and offers a chart showing annual clearances, 27–28.

304 The leader in Providence: Ibid., 213.

304 soon found success: For notes on Sterry, see Walter Smith, *The Sterry Family,* cited at www .zipworld.com.au/~rsterry/gen/wbsmith/notes.html; for Sterry visiting John at home, see Journal of Abby Brown Francis, 1796–1818, HALB.

304 "If you go through the Mozambique channel": John Brown to Thomas Willing Francis, both drafts dated 4/14/91, HALB.

305 In August, he commissioned Peleg Wood: Martin Benson to Brown & Benson, 8/16/95, JCBL.

305 "experiment . . . to try the strength of the law": Moses Brown to John Brown, 3/24/97, RIHS.

305 the abolition societies in New York and Philadelphia: James Pemberton to Moses Brown, 2/11/97, RIHS.

305 John reacted with the same venom: John Brown to Moses Brown, 3/14/97. No copy of this letter survives, but parts of it are paraphrased in letters by William Rotch (to Moses, 3/21/97, RIHS) and Thomas Arnold (to Moses, 3/20/97), and by Moses himself (to John Brown, 3/15/97, RIHS).

307 "Our Lord is said came with a sword": Moses Brown to John Brown, 3/15/97.

307 "He dashed off another letter": John Brown to Moses Brown, 3/19/97. Again, this letter has not survived, but is referenced in Moses' response (3/24/97, RIHS).

308 "Will any slave trader put": Moses Brown to John Brown, 3/24/97, RIHS.

308 Arnold wrote mainly to defend himself: Thomas Arnold to Moses Brown, 3/20/97, RIHS.

309 "I often contemplate": John Brown to Moses Brown, 7/12/97, RIHS.

310 "I have done with the trade": John Brown to Caleb Green, 6/4/97, RIHS.

310 "Both you and he knows": John Brown to Welcome Arnold, 6/15/97, RIHS.

310 "I call on you my brother": John Brown to Moses Brown, 7/29/97, RIHS.

310 It was a victory for the society: *U.S. v. Ship Hope,* Final Record Book, vol. 1, U.S. District Court, Rhode Island. Professor Coughtry treats the prosecution of John Brown in *Notorious Triangle,* 212–16. See also Reilly, *Moses Brown and Rhode Island Antislavery,* 40–43.

311 another round of appeals from John: John Brown to Moses Brown, 11/17/97; David Howell to John Brown, 11/19/97, RIHS.

311 "by the *peculiar turn* of the jurors": Moses Brown to Dwight Foster, 1/30/00, RIHS; emphasis in the original.

312 meetings ceased: Moses Brown to James Pemberton, 11/22/1801, RIHS.

312 Those ships bore away from Africa: Coughtry, *Notorious Triangle,* 27–28.

312 named her son after him: Hazelton, *Let Freedom Ring,* 124.

15. JOHN GOES TO CONGRESS

Page

313 He toyed with the idea of a bid: Henry A. L. Brown has in his personal collection a poster touting John's prospective candidacy for governor.

313 John acted promptly: John Brown to unknown, 12/21/97, RIHS.

313 "one of the best sailers": Navy Secretary Benjamin Stoddert to Capt. Silas Talbot, 8/29/98, in Dudley Knox, ed., *Naval Documents Related to the Quasi-War Between the United States and France* (Washington, 1938), I:351.

313 The navy balked: Navy Department to John Brown, 8/7/98, ibid, I:277.

314 "a complete master of the art of bargain-making": Stoddert to Talbot, 9/20/98, ibid., I:428.

314 "worse than useless": Stoddert to Stephen Higginson, 6/15/99, ibid., III:343.

314 overhaul that cost as much as the original sale: Gibbs & Channing to Stoddert, 11/17/99; 12/7/99, ibid., IV:411, 502.

314 the most respectable men: John Brown to Moses Brown, 8/28/98, RIHS.

314 "all his navigations and distillery": James Brown diary, 12/10/97, quoted in Brown and Walton, *John Brown's Tract*, 105.

315 His last cargo from the *George Washington*: James Brown diary, 5/7/97, ibid., 102.

316 "monomania": George A. Hardin, *History of Herkimer County* (Syracuse, 1893), quoted ibid., 95. Details of John Brown's trips to his Adirondack land are recounted in ibid., 135–40.

316 William Ellery was a diminutive: William M. Fowler Jr., *William Ellery: A Rhode Island Politician and Lord of the Admiralty* (Metuchen, NJ, 1973), 164–80 and passim.

317 "disagreeable business": Samuel Bosworth to Treasury Secretary Oliver Wolcott, August 1799, in Shepley manuscripts, RIHS.

317 "fear and trembling": Quote from William Ellery, in Coughtry, *Notorious Triangle*, 218.

317 Bosworth answered a knock on his door: Samuel Bosworth gave a first-person account of the visit by John Brown and the subsequent kidnapping in his letter to Treasury Secretary Wolcott. The incident at Bristol is recounted in Coughtry, *Notorious Triangle*, 217–18; Howe, *Mt. Hope*, 107–8; and Fowler, *William Ellery*, 175.

318 John set out in November: John Brown to James Brown, 12/23/99, HALB.

319 He won appointment: John Brown's appointment in *Annals of Congress*, X:208.

319 "has congratulated me": John Brown to family, 1/12/00, HALB.

321 his first speech as a member of the House: *Annals of Congress*, X:32.

323 "to encourage the friends of humanity": Moses Brown to Dwight Foster, 1/30/1800, RIHS.

323 Foster replied in February: Dwight Foster to Moses Brown, 2/20/1800, RIHS.

323 The amendments to the slave-trade bill: *Annals of Congress*, X:686–89.

324 Tench Francis had died late Thursday: John Brown to unknown, 5/1/1800, RIHS.

324 The vote was resounding: *Annals of Congress*, X:699.

325 the only surviving letter that he addressed to Moses: John Brown to Moses Brown, 3/13/1800, RIHS.

325 Moses proved to be an assiduous: Undated memorandum, "Matters Need Doing at the Bank," Moses Brown papers, RIHS.

325 John fared especially poorly: Brown and Walton, *John Brown's Tract*, 171

326 The budding romance caused much anxiety: Background for James Mason and the circumstances of his wedding to Alice Brown are offered ibid., 163–64.

326 Herreshoff lost most of his fortune: Ibid., 145.

326 "To judge from your conduct": Sally Brown to John Brown, 11/29/1800, quoted ibid., 170.

327 of nineteen clearances for Africa: Coughtry, *Notorious Triangle*, 222.

328 "He trudged the six hundred steps": John Brown to James Brown, 12/13/1800, quoted in Brown and Walton, op. cit., 170.

328 John gamely managed the stairs: John Brown to James Brown, 1/22/1801, HALB.

328 the aristocratic once stopping by: John Brown to Moses Brown, 1/1/1801, RIHS.

328 a series of letters: Ibid.; see also Moses Brown to John Brown, 12/17/1800, RIHS.

328 Leonard met with Moses in Providence: Thomas Robinson to Moses Brown, 12/24/1800, RIHS.

328 naming the sloop *Fanny*: Coughtry, *Notorious Triangle*, op. cit., 222.

329 "James D'Wolf owes nothing": Ibid., 223.

329 "The violence used in Newport": John Brown to Benjamin Bourne, 2/18/01, Peck manuscripts, RIHS.

329 "This outrageous conduct": John Brown to Benjamin Bourne, 2/22/01, ibid.

330 "I now have the pleasure": John Brown to Benjamin Bourne, 2/23/01, ibid; emphasis in original. See also *Annals of Congress* X:1050.

16. LEGACIES

Page

332 Alice, James, and their children: Brown and Walton, *John Brown's Tract*, 176.

332 John was forced to make amends: Ibid., 177.

333 the dispute became entangled: Ibid., 159.

333 "she succeeded in smuggling": Thomas Willing Francis to John Brown, 3/2/1802, HALB.

333 "All these attentions": John Brown to Charles Herreshoff, 9/26/1801, quoted in Brown and Walton, op. cit., 177.

334 Those were his last words: Abby Francis, John Brown Francis, and James Brown all recorded their impressions of John Brown's final hours. Their accounts are reproduced ibid., 180–81.

335 "before I was seven years old": John Brown to James Brown, 12/7/1782, HALB.

337 "This rage for the traffic": American Convention for Promoting the Abolition of Slavery, *Minutes*, 40.

337 Howell's review of the situation: Ibid., 41.

337 the president gave way: Coughtry, *Notorious Triangle*, 226–27.

338 "He has been bred and brought up": Jonathan Russell to Albert Gallatin, 3/19/04, Shepley Collection, RIHS.

338 "There is now, dear sir": Ellery letter quoted in Coughtry, op. cit., 228.

338 "American citizens are instrumental": Madison quoted in Du Bois, *The Suppression of the African Slave-Trade*, 110.

338 "the African slave trade now prevails": *Annals of Congress*, 15th Congress, 2nd session, 1537.

338 "the actual volume of forced African slave migrations": Herbert S. Klein, *The Atlantic Slave Trade* (Cambridge, 1999), 193.

339 Phebe Lockwood was taken ill: Moses Brown to William Rotch, 6/24/08, RIHS.

339 he derived some comfort: Moses Brown will, 5/12/34, RIHS.

339 "What am I continued so long here for?": Moses Brown to Noah Webster, 10/30/22, quoted in Thompson, *Moses Brown*, 288.

340 Moses took an office: Ibid., 285–87.

340 "our school has become too large": Moses Brown to John Osborn, 12/24/24, RIHS.

340 "Dear Friend": Harrison to Moses Brown, quoted in John Wood Sweet, *Bodies Politic*, 337–40.

341 "Me thinks it is an evidence": Moses Brown to all whom it may concern, 1803, quoted in ibid., 271–72.

341 an ugly race riot: Ibid., 352–70; Moses Brown's petition, 375.

342 A similar society: Ibid., 328–29.

342 Moses made the purchase: Ray Rickman, ed., *A Short History of the African Union Meeting and School-House* (Providence, 1821). Rickman, an amateur historian, discovered a copy of this pamphlet in the archives of the British Museum in 2002 and republished it the following year. Rickman attributes authorship of the pamphlet to Moses Brown.

343 "Successive bereavements": Bulkley, *Chad Brown Memorial*, 39.

344 a "moon shine inheritance": John Brown Francis to John Herreshoff, 8/25/30, quoted in Brown and Walton, *John Brown's Tract*, 284.

344 the tract was sold off in pieces: Ibid., 322.

Acknowledgments

THIS BOOK WAS CONCEIVED during a conversation I had with my brother Bill, a television news reporter who works out of the State House in Providence. During a winter visit Bill pointed out John Brown's mansion, still standing on the shoulder of College Hill, and described the life and the controversies of the man who built that hulking house. My brother was just sharing local lore, but I was surprised to learn that slavery had flourished in New England and intrigued at the feud it engendered in the town's founding family.

From that day forward, my immediate family provided me constant support and encouragement. Bill and my other brother, Tim, immediately saw the story's potential and pressed me to pursue it. My father read the manuscript, made extensive notes, and shared with me insights developed over a career in journalism. My mother Ann Crompton also read the manuscript and was enthusiastic from the beginning, based in part on her bedrock conviction that her sons can accomplish whatever they set out to do. For that, and for all the trials I've put her through over the years, this book is dedicated to her.

My mother's husband Fuzz was supportive as well, providing me with rides, cars, and counsel whenever called upon. Bill's wife Judy Chong made me feel at home during my extended research visits to Providence. And my wife Tulsa Kinney supported me at every turn, from the early months of research, with no contract and no particular prospects, to the long weeks of writing, when she ignored my own doubts and convinced me to press on. She vetted every draft chapter, managing to be my toughest critic and my biggest fan, always finding time for me regardless of the demands of her own professional life. I am fortunate for her love and her loyalty.

This story takes place in Rhode Island, but I was able to conduct much of my research and writing in Los Angeles, thanks in large part to the excellent collections maintained at the Doheny Memorial Library at the University of

Southern California and at the Los Angeles Public Library in downtown Los Angeles. Both maintain superb holdings of early American history; at the central library downtown, for example, I was surprised to find the full ten-volume Rhode Island Colonial Records and two books of colonial Rhode Island genealogy, as well as a bound volume of the extraordinary maps produced by Henry Chace in 1914, which detailed land holdings in Providence in 1798. The staff at the public library was also instrumental in providing me with microfilm reading machines and access to the *Papers of the American Slave Trade*, obtained on loan from the Library of Congress. Librarians Kathy Ellison in the rare books department and Patricia Williams in intramural loans were both helpful and professional.

During my several research visits to Rhode Island, I was able to dig deeply in the collection and archives of the Rhode Island Historical Society. That institution was in a state of transition during the period of my work there, but I am confident the trustees will remain committed to maintaining its invaluable collection as a public resource. At the John Carter Brown Library, Reference and Acquisitions Librarian Richard Ring was cheerful and helpful in guiding me through a vast Brown family archive. The staff at the Providence Public Library was courteous and capable. In Providence, City Archivist John Myers afforded me ready access to a remarkable trove of eighteenth-century ledgers and documents.

Several individuals deserve special mention for their important contributions to this project. Henry A. L. Brown, a descendant of the Francis family of Philadelphia and thus of the Providence Browns, is himself a historian and an author who responded promptly and most generously to my request for assistance. Henry has devoted countless hours to collecting, transcribing, and cataloguing Brown and Francis family journals, letters, and other early materials, and he welcomed me as a friend, opening his files in collegial faith that we both held the truth of the story as our principal object. I hope he finds this volume does justice to his confidence.

Angela Brown Fisher, Halsey Herreshoff, Alice Westervelt, and Sylvia Brown are other Brown family descendants who were kind enough to meet with me and share their insights and their family stories.

Another historian who provided me early encouragement and assistance was Jay Coughtry, author of *The Notorious Triangle: Rhode Island and the African Slave Trade 1700–1807*, the seminal 1981 study that established beyond dispute Rhode Island's leading role among American slavers. Now a professor at the University of Nevada, Las Vegas, Jay was happy to entertain a cold call from a reporter just scratching the surface of a story he knew better than anyone else and to spend several hours showing the ropes to a novice.

John Wood Sweet, who wrote *Bodies Politic*, a penetrating history of slavery in New England, was also very helpful. I met John while reviewing documents in the reading room at the Rhode Island Historical Society; I was just getting familiar with the Brown family papers while John was doing some final culling after publication of his book. He freely shared his knowledge, as well as some crucial letters that had escaped my notice.

Others who were helpful in this project include Robert P. Emlen, the curator at Brown University and a lecturer in the Department of American Civilization, and Ray Rickman, the amateur historian who located and published the 1821 pamphlet, *A Short History of the African Union Meeting and School-House*. Ray was generous with time and sources, and provided me a reference to Ben Gworek, who served me ably as a research assistant. Likewise, Jane Lancaster, still another historian and author, referred me to Elizabeth J. Johnson, perhaps the epitome of the amateur historian. Betty is the single-handed proprietor of the Pawtucket History Research Center, which she runs out of her family home, erected in 1828 and itself worthy of historic designation.

My work on this project was supported in part by a research grant from the Newell D. Goff Institute for Ingenuity and Enterprise Studies; for that assistance I thank Donald W. Gardner and Ronnie Newman. I must also thank several friends and colleagues, including John Seeley, Claude Steiner, Sara Catania, Luis de la Vega, Christine Pelisek, Dean Kuipers, Dave Cogan, and Sam Anson. Frank Culbertson came through with a last-minute copyedit. Mark Cromer provided timely editorial assistance, and must take credit for the title of the book. And I was blessed with the cheerful distraction of my children Dexter and Kelly; perhaps the next time around they will provide me with advice as well as encouragement. In New York, I had the able assistance of my agent Paul Bresnick. Paul also happens to be a former editor of mine, which means I benefit both from his publishing-savvy and his editorial feedback. Victoria Meyer at Simon & Schuster demonstrated early enthusiasm for an untested product. But the most daring gamble was the one taken by my editor Alice Mayhew, who had the audacity to pull my initial proposal out of what must always be a hefty pile and agree to take me on as an author. I can only hope this volume justifies her confidence in me and in this remarkable story.

PHOTO CREDITS

1. Henry E. Kinney (attributed to), oil on canvas, ca. 1898. Rhode Island Historical Society # Rhi X5 9
2. Edward Greene Malbone, *John Brown*, 1794, watercolor on ivory. New-York Historical Society #1948.469
3. Thomas Chambers, *The Ship* George Washington, oil on canvas circa 1898. Rhode Island Historical Society #RHi X5 123
4. George Hall, *Landing of Roger Williams*, engraving from a painting by Alonzo Chappel. New York Public Library #478711
5. Max Rosenthal, *Stephen Hopkins*, lithograph. New York Public Library #419830
6. Willard Rappleye photo
7. John Greenwood, *Sea Captains Carousing at Surinam*, 1755, oil on canvas. Courtesy the Saint Louis Museum of Art
8. Esek Hopkins, detail from Greenwood
9. Anderson, *Abraham Whipple*, lithograph. New York Public Library #478718
10. Watercolor, from R. W. Kelsey, *Centennial History of Moses Brown School*, 1919. Courtesy Moses Brown School
11. Willard Rappleye photo
12. Max Rosenthal, *David Howell*, etching. New York Public Library #419882
13. Willard Rappleye photo
14. Monotint from Henry A. L. Brown collection
15, 16. Courtesy John Carter Brown Library at Brown University
17. S. Hill, *College Hall*, engraving, circa 1800. Courtesy Henry A. L. Brown collection
18. Willard Rappleye photo
19. Joseph Partridge, *President Street, the First Baptist Meeting House, and adjoining buildings*, watercolor on paper, 1822. Rhode Island Historical Society #RHi X3 3058
20. Engraving, *African slave traffic*, from William Blake, *The History of Slavery and the Slave Trade*, 1859. New York Public Library #427778
21. Simeon S. Jocelyn, *Roger Sherman*, etching. New York Public Library #420112
22. Alonzo Chappel, *Gouverneur Morris*, engraving, 1863. New York Public Library #EM3000
23. From an old engraving. Courtesy Betty Johnson
24. G. G. Smith and J. W. Watts, *The First Baptist Church*, engraving from R. A. Guild, *History of Brown University, with Illustrative Documents*, 1867
25. *Original Building*, watercolor from a sketch on the dial of an old clock, from Kelsey, *Centennial History of Moses Brown School*, 1919. Courtesy Moses Brown School

New York Public Library images # 4, 5, 9, 12, 21, 22 are from the Emmet Collection, Miriam and Ira D. Wallach Division of Art, Prints and Photographs, The New York Public Library, Astor, Lenox and Tilden Foundations.

New York Public Library image #20 is from the Manuscripts, Archives and Rare Books Division, Schomburg Center for Research in Black Culture, The New York Public Library, Astor, Lenox and Tilden Foundations.

Index

Index

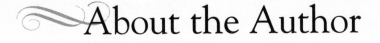# About the Author

Charles Rappleye is an award-winning investigative journalist and editor. He was raised in Cambridge, Massachusetts, attended school at Madison, Wisconsin, and resides in Los Angeles. He has written extensively on media, law enforcement, and organized crime. This is his second book.